Skilled Hands, Strong Spirits

Skilled Hands, Strong Spirits

A Century of Building Trades History

OCLC Record

GRACE PALLADINO

Cornell University Press *Ithaca and London*

First published 2005 by Cornell University Press

Printed in the United States of America

Library of Congress Cataloging-in-Publiction Data
Palladino, Grace.
  Skilled hands, strong spirits : a century of building trades history
  / Grace Palladino.
    p. cm.
  Includes bibliographical references and index.
  ISBN 0-8014-4320-2 (cloth : alk. paper)
  1. Building trades—Employees—Labor unions—United States—
History.   2. Construction workers—Labor unions—United States—
History.   3. AFL-CIO. Building and Construction Trades Dept.—
History.   I. Title.
  HD6515.B9P35 2005
  331.88'124'0973—dc22   2004017450

Cloth printing   10 9 8 7 6 5 4 3 2 1

PRINTED IN U.S.A.

In memory of Stuart B. Kaufman, friend and colleague

CONTENTS

ACKNOWLEDGMENTS

It is a pleasure to thank the many trade unionists, colleagues, and friends who helped make this book a reality. Former president Robert A. Georgine and Mary Ellen Boyd, then at the Building and Construction Trades Department (BCTD), and Professor Lois Gray, at Cornell University's New York State School of Industrial and Labor Relations (ILR), initiated the project. Although this book was a "work for hire," both Cornell and the Department left it to me to research and write as I saw fit. BCTD president Edward Sullivan and secretary-treasurer Joseph Maloney went out of their way to answer questions and to ensure that I had access to Department records, and past and present BCTD officers and staff, including John J. Barry, Marvin Boede, Mary Ellen Boyd, Robert Georgine, Jeff Grabelsky, Joseph F. Maloney, and Robert Ozinga, generously shared their knowledge of the industry and the labor movement. Sarah Springer, at the George Meany Memorial Archives, helped me to locate hard-to-find materials, Vanessa Figueroa, at Cornell, solved more than one bureaucratic problem, and Lynda DeLoach at the Meany Archives and Robert Severn at the BCTD provided crucial help with the photographs. The late Professor John T. Dunlop, whose association with the building trades stretched back more than sixty years, not only sat for a lengthy interview but also read and commented on a number of chapters.

This book could not have been written in a timely fashion without the work of pioneering scholars including William Haber and Marc Linder, for the building trades, and my colleagues at the Samuel Gompers Papers, especially Peter J. Albert, for the early history of the American Federation of

Labor. Professor Linder also read various chapters in record time, as did Melvyn Dubofsky, Jeff Grabelsky, and Richard Schneirov. Janet Greene alerted me to interviews she had conducted for the Robert F. Wagner Archives. Frances Benson, at Cornell University Press, proved to be an enthusiastic booster. As always, Brad Piepmeier kept my spirits up, helping me to stay on track in ways far too numerous to mention.

This book is dedicated to the memory of Stuart B. Kaufman, who gave me my first job at the Samuel Gompers Papers. A professor of history, an early proponent of the George Meany Memorial Archives, and founding editor of *Labor's Heritage,* Stuart dedicated his professional life to making the primary sources of working-class history accessible to scholars and workers alike. At the Gompers Papers, Stuart taught me the value of trying to tell labor's story from labor's point of view, a model I have tried to follow here.

ABBREVIATIONS

ABC	Associated Builders and Contractors
AFL	American Federation of Labor
AGC	Associated General Contractors of America
BCTD	Building and Construction Trades Department
BMIU	Bricklayers' and Masons' International Union of America
BPDA	Brotherhood of Painters and Decorators of America
BTC	Building Trades Council
BTD	Building Trades Department
BTOP	Building Trades Organizing Project
CAC	Cantonment Adjustment Commission
CICBC	Construction Industry Collective Bargaining Commission
CICEP	Construction Industry Cost Effectiveness Project
CIJC	Construction Industry Joint Conference
CIO	Committee for Industrial Organization; later, Congress of Industrial Organizations
CISC	Construction Industry Stabilization Commission
CLU	Central Labor Union
COMET	Construction Organizing Membership Education Training
CPWR	Center to Protect Workers' Rights
EC	Executive Council
GMMA	George Meany Memorial Archives
IABSOIW	International Association of Bridge, Structural and Ornamental Iron Workers
IBEW	International Brotherhood of Electrical Workers

IUOE	International Union of Operating Engineers
LC	Library of Congress
NBJA	National Board for Jurisdictional Awards
NBTC	National Building Trades Council
NCA	National Constructors Association
NCEC	National Construction Employers Council
NECA	National Electrical Contractors Association
NIRA	National Industrial Recovery Act
NJB	National Joint Board
NLRB	National Labor Relations Board
NWLB	National War Labor Board
OPM	Office of Production Management
OSHA	Occupational Safety and Health Administration
PWA	Public Works Administration
RAG	Robert A. Georgine
SBTA	Structural Building Trades Alliance
SG	Samuel Gompers
SGLB	Samuel Gompers Letterbooks
UA	United Association of Journeymen Plumbers, Gas Fitters, Steam Fitters and Steam Fitters' Helpers of the United States and Canada; after 1913, the United Association of Plumbers and Steam Fitters of the United States and Canada; after 1921, United Association of Journeymen and Apprentices of the Plumbing and Pipe Fitting Industry of the United States and Canada
UBCJA	United Brotherhood of Carpenters and Joiners of America
ULLICO	Union Labor Life Insurance Company
UAW	United Automobile Workers
UMCP	University of Maryland, College Park
WAB	Wage Adjustment Board
WPA	Works Progress Administration

AFFILIATES OF THE BUILDING AND CONSTRUCTION TRADES DEPARTMENT, 2004

International Brotherhood of Boilermakers, Iron Ship Builders, Blacksmiths, Forgers and Helpers

International Union of Bricklayers and Allied Craftworkers

International Association of Bridge, Structural, Ornamental and Reinforcing Iron Workers

United Brotherhood of Carpenters and Joiners of America

International Brotherhood of Electrical Workers

International Union of Elevator Constructors

International Association of Heat and Frost Insulators and Asbestos Workers

Laborers' International Union of North America

International Union of Operating Engineers

Operative Plasterers' and Cement Masons' International Association of the United States and Canada

United Association of Journeymen and Apprentices of the Plumbing and Pipefitting Industry of the United States and Canada

International Union of Painters and Allied Trades

United Union of Roofers, Waterproofers and Allied Workers

Sheet Metal Workers' International Association

International Brotherhood of Teamsters

Skilled Hands, Strong Spirits

Introduction:
The Ties That Bind

While New York City was still in shock after the devastating attack on the World Trade Center, union construction workers were already on the job. Within minutes of learning the horrifying news, they raced downtown from construction sites all over the city; a bridge in Staten Island, high-rise projects uptown, a rail job at Kennedy Airport were all shut down fast. "Every tradesman in New York is here," a carpenter reported. "All the construction jobs have ceased." The only non-uniformed workers allowed at the site, they initially ran water to the fire fighters, hauled away buckets of rubble, carried in heavy equipment, and basically did whatever they could to help fire fighters search for victims. Within hours their unions were organizing volunteer rescue squads from all over the country and rounding up the equipment they would need to cut through structural steel, shore up the unstable site, and handle potentially lethal materials.[1]

"The rest of us don't know where or how to begin," the *Washington Post* reported, "but the impromptu volunteer army of workers does. They come in carrying Skil saws and wrenches, spades and Halligan tools. They drive loaders, excavators, backhoes and bulldozers. They commit grand acts of improvisation and problem-solving." Despite the possibility of cave-ins or gas main breaks, and the emotional toll of a heartbreaking job that had to be done "no matter what," as one union member put it, the trades performed as a team. Iron workers cut through heavy steel beams with blow torches, riggers cabled the steel to cranes, and crane operators hauled it away, making it possible for others to start digging. "You just knew there were innocent people under there. . . . You'd do anything in your power to make sure they got out alive," one iron worker (who happened to be female) explained. "If that meant taking [rubble] out piece by piece, digging holes in caves, it didn't matter, you'd do it. . . . We were just individuals working together on one common cause."[2]

Over the next few months iron workers, operating engineers, laborers, steam fitters, carpenters, teamsters, and other trades would work around the clock, demonstrating a measure of skill and compassion that the public rarely associates with union construction workers. "The National Organization for Women won't be suing them for their hiring policies" while they worked at Ground Zero, the *Washington Post* predicted. "And no one is calling them Larry Lunchpail or Joey Six-pack, either." Instead, journalists focused on the dedication these workers displayed every day, portraying their ability to work twelve-hour shifts despite prolonged physical discomfort, their willingness to man the job seven days a week, and their determination to respect the memories of those lost forever and the families who mourned them: New York City's building trades unions lost fifty-nine members in the brutal attack, all brothers and sisters as far as workers were concerned. And union members had plenty of friends and family in the fire department and police force, all union workers, too. So while politicians and contractors soon pressured them to consider Ground Zero a construction site, not a recovery site, construction workers took their cues from grieving fire fighters in the pit. When excavators found something that looked out of place, they put it off to the side so fire fighters could then search through it. If human remains were discovered, work stopped until proper respect was paid. And when Thanksgiving rolled around, there was a crew ready to work through the holiday, since that seemed to be the right thing to do. "If I had people in here, I'd want to know someone was looking too," as one construction worker put it.[3]

In a sense the crisis brought out the best in building trades workers and their unions, a spirit of generosity and competence that is usually overshadowed by controversy. For within the trades, a long history of jurisdictional battles over "turf" has damaged their reputation with employers and building owners. And outside the trades charges of racism, sexism, and soldiering on the job have undermined their credibility with the public. The consequences have been costly: At the turn of the twenty-first century, building trades unions represented less than 20 percent of the workforce, a sharp contrast to conditions in the late 1940s through the 1960s when they claimed well over 50 percent. In those days construction work was one of the highest paid blue-collar occupations. The work was demanding, dangerous, and seasonal, but union workers and their families felt relatively secure. Today lower-waged open-shop construction dominates the market. A wide range of prefabricated building materials and an ample supply of semiskilled nonunion workers and day laborers make union construction—and the training, work rules, and benefit funds that go with it—too expensive, apparently, for all but the largest public works and industrial projects.[4]

No wonder construction workers felt the need to show the union flag at Ground Zero. "You didn't see any day laborers down there. It was all union men," one worker told a crowd of onlookers. "It was the kind of people the media says is paid too much." A fireman working on the site agreed. "We had no deaths, and very few injuries in a work environment that was considered extremely hazardous," he pointed out. "I believe only union workers could have accomplished that." Both men had a point. Except in times of crisis or war, when the value of skilled union work is obvious, the press tends to assume the worst about the building trades. After all, in an industry where time is money, and nonstop production is the key to a contractor's success, what looks like aggressive unionism to rank-and-file workers can seem more like intimidation, or even extortion, to those outside the trades. In fact, ever since building trades unions first organized in the nineteenth century, opponents have portrayed their leaders as corrupt and their members as concerned with nothing greater than their own economic advancement.[5]

But bad publicity is only part of the problem. The unions themselves tended to be insular from the start. The shared exposure to danger, the physical demands of the work, and the fact that knowledge of the various trades was passed from father to son nurtured a strong "insider" versus "outsider" point of view, as one carpenter put it.[6] Consequently the public knows very little about why these unions were organized in the first place or what role they played in stabilizing an inherently risky and highly competitive industry. And they know even less about the ties of union brotherhood and sisterhood that compelled the trades to rush downtown on September 11, 2001. Indeed, the principle that union members take care of their own, no matter what, the practical solidarity that holds a union together, often looks more like narrow self-interest or exclusivity to those outside the trades.

The fact is, building trades unions do take care of their own, and they are proud of it. They could not have built their unions any other way: The tradition is rooted in the struggle for survival that marked the rise of the labor movement. Employed in a highly competitive and seasonal industry, where ten-hour days, subsistence wages, and economic booms and busts were the rule, building trades workers organized unions to protect themselves and their families from price-cutting contractors and cheap competition. And that was a dangerous enterprise at the time. In the nineteenth and much of the twentieth century—up until the passage of the Wagner Act in 1935—workers had no legal right to organize. They had no better means of protection than the trust they placed in one another to uphold the union cause, which meant walking off a job that employed nonunion workers or standing together in general organizing strikes that could be violent on both sides. It took courage, discipline, and a fair investment of money for building trades unions to command a living wage and decent working conditions. In fact, it took at least forty years of strikes, lockouts, and organizing workers and contractors to secure the standards that marked building trades workers as "labor aristocrats" in the twentieth century. These standards included the closed-union shop, the five-day week, relatively high hourly wage rates, and premium rates for overtime, all of which expanded work opportunities for union members and provided a measure of economic security rarely experienced in the working-class world. But securing these standards also required a strong sense of mutual obligation that union members called brotherhood: The union had to be able to count on a member's support, no matter what, and in return, the member could count on the union to protect his wages, train his son for a job, and look after his family in case of death or serious injury. In the days before Social Security laws, this made a significant difference to union families.[7]

Yet the ties of brotherhood that gave building trades unions their strength rarely reached beyond city limits in the early days, especially in well-organized areas like New York, Chicago, or St. Louis. In an industry that was essentially local as far as actual building construction was concerned, local unions were the heart of the building trades movement. Primarily interested in controlling local work for local members, they lobbied politicians to enact building codes and licensing laws to protect work standards and union jobs. They hired full-time business agents to police their trade agreements and to ensure that contractors actually paid the men, and allied themselves with other local unions in building trades councils to support one another's strikes. In order to keep their members employed in good times and bad, some local unions "closed their books" or limited membership to family and trusted friends only. Others entered exclusive agreements with local contractors and material suppliers to preserve the local market. And nearly all believed that new members, including traveling journeymen from the same trade, should be charged a healthy initiation fee if they wanted the benefits a local union provided. "It has cost every one of the old members . . . from $150 to $200 to secure present conditions," an electrician from St. Louis explained in 1899, "and members coming from other cities should not complain that we are hard on them. In a city where wages are from $1.00 to $1.50 more, and the working day two hours less than in surrounding cities, it is absolutely necessary to have some restrictions—a protective tariff if you wish to call it such."[8]

Under the circumstances it made practical sense for local unions to make their own rules. In fact, local leaders in well-organized cities would have it no other way. They wanted no interference from "outsiders," and that included national and international building trades unions that were attempting to centralize authority, and concentrate union power, in the late 1890s. The United Association of Journeymen Plumbers, Gas Fitters, Steam Fitters and Steam Fitters' Helpers, the United Brotherhood of Carpenters and Joiners, and the International Brotherhood of Electrical Workers, among others, all believed that a strong, central organization was the key to standardizing conditions throughout the country: International unions could serve as a clearinghouse for information regarding strikes and local conditions, develop union-wide policies to balance the interests of strong and weak local unions, and address critical issues like traveling journeymen, technological changes, and strike policies and benefits. Practical men that they were, international union leaders knew they had no other choice but to respect local autonomy as far as controlling entrance to the trade was concerned, but they drew the line when it came to jurisdictional matters. As the industry shifted from masonry to structural steel construction in the 1890s, and as increased specialization led to the formation of new specialty unions, including the Cement Workers, the Marble Workers, and the Lathers, the fight to control work and install new materials grew fierce.

When local building trades councils attempted to settle these fights according to local practice rather than international union rules—and established a national organization in 1897 to strengthen their position—the international unions took action. Determined to resolve these disputes once and for all on an industrywide basis and thereby assert their authority, the largest building trades unions (including the Carpenters, Bricklayers, and Plumbers) organized the Structural Building Trades Alliance (SBTA) in 1903, an independent federation of building trades unions that would evolve into the Building Trades Department of the American Federation of Labor in 1908.

The plan seemed simple enough, especially to international union leaders. The national organization would set strict jurisdictional rules, requiring "specialty" trades like the Metal Lathers or Marble Workers to join "primary" trades like the Iron Workers or the Bricklayers; a policy of "one trade one union," they believed, would nip disputes in the bud. At the same time, the national organization would establish a network of local councils pledged to uphold the rules, a network that would forge national ties of brotherhood throughout the industry. In the process, the national organization would strengthen the ability of the building trades to stand together in a fight, providing the power that international unions needed to negotiate and to enforce closed-shop agreements.[9]

There was only one problem. Neither the Structural Building Trades Alliance, the Building Trades Department, nor the international unions, for that matter, had the power to enforce national policy on well-organized local unions or councils determined to go their own way: The strong centralized organization envisioned by SBTA founders never got very far once the constitution was drawn up. On the contrary, the new organization was mired in disputes from the start since it raised far more questions than it solved. If specialty unions refused to join the primary trade, could they be shut out of the building trades movement, or did it make more sense to broaden the organization? If an international union could not compel local unions to join local councils, should its charter be revoked? And how would jurisdictional disputes be settled, if the unions involved could not agree? Would "might make right" as the smaller unions feared, or would disputes be settled objectively, on the basis of logic or merit? When it came to making such crucial decisions, how would votes be apportioned—on the basis of membership and per capita taxes paid, as the larger unions preferred, or would each affiliate have an equal vote regardless of size? Should the national building trades organization set policy on issues like general strikes, arbitration, national agreements, and organizing, or were these matters better left to the international unions to decide for themselves? Finally, where did employers fit into the picture? Was the goal of the building trades movement to improve relations with employers and stabilize the industry, or to make it possible for rank-and-file workers to negotiate the best terms the market would bear?

As this book demonstrates there were no easy answers to these questions when the Building Trades Department was just taking shape. And there are still no easy answers today: Almost a century later these issues are hotly debated in one form or another, at all levels of the building trades. In fact, from the time that building trades unions first attempted to federate in the early 1900s, the Department has struggled to find a workable compromise between local autonomy and centralized authority that addresses the needs of both rank-and-file workers and the industry that employs them. And it has tried to balance the interests of skilled mechanics, semiskilled installers, and general laborers, rising and declining trades, and large and small international unions, interests that have changed over time as the industry has grown more specialized, the workforce more diverse, and the influence of government more direct. In the process, Department leaders have experimented with jurisdictional boards, project labor agreements, grass-roots political organizing, joint labor-management committees, and multi-trade organizing campaigns. These efforts have not always been successful, as the current low rate of union density demonstrates. But despite a long history of internal fights, competing interests, technological changes, and political attacks, the Department has managed to protect the goal of union standards and union construction far longer than critics predicted.

This book follows the evolution of the Building and Construction Trades Department from a loose federation of contentious unions at the turn of the twentieth century, to the recognized voice of the building trades in the 1930s and 1940s, to the leading protector of prevailing wage laws, apprenticeship training, health and safety provisions, and collective bargaining in the second half of the twentieth century. Beginning with the rise of building trades councils in the late 1880s, it tells a story of industrial warfare, inter-union cooperation and conflicts, and experiments with organizational structures and strategies to broaden union membership, reconcile jurisdictional disputes, and overcome, or at the very least challenge, the powerful combination of corporate and judicial hostility that set stark and sometimes unbeatable limits on organized labor throughout the twentieth century. The cast of characters ranges from hard-hitting "walking delegates" who kept their ranks in line, to international union officers determined to protect their members' jobs, to Department leaders seeking a basis for consensus, to an ever-changing roster of "outsiders"—including contractors, politicians, arbitrators, and civil rights activists—all of whom had a hand in shaping the development of the Building and Construction Trades Department.

Part 1 follows the forty-year effort of the building trades to achieve a measure of organizational stability, which was no easy task, given the complex structure of the industry. Bricklayers, carpenters, operating engineers, and laborers, for instance, were employed by general contractors. But painters, electrical workers, pipe fitters, and plasterers worked with specialty contractors, many of whom came up through union ranks. And then there were different sectors of the industry, some requiring more highly skilled and highly paid workers than others. Whether union members worked in building, highway, heavy, or residential construction made a difference when it came to negotiating agreements or setting limits on work rules. And whether union members were skilled mechanics, semiskilled installers, or general laborers also made a difference when it came to organizing a job: workers who could be replaced at a moment's notice had to depend on skilled mechanics to support their strikes. That some unions were large enough to go it alone if they had to further complicated matters, especially when the Department tried to enforce jurisdictional decisions. Indeed, the twenty-year fight between the Carpenters and the Sheet Metal Workers over the installation of metal building trim crippled Department efforts to develop arbitration boards, assert authority over local councils, and speak as the representative voice of organized building trades workers. When recurring jurisdictional conflicts eventually gave way to rival Departments in the early 1930s, around the same time that the industry collapsed in the Great Depression, building trades unions were forced to confront the high price of trade dissension, agreeing to disagree, at least for the time being, so that Department members could work together to survive the crisis.

Part 2 focuses on the federal government's increasing influence in the construction industry, and the Department's increasing preoccupation with politics and labor legislation. It begins with President Franklin D. Roosevelt's attempt to jump-start the economy during the Great Depression through public works projects, and follows the Department's difficult fight to uphold union standards in the face of mass unemployment. Part 2 also examines the Department's alliance with the Associated General Contractors of America to oppose the use of the day labor system on government jobs—an alliance that resulted in a wartime stabilization agreement that not only standardized conditions and wages during the Second World War but also made union construction a real power in the heavy construction industry. When the government desperately needed skilled craftsmen to construct military bases, defense factories, and top-secret, hazardous, atomic weapon facilities at Los Alamos and Oak Ridge, it relied on the Department and its affiliated unions to man these projects quickly and efficiently. When the war was over, however, relations with government changed abruptly. Wartime government-labor boards gave way to the Taft-Hartley Act in 1947 and the 1951 Denver decision that outlawed the secondary boycott, or sympathetic strike—the building trades' most effective weapon in the fight to organize construction jobs. At the same time a postwar civil rights revolution was also challenging the building trades' traditional control of skill, forcing the Department and its unions to confront the consequences of racial discrimination, and develop a system of apprenticeship training that would satisfy the demands of the government, the industry, and the workers themselves.

Part 3 examines the rise of nonunion construction and the Department's efforts to reverse the trend. It begins in the era of the Vietnam War when construction was booming, unemployment was at an all-time low, and the building trades were making the most of the opportunity—or, as critics contended, pricing themselves out of the market. Describing Department efforts to work with government agencies and contractors to stabilize wage rates and improve productivity, Part 3 examines the emergence of the Business Roundtable and the sharp decline in unionized construction that began in the mid-1970s, around the same time that the postwar construction boom went bust. Stepping up its political efforts to enact favorable legislation and defeat employer plans to undermine skill and training standards, the Department also heightened its efforts to organize the unorganized, a radical and controversial shift in building trades policy that ultimately promised more than the Department and its affiliated unions were able to deliver. At the same time, some serious internal fights over questions of representation, jurisdictional rights, Department finances, and the overall direction of the building trades movement threatened to tear the organization apart. When the United Brotherhood of Carpenters and Joiners left the Department in 2001—temporarily, as it turned out—it seemed as if the Building and Construction Trades Department had come full circle. For in a sense, this book ends where the Department's story begins—with a very practical need to build a working monopoly of all qualified construction workers and to strengthen the ties that bind the building trades together and give meaning and power to the concept of unionism.

PART ONE

ERECTING THE STRUCTURE

For loyalty springs from a people's consent,
And the knee that is forced had been better unbent.
— Thomas Osborne Davis, *A True Irish King*

Skyscrapers, Building Trades Councils, and the Rise of the Structural Building Trades Alliance

Even with the advantages of every modern tool and techno-
logical device, skyscrapers are still the work of human hands.
—George H. Douglas, *Skyscrapers: A Social
History of the Very Tall Building in America*

When Chicago's Home Insurance Building opened for business in the fall of 1885, there were no fireworks, no parades, not even a newspaper headline to mark the occasion. At the time nobody recognized the ten-story high-rise as an architectural wonder or realized that major change was under way. In fact, as far as the newspapers were concerned, there was "nothing particularly new in the style of Chicago architecture" that season.[1]

But there was something new in its structure that would reshape city sky-lines for years to come: The Home Insurance Building was the first to employ steel skeleton construction, an innovation that would transform the building industry from the bottom up. In conventional construction, brick and stone walls strengthened a structure; in the new high-rise, cast-iron columns and rolled steel beams carried the load. Although the public was far more interested in the marble entryway and impressive columns of the new building, it was this shift from masonry to structural steel that set the Home Insurance Building apart. Skeleton construction, and subsequent innovations like high-speed elevators, electric motors, and steam-heating systems, would give rise to what one builder called "the most distinctively American thing in the world": steel frame skyscrapers that towered over the nation's landscape by the 1930s, symbolizing the "swaggering vitality of American technology." That they could be erected more quickly, and more profitably, than conventional masonry buildings, and vastly increased the value of rentable space, only added to their allure.[2]

However, it would have been hard to predict this outcome in 1885. The Home Insurance Building may have launched a revolution in building construction, but the industry that erected it was strictly a local, hand-powered affair at the time. Certainly there were factories producing windows, doors, and other building parts by the 1880s, but men, not machines, did most of the work in construction. Carpenters still carved ornate moldings or fashioned beams, pillars, and other heavy work. Stone cutters used chisels and hammers, and worked on site. Laborers did their own heavy lifting. Painters, plasterers, bricklayers, roofers, and tile setters all worked by hand. In those days they were employed by small, unincorporated, and highly competitive contractors whose lives were not so different from their own. Both moved from job to job, scrambling for steady income. And neither qualified as "gentlemen." Contractors and tradesmen tended to be immigrants who started out as apprentices, a pattern not at all unusual. Any competent mechanic with a little money and experience could set up shop as a contractor, making the industry "an open door for small producers to try their luck," as one economist put it.[3]

But the door could swing both ways. It did not take much to put a contractor out of business and a mechanic out of work, especially in a seasonal industry like construction, where short-term contracts and meager profits were the rule. A spell of bad weather, an unexpected rise in prices or interest rates, a business depression all could spell disaster. Marginal "shoestring" contractors, determined to stay afloat one way or another, aggravated the problem. Notorious for cutting prices in order to win contracts during the busy season, they undermined wage rates and, in the process, alienated the city's best workers. Skilled, reliable, "decent" mechanics expected to earn "decent" wages, enough to feed and house their families well, and to educate their children. Employers who could not, or would not, pay such rates did not belong in business, they believed. "When a man is mean enough to try to crush our trade at every opportunity, I say *crush him* in every legal way in our power," one carpenter argued in 1881. "One grand union must be formed" to get the job done, he urged fellow workers, "and that is a union of all the trades."[4]

General Strikes, Walking Delegates, and Building Trades Councils

This carpenter's words were harsh, but his idea was becoming more popular. In an age of ten-hour days, subsistence wages, and virtually no protection, the idea of organizing an army of labor and the vision of achieving justice through general strikes and boycotts were truly inspiring. But how to make those ideas and visions real was another question. After all, even workers within a single trade had trouble cooperating with one another. The tendency in the 1880s, and well beyond, was to stick to your own kind. Skilled carpenters as a group all faced the problem of piece work, for instance; thanks to improvements in woodworking machinery, semiskilled specialists were flooding the market. Yet in cities throughout the country German speakers formed one trade group, English speakers another, and "Hebrews" and Scandinavians were each off on their own, a pattern that was common in the building trades.[5]

Nor was there any guarantee that individuals within these trade groups would agree on strategies or ultimate goals. Some believed that controlling entrance to the trade offered the best protection to skilled mechanics, and they favored craft unions that focused strictly on improving wages and working conditions. Others promoted broader labor reform groups, like the Knights of Labor, which welcomed skilled and unskilled workers with the motto, "an injury to one is the concern of all." Still others supported the recently organized American Federation of Labor, which recognized craft autonomy but urged trade unions to work together on common issues like the eight-hour day in order to achieve success. And finally there were socialists, who believed that political power was the key to social justice, and anarchists, who were willing to do whatever it took to undermine an unfair labor system. But despite all the energy and excitement these various activists expressed, they represented only a small fraction of the workforce. So under the circumstances, it would be no easy task to build "a union of all the trades" and almost impossible to win a general strike in the 1880s.[6]

Consider the case of Chicago's carpenters, who struck for the $3 day at the start of the 1884 season. At first, the most skilled carpenters won their raise without a fight, proving their economic value to the contractors. But their victory was short-lived, thanks to a slowdown in the national economy. As work dried up around the country, the city was soon flooded with carpenters willing to work for less. The local union then called for a general strike to save the raise, but the plan could not be tested. The bricklayers' union, the best organized trade in the city, refused to join the fight. A very practical, survival-oriented group, the bricklayers were willing to contribute $500 to the cause—a remarkable sum that demonstrated the strength of their organization. But they were not willing to jeopardize their own hard-won conditions by striking on the carpenters' behalf. After all, they had battled their own contractors a year before without any outside help. And since union bricklayers regularly collected funds for their own protection through a system of high dues and initiation fees, they believed that their decision was justified. Although the carpenters blamed them for the demise of the carpenters' union, the bricklayers did not consider themselves responsible.[7]

The lesson was not lost on building tradesmen. If they learned anything from the failed strike in 1884, it was the value of controlling their work. For as the bricklayers demonstrated, skill, discipline, and a well-financed organization got results in the building industry. With a long history of organization—the bricklayers' national union dated back to 1865, and some locals were older than that—they did not look to others to win their fights. And they also left nothing to chance. The first of the building trades to establish the closed shop, collective bargaining, and the nine-hour day (which would soon be the eight-hour day in Chicago), the bricklayers were also the first to employ business agents, or walking delegates, to ensure that only union men worked on a job and that contractors honored their agreements. "The Bricklayers' Union has got the bosses' noses to the grindstone," the *Chicago Tribune* noted in 1884, and as long as the work was running, the paper added, "there is no way out of it."[8]

The bricklayers' ability to go it alone may have enraged other trades, but by the mid-1880s their methods were gaining respect. In fact, as the skyscraper boom began to take off, impressively boosting the industry in Chicago and New York City, business agents were collecting dues, keeping the books, and enforcing work rules for more and more unions. And they were getting results, much to the contractors' dismay. The new symbol of power in the building trades, business agents were authorized to "pull a job," or order strikes, when necessary to keep contractors in line. Elected and paid by union members, their jobs depended on getting results, putting a premium on tough, aggressive, business agents who would not take no for an answer. Threatened by this unexpected challenge, contractors equated business agents with gangsters, warning that unless they were reined in quickly, "business would be ruined and the triumph of the walking delegate would be complete."[9]

At the time, however, industrial expansion was on the side of the tradesmen, at least in Chicago and New York City, where business agents were beginning to pool their strength in local building trades councils. New York City's Board of Walking Delegates was established in 1884, and within six years every union but the Bricklayers (which had its own arbitration agreement with employers) had joined. Chicago's first attempt to form a council in 1886 was not as successful, although here the Bricklayers did offer moral support (which meant "the dropping of a brick upon the head of an unwary nonunion workman," according to the press).[10] But in 1890, when the Chicago Building Trades Council (BTC) was launched, every organized trade was a member. Led by a Board of Business Agents, Chicago's BTC was designed to remove "all unjust and injurious competition" through "unity of action for mutual protection." In other words, it would use the power of the sympathetic strike to police the industry: Unions that joined the BTC would honor the strikes of other BTC members to ensure that work went to "fair" contractors who paid union rates and observed union rules. The practical incarnation of "a union of all the trades," these councils equalized the strength of local unions, encouraged labor solidarity, and harnessed the workers' power in the industry, allowing them to flex their economic muscle one building at a time. In the period between 1886 and 1890, for instance, before the founding of Chicago's BTC, building trades unions lost more strikes than they won. In the period between 1890 and 1894, however, victories increased steadily, reaching 85 percent in 1894.[11]

Building trades councils owed their existence to a host of factors, including the burst of labor activity in the late 1880s that gave rise to the national eight-hour movement. But the fact that they took off around the same time as skyscrapers was not a coincidence. The two were linked by economics: In the high-stakes world of skyscraper erection, time was money and competence mattered. "Skyscrapers always called for the best that was available in any given pool of labor," one student of the industry explained. Since steel frame construction required a greater investment of capital, for equipment and material, contractors needed first-class workers if they hoped to turn a profit, workers who could anticipate and resolve problems on the spot. For instance, when contractor W. A. Starrett faced a costly delay early in his career, when a derrick toppled over, he depended on his riveting foreman, Sam Parks, to bail him out. With the mast of the derrick broken, Parks worked all night to improvise a new hauling system, incorporating the upper floors of a building next door as a makeshift mast—an ingenious solution that saved the day for Starrett. An expert rigger, who had the respect of the men who worked under him, Parks would eventually rise to the head of New York City's Board of Delegates, where he would master and then exploit the strategy of the sympathetic strike. But when he worked for Starrett, he was a good example of the kind of worker who made the building trades union an economic power in the industry: He could get the job done right, the first time.[12]

His union, the International Association of Bridgemen and Structural Iron Workers, grew up with steel frame construction, and members who worked on skyscrapers were a breed apart; a cross between mechanics and daredevils, they riveted girders and trusses high atop a building's structure as fearlessly as if they worked on the ground. These "cowboys of the skies" drew public attention as they strode along high narrow beams, working without a net. In their case, nerve was the larger part of skill. In other trades it was efficient, flawless work. Brick walls encasing steel structures had to be watertight and able to withstand years of punishing weather, and roofs and cornices also had to stand the test of time. As skyscrapers grew taller, pipe fitters had to have practical knowledge of hydraulics and pneumatics, and elevators had to be dependable and safe. Electrical work had to be expertly done to prevent fire hazards, a high standard to meet at the turn of the twentieth century, when electrical wiring was still in its infancy. Because a building trades worker had to be "first class or he is of little use," as one organizer put it, building trades unions took skill seriously. The best organized trades trained apprentices, used their union journals to publish expert discussions of technical matters, and expected new members to pass technical exams, especially if they intended to work in high-wage cities. These early efforts to control entrance to the trades paid off, putting building trades unions in a good position to bargain.[13]

The Rise of the National Building Trades Council

Even that process was changing, however, as skyscrapers revitalized the industry. For as steel replaced wood and stone as primary building materials, and steel erectors began to dominate commercial construction, regional and even national contracting companies were entering the business. Men like George A. Fuller, who built Chicago's 1889 skyscraper, the Tacoma, before entering the market in New York City, typified the change. An engineer who oversaw every phase of the business, including financing and materials, Fuller was "a new type of contractor" determined to control expenses and increase profits through careful administration. By the time he died in 1900, general contractors were playing major roles in the industry: They financed the project, purchased and assembled materials, hired craftsmen for foundation, masonry, steel, and carpentry work, and supervised the entire project from beginning to end. In New York City, which was rapidly taking Chicago's place as the high-rise capital of the world, about half a dozen large companies (including the Fuller Company) erected the majority of the city's skyscrapers. And most of these were willing to work with building trades unions, if that was necessary to get a job done. "We favor these companies," a walking delegate explained, "because they're fair. It's not so much that the wages and conditions are better as that they don't try to sneak out of agreements."[14]

However, reaching agreements was getting harder to do: As skyscrapers (and expenses) continued to rise, general contractors began to introduce new building materials and new methods of installation that often crossed traditional trade lines. Building trades councils, which operated in most larger cities by 1897, generally policed a trade's control of work (or trade jurisdiction), but the job was getting complicated. The basic shift from masonry to steel construction, and from wood to metal doors, window frames, and trim (a safety precaution dating back to the 1870s) was shaking up the trades. Who should install these accessories? Carpenters who had always done so? Sheet metal workers who manufactured them? Iron workers? At the same time, the evolution of steel frame construction created entirely new categories of workers, from hoisting engineers who controlled power and delivered materials, to elevator constructors who made "vertical transportation" possible. New questions were also raised. Who controlled the job of wiring electric elevators? Elevator constructors or electricians? And who handled the elevators after they were built? Hoisting engineers or elevator constructors? Finally, new materials were straining trade relations, too. When contractors introduced reinforced concrete as a cheaper alternative to brick and stone work, bricklayers tried to restrict its use, arguing that concrete was unstable, an argument that lost its force in 1904 when the first concrete skyscraper opened for business. But by that time bricklayers, plasterers, and a new union of cement finishers were vying to do the work, while iron workers, lathers, sheet metal workers, and laborers all claimed the right to install metal reinforcing rods.[15]

It was one thing for local unions to defend their jurisdictional rights on the floor of the building trades council. It was quite another to force general contractors to honor their claim on a job site. Sympathy strikes to enforce jurisdictional claims, or to restrict the use of new materials or tools, raised issues more complicated than merely shutting work down. Should the trades unite behind the Stone Cutters' efforts to outlaw the use of the mechanical stone planer, for instance? Or should new workers using these tools be organized? And if they were organized, should they form their own "specialty" union, or were they part of the established trade? Changes in the plumbing industry posed a similar problem. Should building trades councils support the Plumbers' claim to steam fitting as an auxiliary trade, or should they stand by the more recently organized Steam Fitters union? The United Brotherhood of Carpenters and Joiners of America (UBCJA) also kept local councils busy. Did its members have a "vested interest" in work that was once done in wood, as the union claimed? And was it worthwhile to back the UBCJA fight against a rival union, the Amalgamated Society of Carpenters, that had already torn New York City's Board of Delegates apart? And what about the Painters? In that case, rival eastern and western factions had been testing each other's strength since 1894, wrecking local councils in the process. The Bricklayers union wanted no part of these fights and urged local unions to steer clear of building trades councils. But other trades saw no future in going it alone.[16]

Determined to find a permanent solution to these ongoing fights, a group of building trades leaders from midwestern cities—including Chicago, Milwaukee, Toledo, St. Louis, and Kansas City, Missouri—decided it was time to get together and talk. According to Herman W. Steinbiss, a St. Louis painter, they were inspired by the success of the St. Louis BTC in establishing an arbitration system that prevented strikes and encouraged "a more friendly feeling between employers and employe." Gathering in St. Louis in 1897, delegates representing local councils, international unions, and independent local unions organized the National Building Trades Council (NBTC) to encourage the formation of local councils and unions, enforce the eight-hour day, equalize wages between the trades, and secure a mechanics' lien law and other beneficial legislation. Led by president Ed Carroll (an officer of the Plasterers international union who was also president of Chicago's BTC) and secretary-treasurer Steinbiss, the new organization intended to establish a national working card, a correspondence league to improve trade relations, and a system to "adjust differences in our own ranks" without outside interference. There would be no jurisdictional strikes, the NBTC proclaimed. All differences would be settled "off the work" either by committees representing the trades in dispute or, if that failed, by the NBTC governing board. In the meantime, the men would continue to work "refraining from outward show of antagonism," for the NBTC's ultimate goal was the "closer amalgamation of building trades workmen." According to Steinbiss, who would emerge as the strongest promoter of the NBTC, the new organization would prove to be "a powerful aid" to the American Federation of Labor, and a "powerful factor in unionizing the building trades all over the land."[17]

The international unions were not so sure. Although building trades councils welcomed the new organization, only the Painters, Plasterers, Electrical Workers, and Steam Fitters offered strong support. The other building trades unions were wary of the NBTC's emphasis on local authority. Because local councils held the balance of power in NBTC conventions (both local councils and international unions got one vote each), they also had the power to set policy and decide trade disputes. Thus trade jurisdiction would vary from city to city, depending on the strength of a local union, regardless of international union claims or trade agreements. "In other words, the affairs of the council as they affected the affiliated internationals were disposed of by representatives of local bodies," one opponent explained. As far as he could see, international unions had no real function in the NBTC except "to bear the expense."[18]

The NBTC's policy of encouraging "specialty" trades to organize new unions likewise kept the Bricklayers, Granite Cutters, Plumbers, and Carpenters officially on the sidelines (although carpenters' locals were permitted to join and actually played a strong role in the new organization). NBTC efforts to strengthen building trades councils did not suit these unions either, especially since local councils often backed so-called dual or independent local unions that would not, or could not, join the international union.

When NBTC officers tried to compel local unions to join local building trades councils, for instance, the Bricklayers made it clear, in 1898, that the new organization had gone too far.[19]

The American Federation of Labor (AFL) was not enthusiastic either. In fact, at the very time the NBTC was meeting in St. Louis, AFL officers were protesting the new organization. The problem was not that building trades workers wanted to legislate for themselves, insisted AFL president Samuel Gompers. In 1888 he had suggested that very idea himself. But an organization like the NBTC, which strengthened local power at the expense of international union discipline, was not part of his plan. Gompers wanted building trades workers to organize councils, but he expected those councils to be part of the AFL. Convinced that the NBTC would only invite rivalry and increase strife, he steadfastly opposed it. Backing him up in 1899, delegates to the AFL convention declared the NBTC a dual organization, which made it "unfair," or illegitimate. At the same time they urged local building trades unions to affiliate with city central labor unions, the AFL's voice in the local community, and establish separate building trades sections within these councils.[20]

This action effectively checked the growth of the NBTC: Although the organization survived until at least 1907, it was never strong enough to enforce trade decisions or to erect a national network of building trades councils. But AFL-approved central labor union building trades sections could not do the job either. Bricklayers, for instance, were crucial to building trades strength since they were one of the first trades on a job. But the Bricklayers union was not a member of the AFL at the time, and it wanted nothing to do with central labor unions or building trades sections. Like most building trades unions, the Bricklayers did not want the "miscellaneous" trades in a central labor organization to interfere with building trades affairs. As a consequence, however, jurisdictional claims still varied from city to city, and sympathetic strikes to enforce these claims continued to disrupt the industry.

The Rise of the Structural Building Trades Alliance

The contest grew so intense that in 1903 strikes or lockouts shut down construction in nearly every organized city, seriously damaging the reputation of building trades councils. The image of iron-fisted council leaders, like Sam Parks in New York City and "Skinny" Madden in Chicago, revived the 1886 complaint that walking delegates were "blackmailers" bent on ruling or ruining the industry. Their supporters in the ranks did not fare much better. Critics inside and outside the labor movement were outraged when high-priced trades "built a wall" around their locals, charging high initiation fees or even "closing the books" to new members, including union brothers from out of town. Complaints grew loudest in Chicago, where local contractors and material manufacturers signed exclusive agreements with building trades unions to keep local industry in local hands, thus putting a brand new spin on the concept of solidarity. "Collective bargaining became a tool for the joint control of competition," one student of Chicago's industry explained. "National firms . . . desiring access to the nation's second largest market, were forced to conform or disappear."[21]

Or they could organize, of course. In 1899 a group of contractors, bankers, architects, and material manufacturers established the Building Contractors Council (BCC). Backed by a variety of corporate interests, the BCC was determined to win control of the industry by locking out building trades unions until they agreed to dissolve their council. This was not an easy task in a union town like Chicago. The mayor, for instance, did not order police to protect the contractors' new (nonunion) workers, which meant that both sides fought it out on the streets. Newspapers reported some 250 cases of assault during the first five months of the lockout.[22]

Such dramatic evidence of deep-rooted conflict drew the attention of the U.S. Industrial Commission, a fact-finding government agency that sent investigators to take testimony from participants on both sides. The publicity that resulted, however, backfired on the unionists, according to George Perkins, a labor leader with strong ties to the AFL. "The Contractors seized the opportunity and made the Commission a means through which . . . trades unions were unmercifully flayed and their officials vilified," he informed Samuel Gompers. "Everything that the Contractors said against Labor or labor organizations or labor officials, was freely and fully chronicled in the Chicago daily press, while the manly, dignified and flat denials on the part of labor officials and Union men were entirely ignored." His hopes were still strong for the Chicago Building Trades Council, he added, but "my judgment . . . leads me to say that the unions involved in the building trades lock-out . . . are in a somewhat critical condition."[23]

That was putting it mildly. With more than fifty thousand men out of work, and strike funds running low, many unions had no choice but to make separate agreements with contractors, and by April 1901 the Building Contractors Council had won the fight: New agreements included the so-called Cardinal Principles that banned exclusive agreements and union restrictions on the amount of work a man might do, the introduction of machinery or new materials, or the number of apprentices. New agreements also prohibited unions from joining building trades councils or participating in sympathetic strikes; contractors wanted conflicts settled through arbitration boards, but they were not always able to enforce the rules. "They say they've abandoned sympathetic strikes in Chicago," one union president told a reporter. "So they have. They're all 'individual walkouts' now." Another Chicago unionist agreed that since the sympathetic strike was "practically abolished" the men now walked out as individuals to help fellow tradesmen, "without orders from headquarters, of course." If Chicago's building trades workers proved to be better organized than contractors at the time—by 1903 another trades council was on the rise, but the contractors' council was on its way out—this was a devastating defeat nonetheless.[24]

But the problem was not confined to Chicago. "If these sympathetic strikes continue," a contractor in New York City predicted in 1902, "we're going to have another 'Chicago lockout.'" He apparently knew what he was talking about, for by June 1903 New York City's building industry was at a standstill. The trouble began when ten thousand carpenters struck a rival union, generating a sympathetic strike that tied up half the buildings in the city. Around the same time the Board of Delegates admitted two unions of building teamsters, stipulating that these unions would now handle all building supplies. This move was designed to organize the rest of the industry, since teamsters would deliver material only to "fair" union employers. Material dealers refused to comply; instead, they shut down their yards and promised not to reopen until the Board expelled the teamsters unions. Backed by some thirty trade associations, employers declared a general lockout, putting one hundred thousand men out of work. "We are not opposed to labor unions so long as they are fairly and justly managed," a spokesman explained. "But of late the exactions of this union and of that union have become so oppressive that many of us honestly prefer to close our shops and retire from business rather than continue as we have been doing." Pledging to "stand for the right of the employer to manage his own business," they organized the Building Trades' Employers' Association (BTEA), a federation of trade associations designed to abolish sympathetic strikes, eliminate jurisdictional disputes, and reduce the power of walking delegates, or at least "throw their ringleaders into jail," as one reporter put it. They were not trying to destroy unionism, the BTEA insisted, since contractors still depended on unions to supply skilled labor. They were merely trying to keep the sides even, they maintained.[25]

Their plan rested on settling disputes through a board of arbitration whose members would be "neither business agents nor members of any central body of employees." But what the BTEA considered "a new constitution for the building trades," sounded more like "a one-sided business" to building trades leaders, one calculated to blunt the union's economic power in the industry. When the vast majority voted to table the BTEA plan, union leaders assumed that the matter was settled, since they did not believe that large construction companies, like the Fuller Company, would come to the plan's defense. They were disappointed, however. The Fuller Company not only shut down work, but the BTEA organized its own unions, a move that pushed the unions to fight back. Ignoring the employers' ultimatum to accept the arbitration plan or be replaced, they declared a citywide strike. "Resume work and we will talk over the plan," union leaders offered. "Sign our arbitration plan," employers countered, "and then we will resume work." After a deadlock of some three weeks, a joint conference was finally arranged, and after achieving some compromises, the majority of unions signed on to the plan and went back to work.[26]

Sam Parks and his supporters, a force of about fifteen unskilled unions including the teamsters, would not give in. But by this time their defiance made almost no difference. With most of the skilled trades back at work, Parks's army had no real power. More important, however, Parks was on his way out as a building trades leader. Embroiled in a losing fight with steel erectors, he was also convicted of extortion in 1903 after contractors testified that they had paid him to prevent strikes. The story made all the papers; in fact, before the year was out, "Parksism" was another name for graft.[27]

However, in an industry that thrived on collusion—in the form of exclusive agreements between material manufacturers, building contractors, and unions—the sin Parks committed was hardly original. It was just the cost of doing business, his supporters believed, and it was strictly his own affair. If he made "a bunch of money," as one iron worker put it, "he did not get it out of us." On the contrary, his iron-fisted, aggressive leadership had won New York City's building trades workers the highest average wages in the country. But those days were over now. By the time Parks died in Sing Sing Prison in 1904, the contractors' arbitration plan was in full force, walking delegates had lost their power, and the industry was primed for something new. "The lesson of this epidemic of sympathetic strikes and lockouts is, that the building trades must be considered as a single industry," one reporter noted, "and that their labor problem must be treated as a single problem, not as a problem of thirty different trades. Both capital and labor must be organized and a constitution must be provided for the trade."[28]

It seemed to be an idea whose time had come. Indeed, in the summer of 1903, at the same time New York City's industry was fighting it out, building trades unions were searching for new solutions. Frank Duffy, secretary-treasurer of the Carpenters, was particularly fed up with the state of affairs. However he blamed jurisdictional conflicts on the American Federation of Labor, not on walking delegates: The Carpenters had been fighting rivals like the Amalgamated Carpenters and Amalgamated Wood Workers for years, and Duffy strongly resented the AFL's willingness to accept these unions as members. Their membership as well as their work rightly belonged to the United Brotherhood of Carpenters and Joiners, as far as Duffy could see. Determined to force the AFL to act, he began corresponding with Herman Steinbiss, secretary of the National Building Trades Council, to investigate whether the Carpenters would be better served by joining the rival federation. Ultimately the Carpenters decided against that move, since the NBTC was still heavily weighted in favor of local councils. But since he found the idea of a federation of building trades unions intriguing, Duffy issued a call to union officers to meet in Indianapolis to discuss the plan. When representatives of the six largest unions—the Bricklayers, Carpenters, Painters, Iron Workers, Laborers, and Plumbers—met in August, they agreed that it was time to develop a central organization of amalgamated building trades unions, designed to face the challenge of rapid technological change by avoiding the pitfalls of jurisdictional conflicts.[29]

According to NBTC veteran Michael P. Carrick of the Painters, the new organization intended to prevent the rise of dual unions, keep control of jurisdiction in the hands of the men involved, and establish an "allied force" of building trades unions to improve conditions without resorting to strikes. It also intended to work in harmony with the American Federation of Labor, he hastened to inform Samuel Gompers. "We did not meet with the intention of interfering with the A. F. of L. as the men . . . one and all, believe that the American Federation of Labor is doing good work for the cause of labor in general," Carrick informed him. Specifically, however, the building trades unions thought that more could be done on their behalf. "We felt by getting our forces together we could induce the A. F. of L. to give some attention to building trades matters."[30]

Infuriated by this comment, Gompers immediately sent the letter on to the AFL Executive Council, along with a list of AFL actions to prove Carrick wrong. First, he pointed out that the Bricklayers and Iron Workers were not even affiliated with the AFL. Then he made it clear that Gompers himself had organized the laborers' international union, and that the AFL had raised funds for the Carpenters' eight-hour strike, had worked hard to reunite the Painters, and was still assisting the Plumbers union in its fight against the Steam Fitters. So while he did not oppose "a National Building Trades Council or Section . . . in full loyalty to the American Federation of Labor," as he told Executive Council members, Gompers was not at all persuaded that the men in Indiana truly intended to work in harmony with the AFL.[31]

Only time would tell. In the meantime, the Structural Building Trades Alliance, as the new organization was called, began to take shape. Meeting in Indianapolis once again a few months later, a broader delegation of Bricklayers, Carpenters, Electrical Workers, Engineers, Iron Workers, Laborers, Painters, Plasterers, and Plumbers hammered out a program to "arbitrate, adjudicate, and conduct building trades affairs." Their initial decision to admit "none but the basic trades" as members proved controversial: It put

the SBTA firmly on the side of large, amalgamated unions, like the Bricklayers and the Carpenters, and against the specialty trades, like the Steam Fitters
and Cement Workers. Specialty trades would have to join the "primary"
union, if they wanted to be part of this new organization. Delegates also
made it clear that international unions would govern labor affairs; in fact,
building trades councils had no official voice in the new organization. Delegates also endorsed arbitration boards (but promised sympathetic support if
no agreement could be reached), pledged to work in harmony with both the
AFL and the NBTC, and agreed that dual unions should be annihilated, if
not prevented. Finally, they drafted a constitution that gave centralized
power to a Board of Governors: The SBTA's president, secretary-treasurer,
and eight vice presidents would make final decisions on all trade matters, including jurisdiction, based "on the principle of the strict trade vote."[32]

Confident that the hardest decisions were behind them, delegates elected a
Board of Governors to lead building trades unions into a new era of national
trade agreements, international union disciple, and centralized organization. George P. Gubbins, president of the Bricklayers union and a well-
known leader in Chicago, was elected president. William Spencer, general
organizer for the Plumbers and a Canadian immigrant, was elected secretary-treasurer. Seven vice presidents were also elected: J. G. Kavanaugh
(Plasterers), Frank Buchanan (Iron Workers), Frank Duffy (Carpenters),
Alexander Bainbridge (Painters), Herman Lillien (Laborers), James Hannahan (Engineers), and W. J. French (Electricians). Election of the eighth vice
president was postponed, however, until the SBTA decided whether the
Granite Cutters, Marble Workers, or Stone Cutters constituted the "basic"
trade. In the meantime, a special committee planned to meet the following
week to finish drafting the constitution, which would then be submitted to
the board for approval and sent out to affiliates for final ratification.[33]

There was nothing left to do but wait, or so it seemed at the time: The men
in Indiana were confident that the Structural Building Trades Alliance was
on the right track. By speaking in one authoritative voice, the new federation
would prove to be "the most powerful labor body in any one line" of work,
they believed.[34] And by setting up a strict chain of command, the SBTA
would function as an integrated whole, ready and able to meet the challenge
of organized employers head on. Their confidence in the fall of 1903 was inspiring; even the newspapers seemed to agree that the rise of the SBTA promised to solve the industry's problems. Unfortunately they spoke too soon.
Long before the constitution was even ratified, the ground began to shift. By
the time the SBTA called its next convention to order, in 1904, leaders would
be grappling with a hard fact of life: It was far easier for building trades
workers to erect a skyscraper than it was to organize a "union of all the
trades."

The Founding Brothers: From the Structural Building Trades Alliance to the Building Trades Department

> Where so much is needed, and harmony should prevail so that we could show a solid front to the common enemy, we waste time over technicalities and the only lesson we have learned in our first year of existence is how not to do it.
> —Charles Metee to William J. Spencer, April 26, 1906

Their idea seemed simple enough at the time: If building trades unions intended to improve conditions, prevent conflict, and retain control of their work, they would have to join forces in a national organization. Under the circumstances, it seemed the only choice. The introduction of new materials and methods of work, and the rise of specialty trades, rival unions, and jurisdictional strikes, were wreaking havoc in the industry. At the same time, employer-sponsored Citizens' Alliances were launching a national campaign for the open shop in 1903, persuading the founders of the Structural Building Trades Alliance that it was time for the building trades to call a truce. "Unless we hang together, we will hang separately," warned William J. Spencer, one of the SBTA's strongest advocates. Positive that the Alliance plan to unite the "basic" trades, annihilate rivals, and regulate jurisdiction would produce "harmony, equity, and rightful ownership in the building industry," Spencer conveyed the confidence that characterized the SBTA's founding brothers: "Here at last . . . the internationals would stand as a unit one with the other," he attested. "Here an injury to one would be . . . the concern of all."[1]

Thirty-six years old when he first took office as secretary-treasurer, William J. Spencer would emerge as a key player in building trades affairs. The only STBA officer elected in 1903 to make a lifelong career of the job, Spencer would serve almost thirty years as secretary-treasurer, first with the SBTA and then with its successor, the AFL Building Trades Department. A dedicated organizer and promoter, Spencer was also the keeper of the building trades' institutional memory: He attended every convention and Executive Council meeting, handled vital correspondence with local councils, contractor associations, AFL officials, and government leaders, and participated in every significant triumph and crisis. A member of Plumbers Local 36 since 1894, he brought a wealth of experience to the job, having served three years as international secretary-treasurer and another three years as general organizer. In the process he had helped to reform the Plumbers' financial system, negotiated settlements with independent (and sometimes hostile) local unions, and promoted the benefits of a strong international union through his monthly column in the Plumbers' journal (which he wrote under the pen name Bosco). In fact, he was still on the international union's payroll when he first took office with the SBTA, an advantage that proved crucial since the Alliance had no funds at the time.[2]

The Plumbers' investment was worthwhile, because Spencer also brought a determined point of view to the job. A battle-scarred veteran of the Plumbers' fight against the Steam Fitters to control the pipe trades, he took it for granted that "primary" or "basic" trades (like plumbing) should control the work of "tributary" or "subtrades" (like steam fitting). And he made no bones about it: Spencer fully expected the SBTA to help the Plumbers "subdue its rival." That, after all, was the real point of the new organization. In fact, as Spencer later explained, each of the nine basic trades had a "score to settle" with an "outside" rival. The Bricklayers, for instance, helped organize the Alliance in order to defeat the Stone Masons, the Carpenters backed the Alliance to win its fight against the Wood Workers, the Painters participated to put an independent rival in New York City out of business, the Plasterers hoped to beat the Cement Workers, the Laborers union was fighting a series of independent rivals, and the list went on. Ultimately this fight to defeat (and then incorporate) rivals "outside the fold" proved to be a major source of solidarity for the primary trades of the SBTA. It not only compelled Alliance members to "combine and act as a unit," as Spencer put it, but it eclipsed, for the time being at least, some serious grievances the primary trades had against one another.[3]

Indeed, in the winter of 1903–1904 when the Alliance was just getting started, solidarity, or at least the appearance of solidarity, seemed essential: No one was talking about internal conflict at the time. If the Iron Workers,

Painters, and Laborers bitterly resented the Carpenters' ever expanding jurisdiction, or the Plumbers and Electrical Workers waged fierce battles over the installation of iron tubing, or conduits, used for electrical wiring, the early Alliance kept these conflicts quiet. Cooperation and unity were the watchwords, SBTA founders agreed, and Spencer made a real effort to present the fledgling organization in the best light possible. "Complete unanimity of feeling prevailed" at the founding convention, he reported. And why not? The very structure of the new organization promised to establish order, reciprocity, and goodwill. Majority rule and a one union–one vote strategy, the founders attested, would ensure that common trade interests would determine jurisdiction or decisions to order general strikes. Whether a trade was large or small, it would have an equal voice in industrywide matters, and thus no single trade would be able to impose "unwarranted and unreasonable" demands on the others. There would be no room for petty arguments or for power plays, Spencer noted. Affiliates who rejected official decisions would forfeit group support, and that could prove costly: Alliance members had promised to band together to fight rival unions and defend one another's jurisdictional claims, a first in building trades history. According to carpenter T. M. Guerin (who had helped Spencer draft the SBTA constitution), the Alliance offered "what no other central body has ever given: direct sympathy and support to the men in the Building Trades," guaranteeing, in effect, the old labor slogan, "One for all, and all for one."[4]

Moving from Rhetoric to Reality

Whatever SBTA founders hoped, there would be no solidarity among Alliance members without rank-and-file support, an organizational fact of life that building trades leaders knew only too well. In 1903–1904 international union constitutions generally required referendum votes on significant issues, and deciding whether to affiliate and endorse the SBTA's program certainly qualified as significant. Alliance supporters had no reason to worry, according to Spencer's reports. Early returns clearly indicated what Alliance leaders already believed: "the bonds of unity" would be drawn "still tighter, if that were possible, by the approval of the general membership." "Already the Plumbers . . . and the Building Laborers have acted favorably," Spencer noted. And the Plasterers, Painters, Iron Workers, Electricians, Bricklayers, and Carpenters were well on their way.[5] However, when the SBTA met in convention that summer, these confident predictions fell flat. Only six of the nine founding unions—the Painters, Plumbers, Laborers, Carpenters, Iron Workers, and Engineers—sent delegates. And only six of the nine officers elected in 1903 were present. In fact, when the meeting was called to order, SBTA president George P. Gubbins of the Bricklayers, was not on the floor.[6]

It was certainly no secret, in 1904, that the Bricklayers preferred to go it alone: Local unions of the Bricklayers' and Masons' International Union (BMIU) were notorious for refusing to join local councils (and general strikes), and the membership regularly voted against joining the American Federation of Labor. Yet Gubbins, a veteran of BMIU Local 21 in Chicago, had been an Alliance proponent from the start; in fact, there were those who traced the rise of the SBTA to the BMIU's successful fight, in 1903, to incorporate stone masons in Pittsburgh into the BMIU local.[7] But he was taking no chances. As international union president, Gubbins worked hard to ensure that the SBTA met the Bricklayers' specifications: Because his membership would never endorse a broad organization, it was Gubbins who led the fight to restrict the Alliance to basic trades only; there would be no tile setters' union or wood lathers' union in the new organization. As Spencer recalled, the Bricklayers' delegation had been adamant. They had no intention of associating with trades whose members did shop work or fabricated materials, partly because they were installers, not tradesmen, in the Bricklayers' view, and partly because the growing number of "installer" trades might dominate the organization and thus force the Bricklayers to support their jurisdictional strikes. Although other delegates strongly objected at the time (a measure of dissent that was not recorded in Spencer's reports) Gubbins and the Bricklayers' delegation would not yield. If the other trades wanted the Bricklayers in the fold, they would have to follow its lead. That SBTA founders not only adopted the Bricklayers' proposition but also elected Gubbins president attested to the superior strength of the BMIU as an organization.[8]

However, Gubbins had less success with his own membership. He quickly issued a special circular urging locals to endorse the SBTA, but without much effect. BMIU secretary William Dobson backed him up, more or less, but the strong voice that apparently swayed Alliance founders was silent. "You are the sovereign power," Dobson assured the membership. "Your Executive Board simply authorized your president to attend [the SBTA's] preliminary conferences, with the understanding that our organization was not to be pledged to anything whatever." Disappointed when the referendum failed, the leadership raised the issue again at the Bricklayers' convention in 1904. But this time it was Frank Buchanan, president of the Iron Workers and an SBTA vice president, who did the talking. Delegates apparently applauded his rousing speech, demonstrating their approval of the SBTA's "high sentiments," according to convention reports. When rank-and-file bricklayers voted in another referendum, however, the results were the same: Bricklayers, by and large, were still determined to go it alone.[9]

Frank Duffy to the Rescue

The Bricklayers' defection left the Alliance without a president, but not without a leader. When George Gubbins failed to appear for the opening of the 1904 convention, Vice President Frank Duffy immediately picked up the gavel, and the meeting went off as planned. Secretary of the Carpenters, and an Irishman by birth, Duffy had been promoting the Alliance ever since he issued the call for the very first meeting. In fact, many considered him the real power behind the SBTA throne: Some presumed that Duffy had launched the Alliance to force a change in the AFL policy of granting jurisdiction to specialty unions, a charge he would probably have denied but one that had some basis in fact. For there was no denying that Frank Duffy was fed up. "To be plain I might here inform you that the men of the Building Trades will have to look out for their own interests, welfare, and protection," he once told Frank Morrison, secretary of the AFL. What else could they do, since the Federation had a habit of referring complaints to committees whose members "knew nothing whatever of the Building Trades, and who rendered decisions that the Building Trades would not stand for or tolerate." Alliance supporters had no intention of antagonizing the AFL, he added, but the fact remained that they needed an organization to "take care of the men of the building industry."[10]

Whatever his motives, Duffy did his best to make the new organization a success. Like Spencer, he used his position as UBCJA secretary (and editor of the monthly journal *The Carpenter*) to promote the Alliance. And like Spencer, he brought a lot of experience and a determined point of view to the job. A man who never hesitated to speak his mind, Duffy ably defended his membership's broad jurisdictional claims against all comers. He also put his considerable management skills to good use. By the time Duffy assumed office as SBTA vice president, at age forty-two, he had worked in New York City as a local officer, business agent, and financial supervisor for the District Council. In Philadelphia, and then in Indianapolis, he had gained valuable experience as a general organizer, executive board member, secretary treasurer, and then secretary of the international union, a job he held until 1948. A brutally honest and relentless critic, Duffy would play a crucial role in the development of the SBTA and the Building Trades Department, sometimes as an officer, sometimes as an AFL Executive Council member, and sometimes as an opponent determined to preserve his members' rights.[11]

But in 1904 Duffy was at center stage, proceeding as if he had expected to chair the convention all along: He delivered an opening speech, appointed committees, made a report on the year's activities, and basically performed as if nothing were wrong. What choice did he have? It was true that the Bricklayers, Plasterers, and Electrical Workers had apparently lost interest in the SBTA, but no one believed that they were gone for good. In fact, when

Gubbins and a colleague finally arrived, bearing bad news of the Bricklayers' vote, delegates invited them to observe the proceedings and offer advice anyway. And despite the fact that no progress had been made on settling jurisdictional claims, arbitrating strikes, and setting up local councils, there was no sense of crisis or defeat. On the contrary, delegates pushed forward with the business at hand, voting to promote local councils, establish an arbitration plan, set up official headquarters (in Dayton, Ohio), and make the office of secretary-treasurer a full-time, salaried job. With a balance of $18 in the treasury and a newly elected slate of officers, including Frank Buchanan as president, Spencer as secretary-treasurer, and James Kirby, of the Carpenters, as first vice president, the SBTA set out to face another year.[12]

And what a year it was. Although some forty local alliances were organized, serious jurisdictional fights led to dueling organizations in Buffalo, Baltimore, and Pittsburgh, with the rival usually taking the form of an AFL-affiliated building trades section of the local central labor union (CLU). At the same time, the failure of the Plasterers and Bricklayers to join the Alliance complicated local matters. Should delegates from these important trades be seated in local alliances, if they were willing to join? And what about independent locals of Plumbers, Painters, and Laborers? Since local alliances needed their support on a job site, could they not qualify as members, too? Local conditions pointed one way, international union politics and policy another, and in the meantime, rank-and-file building trades workers and their families were suffering. Specialty trades also raised thorny problems. The Steam Fitters union, for instance, was eager to join the Alliance, and it was beginning to look as if the Plumbers union was the only one to consider it a dual organization, a fact that Spencer found alarming. "Beyond question it is expecting too much for one or two organizations to stand religiously for the principles, aspirations and objects of this Alliance," he bitterly complained, "while the remaining affiliated organizations ruthlessly and wantonly disregard them when applied to others but expect and demand unswerving support when they are in need of it." It was a complaint that would be heard repeatedly in the years to come.[13]

Broadening the Organization

The question of broadening the organization was also causing problems. In fact, newspapers publicly criticized the SBTA for ignoring "specialty" unions like the Lathers which had organized in 1899 (and whose members put up the narrow strips of wood, or lath, that served as backing for plaster). The Painters, in particular, apparently agreed; Michael P. Carrick had been pushing for a broad organization from the very beginning, and after his death in the spring of 1904 Brotherhood of Painters and Decorators (BPDA) president Joseph Balhorn and his colleague Alexander Bainbridge, an SBTA vice president, kept up the fight. The Iron Workers, on the other hand, saw things differently, especially with regard to the Lathers. This union had not only changed its official name from the Wood Lathers to the Wood, Wire, and Metallic Lathers, the Iron Workers complained, but it had broadened its jurisdiction in the process, claiming the right to install the metal lath that supported reinforced concrete, and thus trespassing on Iron Workers' turf. What if the Carpenters had tried a similar trick, the Iron Workers wanted to know. What would have happened to the Iron Workers had the Carpenters changed its name to the Wood, Steel, and Iron Carpenters when structural steel had replaced wooden frames in buildings? The answer was obvious. "If they had been as successful in spreading this claim as . . . the Wood, Wire, and Metallic Lathers, there would have been no Bridge & Structural Iron Workers' Union." According to the Iron Workers, admitting the Lathers to the SBTA spelled certain defeat for its members.[14]

As the newly elected president of the SBTA, Frank Buchanan was in a difficult spot. He knew that the struggling organization needed all the support it could muster, and that the Board of Governors was seriously considering the Lathers as a new recruit. But as president of the Iron Workers, an office he had held since 1901, he also knew that his members would take only so much. On the verge of a serious fight with open-shop steel erectors, at the same time that the union battled the Carpenters and Lathers for work, the Iron Workers did not expect much help from the SBTA. In fact, by March 1905 the membership decided to leave the Alliance, forcing Buchanan to offer his resignation, but it was not accepted, at least not yet. The Iron Workers executive board had already scheduled another vote, and Buchanan, like the optimistic leaders of the Bricklayers and the Plasterers before him, had high hopes that the Iron Workers would soon return to the fold. However, by May 1905, when the SBTA met in convention, the Iron Workers union was still outside, and carpenter James Kirby replaced iron worker Frank Buchanan as SBTA president.[15]

The 1905 convention marked more than a change in personnel. It also marked a decided shift in strategy. For before the meeting was over the "primary" trades had been broadened considerably, and four more unions—the Lathers, Tile Layers, Composition Roofers, and Elevator Constructors—had joined the list of eligible trades. Although just a few months earlier Spencer had made it clear that the SBTA did not intend "to indiscriminately accept to membership the several trades engaged upon building work," unless they were "strictly building men" and not installers or specialists, circumstances proved otherwise. The primary trades he was trying to woo at the time—the Bricklayers, Plasterers, and Electrical Workers—had all turned the Alliance down flat. As if to underscore the message, the Bricklayers then retired George Gubbins as international president, and the Iron Workers replaced Frank Buchanan with Frank M. Ryan, a man who had declared the SBTA a "gold brick" in 1905.[16]

So when the Tile Layers and Lathers affiliated that same year, SBTA officers breathed a sigh of relief. They still had a long way to go, however. Serious jurisdictional conflicts pitted the Electrical Workers against the Plumbers and Engineers, making it clear that this former affiliate would not be seeking an Alliance charter soon. The Electrical Workers union was also contesting the Elevator Constructors' jurisdiction, further complicating matters, for if the Alliance accepted one of these eligible trades, it would ensure the hostility of the other. The Plumbers had problems with the Elevator Constructors, too, since both claimed work on "hydraulic arrangements" or water pipes. "We could not consistently surrender any kind of pipe fitting whatsoever," the United Association of Journeymen Plumbers, Gas Fitters, Steam Fitters and Steam Fitters' Helpers (UA) declared, and it intended to stand firm. In the meantime, Carpenters' locals were battling the Iron Workers, Plasterers, Building Laborers, and Wood Workers, between 1904 and 1906, wreaking havoc on local alliances in the process. For with a large and demanding membership, and a national network of local unions and district councils, the Carpenters could not be ignored. "We carpenters must and will claim all bench-work and everything made of wood and used on or around a building of any kind or construction," insisted a UBCJA member from Toluca, Illinois. "We won't give it up for no one." Echoing this determination, Duffy made it clear that the Carpenters and the Carpenters alone would decide "what our jurisdiction claims shall cover, and we don't propose that they shall be curtailed, altered or amended through any other agency." Apparently the original Alliance idea that the primary trades would adjust their differences through "friendly intercourse" and the "Golden Rule" had given way to the older rule of the jungle. And Spencer, for one, was not surprised. "The boasted fealty of the trades to each other," he later admitted, "was never in evidence after the first convention."[17]

For Herman W. Steinbiss, leader of the National Building Trades Council (which changed its name to the International Building Trades Council [IBTC] in 1904) this was heartening news indeed. A headline in the IBTC paper, *The Labor Compendium,* fairly shrieked the news: "Structural Building Trades Alliance Proves a Dismal Failure." Positively gloating over the Iron Workers' decision to go out and the Electrical Workers' reluctance to go in, Steinbiss had no trouble assigning blame: Arrogant, short-sighted, and vindictive founders of the SBTA should have known that rank-and-file building trades workers could not "be led blindfolded" into anything. "Four of the most powerful organizations, who have been advertised as part of the Structural Building Trades Alliance and whose national officers were prominent in its promotion"—the Bricklayers, Plasterers, Electrical Workers, and Iron Workers—"are decidedly 'not in it,' " he reported, "and will have nothing to do with that dual body, which has so far proved successful only in . . . disrupting the building trades movement" and the IBTC.[18] Dismissing the SBTA's founders as disappointed national officers, like "Slippery Willie" Spencer (who had lost his bid for international president in 1904), Steinbiss castigated what seemed to be their rule-or-ruin philosophy. For as far as he could see, the SBTA was the product of spite, pure and simple. Because the IBTC chartered "specialty" unions, like the Stone Masons, Steam Fitters, and Cement Workers, Steinbiss explained, the founding brothers of the SBTA had organized to destroy it. And they were apparently hell-bent on the task: Steinbiss suspected a link between the SBTA and the open-shop movement since, as he reported in his paper, both had been established around the same time, and both had been organized in Indianapolis.[19]

Repairing Relations with the AFL

Although he was not a fan of the SBTA, Samuel Gompers proved more circumspect; the AFL president was willing to wait and see how the SBTA developed before he took a stand. On the one hand, he was naturally wary of a building trades competitor: If these unions managed to stand together, they would be hard to beat. But as a seasoned organizer he was not looking to create enemies either: The AFL may have been on firmer ground than the SBTA in 1905, but it depended on its building trades members for stability and survival. After all, building trades unions were the oldest and best-organized unions in the United States and Canada, and they made up about 20 percent of the AFL's membership. Taking no chances, the AFL Executive Council began to take the building trades more seriously: When William Spencer joined the Council as seventh vice president in 1905, it was tacitly assumed that he now held the building trades' seat. Relations remained rocky, nevertheless, largely due to serious friction between SBTA local alliances and CLU building trade sections in critical cities like Boston and Philadelphia. For instance, in 1905 the secretary of Philadelphia's CLU (a glassworker by trade) expected Gompers to back the AFL affiliate in a fight against the SBTA. "The CLU . . . desires the A.F. of L. to inform the Bro[therhood] of Carpenters, and all other Trades in the building line, that, if they desire to be members of a combination of Building Trades . . . they [should] join the legitimate Building Trades Section of the Central Labor Union of Phila[delphia] and vicinity."[20]

Gompers, however, decided to leave the matter in the hands of the SBTA, a strategy that proved central to improving relations. For while the Alliance's seven affiliates were also AFL members in good standing, almost every one of these unions had a serious grievance against the Federation either because it had chartered an obvious rival union, allowed the "miscellaneous" crafts to have a voice in building trades affairs, or failed to provide the level of support that building trades unions expected in a crisis. The sense that the AFL needed the building trades more than the building trades needed the AFL added to the conflict. When AFL treasurer John Lennon, a tailor, asked the SBTA to send fraternal greetings to the AFL's 1904 convention, for instance, the Laborers and the Carpenters were dead set against it.[21] However, by 1905 mutual ties were beginning to grow, a shift that probably reflected both the SBTA's slip in membership and the AFL's willingness to respect building trades turf: At a meeting in March with President Gompers and AFL secretary Frank Morrison, SBTA leaders pledged both "friendliness and cooperation," and expressed the hope "that when matters of general interest demanded joint consideration, no hesitation or reluctance would be shown by either organization." Returning the favor, Gompers turned over some important documents related to serious building trades fights in New York City, making it clear to the Board of Governors that this was SBTA, not AFL, business.[22]

Internal Conflicts

For James Kirby, first full-time president of the SBTA, this was a healthy turn of events since it demonstrated the AFL's belief in the organization's potential: If the Alliance could only muster its forces in fact as well as in name, building trades unions could set the pace for the national and international labor movement. But there was still important groundwork to be done, and it was up to Kirby to get rank-and-file workers behind the Alliance. As a former millwright and a member of Carpenters Local 199 in Chicago, and the current leader of the District Council there, Kirby knew firsthand the power of local solidarity. But he also knew the value of trade agreements, arbitration boards, and industrywide solidarity. As the newest leader of the SBTA, it was his responsibility to get the word out.[23]

On the road almost constantly from the start of his administration, Kirby spent the rest of 1905 and the better part of 1906 trying to prove the value of the SBTA to building trades workers. Charged by the convention to visit "eligible" unions in the hope of building confidence in the Alliance, he also worked as an organizer, negotiator, peace maker, and trouble shooter. In Bloomington, Illinois, for instance, he established a local alliance, and in

Champaign he put a dual union of building laborers out of business. He straightened out a dangerous fight in Cedar Rapids, Iowa, and then helped to organize a painters' local there, with the approval of the BPDA, of course. In Toledo, Ohio, Kirby convinced painters and carpenters to join the local alliance, but he had no such luck when he tried again in Columbus and Cincinnati. But in Louisville, where the local alliance and the Central Labor Union were "at swords points," he apparently resolved the conflict with the help of Samuel Gompers.[24]

These trips were as educational as they were exhausting. For they demonstrated that "petty disputes" and personality conflicts could be as potent as working conditions and jurisdictional claims when it came to local conflicts. "It is surprising," Kirby reported, "what length some will go to avenge some fancied insult or neglect that occurred long ago."[25] Tensions between skilled and unskilled unions were also an issue. Many of the conflicts that drew Kirby's attention grew out of the Laborers' struggle to organize and defeat rival unions. But given the Laborers' basic inability to defend the union's ground without the assistance of the skilled trades—whose members could not be replaced so easily—conflict over sympathy strikes was inevitable. According to the Laborers' leader, Henry Stemburgh, there was a general belief among the trades that "most anyone could do the work that was performed by . . . our organization" for a much lower wage. Given those circumstances, building trades workers were not always eager to help. When laborers in Syracuse, New York, for instance, wanted carpenters to strike on their behalf, they were sorely disappointed. "We believe that the Hod Carriers and Building Laborers are not a bona fide trade of the Building Craftsmen," the Carpenters explained, "and we firmly believe that the interests of the organized mechanics would be best subserved by not accepting the proposition submitted."[26]

A similar conflict arose in Washington, D.C., where the Laborers union was classified as "unskilled" and was not admitted to the local alliance. But in this case, Kirby noted, there was more going on. In Washington, D.C., as in many southern cities, race, not skill, was the sticking point. "This is not a fight on the Laborers," Kirby reported soon after visiting the city. "[It] arises purely from the race situation." Blaming the trouble on the Laborers' black representative and his "indiscreet language," Kirby believed that his hands were tied in this case. And since the issue was social, not industrial, Spencer apparently agreed. Washington was a segregated city, and it was not unusual that local alliance members were "unwilling to seat colored delegates," as he put it. When Stemburgh complained that the Board of Governors was not doing enough to resolve the situation, Spencer stood his ground. "It should be borne in mind that as yet not one cent of per capita tax has been paid to this office by [the Laborers]," he noted in the summer of 1905. "We have been the soul of leniency," he concluded, at least where the Laborers' finances were concerned.[27]

But the conflict in Washington, D.C., could not be so easily dismissed. Whether Kirby and Spencer acknowledged it, they knew that social conflicts undermined labor solidarity nationwide. Jacob Tazelaar, a painter and building trades organizer, put the issue plainly: "What you find here in the 'Sunny South' between the white man and the negro you find in the East between the different races and nationalities, one arrayed against the other, whilst the corporation and employers stand aside enjoying our blind fight. . . . Keep it up! Keep it up! Keep it up!" he quipped. "But you will be the sufferer."[28]

Those who doubted his advice had only to travel to places like New Orleans, Chattanooga, Jacksonville, or Birmingham, where building trades workers paid a very high price for their attitudes: Some trades managed to enjoy fairly good conditions, President Kirby noted, after a southern tour in 1906, but no trade commanded a closed shop. And given the high level of distrust "not only among the different trades, but in the organizations themselves," as Kirby put it, he did not see much room for improvement. A return visit in 1907 confirmed his view. "Generally speaking, the trouble in the South is the inclination to scrap among themselves," he noted. "Too much energy is wasted on trivial matters and [they are] losing sight of the nonunion man in their efforts to control their Local organizations." As to the "race question which affects the southern states so vitally," Kirby was keeping out of it. He did, however, offer this statement: "Follow the advice of your officers! For during my entire visit," he explained, nearly "every union official I met, and even every man actively connected with the labor movement, realized the necessity of thorough organization of every individual who labors for a livelihood."[29] A carpenter from Birmingham, Alabama, put the issue more plainly: "The colored member's card is as good as ours. . . . Let us give [him] a chance to hold a job and earn a living for himself and his family." True brotherhood, he insisted, demanded nothing less.[30]

This native son of Alabama offered some general advice, too. Tired of all the squawking over whether to endorse the SBTA, he challenged workers to give it a chance. "Let us bury the hatchet, quit quarreling and do [un]to others as we would have them do unto us"—words to live by if the SBTA had any hope of accomplishing its goals. But words were no longer enough. Leaders like Kirby and Spencer were still struggling with a very practical problem: how to make the promise of solidarity, or "true Brotherhood," a reality across the board. Everyone agreed that "combined action was the remedy," as Spencer acknowledged with some frustration, "but how to obtain it" was still an open question.[31]

There were those who believed the solution was obvious: The Board of Governors should use an "iron fist" to keep affiliated unions, and specifically local unions, in line. Those who failed to follow SBTA rules and jurisdictional decisions should be heavily fined and suspended immediately. After all, that was the policy adopted at the founding convention. Others, however, valued stability over strict discipline. When the local alliance in Spokane fined the Plumbers $325 for refusing to comply with a decision to issue quarterly working cards, for example, the Board of Governors would not back them up. "It will be well to remember," Spencer wrote, "[that] to heavily fine locals, even though they may be derelict in duty, may work to the ultimate dissolution of the Alliance." Outraged by this failure to act, the local alliance made its dissatisfaction clear: "We were led to believe when we applied for a charter . . . that the General Board of Governors . . . would compel local unions to obey the local laws or lose their charter. If such is not the case please notify us at once."[32]

Local alliances also complained regularly that SBTA affiliates often failed to join local councils, or to support approved strikes. "They have refused to do anything to help the Alliance in any form since they have been affiliated with us" a local leader wrote when carpenters in Syracuse worked through a laborers' strike. And that threatened conditions for the rest of the trades. "Contractors [state that] they are not afraid of the Alliance, as they have assurance that we can get no support from the Carpenters or Plumbers or Bricklayers," he complained. But neither Kirby nor Duffy nor Spencer nor William Merrick (president of the Plumbers) was sympathetic. They believed that there were two sides to every strike story, and they were tired of local attempts to threaten affiliates into submission, especially affiliates that had more members than the other unions combined. "Now, while the Carpenters have not acted, at all times, in a manner intended to promote harmony and advance the interest of all concerned, . . . had other delegates . . . assumed a less radical attitude towards them I feel sure that instead of hindering, they would have assisted," Kirby maintained. "Had personalities not been allowed to prevail," he added, the carpenters would have cooperated.[33]

There was also the ongoing problem of independent local unions that refused to join the international union, for example, independent unions of steam fitters, painters, plumbers, carpenters, and laborers. As long as they proved dependable, many local alliances welcomed their support, a serious break in discipline that international unions could not ignore. However, when it came to independent unions in New York City, many international unions refused to get involved. New York City's unions tended to be a law unto themselves. Because they were often stronger than many international unions at the time, they brooked no interference from outsiders. "The conditions of affairs in the building industry in New York City is different from that of any other city in the United States," Frank Duffy explained. "They are peculiarly located, have peculiar notions and ideas of their own and they are opposed to the SBTA at the present time." And that being the case, the Carpenters saw no good reason to start a fight the union could not win.[34]

The Painters, however, disagreed: Determined to beat the Amalgamated Society of Painters, which controlled the trade in New York City, the Painters planned to enlist the SBTA's help by launching a local alliance there. This aggressive strategy startled William Spencer, who immediately alerted the Board of Governors when an application for a New York City alliance arrived in the mail. "The application is undoubtedly the work of Vice President [Jacob] Tazelaar [of the Painters]," he noted, "and . . . ordinarily should be acted upon favorably." But under the circumstances Spencer wanted approval from the Board of Governors before taking action. When the subject came up at the next board meeting, the majority apparently agreed that opposition in New York City, especially in Manhattan, Brooklyn, and the Bronx, was too strong to take on. But the Painters, Plumbers, and Tile Layers, who backed the plan, refused to give it up, forcing Duffy to enter a formal protest to make his position clear: "There is no use in looking for the support of the carpenters in New York at the present time," he said, a refusal that doomed the plan.[35]

Seriously frustrated, the Painters union believed it was time to restructure the Alliance. More convinced than ever that it needed the support of those building trades that were still outside the Alliance, the Painters introduced a resolution at the 1907 STBA convention to "admit to membership . . . all international unions of building men that are affiliated with the American Federation of Labor." The Painters also called for an end to full-time Alliance officers, offering a plan for a new Board of Governors that would include the officers of every affiliated union and meet whenever conditions required it. Spencer was not surprised that these resolutions were defeated, since "their object was to bring about a dissolution of the Alliance." But he was disappointed when the Painters union took its next step: it dismissed the Alliance as "a revenue collecting organization . . . without serious intent to . . . promote the welfare of our local unions," and left the SBTA. "None of the International organizations affiliated are prepared to compel their local unions to affiliate with, or to discipline them for withdrawing from local alliances," President Balhorn explained to the membership. And that being the case, it was time to move on.[36]

Although Spencer and the Painters' representative on the Board of Governors, Alexander Bainbridge, tried to make the case that the Painters had actually gained members with the help of the Alliance, the Painters' decision was final. "The principle upon which [the Alliance] is founded is sound," President Balhorn admitted, "but I fear the time is not ripe for the conversion of the theory into practice." Whether he liked it or not—and he certainly did not—William Spencer was forced to agree. "The truth is, the failure of the bricklayers and the plasterers to make good, coupled with the desertion of the iron workers and the painters," he later admitted, "caused a general weakness in the structure that all known restoratives failed to relieve. Its inertness foreshadowed collapse."[37]

At the time, however, neither Spencer nor Kirby was ready to admit defeat. On the contrary, they were more determined than ever to keep the Alliance afloat. Since local alliances often found themselves fighting with AFL-affiliated building trades sections of central labor unions, President Kirby now called on the AFL to dissolve them. Addressing the AFL Executive Council in the summer of 1907, he complained that AFL organizers (including a cigar maker and a machinist) were using these building trades sections to undermine local alliances, since they considered the SBTA a dual union. Eager to resolve this "misunderstanding," the Executive Council authorized AFL president Samuel Gompers, Carpenters' president William Huber, and Granite Cutters' secretary-treasurer James Duncan to meet with the SBTA's Board of Governors to straighten things out. When they finally got together that October (with Kirby, Spencer, and James Hannahan of the Engineers representing the SBTA) they cleared the air. The AFL representatives criticized the narrow "structural" base of the SBTA, but Alliance members pointed out that local alliances "safely" accepted any building trades union that wanted to join, whether or not the international union was eligible for membership. They also responded to the AFL organizers' charge that the SBTA was a dual union, hostile to the AFL: "For the purpose of guaranteeing the good faith of the Alliance that it is in harmony with . . . the AFL," Kirby, Spencer, and Hannahan suggested "that a charter be issued to the Structural Building Trades Alliance on the same conditions as charters are issued to central bodies."[38]

The Rise of the Building Trades Department

When the AFL met in convention the following month, the Committee on Building Trades took up the suggestion. Chaired by Carpenters' president William Huber, the committee represented a real mix of building trades unions, including some that had been "at each 'other's throats' for years," as one member put it. The Plumbers and Steam Fitters, Electrical Workers and Elevator Constructors, Soft Stone Cutters, Granite Cutters, Tile Layers, and Roofers, among others, were all represented. In fact, only the "trowel trades" were missing, as neither the Bricklayers nor the Plasterers were AFL members at the time. Convinced that it would be better for everyone if the building trades were part of the general labor movement, a five-man subcommittee—Joseph Balhorn (Painters), Henry Stemburgh (Laborers), John Mangan (Steam Fit-

ters), Joseph Evans (Stone Cutters), and William Kennedy (Electrical Workers)—hammered out a "skeleton plan" for a new AFL affiliate: a national Building Trades Section with "undisputed jurisdiction" over building trades matters
and final authority over local building trades sections. Because broad support
was essential, Chairman Huber invited every building trades delegate at the
convention to weigh in on the plan. He also made sure that representatives of
the Bricklayers and Plasterers joined the discussion, so that the final result
would truly reflect the best interests of the building trades as a whole. After another subcommittee amended the plan to ensure that it was constitutional, this
wide-ranging group of building tradesmen voted to present a new recommendation to the convention: that the American Federation of Labor create and
charter "a department" with "autonomy over the building trades" and "authority to issue charters to local building trades sections."[39]

Not at all sure what kind of reception the plan would meet, building
tradesmen left it up to Frank McNulty, president of the Electrical Workers,
to make their case. "I want to say that for the first time in the history of the
American labor movement, the recognized, bona fide building trades . . .
have united for the purpose of creating a Building Trades Section that will
unite the labor movement of this country," he said. "I hope you will not
think for a moment that . . . the building trades [intend] to separate our
labor movement. That is far from the idea." For as McNulty explained, "The
purpose is to have the building trades and the miscellaneous trades work
hand in hand . . . to eliminate . . . the continual fighting of building trades
over jurisdiction. In the past we have made enemies of our friends among the
employers. We realize that unless the building trades can be united under
one head it will be impossible to eliminate these fights."[40] James Duncan,
AFL vice president and another building tradesmen, backed him up. "When
it is remembered that here has been a National Building Trades Council
which has failed, when it is understood there is a Structural Building Trades
Alliance about which there is some misunderstanding . . . you will see this
will take its place and gives us a Building Trades Department in which matters . . . can be handled with authority. . . . If the affairs are turned over to
those who know the conditions best they will have a better system of government than they have ever had before."[41]

One of Samuel Gompers's closest and most outspoken confidants, James
Duncan proved crucial to winning support for the new department. His
own union, the Granite Cutters, had steered clear of both the National
Building Trades Council and the SBTA, but when it came to organizing an
AFL department Duncan had been there from the start. Before Gompers
was ready to follow Duncan's lead, however, he had some questions of his
own for the building trades representatives. Taking the floor, Gompers wondered whether charters issued by the new department would indicate that

the department was part of the American Federation of Labor. Quickly getting the point, McNulty answered with a resounding "Yes; with 'American Federation of Labor' in big letters ... [s]eventy-two point letters," to be exact. McNulty also accepted the suggestion Gompers made that the building trades set up headquarters with the AFL in Washington, D.C., and agreed that the department would report regularly to the AFL Executive Council. Satisfied that the building trades acknowledged the AFL's leadership, Gompers gave his blessing. "I desire to say that as a trade unionist ... as well as the President of the American Federation of Labor, the project has my hearty endorsement."[42]

And that, according to William E. Kennedy, secretary of the Building Trades Committee, made all the difference. With Duncan and Gompers squarely on board, convention delegates offered a unanimous vote of support for the new department, and Kennedy credited both men, along with McNulty and Kirby, with the victory. "It is now only a question of a few weeks when this ... magnificent structure will be launched, and when it does get started," he reported, "when all the building trades ... all over the country, all stand shoulder to shoulder, can any one doubt as to the results when we are right?"[43]

James Kirby was equally pleased, but he took a different view of the proceedings. "I want to say right here and I fear no successful contradiction that the agitation created and success attained by the SBTA is the main reason why the building trades were granted complete autonomy over their own affairs without a dissenting vote. ... The laws of our organization will have to be completely rewritten and maybe we won't know ourselves when we come out of the work. But I want to say it is better for all concerned as we will then be in a solid body and able to bid defiance to all our enemies, come where they will." As if to prove his point he made sure that when the call for a convention went out, it was the SBTA and not the AFL that invited building trades leaders to meet in Washington, D.C., to form a new organization.[44]

With delegates from eighteen trades (including stone cutters, marble workers, cement workers, and most of the "primary" trades) answering the call, the convention that opened on February 10, 1908, represented a real cross-section of the industry—only the Bricklayers and Plasterers were missing. There were delegates from two unions of carpenters (the United Brotherhood and the Amalgamated Carpenters) and two unions of roofers (the Slate Roofers and the Composite Roofers), demonstrating a major break from SBTA policy. And delegates were apportioned according to membership, with one delegate representing every four thousand union members, another major change. But in Kirby's view, that was a change whose time had come. As a member of the SBTA's largest affiliate, Kirby knew firsthand that carpenters, for one, had had enough of the Alliance's one trade–one vote policy: It was not fair, they complained, that an organization one hundred and eighty thousand strong should have the same representation as one with a thousand members, and Kirby frankly agreed with them. The Alliance had made a valiant effort to give "voice to weak and strong alike," but experience had proved, he now contended, that "a movement that permits taxation without a just and equal representation cannot be successful for long."[45]

The same was true of a central organization that did not have the power to enforce its own rules, another lesson Kirby had learned the hard way. "If this is going to be a voluntary institution," he warned, "we are wasting our time, and spending . . . money . . . needlessly." Affiliates that could not compel their local unions to join local councils would have to change their rules, especially if they expected other organizations to back *them* in a fight. And affiliates would have to take more practical and less selfish approaches to jurisdiction, Kirby urged. "I tell you, my friends, if you will read the claims set forth . . . [by some of the] different crafts here assembled, you will smile, sure, but don't forget your own constitution may look just as foolish to others. . . . Let us be sincere among ourselves," and "claim what we are entitled to, nothing more."[46]

Devoting the next four days to the vital business of crafting a constitution, delegates debated whether to accept the Machinists union as a member of the department (it was not accepted), whether to charter state councils (they would be chartered), and whether local councils would have a vote at conventions (they would not vote). The discussion heated up when the issue of apportioning convention votes was raised. The Carpenters pushed hard to have the AFL's policy of proportional representation on roll-call votes adopted, but the other trades preferred sticking with the SBTA policy of one delegate, one vote—a decision that hardly seemed controversial at the time but one that would irrevocably shape the future of the new organization. Meanwhile, questions of leadership and authority took precedence. With James Kirby and William Spencer reclaiming their seats as president and secretary-treasurer, and a mix of old and new faces rounding out the Executive Council—George Hedrick (Painters), James Hannahan (Engineers), Frank Ryan (Iron Workers), William McSorley (Lathers), and Charles Leps (Tile Layers)—the Building Trades Department was ready for business.[47]

When Samuel Gompers issued the Department's charter on March 20, 1908, he did so with pleasure. He still had his doubts about a separate building trades organization; for instance, he believed that the new Department had already broken its deal with the AFL when it voted to charter state building trades councils. But he took it on faith that the building trades' determined struggle for autonomy would be tempered by an equally strong commitment to cooperation with the larger movement. For the Building Trades Department was not, as some contended, a radical departure from the AFL's program, he maintained, or a response to the AFL's alleged mistreatment of the trades. On the contrary, he told William Spencer, the new Department was the next logical step in the "development of the federated idea of the trade union movement." And, to bolster his argument, he quoted part of his 1888 presidential address, when Gompers had first raised the idea of industrial departments.[48]

Now extending a hearty welcome to the AFL's newest affiliate, Gompers offered to help in every way possible to make the Department "entirely successful." But he also made it clear that success would depend on mutual cooperation and respect: As long as the Building Trades Department valued the "underlying principles of the trade union movement" and stood by "the conditions set forth by the Norfolk Convention of the American Federation of Labor," the movement would flourish. But just to be sure that there would be no misunderstandings regarding relations between the AFL and the new Department, Gompers took one more step: Along with the charter, he included a transcript of the questions he had asked—and the answers Frank McNulty had provided—at the AFL's 1907 convention.[49]

CHAPTER THREE

"Sticking Apart": Work, Jurisdiction, and Solidarity

> Memories of old conflicts and defeats rankle and some think
> and talk more of the past than of the present and future—so
> much so that whenever a move is made looking to concerted
> action cold water is at once thrown on it. . . . We gain nothing
> by sticking apart and listening to tales of treachery . . . spread
> by the contractors, whose interest is to keep us divided so
> that they may whip us in detail.
>
> —Jacksonville *Artisan,* 1916

Frank Duffy had held no "official" position with the building trades
since 1904. Nor did he seek one in 1908, when the Building Trades Department (BTD) was launched. But that did not mean he intended to steer clear
of department affairs—far from it, as anyone who knew the Carpenters' secretary could attest. Officer or not, Duffy had been a key player in the Structural Building Trades Alliance, and he fully intended to reprise his role in the
new organization. "You can count on [my] warm feeling and willing support," he let William Spencer know early on. "I will not promise . . . that all
my communications will be love letters; on the contrary, you may expect
that if things don't go right, you will hear from me in no uncertain terms. Let
us hope that the Building Trades Department of the American Federation of
Labor will be a success," a hope that Spencer undoubtedly shared, if only to
keep Frank Duffy at bay.[1]

Under the circumstances, however, that hardly seemed possible: The very
structure of the new Department all but guaranteed a fight. The nineteen
unions that organized the BTD varied considerably in size and strength. The
Painters, for instance, counted more than sixty thousand members, the
Plumbers approximately twenty-three thousand, and the Tile Layers around

two thousand. But the Carpenters towered over the rest with well over one hundred eighty thousand members, a total that surpassed the combined membership of the four next largest unions. With an aggressive national network of local unions and district councils, the Carpenters union had more resources than most to protect its interests. Yet in the Building Trades Department its impressive numbers did not matter much—until it came to paying per capita taxes, or bailing out weaker unions in a strike, Duffy complained. The Carpenters may have constituted more than 40 percent of the Department's membership, but its voice was not proportionately louder than the rest when voting on Department policy: The Carpenters union (which paid about $425 a month in per capita taxes) was entitled to cast one vote per delegate on the convention floor, the same as every other Department member, including the Elevator Constructors (which paid $6.60) or the Marble Polishers (which paid $5.52). And that would prove to be a recipe for disaster.[2]

Size and Strength

Department leaders could not have been surprised, however. After all, the Structural Building Trades Alliance had employed similar rules and the Carpenters had fought them for years. "The carpenters and the Building Trades Alliance do not jell," as one member put it. Their lack of representation, they believed, encouraged weaker unions to exploit their strength in a fight, and carpenters bitterly resented it. In fact, Duffy had been ready to pull the Carpenters out of the SBTA in 1906, after a local alliance declared the union "unfair" for refusing to support a Plumbers' jurisdictional strike. "I am not making threats," he told Spencer. "I am out to see that the carpenters are protected and that they receive fair treatment." Enraged that SBTA officers might take the local alliance complaint seriously, he made it absolutely clear that his members would "not stand to be bull-dozed, forced into or compelled to do things" no matter the issue at hand. "Do you realize you are doing us an injustice?" he wanted to know. "An organization of over 181,000 members in good standing has the same representation and the same vote as an organization of 1,000 members. Is this fair?" Obviously Duffy did not think so.[3]

Carpenter James Kirby, president of the Building Trades Department, did not think so either. In fact, just days before the BTD's founding convention Kirby had discovered that most of the delegates wanted to save the SBTA's one union–one vote policy, and that made him livid. The majority of the small organizations, Kirby complained, "want to make the laws, have the officers, run things to suit themselves and let the Carpenters pay the freight."

But if they intended to keep this up in the new Department, he told William Spencer, "I am through with the works for good. The taxes we have paid and will have to pay would employ a couple of organizers, and I am not sure but that would do the United Brotherhood more good." Admitting that he was "good and sore" at some of his colleagues, Kirby also confessed that his hopes were not very high for the new organization. "I was told that unless the Carpenters blocked it, [the Building Trades Department] would be the greatest institution ever created," he noted. "My reply was that the Carpenters would block any d—— thing that did not give them their rights, if it put them all on the hog."[4]

There was no doubt that the Carpenters union could do just that, if it wanted to, but in the end it was a coalition of smaller unions that ultimately did the blocking. They had no trouble agreeing that the larger unions deserved greater representation on the convention floor: The Carpenters union was allowed seven delegates, the Painters five, and the Electrical Workers, Engineers, and Plumbers four apiece. But they firmly drew the line against proportional voting. Democracy was one thing, survival another, and the smaller unions believed that they had no other choice if they wanted a voice in Department affairs. If the larger unions were allowed to vote their memberships, what would stop them from controlling jurisdiction, and swallowing up the smaller trades, as they had been trying to do for years? And if the Carpenters could control a full 40 percent of the vote, what incentive would the smaller trades have to remain in the organization? Yes, the Carpenters had the membership, no one was disputing that. But numbers were not everything in the building industry, where five operating engineers had more practical power than fifty carpenters or one hundred laborers. If the Building Trades Department really intended to forge an industrywide organization, could might really equal right when it came to making policy? The smaller trades did not think so, and they were willing to vote together in convention and to stand together in local building trades councils to prove their point.

For instance, when the Carpenters' local union in Cedar Rapids, Iowa, pushed the BTC to submit its laws to a referendum vote, eight smaller unions voted the Carpenters down, according to the Council secretary. "The majority of the trades . . . do not want the referendum as it would be putting the control . . . in the hands of the Carpenters and the Building Laborers," he reported. "This . . . would disrupt the Council, as . . . the [smaller trades] would soon get disgusted and their delegates would not attend the meetings." Kirby replied that his hands were tied, since the Carpenters' constitution ensured that local unions could not be forced to comply with any law unless they voted on it. But he also thought that the Council was making a tactical mistake: There was no good reason to fear the outcome of a referendum or to expect that rank-and-file carpenters would vote as one. "I have yet to see the time when my organization or any organization was united upon a question of law," he pointed out, "and it is very seldom that they are united . . . upon a question of electing a representative, even though the opponent may be from another craft." Unable to counter the Council's fears, Kirby was also unable to force the local to retain its membership—a real loss, he added, since there were more carpenters than there were Council members in Cedar Rapids.[5]

Carpenters all over the country voiced similar complaints. In Passaic, New Jersey, where the other trades were "badly organized and don't control their work," as one carpenter put it, the local wanted nothing to do with a building trades council. In the first place, affiliation cost too much: "We will have to pay two-thirds of the expenses of the local branch, which we are not in a position to do," this carpenter told Duffy. And second, long-standing conflicts with the Plumbers and Sheet Metal Workers had destroyed any chance for local harmony: "They see that we have the strength which they have not, and they want to ruin our locals some way," or so it seemed to this carpenter. "If it is not compulsory on us to affiliate with these fellows, don't ask us to," he urged. In Washington, D.C., local carpenters were not even willing to go this far; they made their decision without seeking anyone's advice. According to Kirby, they gave the Department "a hard bump at their meeting, voting something like seventy to four against affiliation. They certainly are the limit here in Washington," he told Duffy, "and it seems strange to me that some of them can affiliate with their wives."[6]

The problem dominated Department debate for the next two years, disrupting local councils from Savannah to Denver in the process. With nineteen out of seventy-five local councils already at war, prospects for the future looked dim. Department law clearly required local unions to join local councils, but Department officers were not eager to take a stand. Instead, they agreed that it was up to the international unions to keep locals in line, a conclusion that some affiliates had a hard time swallowing. "May we ask why there is any necessity for the existence of the Department?" the Laborers wanted to know. "We fail to see how an organization could be maintained under such a plan."[7] "Kick 'em out," the critics of the Carpenters agreed. But suspension held no threat to the union. When Spencer merely hinted that the Executive Council was considering this plan, Duffy assured him that "the Brotherhood of Carpenters can get along very well without affiliating with the Building Trades Department." For good measure, he also held back the Carpenters' per capita tax payment until the Executive Council was ready to make a final decision, a practical move that Spencer took seriously since Department funds were already running low at the time.[8]

The issue exploded at the BTD's 1909 convention, where Duffy made his position clear. If the other trades wanted the Carpenters in line, they knew what they had to do: amend the constitution so that a majority of rank-and-file council members—and not just a majority of trades—approved local council law. He did not rely on numbers alone to make his case, and he did not plead for justice. Instead, he based his argument on practical politics pure and simple; he argued on the basis of what would work. "It is not a question of the Carpenters wishing to take advantage of any other trade," he said. "But we want our local unions to become affiliated, to become part and parcel of the local Building Trades Councils. They state that they refuse to go in there because they have nothing to do with making the laws," and Duffy had no choice but to respect that. In the Carpenters union, "we let the rank and file make the law and we abide by it," he said. "If [the councils] make a law and the carpenters vote on it, I will not allow a local union to say to me that they will not affiliate; I will see that they are compelled to go in, if they help make the law."[9] The equation was simple and the outcome guaranteed. If local councils adopted the referendum vote, Duffy would deliver local carpenter unions and the influence of the Department would grow.

Majority Rule?

There was only one problem. In 1909 there were not many delegates who trusted the Carpenters. The union's long-standing fight to incorporate the Wood Workers and other rivals had turned the smaller, craft unions against it, and a series of jurisdictional battles—against the Iron Workers, Asbestos Workers, Marble Workers, and Sheet Metal Workers, for instance—persuaded a majority of delegates that the time had come to cut the mighty Carpenters down to size. Picking up where the Structural Building Trades Alliance had left off, they now demanded that the Executive Council enforce the rules, and let the chips fall where they may. "I do not think this Department should change the laws to satisfy any one affiliated organization," Arthur Huddell, the Engineers' delegate noted, and Herbert Crampton, from the Amalgamated Society of Carpenters, agreed. "This is basing a humanitarian movement entirely on commercialism," he argued. "This is an attempt to make a powerful organization the whole thing."[10] The arguments were stirring, the sentiments strong, and the votes decisive. And just in case the Carpenters did not get the message, delegates also instructed the Executive Council to expel those unions that continued to break the rules. "If we are to have a Building Trades Department that amounts to anything," insisted Frank McNulty, delegate for the Electrical Workers, "we must have laws that can be enforced, and we must be able to punish organizations that violate those laws." It was one thing to debate and dissent on the convention floor, these delegates agreed, but once the vote was cast, as the Sheet Metal Workers put it, "the will of the majority must rule."[11]

It was a phrase that was often heard in labor circles and for good reason: Who could argue with the concept of majority rule? It was, after all, a central tenet of trade unionism. Under the circumstances, however, the phrase had no meaning. A majority of delegates may have defeated the Carpenters in 1909, but these delegates had evaded the larger questions behind the Carpenters' complaint: What constituted a true majority in central labor unions—rank-and-file members or the organizations that represented them? And how could justice be served when these organizations varied so greatly? Was "one delegate, one vote" a reasonable compromise, as the smaller unions maintained? Or was it the means of disenfranchising larger unions? Was "one member, one vote" the only fair way to run an organization, as the Carpenters charged? Or was it merely a democratic ruse to impose the larger union's will? Who should exert the greater influence on Department policy—the large affiliates that paid the highest taxes (and kept the organization afloat) or the smaller unions that depended on the organization to defend their claims? And what should take precedence—the trade interests of a particular union or the stability of the Department as a whole? These were not questions that could be answered easily; both sides could come up with credible arguments to prove the justice of their cause. But they were not questions that could be overlooked for long: Issues of representation and control were not abstract matters in the building trades. They were directly related to more practical matters of jurisdiction, jobs, and wages. The coalition of smaller unions that defeated the Carpenters in 1909 had more than democracy on its mind when it voted to preserve the smaller unions' version of majority rule: These smaller unions were determined to protect their trade jurisdiction from the greedy grasp of the Carpenters.

In a volatile and demanding industry like construction, jurisdiction was the key to economic security. A building trades worker might command relatively high hourly wages, but the well-being of his family depended on steady employment, which was getting harder to obtain, or so it seemed at the time. With the introduction of new materials, new methods of work, and new specialties conditions were changing every day, limiting work opportunities for some trades, creating jobs in others, and increasing friction all around. When one union challenged the right of another union to install pipes, build scaffolding, drive piles, or reinforce concrete, for instance, the conflict could be brutal. "Civil war is not too strong a term to describe some of these inter-union struggles," as one observer put it. Men who had put in their time, learning a trade from the bottom up, believed they had a vested interest in the job—and if new work opened up, that was their work, too. After all, they had sacrificed to build up a trade, and they could not be expected to step aside quietly when contractors tried to replace them with less-skilled, less-experienced, and lower-paid men. From their perspective, they could not afford to be so generous. Because construction work fluctuated with the seasons and the business cycle, building trades workers took it for granted that there was only so much work to go around—only more reason to protect their turf from trespassers. What looked like "narrow" trade interests and "fratricidal war" to those outside the industry seemed more like family survival to those who made their living in the trades.[12]

And no union was more determined to survive than the Carpenters. " 'Hold what we have and get all we can,' [that's] our motto," as one carpenter put it, an aggressive jurisdictional strategy that the union took seriously. By 1909 the Carpenters claimed not only wood work but also any work that had once required wood, a creative shift that broadened job opportunities for its still growing membership. Given the realities of technological change, and the rise of steel frame buildings, what choice did carpenters have? They could follow wood out of the industry, or their union could change along with the times. "The steel and iron worker, the stone and brick mason, the plasterer, the marble setter and tile roofer are rapidly usurping the place of the carpenters in all the large city buildings," Duffy explained. "Wood has disappeared altogether except for doors and window frames," and even that work was on its way out. In New York City, for instance, fire codes now required metal trim, metal doors and window frames, and metal roofing in most tall buildings, and wood was becoming "as extinct as the dodo," one carpenter noted. "As a consequence," he added, "the carpenters have to fight for the right to erect this work," a logical conclusion, according to the Carpenters union, especially since its members were already on the job.[13]

Armed with the decision of New York City arbitrator Judge William J. Gaynor of the State Supreme Court, the Carpenters officially claimed metal trim work in the spring of 1909. With the help of city architects (who now wrote that claim into installation specifications), they continued on their way. Trim was trim, the union insisted, and if metal had replaced wood, what of it? "It goes up identically the same as wood, it is finished in exactly the same manner, it is erected by carpenters with carpenters' tools, and with the skill the carpenter learned on wood," one member of the Carpenters explained. Carpenters installed trim, and they would continue to do so: A shift in material was not enough to put the Carpenters union out of work.[14]

But it was enough to arouse the Amalgamated Sheet Metal Workers' International Alliance, which also expected to control this work. Since union members fabricated metal trim, they believed that they should install it, and they were ready to go to war, if necessary, to protect their rights. If carpenters were stuck in an obsolete trade, that was their problem, the union maintained. The Sheet Metal Workers had no intention of bailing them out with jobs. There was only one honorable way to move into metal work, according to President Michael O'Sullivan. Carpenters could get the proper training and then join the proper union—the Sheet Metal Workers. Otherwise they were nothing but "pirates"—and tyrannical pirates at that. "They . . . feel their numerical strength gives them a voting power in the councils of labor . . . that would crush all opposition." But they were bound to fail, O'Sullivan added. And his prediction was right. When the Sheet Metal Workers raised the issue at the 1909 BTD convention, delegates rejected the Carpenters' claim by a 3 to 1 margin: The Tampa decision, as it came to be called, awarded metal trim to the Sheet Metal Workers. "We protected and safeguarded the interests of our craft to the best of our ability," O'Sullivan proudly reported. "Our cause was just and we won, and as nothing succeeds like success, we are all happy."[15]

Exit the Carpenters

A political victory on the convention floor, however, was not the same as a practical victory on the job. For no matter how the majority ruled in 1909, carpenters continued to do metal-trim work. Possession was nine-tenths of the law, as far as carpenters were concerned, and with architects, general contractors, and manufacturers on their side, they had no intention of complying with the Tampa decision. And to prove they were serious, carpenters made their position official: In 1910 the United Brotherhood of Carpenters and Joiners "emphatically and unequivocally" declared its intention to "retain the erection of steel and hollow metal trim, sash, and doors," as if that settled the matter once and for all. "If this holds good we might all just as well become carpenters, or form an industrial organization," O'Sullivan complained. Astounded that the Carpenters union presumed it could dictate Department and AFL policy, the Sheet Metal Workers vowed this would not stand. "We did everything in our power to straighten matters out," Vice President Thomas Redding explained, but the Carpenters would not yield. "They felt as though they were greater than the Department," he reported, "and . . . if they do not get what they want they will put the Department on the bum."[16]

These were fighting words to delegates at the 1910 BTD convention, and a majority promptly voted to suspend the Carpenters. The law was clear, the infraction was blatant, and the Department had to show the Carpenters, once and for all, who was boss. Getting the message loud and clear, the Carpenters wasted no time. "It is up to us to get out of here," Daniel Featherston announced and, with that, the Carpenters' delegation walked out. Because he was convention chair, James Kirby remained, but he was only doing his duty as Department president. Otherwise, he added, he would be out the door, too. At the time, however, no one seemed to care since many unions believed that the Department would be better off without the Carpenters. In fact, the convention proceeded as if nothing much had happened. Delegates elected a new president (James Short, of the Journeymen Stone Cutters) and a new Executive Council member (Olaf Tveitmoe of the Cement Workers) to join incumbents George Hedrick (Painters), Frank Ryan (Iron Workers), Frank McNulty (Electrical Workers), and Michael O'Sullivan (Sheet Metal Workers). They also took one last shot at the Carpenters before they adjourned: Adopting an emergency motion, delegates instructed Secretary-Treasurer Spencer to notify local councils to recognize "only those trades that are affiliated with this Department."[17]

Not everyone was pleased by the outcome. James Duncan, a leader of the Granite Cutters and an AFL vice president, considered the Department's decision to expel the Carpenters "a knockout blow." Although Duncan had provided crucial support when the Department was just starting out, he had always doubted its ability to settle conflicts, especially jurisdictional conflicts. And after the events he had witnessed at the 1910 convention, his doubts were stronger still. "A spirit of rancor seemed to prevail," he told AFL president Samuel Gompers, and he blamed Michael O'Sullivan, Frank McNulty, and especially Frank Ryan for stirring up trouble. Ryan was "a veritable bear," he complained, "and he seemed to be filled with joy at the prospect of cutting out the heart of the Department. He was doing it with what he considered good intentions . . . namely 'discipline of the Department' in which the word 'compel' was so frequently used one would have thought they were . . . living under the rankest kind of imperialistic government." Now Duncan wondered "just what they will do about revenue, . . . for they needed to double the per capita tax even with the carpenters . . . in." Worse yet, he added, "the clamor for discipline in the convention will not be safely duplicated now on buildings. The bricklayers have always been looking for some one to remain on buildings with them when other trades went out, now the carpenters will remain, so will the steam fitters [who were also expelled in 1910]. . . . How the balance of the trades are to maintain 'discipline' on the buildings is not clear to me." In Duncan's opinion, the results of the 1910 convention "can be written in a single word, 'chaos.'" Gompers was inclined to agree. The actions at the convention reminded him of earlier fights in the Knights of Labor. "They sought to 'compel' the doing of things and when they found that did not work they [began] the process of decapitation . . . [leaving behind] a very sad record of corpses littering the field of Labor."[18]

As a man who had spent most of his life building up the American Federation of Labor, Gompers had no intention of letting the Building Trades Department fall apart now. He was a believer in justice and discipline, to be sure, but he was also a practical politician. And he knew from long experience that revenge often passed for justice in the heat of union fights. That being the case, he was in no hurry to act when Department leaders urged the AFL to revoke the Carpenters' charter. Carpenters were making a mockery of the Department, Spencer complained, striking jobs that employed sheet metal workers until local councils reversed the Tampa decision. But as Gompers saw it, expelling the Carpenters would not solve the problem; it would only lead to "bitter conflict, relentless antagonisms, and disintegration."[19]

Gompers had no illusions. He knew firsthand how aggressive the Carpenters could be since the AFL president had gotten more than his share of blistering letters from Frank Duffy. But he also knew that the Carpenters played a vital role in the labor movement. After all, it was one of the AFL's largest affiliates (second only to the Miners) and it was a crucial source of organizers, troubleshooters, and funds—assets that far outweighed arrogance, in Gompers's view. For instance, thanks to the Carpenters' per capita tax, James Kirby had been able to serve as a full-time organizer for the building trades, spending most of his time on the road. Now the Department was forced to seek an AFL organizer, and they were always in short supply. At the same time the Department was learning the hard way that local councils valued the Carpenters' support more than they did their BTD charters. So it seemed clear to Gompers that whatever satisfaction Department officers had derived from tossing the Carpenters out, the price was far too high. "If it is unwise to cast aside a weak link," when it came to maintaining "the chain of unity" among rank-and-file workers, he now asked Spencer, "how much more injurious is it to cast out the stronger?"[20]

Gompers was determined to reunite the building trades from the start, but Frank Duffy proved far more aloof. He deeply resented the Department's action, especially after William Spencer coupled the official suspension notice with a request for back taxes. "We are considered . . . such a despicable lot we were afraid our money would not be accepted," Duffy replied, reminding Spencer that this was not the first time the Carpenters had saved the Department financially. He also reminded him of his long record of service. "You know . . . that no other officer of a Building Trades organization spent more of his time and wrote more often to his Local Officers and members than I did. Yet I am looked upon as a renegade." But there were no hard feelings, Duffy insisted, for the Carpenters union was doing just fine. In fact, most local unions considered suspension "a relief," not a hardship, he added, that is, if they even considered it at all. "The longer we are away from you, the less interest we take in you," Duffy told Spencer, making it clear that neither he nor his organization "could be induced to come back to the Department. . . . under present conditions." So when the AFL ordered the Building Trades

Department to reinstate the Carpenters, and delegates to the 1911 convention complied, the union was in no hurry to return. The General Executive Board would take up the question in April 1912, Duffy told Spencer, but only if well-known jurisdictional and representation problems were resolved. "Chagrined" by the delay, Spencer and President Short not only met with Carpenters' officials to hammer out their differences but also agreed to act on the Carpenters' complaints. All they had to do was reaffiliate, Spencer told them, which meant paying per capita taxes back to December 1, 1911, the date the suspension had been officially lifted.[21]

That did not happen, of course. With rank-and-file support noticeably weak, the Carpenters began payments in May 1912—and getting union members to agree even to that had not been easy, Duffy said. "If it had not been for that note I attached at the bottom of the circular [supporting reaffiliation] . . . the question would be hopelessly beaten." And if the Department and the AFL Executive Council had not promised to reopen the question of representation, and settle the metal trim controversy, Carpenters' leaders would never even have called for the vote. These were nonnegotiable issues, as far as the union was concerned. Yet when the Department convention met in November 1912, nothing much had changed. The Carpenters' complaints were aired once again and then sent on to the AFL Executive Council. The following year the AFL's recommendation to double the Carpenters' vote fell flat: Delegates rehashed many of the same arguments they had made back in 1909, and then voted to retain the status quo.[22]

The Carpenters fared no better on jurisdictional matters. When James Kirby called for a joint conference with the Sheet Metal Workers, for instance, delegates quickly shot down the idea, and in no uncertain terms. "The Sheet Metal Workers own this work and they defy any one to take it away from them. We will die fighting," Thomas Redding replied. Arguing that there would be no conflict if Department leaders would just enforce the rules, Redding made it clear that he did not care how much per capita the Carpenters paid.[23] And neither did a majority of delegates, apparently, who not only backed the Sheet Metal Workers in this fight but also favored the Department's newest affiliate, the International Association of Machinists (IAM), over the Carpenters. Both unions claimed millwright work, that is, the right to install machinery (which, the Carpenters argued, had once been made of wood). Awarding this work to the IAM (which had joined the Department in 1910), delegates to the 1913 convention made their intentions clear: Largest union or not, the Carpenters could expect no special treatment. Unwilling to accept these conditions, the Carpenters again withdrew. The union had already stopped paying per capita taxes by the fall of 1913, and by early 1914 it had officially cut its ties to the Department.[24]

Jurisdiction and Justice

The break with the Carpenters would prove to be more serious than it first appeared. But it was a symptom, and not a cause, of Department troubles. For there was still no answer to the central question of how to resolve jurisdictional conflicts, the very question that had given rise, back in 1903, to the Structural Building Trades Alliance in the first place. At that time the SBTA's original plan for "primary" trades and clearly defined jurisdictions had promised a logical solution, at least on paper. A few years later the Building Trades Department's plan for joint conferences and executive decisions when all else failed proved equally logical—and unenforceable. The underlying idea that "justice" could be achieved through objective, merit-based decisions seemed eminently fair and practical, that is until a decision was reached, and one side lost the case. Then the conflict started anew. For when it came to awarding jurisdiction and jobs, justice was in the eye of the beholder. No union member was willing to give up work, and no union leader was willing to concede jurisdiction, without a fight. Samuel Gompers may have been right when he told the Department that modern construction methods "compelled . . . the building trades to cooperate more generally" than ever before. But the fact remained that cooperation was still easier to talk about than to achieve, especially when both sides in a jurisdictional war were determined to win.[25]

In fact, over the course of the Department's first five years jurisdictional wars seemed endless: Plumbers and Steam Fitters, Laborers and Cement Workers, Sheet Metal Workers and Painters, Lathers and Iron Workers, Plasterers and Cement Finishers, and even two groups of rival Electrical Workers regularly challenged each other on the job, in local building trades councils, and on convention floors—and when they could not win one way, they tried another. To be sure, they all pleaded with each other to obey the rules and make the Department a real power in the industry. Yet they attacked the same rules whenever decisions did not go their way. For instance, when the Department awarded reinforced concrete work to the Iron Workers in 1910 (reversing a 1909 decision that had given it to the Lathers) William McSorley, the Lathers' president, refused to stand for reelection to the Executive Council. How could he, after the Department had robbed his members? However, the Department's decision made no practical difference. As Lathers in New York City demonstrated every day, they had every intention of doing this work.[26]

The Plasterers union was equally enraged when it lost an important decision. After the Department awarded certain finishing work to the Cement Workers, international secretary T. A. Scully instructed Spencer to "kindly drop the Operative Plasterers International Association off of your books."

When Spencer replied that he could not oblige, since Department membership was mandatory for AFL members (except, apparently, for the Carpenters, as critics often complained), Scully was not impressed. "Be that as it may," he answered, but "it will be useless for you to check us with any more per capita tax for it will not be paid." That the Painters and the Laborers, the Department's two largest affiliates, were also threatening to leave over jurisdictional decisions only added to the tension of the times.[27]

Jurisdictional wars were as costly to the industry as they were to the BTD, since they stopped work and consequently raised the cost of construction. Determined to find a long-term solution, Department leaders began to look to contractors for help. Just as the Carpenters union had relied on the architects to enforce its claim on metal trim, Department leaders now invited general contractors to join a campaign to enforce Department decisions. The idea was to design "a mutually satisfactory plan" to abolish "internecine dissension," William Spencer explained, and the goal was to keep the industry healthy for building trades workers and contractors alike. The idea seemed promising, since almost every contractor on Spencer's list expressed interest in a joint conference. But when the meeting was called to order on January 8, 1912, not a single contractor appeared. Whether this reflected the Department's lack of standing in the industry or, as President Short suspected, the influence of powerful New York City unions that opposed the Department, the result was the same: As long as Department members would not follow the rules, the BTD could not expect contractors to enforce them.[28]

Forced to rely on their own devices, President Short and the Executive Council now turned their attention to amalgamation, that is, the consolidation of related unions, like the Steam Fitters and the Plumbers. "If we can demonstrate our ability to settle trade grievances among ourselves," they explained at the 1912 convention, "we will immediately inspire confidence in the mind of the investing public," and industry would boom. Delegates, however, had another plan. Although they were willing to concede that amalgamation made sense (as long as it was not their union that was "gobbled up") they also thought a change in Department structure would help. Because many believed jurisdictional decisions depended on political connections, not "merit," in 1913 they voted to expand the Executive Council to give every affiliate a seat. Although James Duncan pronounced the plan a bureaucratic nightmare, John Donlin did not agree. Speaking on behalf of the Plasterers union (which had recently, but reluctantly, come back to the Department) he made it clear that broad representation was the key to achieving justice in jurisdictional disputes. "My organization never got a fair show," he insisted. "We were not represented on the Board and those whom we contended with always had a friend in court." Under the new system, every union would have a vote. And every union would pick up its representative's expenses, instead of using per capita taxes, which, in Donlin's view, was a real improvement. "We will pay the expense of our representative . . . but we don't intend to pay the representatives of other organizations who in every way shape and form oppose our existence," he said. Although Executive Council members, past and present, resented the criticism implied, the resolution passed by a comfortable margin.[29]

The delegates' attempt to find a political solution to jurisdictional fights offered a sharp contrast to the Carpenters' more practical approach. In 1914 the union entered an "offensive and defensive alliance" with the Bricklayers, the second largest (and still unaffiliated) building trades union. Since the Bricklayers also had agreements with the Operating Engineers, the Plasterers, and the Stone Cutters, this alliance commanded respect. When the Bricklayers refused to handle material hoisted by nonunion engineers, or to work on jobs that employed sheet metal workers instead of carpenters, contractors paid attention. And when these alliance unions began to break their ties to local councils, and threatened to set up rival "structural trade alliances," the BTD paid attention as well. In Kansas City, Missouri, for instance, an alliance between the Plumbers, Electrical Workers, and Bricklayers had persuaded rank-and-file marble workers to leave their AFL union and join the Bricklayers. After the pattern was repeated in other cities, the Department pledged to support the Marble Workers "with all the power at its command." But that was not enough. When Department officers tried to get leading contractors, like Paul Starrett of the Fuller Company, on their side, they were disappointed. "Mr. Starrett practically acknowledged that the Fuller Company would have to go along with the strongest combination, and therefore could not do anything for us on this subject," the officers admitted.[30]

An Uneasy Truce

That was reason enough, in Samuel Gompers's view, to get the Carpenters back into the Building Trades Department—and the sooner the better. The alliance unions were determined to control the building industry by any means possible. They were already granting concessions to take all the work they could get, regardless of jurisdiction. And like it or not, they were getting results, a practical fact of life that Gompers could not ignore. Rejecting the Department's request to throw the Carpenters out of the AFL and be done with it, he instead asked Frank Duffy (who had joined the AFL Executive Council in 1914) for his recommendations. Assuring Gompers that his union was "as loyal and true as ever" to the AFL, he made it clear that the Carpenters opposed the Building Trades Department's "rotten methods and system of doing work, and its trickery in getting decisions."[31]

Apparently in agreement, Gompers ordered the Department to reinstate the union. He also appointed a committee (that included James Duncan) to amend the AFL's constitution regarding Departments, a move designed to implement changes that the Carpenters now demanded. When the BTD convention agreed to give unions as large as the Carpenters two roll-call votes per delegate, to reestablish the seven-member Executive Council, and to make Department (and local council) membership voluntary, the door was open to the Carpenters once again. But as usual, the road to reunion proved rocky. When the union sent a delegation to the 1915 BTD convention, for instance, the Machinists, the Sheet Metal Workers, and the Iron Workers protested vigorously. But the Carpenters stood firm. By the time the convention had adjourned, the Carpenters had not only managed to get the Tampa decision annulled, and the Machinists dropped from the Department, but it had elected its own man to the Executive Council—William L. Hutcheson, the Carpenters' newly elected president, who would prove to be an even tougher opponent than Frank Duffy.[32]

The Carpenters' renewed affiliation boosted the Department's stature in the industry, but it did little to resolve jurisdictional wars: The steady introduction of new materials and more easily mastered methods of work, together with an industry depression beginning in 1915, kept tensions high. Likewise, while the AFL's amended constitution satisfied the Carpenters' demand for a greater voice in Department affairs, it did not resolve the underlying conflict between large and small unions. On the contrary, the AFL's new rules only strengthened the general, and increasingly dangerous, perception that the Carpenters union was now in charge. A long-standing fight between the Carpenters and the Plasterers, for instance, that started over jurisdiction in 1913 took a decidedly political turn in 1916, demonstrating the power of this perception and the hostility it generated. For when the Carpenters claimed the right to erect plaster staff (a mixture of plaster and fibrous material used in ornamental work), and the AFL Executive Council supported the union, the decision set off a fight within the Department that picked up where the metal trim fight had left off—and proved to be just as damaging in the long run.

When the fight to erect plaster staff erupted at the San Francisco Panama Pacific Exposition, it had all the markings of a great drama. Plasterers Edward McGivern and John Donlin were as aggressive and outspoken as carpenters Duffy, Hutcheson, and P. H. McCarthy, the legendary leader of the California building trades (and the former mayor of San Francisco). The sides seemed equally matched, with the Department's largest union (the Carpenters) pitted against its highest-paid trade (the Plasterers). Whatever the Plasterers lacked in numbers, its members made up for in skill, and that carried a certain weight on the job site. Like the Carpenters, the Plasterers union believed it could go it alone, if necessary; after all, the Plasterers had waited until 1908 to join the AFL and had broken with the Department when a decision did not go its way. And also like the Carpenters, the Plasterers union was willing to seek outside agreements if that became necessary to protect work. In fact, the Plasterers had a long-standing agreement with the Bricklayers that allowed both unions to share jurisdiction in some cases, an alliance that had proved to be as important as skill to the Plasterers' overall success.[33] In a relatively strong position to push the Plasterers' case in San Francisco, McGivern was willing to cooperate when McCarthy offered to split the work, fifty-fifty—surely an honorable compromise was better than a strike under the circumstances. But the deal fell apart almost immediately, when contractors refused to hire plasterers. "We believe this is unfair to us," they told William Spencer, since they had figured their costs on the basis of carpenters' wages, and had signed an agreement with McCarthy's BTC that promised there would be no jurisdictional strikes. Whether the contractors were sincere or merely doing McCarthy's bidding, no one was certain. But plasterers in San Francisco had their doubts. "What a lovely joke it is to be affiliated with the supposed ideal Building Trades Council," one complained, "and expect that your trade rules and jurisdictional rights are being respected and protected." Although the Plasterers vowed "to enforce the rule even if every job in San Francisco is shut down," ultimately carpenters did the work.[34]

Although the fight in San Francisco ended with the Carpenters' victory, the Plasterers union was not exactly defeated. In fact, John Donlin emerged from the conflict as the president of the Building Trades Department. Just as Hutcheson and Duffy knew how to leverage the Carpenters' large membership to protect their union's interests in the AFL, Donlin was equally skilled at building political coalitions to balance the Carpenters' power in the Department. And he had plenty of material to work with; by 1916 the Carpenters had managed to alienate almost every other trade! The ties that bound Donlin and his supporters were closer to shared hostility than solidarity, but they were strong nonetheless. The bitterness of jurisdictional fights, and the humiliation many trades suffered at the Carpenters' hands, gave rise to a lasting sense of anger and outrage that may not have benefited the Department as a whole but certainly kept political factions tight. For instance, as late as 1920, opponents could still get a rise out of Donlin with the question, "Who put up the plaster staff on the San Francisco exposition?"[35] And as late as 1930 the political alliances generated by this fight would give way to rival Building Trades Departments.

At the time, however, no one could foresee the future. In fact, in 1916, when Donlin took over as president, the Department was feeling more successful than it had in years. Despite ongoing conflicts, and a business depression, it had not only survived but had grown, a real accomplishment under the circumstances. It was even celebrating some hard-won achievements: After years of Departmental preaching, pushing, and prodding (to say nothing of revoking charters) to amalgamate small related trades, the Steam Fitters had finally joined forces with the Plumbers, the Cement Workers had gone into the Plasterers (if members were finishers) or the Laborers (if they were not), the Art Glass Workers had joined the Painters, and the Amalgamated Society of Carpenters and the Amalgamated Wood Workers had finally bowed to the inevitable and given way to the United Brotherhood of Carpenters and Joiners.[36] Adding to the generally good news, the Department was also pleased to report the affiliation of the Bricklayers in October 1916 and the addition of seventy thousand new members, a direct result of the decision to make local council affiliation voluntary (and an acknowledgment that technological change and jurisdictional conflicts were finally catching up with the Bricklayers, too). "For the first time in the history of the Building Trades movement ... we are all united," outgoing president Thomas J. Williams proudly proclaimed at the 1916 convention. "What an era of possibilities stretches in front of us! What an opportunity to make our united Building Trades Department respected by our own membership in the first place, and by the contractors and the public in general."[37]

World War and the Promise of Peace

But if the future looked promising, it would also prove to be demanding. World war had been raging in Europe since 1914, and by the close of 1916 American involvement seemed imminent. Determined to make the world and the workplace safe for democracy, AFL president Samuel Gompers had already accepted an appointment to the Advisory Commission of the Council of National Defense, a government agency established to organize the nation's preparedness program. In March 1917, just a few weeks before the United States officially joined the fight, Gompers called a meeting of leading trade unionists, including Department leaders, to hammer out the AFL's "Position in Peace or in War." Frankly debating the meaning of patriotism, the consequences of war, and the overall value of labor's support, participants revealed a broad range of opinion. There were those who agreed with Congressman Frank Buchanan, past president of the Iron Workers (and the Structural Building Trades Alliance), that this was not America's fight. Others shared Bill Hutcheson's fear that Gompers's wartime cooperation would undermine labor's right to strike. Even James Duncan, Gompers's most reliable link to the building trades, doubted the wisdom of granting the military too much authority during war. But after registering their dissent and debating their options, the union representatives reached a decision. "Our labor movement distrusts and protests against militarism," they proclaimed. But in the face of war they saw no other choice but to "offer our services to our country." They made it clear, however, that patriotism was not blind. "War has never put a stop to the necessity for struggle to establish and maintain industrial rights," they added. "Wage earners in war times must . . . keep one eye on the exploiters at home and the other upon the enemy threatening the national government."[38]

From Gompers's point of view, the war offered organized labor a real opportunity to prove its worth. By "pulling in harness" with the government, as U.S. president Woodrow Wilson put it, AFL unions would take their place as vital partners in the nation's war effort, a first in American history.[39] For the building trades, this meant working with the federal government to build military cantonments (or training camps), air fields, and other necessary structures as quickly and professionally as possible, demonstrating, in the process, the practical value of a skilled labor force ready and able to meet a crisis. The goal was laudable, but the partnership was not easy to sustain, as building trades workers soon realized. "Our office was besieged with complaints from all sections of the country," President Donlin reported to the 1917 BTD convention. "The Government had awarded contracts amounting to hundreds of millions of dollars in construction work and . . . more than 50 percent of this . . . had been awarded to contractors" who had no experience working with skilled union labor. Understaffed and overworked, Donlin and Spencer could not cope with the avalanche of serious grievances. But after the Electrical Workers appointed a representative to handle government affairs, and the Bricklayers, Carpenters, and Plasterers followed suit, the Department got back on track. With the help of President Gompers, "we succeeded in having the different Government Departments instruct all contractors to comply with . . . established labor conditions," Donlin added. "But this only in a measure relieved the situation."[40]

Donlin was referring to the "Cantonment Adjustment Accord"—also known as the Baker-Gompers Agreement—a controversial compromise that was designed to avoid strikes: The agreement ensured that building trades workers would be paid according to union scale, and that grievances would be settled through the Cantonment Adjustment Commission (CAC), a board representing labor, employers, and the public. The model for a series of similar boards (notably the National War Labor Board that was organized in the spring of 1918), the CAC stood for the eight-hour day, equal pay for equal work, and labor's right to organize and bargain collectively with employers. But while the CAC gave labor a seat at the bargaining table and a voice in actual settlements it did not guarantee the closed shop. To Gompers, who had made the agreement without consulting building trades leaders, the decision not to fight for a closed shop was a necessary compromise, since that was a fight the AFL could not win. But to Bill Hutcheson and the Carpenters it seemed more like a sellout. "While we have every desire, intention and thought of assisting the . . . Government in the crisis we are now passing through," the Carpenters' president noted, "we have no . . . intention of waiving or giving up our rights to maintain for ourselves the [closed-shop] conditions we have established." Underscoring his point, Hutcheson refused to recognize the Baker-Gompers agreement or to serve on the CAC or similar labor boards.[41]

John Donlin's approach was different. While he shared some of Hutcheson's objections, as president of the BTD he basically followed Gompers's wartime lead and, in his estimation, cooperation had paid off. Even without a closed-shop mandate, union membership in general government construction was higher than ever. And while union leaders did not win every grievance they brought before the CAC or other boards, "in the aggregate we were treated very fairly," Donlin said. Moreover, he had worked with some of the biggest contractors in the industry and had learned a lot from the experience. "These men . . . were always more than considerate toward me. . . . [They] did not have any selfish interests, nor did they allow any feelings, friendly or otherwise, to prevail in the selection of contractors for any project; the project itself recommended the contractor," he explained, marveling that decisions could be made quickly, without the endless wrangling that plagued the building trades movement.[42]

This wartime example of "merit-based" decision making seemed like a valuable lesson to Donlin, one that could be readily applied to jurisdictional disputes. "Just as in winning the war it was necessary for us to forget our individuality and make personal sacrifices in order to attain our national objective, so we must apply . . . the principle of setting aside petty individual grievances for the sake of . . . the whole movement," he told the 1919 BTD convention. "Both right and might won the war," he added, "might being a very great essential." But if the Department had right on its side, it clearly lacked the might to enforce jurisdictional decisions; every delegate knew from experience that Department law was not enough to force affiliates to comply. They also knew that craft fundamentals were not the issue; no one was challenging the bricklayers' right to erect brick walls or the iron workers' right to erect structural steel. It was "incidental" work requiring no special skill, knowledge, or training that fueled jurisdictional wars. And that being the case, Donlin advised, it was time "to allow some tribunal to adjust those disputes," to create "a board for the maintenance of industrial peace and the elimination" of jurisdictional strikes. "Our Department is today in a better condition than ever before in its history," he added. "It only awaits your hearty cooperation to make it more effective."[43]

The plan to create the National Board for Jurisdictional Awards in the Building Industry was originally sponsored by John B. Lennon, longtime leader of the Tailors (and former treasurer of the AFL) who now served as a conciliator for the U.S. Department of Labor. Meeting with representatives of the American Institute of Architects, the Associated General Contractors (AGC), the National Association of Builders' Exchanges, and the Building Trades Department, Lennon had proposed an eight-member board (including three BTD representatives, two contractor representatives, and one each from the architects, engineers, and builders groups). With an ambitious plan to "encourage the resumption of building operations . . . to eliminate waste . . . and to create complete harmony among the several units entering into building construction," the National Board for Jurisdictional Awards (NBJA) had been initially endorsed by the Iron Workers, the Elevator Constructors, the Laborers, the Painters, the Plasterers, the Stone Cutters, the Tile Roofers, and the Composition Roofers by the time the 1919 convention met.[44]

But the Granite Cutters, as James Duncan told the convention, could not sign on as long as international unions were required to suspend locals that did not abide by the Board's decisions. Although a predictable debate ensued over the value of punishing transgressors, when John Lennon took the floor he was able to keep the majority on board. "I want to say that the final working out of the plan is the work of building tradesmen," he said. "I found not one trade unionist that was not in favor of some plan that would eliminate jurisdictional disputes in the building trades. . . . If the general idea is approved and your officers are instructed to cooperate with the other elements in putting it into effect, you will find the disagreeable features as they arise will, under the plan itself, be possible of elimination . . . and such changes made as may be necessary." Although he did not persuade the Granite Cutters' or the Laborers' delegation to give final approval to the Board, both Lennon and Donlin were relieved when the rest of the trades voted "Aye." For as Donlin told the delegates, "unless some plan was adopted for the elimination of jurisdictional disputes, the Building Trades Department would not last."[45]

At the time the NBJA offered a promising solution to a long-term conflict: Even the Carpenters had agreed to sign on to the plan by the summer of 1919. Within a year the Board had settled some long-running feuds (awarding reinforced concrete to the Iron Workers, for example) and it had managed to compromise a good many fights without incurring any serious backlash. "The work of the Board proceeds satisfactorily and there is a feeling among the labor men," chairman Rudolph P. Miller noted with relief, "that the work of this Board will be very helpful . . . in avoiding trouble especially in the way of strikes."[46]

His optimism, however, would soon give way to frustration, especially after the NBJA attempted to settle the Carpenters' fight with the Sheet Metal Workers over the question of installing metal trim. By the fall of 1920 the Carpenters union was already questioning the structure of the NBJA, pointing out that the Board represented only a small fraction of the nation's contractors. And by the time the Board finally settled the question and awarded metal trim to the Sheet Metal Workers in December 1920, both the Board's and the Department's claims to authority were in serious jeopardy: The Carpenters had not only decided to break all ties to the NBJA, but the union was ready to leave the Department once again over longstanding and still contentious issues of jurisdictional rights, representation, and the Department's interpretation of majority rule.

The High Price of Unity: Conflict, Crisis, and Coming Together

> Before the Building Trades Department can function success-
> fully . . . a solution for jurisdictional dissension must be found.
> —William Haber, *Industrial Relations*
> *in the Building Industry,* 1930

The year 1919 was a year of possibilities. The war was over, spirits were high, and the promise of industrial democracy burned bright. Thanks to wartime labor boards, and the partnership forged between the American Federation of Labor and the Wilson Administration, collective bargaining had finally come of age, or so it appeared. And now that peace was on the horizon, wage earners fully expected "a new deal all around . . . a square deal," as one machinist put it. After years of meeting wartime demand for training camps, armaments, uniforms, and soldiers, organized labor now looked forward to sharing the benefits of postwar reconstruction. For in 1919 there were houses and schools, office buildings and factories to plan. There were bridges to erect and roads to improve. There were cars and radios and appliances to be manufactured. And there were almost four million members of the AFL—the largest membership to date—who believed that they had earned the right to "a voice on the job" and to American standards including the eight-hour day, union wage scales, safe working conditions, and collectively bargained agreements.[1]

"This is a country of wonderful opportunity," BTD president John Donlin proclaimed, and he urged Department affiliates to make the most of it. With almost nine hundred thousand members by 1920 constituting 17.6 percent of total union membership, building trades unions were in a good position to prosper. They had not only successfully defended their rights and standards during the war (despite the government's adamant refusal to recognize the closed shop) but they had also increased their numbers significantly. Since 1914, when war first erupted in Europe, both the Iron Workers and Engineers had added ten thousand members, the Laborers sixteen thousand, the Painters almost thirty thousand, and the Carpenters and Electrical Workers one hundred thousand members each.[2] With the newly established National Board for Jurisdictional Awards ready to take care of inevitable conflicts, Donlin looked forward to forging a partnership with industry leaders to revive the commercial construction industry. Indeed, if anyone had told him that within two years the industry would be mired in depression, and building trades unions would be fighting bankers, building owners, and contractors for their very existence, he would not have believed them.

It was not that Donlin was naive or hopelessly optimistic. On the contrary, he was a blunt and practical man. But he believed that industry worked best when unions and employers respected each other, especially in a local market industry like construction, where speed and skill were as valuable as capital. Anyone with common sense and a conscience, he presumed, understood why unions were necessary for building tradesmen "whose employment is hazardous, intermittent, and seasonal, and who necessarily must work for different employers with the completion of each operation," as Donlin put it. And anyone with an interest in the industry had to know by now that economic justice was the key to productivity. Since the alternative had produced only strikes and mutual hostility so far, Donlin fully expected improvements in the future. And why not? Industrial democracy was not only fair, he insisted, it was good for business.[3]

A man who considered "class feeling" to be "un-American," Donlin did not share the contempt for business or profits that fueled radical labor groups like the Industrial Workers of the World (IWW), or the One Big Union movement that was growing in Canada. On the contrary, he believed that union growth and improved conditions were inevitably linked to industrial prosperity. And his union, the Operative Plasterers, had a good working relationship with its contractors. He had no illusions about capitalists, however, and no intention of blindly following the employers' lead: His wartime experience had persuaded him that "presumption" was a greater asset than ability in the world of big business. Nor did he have any illusions about his fellow workers. Labor and capital were both seeking money, power, and personal aggrandizement, he noted, and each would destroy the other, and the industry in the process, if given half a chance. That being the case, it only made sense to seek a practical basis for cooperation. "Business is business," he told delegates to the 1919 convention, "and it will be considerate toward labor only when labor proves that it is in a position to compel consideration. In all times past this has proved to be true."[4] As long as building trades unions organized their ranks, provided skilled and efficient workmen, and averted jurisdictional strikes, he maintained, there was nothing to fear from capital. After all, the public had embraced the concept of industrial democracy during the war. Now the question was: How far were they willing to go with it?

The Rise of the American Plan

The answer proved disappointing, since the public could be fickle with regard to organized labor. As long as war raged on in Europe, for instance, no civilian leader was better known or more respected than AFL president Samuel Gompers, and no domestic issue was more pressing than bringing order, fairness, and representation to the workplace. But once the crisis had passed and the federal government no longer needed the AFL as an ally, organized labor lost its patriotic glow. Labor boards were dismantled and "monopolistic" unions were blamed for postwar inflation and a sluggish economy. This change in policy became official in the fall of 1919, when an AFL delegation (which included John Donlin) walked out of an industrial conference sponsored by the Wilson administration. The conference had refused to endorse collective bargaining, a public indication of how quickly the tides had turned against labor.[5]

No longer hailed as public champions of social justice, union workers, and specifically building trades workers, were now targeted as a greedy, corrupt, and dangerous group. Their Byzantine work rules and high wage rates had scared off investors, critics charged, and their business agents had only one interest—their own power and personal wealth. In 1919, a record four million workers in the United States and Canada had joined almost four thousand strikes, including coal and steel strikes, a policemen's strike, and general strikes in Seattle and Winnipeg, adding fuel to the anti-union fire. "The whole nation is tired of strikes and lockouts, and disgusted with such institutions that make lockouts and strikes possible," Donlin complained, and if press coverage was any indication, he was right. Union workers were either Bolsheviks or thieves, according to the newspapers, and the distinction hardly mattered since the outcome was the same: Collective bargaining and labor organization had lost public support.[6]

It was hardly surprising that Donlin and the Department were on the defensive by 1920. No longer making plans for a prosperous future, they were debating strategies to counter a national open-shop movement that was backed by the Chamber of Commerce, the National Erectors Association, the National Association of Manufacturers, and national employers like U.S. Steel. Characterizing the open shop as the embodiment of American principles including independence and fair play, supporters not only promised "equal opportunity for all and special privileges for none," but insisted that closed shops threatened economic prosperity, ideas that were rapidly catching on. The Associated Industries of Seattle, for instance, an employers' group that organized following the 1919 general strike, launched what they called the open-shop "American Plan" to make the city union-free, and by 1920 Seattle's building trades had lost the closed shop. In Detroit the Dupont Engineering Company, which was building three new plants, also repudiated closed-shop agreements. Even after seven thousand building trades workers walked off their jobs, Dupont's management stood firm. The situation was equally grave in Boston, where union workers had been locked out (after refusing a wage reduction) and nonunion workers were erecting the John Hancock Insurance Company building, one of the city's major construction projects.[7]

These were not isolated complaints, for by 1921 the American Plan had made its way to large and small cities alike. Open-shop construction reigned in Duluth, Los Angeles, Minneapolis, Philadelphia, St. Paul, and San Francisco, disrupting the industry and building trades councils in the process. "There is no question that there is national propaganda to defeat building trades organizations," sheet metal worker John Hynes reported in 1921. "The moneyed interests of America, including the railroad officials and so on, realize that if they can beat the building trades crafts and put us back to prewar conditions, it will be quite easy to take the other men and women in the American Labor Movement and put them in any category they feel like putting them in." J. C. Bulger of the Colorado Federation of Labor wholeheartedly agreed, adding that the American Plan was closer to a "scab plan" since it was obviously closed to organized labor. The Electrical Workers were even more frank. The American Plan was the product of the same "wonderfully patriotic profiteering employers" who had cheated the nation during the war. Now they were using the flag to "camouflage industrial slavery."[8]

Canadian workers were having their share of postwar troubles, too. The building trades had been hit especially hard during the war, and recovery seemed exceedingly slow. Worse yet, the combination of economic depression, and the rise of a militant One Big Union movement in the west, had put Canadian employers on guard. Echoing the same complaints of Bolshevism and corruption that fueled the American Plan, they now believed it was time to put Canadian labor in its "place," and nip collective bargaining and union standards in the bud.[9]

The fact that Canadian workers often divided along regional, religious, and language lines played right into the employers' hands. For instance, when the Montreal Building Trades Council tried to organize an industrywide strike in 1919, the movement fell apart. "First there is the racial problem to be overcome," explained John Bruce, an organizer for the Plumbers. "We have locals with English speaking branches and French speaking branches. . . . In some instances the distinctly French organizations were not willing to go along with the others." Even after the Carpenters, Bricklayers, Plumbers, Sheet Metal Workers, and Plasterers arranged a series of mass meetings, "it was impossible to get [the men] to attend." Some favored strictly Canadian unions, including those that were being organized through the Catholic Church. Others favored international unions and the American Federation of Labor. And then there were those who had given up on the labor movement entirely. "[They] feel that the situation . . . has not been given . . . serious attention," painter James Skemp reported and, as a consequence, "working conditions and wage rates are demoralized and the building industry largely disorganized."[10]

Trades versus Industry

Internal divisions were certainly nothing new in the building trades, and they were by no means confined to Canada. In the United States it was not unusual to have black and white Plasterers locals, Jewish Carpenters locals, or Italians, Germans, and Irishmen working and organizing with "their own kind." Nor was it unusual for tradesmen to avoid entangling alliances that could involve them in sympathetic strikes. "Sticking apart," a phrase coined by a building trades worker in 1916, still applied in 1921. The tendency to go it alone, if possible, had great appeal for skilled workers more interested in securing work for their trade than in solving industry wide problems. Economic survival, after all, was a union's first law. In 1921, when work was scarce and opposition strong, many building trades workers saw no good reason to enter or even support a fight unless their particular interests were directly at stake.[11]

The Granite Cutters, for instance, refused to support Department efforts to fight an injunction law in Omaha, Nebraska. When the union was asked to pay its $550 share of the legal bill, it was polite but adamant. "We have no building cutters in that part of the country," James Duncan explained. "We will continue to give service to the Department and fight for it in whatever way we can . . . but if you insist on our paying this we will . . . gracefully retire." Although John Hynes argued that the fight in Omaha affected all the trades, since it would have spread throughout the nation had it not been stopped, the Granite Cutters did not see it that way. When the union finally paid the bill, it did so under protest. Yet the very next year, when members of the Granite Cutters were locked out in an open-shop fight in California, the union's attitude had changed radically. This time, the Granite Cutters expected everyone's help. Duncan even requested that the AFL assess its entire membership on the Granite Cutters' behalf, and he was not at all pleased when his good friend Gompers turned him down.[12]

Keeping the trades together on the local front proved no easier. At times it seemed as if the 1920s motto was "every trade—or even every local union—for itself." In Portland, Maine, the building trades "seem to be working as individuals instead of cooperating with each other," one organizer reported. And in Norfolk, Virginia, "a number of the . . . trades [are] not playing the game fairly," said another. They were "only pulling jobs in theory—the men going back on the job, with the consent of their craft, the day after it was pulled." In Wichita Falls, Texas, the Plumbers did not even bother to consult the other trades when they struck for $15 a day, a "radical step," according to a painter there, that "plunged organized labor . . . into the clutches of the 'Open Shop' advocates." With no support from the other trades, a state of affairs that would undoubtedly fuel future fights, both the strike and the closed shop were lost.[13]

There were also local unions that refused to accept new members or to allow tradesmen in nearby towns to charter new locals; they preferred to keep all available work for themselves. Others set initiation fees so high that few were willing to join. This closed-door policy particularly irked John Possehl, vice president of the Engineers. "I can't get [the hoisting engineers in Cleveland] to take in everybody that comes along," he complained. "They would rather pay $100 in assessments than take in a new member. It seems that when a hoister dies, they go to the funeral with a long face, and then laugh up their sleeves because there is another one out of the way." With no faith in the economy or the future, these local unions were determined to protect their members' security at all costs. Some employed a "permit system" (which allowed nonmembers to purchase the right to work on union jobs as needed) rather than organize. Others were accused of employing threats and violence to keep control over work.[14]

The cost, however, proved high, especially when supporters of the American Plan publicized stories like these. Newspapers thrived on scandal, and building trades scandals were the talk of the town in the early 1920s. Strong-armed business agents, restrictive work rules, and closed memberships were all linked to high construction costs, inflated wages, and soaring rents. Although no one in the industry kept production records at the time, and no one was able to measure labor productivity or its relation to prices, that made no difference. Newspapers promoted sensational stories detailing high hourly wage rates (but overlooking seasonal unemployment), strike-happy business agents (whether they represented the majority or not), and dishonest union workers who apparently soldiered on the job (although the conditions of their work were rarely mentioned).[15]

No wonder the public was tired of unions. The link between union rules, corruption, and inefficiency was repeated so often that those outside the industry naturally assumed it was true. "Big Wages and Little Labor is the slogan of your labor unions," a banker's wife wrote to Samuel Gompers, outraged that carpenters apparently made more money than her husband did. Even if that were true, Gompers replied, that did not mean they were dishonest. "A great many persons think that the services of carpenters are actually worth more to society than the services of bankers," he pointed out.[16] But as he proved to another critic (who complained about bricklayers), wages were not as high as the public presumed. "Bricklayers . . . may earn $1.00 an hour, $8.00 a day," he explained, but they worked only 150 days a year, for a total of about $1,200. "The man who spends that much for noonday lunches in a year only sees the $1.00 an hour," he added, "and accepts without thought the idea that the bricklayers work 300 days in a year and therefore earn $2,400."[17]

The public also overestimated the amount of time wasted on construction sites. For instance, an open-shop supporter wanted to know why union bricklayers were allowed to slack off. Although they were capable of laying two thousand bricks a day, he insisted, they restricted themselves to a mere eight hundred, thereby seriously jeopardizing profits. "You did not stop to figure out the possibility of such a charge," Gompers replied. "A bricklayer to lay 2,000 brick[s] a day would have to lay four brick[s] a minute, one every fifteen seconds. Some day try it yourself and see whether you can lay one brick every minute in an eight hour day, or even one brick every five minutes." As Gompers demonstrated, it was "easy to make such charges but . . . easier to puncture them."[18]

Scandals and Citizens' Committees

These arguments got lost, however, in a new flurry of bad publicity. In 1921 two state investigating bodies—the Dailey Commission in Chicago and the Lockwood Committee in New York—had linked the high cost of building to collusion between business agents, contractors, and building material suppliers. "Graft has been imposed upon builders to the extent of millions of dollars every year," reported the Dailey Commission, a conclusion that was upheld by the testimony of a Chicago judge. "Many of the important unions of the city . . . are controlled by criminals," he attested, and they were "destroying law and order in this great community."[19] Similar conclusions were reached in New York where, according to the Lockwood Committee, every kind of building material "from structural steel and bricks to doorknobs and sandpaper" was "under the control of merciless, gouging, monopolistic combines." And every contractor in New York City, apparently, was under the control of Robert P. Brindell, a dock builder turned Carpenters official, who not only reorganized New York City's cantankerous Buildings Trades Council (BTC) but also built a sizable fortune collecting what he called "strike insurance."[20]

Eventually convicted and jailed, Brindell was the most notorious building trades leader to fall in 1921, but he was not alone. In San Francisco P. H. McCarthy, who had ruled the Building Trades Council since 1898, also lost his power, and the closed shop, when he agreed to settle a strike through arbitration, and the decision went against the BTC. True to form McCarthy rejected the award, declaring it "null and void," and announced that the BTC would no longer participate in the process. But this time opponents called his bluff. General contractors locked out union workers on nine downtown buildings, and material dealers agreed to supply only those contractors who reduced wages and rejected union work rules. Finally, businessmen outside the industry formed a Citizens' Committee to support the fight, raising funds from corporations including Standard Oil and Wells Fargo Bank. By June contractors and material dealers were working on an open-shop basis, and McCarthy was forced to surrender. "He has not only eaten crow," a critic noted, "but he is rolling in the mud." In January 1922 he resigned his position as BTC president.[21]

The story followed similar lines in Chicago, where the Dailey Commission's spectacular "revelations" drew widespread publicity. After more than a dozen business agents were indicted for conspiracy, the public apparently agreed that building trades unions needed a policeman, as one observer put it. And Judge Kenesaw Landis thought he was the right man for the job. When he was chosen to arbitrate a wage dispute in 1921, he used the opportunity to regulate relations between contractors and building trades unions. Issuing a decision known as the Landis Award, he not only reduced wages (by 25 percent) and abrogated union work rules, but he also abolished jurisdictional strikes and weakened the closed shop. In the process he divided Chicago's BTC into rival forces, with one side accepting the decision and the other determined to fight. At that point almost two hundred businessmen (representing major department stores, manufacturers, and utilities) organized the Citizens' Committee to Enforce the Landis Award to support trades that accepted the agreement and to wage a battle against those that did not. Even after the award had expired, the Citizens' Committee kept up the fight, refusing to recognize "outlaw" unions, including the Carpenters, Elevator Constructors, Engineers, Painters, Plasterers, Plumbers, and Sheet Metal Workers, a group representing the vast majority of Chicago's building trades workers. Although President Donlin tried to negotiate a solution, the committee would not budge. "To recognize these unions and again restore them to full control of their respective trades," the committee argued, "would . . . be even worse than before. . . . No effective opposition . . . could again be organized within a generation."[22]

A Chicago man himself, Donlin was not completely surprised by the Dailey Commission's findings; ties between local unions, local contractors, and local building materials men had always been strong in the city. He was not surprised either that the men behind the Citizens' Committee were some of the largest employers and building owners in Chicago. Like many trade unionists, he took it for granted that these "Citizens" were more concerned with destroying collective-bargaining rights than they were with corruption. He also linked them to the economic depression that had been stalling the building industry since 1921. Once the open-shop "citizens" campaign had done its damage, he predicted, bankers would find the money to fund construction loans again, and to a large extent he was right. By 1923 almost 40 percent of communities were building on an open-shop basis, according to the National Association of Manufacturers (NAM), and by 1924 the industry had not only recovered but was setting new records.[23]

Thus Donlin saw no advantage to an all-out fight. It made more sense, he believed, to "retreat successfully" and live to fight another day. In fact, he advised Chicago workers to make their peace with the Landis Award, since it was, after all, a closed-shop agreement. But that kind of conservative advice cost him, and the Building Trades Department, valuable support. The Carpenters union, for instance, which was leading the anti-Landis fight, had no intention of letting an outsider "run their business" and had no respect for a labor organization that allowed employers to set the rules.[24] Donlin, however, did not consider the Landis agreement to be the real problem. He was far more worried about building trades unions, like the Carpenters and the Painters, that went their own way, regardless of public opinion or of the consequences. Militant building trades councils and sympathetic strikes may have launched the building trades movement, but Donlin firmly believed that in the 1920s they were no match for militant corporations determined to break that movement down. For even if the Carpenters and Painters won their fight against the Landis Award, which they eventually did in 1924, that had more to do with the level of organization in Chicago than it did with militant tactics, he believed. Like it or not, there were few cities as well organized as Chicago and even fewer ready to challenge corporate interests and win.[25]

"The trouble with our movement is the absence of International influence over local matters," Donlin told the 1922 convention. Local rabble-rousers and "would-be leaders" were behaving in ways that proved to be both "stupid and economically wasteful." They pandered to every "whim and caprice" of the membership, he complained, incorporating into their laws "the most absurd of economic fallacies." And in the process they had paved the way for the American Plan and undermined the "mutual interdependence" that gave building trades unions their strength. "Organization demands management and supervision," Donlin insisted. If the building trades movement hoped to advance, international union officers would have to take charge, and pay more attention to local matters and their effect on the industry as a whole. "We must establish mutual respect and a feeling of mutual interdependence among crafts," Donlin pleaded. "We must consult each other in our difficulties." For until communication between building trades leaders greatly improved, there was really no hope of keeping local unions in line. It was time to revitalize the Department, Donlin believed, and to bring the general presidents together at regular meetings to discuss and to supervise local unions and building trades councils. "This Department, the wonderful potentiality of this Department, can only be developed in this manner," he said.[26]

The Carpenters and Civil War

The plan sounded sensible enough, especially to a gathering of international union officers. But there was a serious problem. The United Brotherhood of Carpenters and Joiners, the union that was causing Donlin the most trouble on the local level, was not represented at the 1922 convention. The Carpenters had left the Department, once again, and local unions were successfully challenging Department authority and Department councils throughout the country. It was a dangerous conflict, since a full-fledged labor war could only advance the open shop, Donlin and his supporters believed. But it was hardly new. The break between the Carpenters and the Department in the 1920s stemmed from some very basic conflicts that dated back to the rise of the Structural Building Trades Alliance: Did unity develop from the bottom up, or could it be imposed through a constitution and "discipline"? Were international unions required to compromise trade interests, for the general good, even if local unions protested? And if they were, which union had the greater obligation to make concessions—the union that represented the larger membership or the one that could garner the most votes at a local council meeting or Department convention? In the past this conflict had usually exploded over the question of jurisdiction, and the 1920s fight was no exception. This time, however, the point of contention was the National Board for Jurisdictional Awards, the labor-industry conference that had promised to resolve such conflicts once and for all.

Department affiliates had endorsed the NBJA, more or less enthusiastically, in 1919. But as early as 1920 the Carpenters union was having second thoughts. President William L. Hutcheson, the Carpenters' no-nonsense leader, was willing to serve the Board as vice chairman. And he was willing to cast his vote and decide jurisdiction for other trades. For instance, he did not question the Board's authority or intent when it awarded corner beads to the Plasterers (over the Lathers), or threaded pipes to the Plumbers (over the Iron Workers). But he had no intention of letting "outsiders" on the Board determine the Carpenters' jurisdiction. When BTD president John Donlin asked the Board to consider five metal-trim cases involving the Carpenters and the Sheet Metal Workers, cases that had been festering for more than a decade, Hutcheson called a halt. At first he merely tried to postpone the hearings, a familiar tactic in jurisdictional disputes. When that was not enough, he raised some serious questions about the Board's makeup (since it represented only a fraction of construction employers) and managed to link some prominent Board supporters to the open-shop movement.[27]

Still he could not stop the hearings. But he did not participate in them. When the NBJA finally met to take up the metal-trim cases on November 29, 1920, Hutcheson's seat was empty. The following day he made the break official, informing William Spencer that the Carpenters would no longer participate in the National Board for Jurisdictional Awards. "Neither will we be in a position to recognize findings as made by that body," he added, "or compel our members to observe the same." The very next day the Board awarded metal trim to the Sheet Metal Workers, but that made no difference at all. Carpenters continued to do the work wherever they could get it, just as they had been doing since the days of Judge Gaynor's award in 1909. And manufacturers, for the most part, backed them up.[28]

Disappointed by the outcome, Donlin took the case to the 1921 BTD convention. "By all the laws of honor upon which civilization rests, we building tradesmen are committed to this board," he said. After all, the NBJA had been "conceived, established, and ratified" by building trades workers, including the Carpenters' "Big Bill" Hutcheson. And it was doing an excellent job for the industry, as far as Donlin could see. "The National Board for Jurisdictional Awards is our Supreme Court," he contended, "and this court is indispensable." But now "a certain organization" was threatening its future, and it was up to convention delegates to decide what to do. Would they stand behind the National Board for Jurisdictional Awards? Or would they support the Carpenters' right to ignore Board decisions?[29]

The vote overwhelmingly supported the Board, but Hutcheson wanted to know what this meant for the Carpenters. "It means that they are expected to carry out the laws of this Department," Donlin responded. "The general contractors, the architects and the engineers [on the Board] . . . do not feel that any one organization is bigger than the rest of the building trades industry, and that is the attitude of this convention." Unwilling to "let the whole world know that we are unable to settle our inter-union disputes," Donlin made his position clear. "We do not want to fight each other. We have to fight the united interests of capital, material men, bankers and everyone else, and we must have harmony." But Hutcheson was having none of it. A man who would argue with the Pope, if he thought the Pope was wrong, as one of his friends put it, Hutcheson was not about to let Donlin or anyone else tell the Carpenters what to do. So when the delegates refused to change their vote, Hutcheson's choice was clear. He led the Carpenters' delegation out of the convention, and into a serious war with the Building Trades Department.[30]

Department leaders not only expected but required the support of the American Federation of Labor in this fight. The AFL constitution was on their side, they told Samuel Gompers, and they wanted him to follow the rules and toss the Carpenters out. "The integrity of the unions in the Building Industry is at stake," William Spencer contended.[31] But the Carpenters argued just as strongly for AFL support. After the NBJA declared the Carpenters an "outlaw" union, and ordered building trades councils to act accordingly, Frank Duffy made it clear that his union would leave the AFL if the NBJA was allowed to rule the building trades. "How a body outside of the labor movement can give mandatory orders . . . [to unseat the Carpenters] is beyond my comprehension," he told Gompers, particularly since no similar rules apparently applied to the architects, engineers, contractors, builders, and employers represented on the Board. "They are not instructed, directed or ordered to hire Union men only; they can hire non-Union men as well, and they have no power or authority to make these non-Union men observe their decisions." In Duffy's opinion the NBJA had one interest only: "Tying down, hand and foot, the Union man." And that being the case, the Carpenters believed, the Board had to go.[32]

The Carpenters' claim to AFL support grew even stronger after the Department backed the NBJA. The BTD not only endorsed the Board's resolution against the Carpenters, but it did its best to carry it out. In California, for instance, where the Carpenters publicly rejected the Board's authority, the BTD set up a new council in Los Angeles (since the old one refused to unseat the Carpenters) and threatened to revoke the charter of the State Building Trades Council. In Detroit it approved a general strike against union carpenters hired to work on a new baseball field, and in Cleveland a meeting of Department general presidents called a strike against union carpenters who were installing metal trim. "Is it not strange that Bricklayers will work with nonunion men on some jobs," Duffy asked Gompers, "but on a thorough union job like [this] . . . they pull their men against union carpenters?" If the AFL Department had the power to order strikes against an AFL affiliate, then Duffy and the Carpenters wanted no part of either organization.[33]

Embarrassed by this public spectacle, and unwilling to lose a large and dependable affiliate, the AFL took the Carpenters' side. "Strikes of union workmen against other union workmen are intolerable," the Executive Council informed the Department, "and must be instantly discontinued." But neither side took the lesson to heart, and for the next three years this destructive civil war raged on. In Baltimore and Chicago, in New York City, Cleveland, Dayton, and St. Louis, local unions were forced to take sides, and the open-shop movement flourished in the meantime. Although Samuel Gompers never stopped trying to bring the sides together, he died before any compromise could be reached. William Hutcheson was willing and able to keep up the fight as long as the Building Trades Department recognized the NBJA. And John Donlin was equally determined not to give in, with or without AFL support. If trade unionism stood for justice, and not expedience or mere numerical strength, he believed, there could be no other choice.[34]

The Rise of the Tri-Party Alliance

By this time, however, Donlin was on his way out. Although Department affiliates officially supported his hard-line stance, by 1924 most building trades leaders were tired of the fight. Like painter George Hedrick, a Department vice president since 1908, they believed it was time for a change. Favoring Hedrick's plan for a "100 percent Building Trades Department," which included the Carpenters, delegates elected him president and also elected a new secretary-treasurer, William Tracy of the Plumbers. At that point the tide began to turn. Within a few months, Hedrick and Hutcheson were carrying on a more-or-less cordial correspondence, and by May 1925 the Department's Executive Council met with a committee from the Carpenters to try to work things out. "Now while nothing definite was accomplished," Secretary Tracy told AFL president William Green, "I believe a better feeling exists."[35]

At the same time relations between the Carpenters and the Sheet Metal Workers were also improving. In 1926 the Sheet Metal Workers accepted the Carpenters' terms and ended the metal trim controversy: The United Brotherhood of Carpenters and Joiners would erect and install most interior trim, and the Sheet Metal Workers would hang and adjust metal sash, install metal lockers and shelving, and do work on storefronts and column forms. It would take another two years to formalize the agreement, since rank-and-file sheet metal workers demanded some changes before they accepted the compromise, but the fight was basically over.[36] And that made a tremendous difference to the building trades movement. With business booming by 1926, local unions were able to focus on improving conditions and restoring the closed shop, instead of wasting time and resources on endless jurisdictional wars.

The Department benefited from the change, too. In 1926 BTD president William J. McSorley (who had succeeded Hedrick at the 1925 convention) was pleased to report that state and local building trades councils were gaining strength. The following year he welcomed back three hundred thousand carpenters to the fold. Apparently the Department had agreed to accept the Carpenters' terms for reaffiliation: Delegates to the 1927 convention not only voted to withdraw from the National Board for Jurisdictional Awards but also elected William Hutcheson to the newly created office of sixth vice president. Since Hutcheson represented "one of the greatest, if not the greatest organization in the building trades," according to Department vice president James Noonan, his election promised to "cement the building trades movement of the country."[37] For with the Carpenters' help, building trades unions were reclaiming their turf. In 1927 the percentage of cities building open shop dropped down to 29 percent (from a high of 40 percent in 1925), and between 1927 and 1928 building trades unions regained almost all the ground they had lost since 1921. "I think we can truthfully say," AFL president Green told the 1928 BTD convention, "that . . . the Building Trades organizations enjoy today better wages and better working conditions than they have ever enjoyed in the history of our country."[38]

If the Carpenters' reaffiliation proved that unity was the cornerstone of building trades success, it also proved that the price of unity was high, too high, perhaps, for Department affiliates. Carpenters were willing to cooperate with the other trades, as long as no one interfered with UBCJA plans. As history demonstrated, the union would defend its trade interests aggressively, no matter what the other trades thought, and it would leave the Department any time an important decision did not go its way. This militant attitude reinforced loyalty among rank-and-file carpenters. But it also stirred up serious resentment within the Department that could not be contained for long. Small specialty unions, like the Lathers and the Elevator Constructors, would not easily forget the Carpenters' unwillingness to compromise or its ability to command AFL support even when the union broke the rules. And large affiliates like the Bricklayers would not simply stand by if members thought the Carpenters union was trampling on their rights.

The test came sooner than anyone had imagined: Right after the close of the 1927 convention, the Bricklayers decided to leave the Department. The union had lost an important fight to the Plasterers over the question of setting artificial stone, and the Bricklayers blamed the Carpenters for the outcome. The Plasterers and the Carpenters had colluded in "rival" councils when the Carpenters were still on the outside, bricklayer James Bowen complained, and now that the union was back on the inside, they were colluding on the convention floor. According to Bowen, the Plasterers union and its supporters in the Department had agreed to accept the Carpenters' terms for reaffiliation in return for the Carpenters' vote against the Bricklayers in a jurisdictional fight. Under such "deplorable" conditions, Bowen noted, the Bricklayers had no choice but to go it alone. "We will secure justice by the strength of our membership," he concluded, "rather than secure it by trades made in the dark with those who will not give justice unless they can secure in return some favor for themselves."[39]

They were not alone for long, however. By 1929 the Carpenters had left the Department after it failed to lower per capita taxes. The Carpenters also feared that a new jurisdictional board was imminent, a prediction that proved true in 1930 when the Department established the Board of Trades Claims. The very next year the Bricklayers and Carpenters had formed an alliance. These longtime opponents now agreed to defend and protect their mutual interests. And they also agreed that their international presidents would handle jurisdictional conflicts, which did not bode well for the other building trades. Before the year was over the threat of jurisdictional war was on the rise again. The International Brotherhood of Electrical Workers (IBEW), another large building trades union, had also signed the pact; it had left the Department in March, apparently to protest the new Board of Trades Claims. But it was just as likely that the IBEW's unconventional president, Harry Broach, thought that the new alliance offered better opportunities to expand his union's jurisdiction.[40]

The "Tri-Party Alliance," as it came to be called, had a strong basis for power in the industry: The Carpenters, the Bricklayers, and the Electrical Workers not only represented a majority of organized building trades workers, but these unions organized their industries as well as their crafts. The Carpenters' claim to "all who worked in wood" extended to mill workers, pile drivers, and specialists of all kinds, whether they worked in factories, on the docks, or in construction. The Electrical Workers included linemen, shopmen, and utility workers, as well as building tradesmen. And the Bricklayers organized stone masons and stone setters, plasterers and modelers, marble masons, tile setters, terrazzo and mosaic workers, as well as cement finishers.[41] All three organizations were large, amalgamated "craft-industrial" unions, willing and able to expand their jurisdiction to keep up with technological change. And working together, these three unions posed a serious threat to Department affiliates, especially when the Tri-Party Alliance abrogated long-term treaties between the Carpenters and the Iron Workers, for instance, or negotiated new treaties with the Machinists that infringed on the Elevator Constructors, the Iron Workers, and the Sheet Metal Workers.[42]

Denouncing Alliance members as "pirates" at the 1931 BTD convention, elevator constructor Frank Feeney made the danger clear. "If the Building

Trades Department is going to allow this . . . Mr. President, you had better adjourn this convention . . . and let those of the unions that are in here take advantage of an opportunity, probably, of joining that group." Delegate Ryan, of the Iron Workers, agreed. "If the Department doesn't nip this thing now, before it goes any further, I don't think you will have enough left to adjourn, because nearly every organization here will walk out. . . . If we do not get the assistance from this Department we are entitled to, you will have more alliances and your department will be shot to pieces." And that, he added, "would be the worst thing that could happen to the labor movement."[43]

But while delegates debated the best way to beat the Tri-Party Alliance, John Hynes made it clear that the decision would have to come from the ranks. "This Department will be as strong as the Local Councils will allow it to be," he pointed out. "Why not go back to your respective cities and clean house so far as our Local Councils are concerned? . . . Let us start and say: 'Everybody that is in here . . . will have to go along with the laws of the Building Trades Department.'" Local councils would have to unseat the Bricklayers, Carpenters, and Electrical Workers (whether these unions paid the bulk of council dues or not), and international union presidents and Department officers would have to lead the fight, setting up new councils, if they had to. "If the other trades combine themselves as they ought to they can go out and battle," another delegate insisted, "and in short time the [Carpenters, Electrical Workers, and Bricklayers] will be rapping at the door to get into this Department."[44]

The Great Depression

Under normal circumstances the rise of the Tri-Party Alliance would have erupted into another civil war. But there was nothing normal about circumstances in the 1930s. The stock market had crashed in 1929, ushering in the Great Depression, and building trades unions were looking for work, not fights. Between 1929 and 1933 prospects grew progressively dim: Corporate profits fell from $10 billion to $1 billion, the gross national product was cut in half, and 25 percent of the workforce was unemployed. Times were equally tough in Canada, where the gross national product fell from $6.1 billion in 1929 to $3.5 billion in 1933, and unemployment reached 30 percent.[45]

As these national economies ground to a halt, the construction industry went with them. Private construction expenditures fell almost 80 percent between 1929 and 1933 (from about $11 billion to $3 billion) and public expenditures dropped 40 percent between 1931 and 1933. By that time seven out of ten building tradesmen were out of work, and the rest saw hours drop, average wages fall (by 15 percent), and annual earnings cut in half.[46] Even the most loyal union workers had a hard time keeping their memberships current. At the height of the Depression, the Engineers saw paid-up memberships drop by about 36 percent, while the Iron Workers, Painters, Plumbers, Plasterers, and Sheet Metal Workers lost at least half their members. The Laborers were hit hardest of all, losing more than 80 percent. And while the Elevator Constructors union was able to offset some losses by taking on lower-paid maintenance and repair work, only the Roofers (the Department's smallest affiliate) counted no losses during the Great Depression.[47]

Struggling to survive the crisis, the Department did its best to hang on. It accepted two new affiliates: the Teamsters in 1928 and the Boilermakers in 1931. It protested when federal government contracts went to "unfair" employers who undercut union standards, and lobbied hard in favor of public works projects (such as rebuilding depressed "slum" areas), a shorter work week, and labor legislation (including the 1931 Davis-Bacon Act that required workers employed on government building projects to be paid at rates prevailing locally, a law designed to protect local tradesmen and contractors from outside competition from lower-waged areas).[48] But it was fighting without the help of its most experienced leaders. James Duncan, longtime liaison to the AFL (whose labor career dated back to the 1890s) had died in 1928, and George Hedrick, who had served on the Executive Council from the very beginning, died the following year. William Spencer, who had helped to organize the Structural Building Trades Alliance (and had resumed his post as Department secretary-treasurer in 1927) died in 1933. And long-time Executive Council member Arthur Huddell of the Engineers (who had served from 1921 to 1931) was also gone.[49] In fact, former president William McSorley (who had signed the BTD's charter in 1908) and Sheet Metal Worker John Hynes (who was first elected vice president in 1914) were the only "old hands" on the Executive Council by 1933. BTD president Michael J. McDonough, of the Plasterers, secretary-treasurer William O'Neill of the Plumbers, and vice presidents Lawrence P. Lindelof (Painters), Joseph V. Moreschi (Laborers), Paul J. Morrin (Iron Workers), and John Possehl (Engineers), rounded out the leadership.

The most significant change during these critical years, however, involved the Department's mission, not its personnel. With the election of U.S. president Franklin Delano Roosevelt in 1932, the Department's political activities increased dramatically. As leader of the American Construction Council in the 1920s, Roosevelt had long preached a gospel of voluntary standards and self-regulation to stabilize industry. And now he had a golden opportunity to put those ideas to work. In 1933 he used New Deal legislation—the National Industrial Recovery Act (NIRA)—to develop "fair codes of competition" and to regulate wages, prices, hours, and production in order to get people back to work. But while the NIRA recognized labor's right to organize and bargain collectively through unions, it left unions out of the code-making process. Trade associations, like the Construction League (an organization of contractors, architects, engineers, and material dealers) were expected to set industry standards.[50]

Perhaps because he was a former legislator himself, BTD president Michael J. McDonough had no intention of sitting the process out. Ever since the crash of 1929, the Department had taken politics more seriously, and in the case of the construction code, McDonough made sure that the Department's voice was heard—whether government officials wanted to hear it or not. Building trades unions were seeking a five-day, thirty-hour week, and the wages they commanded before the industry had collapsed. But the code developed by the Construction League endorsed a six-day, forty-eight-hour week, and wages that fell far below union standards. "This is an industry with highly skilled workers," McDonough protested, workers who had organized and won the forty-hour week years earlier. "Their standards . . . must be met frankly," he insisted, "if mass purchasing power is to be increased."[51]

McDonough pressed the Department's case on anyone who would listen, including National Recovery Administration General Counsel Donald Richberg, Deputy Administrator Malcolm Pirnie, Administrator General Hugh Johnson, Secretary of Labor Frances Perkins, Senator Robert Wagner, and, finally, President Roosevelt himself. And ultimately the Department got results. Early in 1934 President Roosevelt not only abandoned the Construction League's code but also assigned Major George Berry (a longtime AFL leader and government labor representative) to consult with building trades unions and draw up a new code. The result was a compromise the Department could live with: a forty-hour week, a minimum skilled wage of $1 an hour (unless unions had negotiated a higher rate), and union representation on the National Construction Planning and Adjustment Board that would administer the code. "The methods of code writing did not offer much opportunity for the exercise of labor's bargaining power," the Department admitted. But despite obvious shortcomings, "more progress was made in this code than in many others where labor was not organized and no stout defense could be raised."[52]

But before Roosevelt would sign off on the code, he required one more change. The Planning and Adjustment Board would have to come up with a plan to settle jurisdictional disputes. Eager to comply, the Board declared jurisdictional strikes "intolerable" at its first meeting in August 1934. It also established a Committee of Temporary Adjudication (to be manned by the chairman of the Board and the president of the Building Trades Department) and a National Jurisdictional Awards Board (to be administered by three government employees) to make final decisions. Satisfied by the outcome, President Roosevelt took one more step. He issued an Executive Order that made the board federal law, and amended the construction code to outlaw jurisdictional strikes. And in the process he boosted the Department's power in the industry, making its president the leading labor negotiator for the building trades.[53]

The significance of this change was not lost on the Tri-Party Alliance. In fact, Department officers and Alliance leaders had been consulting regularly since the start of the construction code campaign, and both had a hand in designing the new jurisdictional plan: Representatives of the Bricklayers, Carpenters, and Electrical Workers sat with Department members on the Planning and Adjustment Board. Moreover, by the time the new jurisdiction board was announced, the Alliance unions had already negotiated their reaffiliation with the Department. If the next president of the Building Trades Department was going to make jurisdictional decisions, it only made sense that the three largest building trades unions, the Bricklayers, Carpenters, and Electrical Workers, take their rightful place in the Department.[54]

But what exactly was their rightful place? In the view of the Alliance unions, once the Department's Executive Council approved their applications and accepted their per capita taxes, they were full-fledged Department members, like everybody else. And on June 14, 1934, the Executive Council had apparently agreed. Accepting and approving applications from the Bricklayers, the Carpenters, and the Electrical Workers, the Council reported that they were now affiliated organizations "entitled to all rights and privileges . . . in the conventions of the Department." But within a few months the Department changed its mind. On the eve of the 1934 convention, which met in San Francisco the last week of September, it was rumored that the "big three" affiliates had plans to shake up the Department. The current officers were not aggressive enough, the newspapers reported, so the Tri-Party Alliance was running a slate of its own. Alliance supporters had already "parceled out the offices," through pre-convention "deals," according to the *New York Times*. "An officers' fight was in full blast," as the Stone Cutters put it, "and definite lines were drawn."[55]

The realization that the "big three" unions had no intention of reelecting Michael McDonough, or his supporters, put a brand new spin on reaffiliation. Employing a strategy perfected by the Carpenters, the Department now decided that it was up to convention delegates to accept or reject the three unions. Thus, despite warm welcomes in both the president's and the Executive Council's reports—"It is indeed a pleasant duty to report . . . the reaffiliation," as the council put it—the credential committee now refused to seat delegates from the "big three," and the convention agreed. "The Building Trades Department has weathered the depression . . . through the solidarity of those trades now in affiliation," delegates noted, "and fearful that this solidarity will be disrupted . . . we do not concur in the action of the Executive Council in accepting . . . these organizations and therefore recommend that . . . their affiliation be denied."[56]

Daniel Tobin of the Teamsters and President William Green of the AFL argued forcefully against this interpretation since the Department had been accepting the unions' per capita taxes for months. But the delegates stood firm. They not only refused to recognize the three largest building trades unions, but they also adopted an amendment eliminating the "double vote" on roll-call votes that empowered large unions on the convention floor. For that was the real crux of the fight. If the "big three" unions were going to reaffiliate, delegates wanted to make sure that the smaller specialty unions maintained their influence in the Department and their ability to protect their jurisdiction.[57]

The delegates' vote, and President McDonough's reelection, ended the fight as far as the convention was concerned. But President William Green and the AFL Executive Council were not at all satisfied. The very next week the AFL declared the entire BTD proceedings "illegal," and in November President Green called another convention at AFL headquarters in Washington, D.C. Gathering in the seventh-floor auditorium, seven building trades unions—the Bricklayers, Carpenters, Electrical Workers, Engineers, Marble Polishers, Laborers, and Teamsters—adopted a new constitution and elected a new set of officers. When the meeting adjourned, President J. W. Williams (Carpenters), Secretary-Treasurer Herbert Rivers (Laborers), and Vice Presidents John Possehl (Engineers), Richard Gray (Bricklayers), Daniel Tracy (Electrical Workers), William McCarthy (Marble Polishers), Thomas Hughes (Teamsters), and Joseph V. Moreschi (Laborers) were ready to set up a new Building Trades Department.[58] But two floors down, President McDonough remained at work in his BTD office. "All that won't affect us in the least," he told the *Washington Post*. "Our twelve unions will go on just as before. . . . Although the other side has more members, our unions have the greater economic strength. In case of a strike, our twelve trades would stick together with more solidarity than the others."[59] To prove his point, McDonough and the Executive Council that had been elected in San Francisco—Hynes, Lindelof, Morrin, McSorley, Feeney, and J. A. Mullaney of the Asbestos Workers—made it clear that they intended to "continue to function as the Building Trades Department." They refused to turn over Department books and funds, and they did not give up their fifth-floor office at first. "Our Department will carry on the same as in the past, irrespective of the decisions of . . . the American Federation of Labor," the McDonough group insisted, especially since those decisions were "autocratic, dictatorial, and a flagrant violation . . . of democracy."[60]

Before the year was over, there were two bona fide Building Trades Departments fighting it out in the courts, in the newspapers, in union journals, and at AFL conventions. The Williams Department operated out of AFL headquarters. The McDonough Department was housed directly across the street, in the Machinists' Building. "Each carries on its business as if it were the one and only building trades department," the *New York Times* reported. "The only thing they agree on, is the need for an extensive low-cost home building program."[61] In the meantime, however, neither Department president was able to claim the prize, the coveted seat on the Temporary Adjudication Board. Even though AFL president William Green vouched for J. W. Williams's credentials, the Planning Board's chairman refused to recognize either Department as long as the fight raged on. But ultimately the issue proved moot. In May 1935 the U.S. Supreme Court declared the National Recovery Administration unconstitutional and the jurisdictional board ceased to exist.[62]

At around the same time a court decision further underscored the futility of this leadership war: According to Judge Adkins, of the Washington, D.C., Supreme Court, there was only one legal Building Trades Department, and that was the Department that had called the San Francisco convention in 1934. The AFL had been within its right to declare the proceedings of that convention illegal, but it had no right to call a new convention, according to the judge. Thus the court recognized the McDonough Department as the legitimate department, but it did not recognize its current officers, since their lawful terms had ended in 1934. Given these legal complications, Judge Adkins agreed that there was only one solution. Both sides would have to come together and start again. When Adkins offered his services as a mediator, however, both sides turned him down.[63]

There had to be a compromise: The federal government was funding most construction work, and it would not stand for jurisdictional fights or rival Department wars. But it would take another year of meetings, threats, and counter threats to reach a truce. Neither side trusted the other, and neither had a ready solution to conflicts that had undermined unity since the days of the Structural Building Trades Alliance. More than a decade of hard-fought jurisdictional battles had demonstrated that neither side would be easily defeated regardless of membership size, for both groups brought a measure of strength to the Department. What the McDonough affiliates lacked in numbers, for instance, they made up for in solidarity on local job sites—and that could not be ignored. So in order to reach a workable compromise, both sides would have to be satisfied that their voices would be heard on the Department's Executive Council, at conventions, and in the American Federation of Labor. There could be no going back to the days when the smaller unions controlled Department policy by limiting the larger unions' vote. But there could also be no going back to brutal "might makes right" politics.

With the help of AFL vice president George Harrison, who acted as a conciliator, the rival Departments came together at a special convention in March 1936. Delegates acknowledged some irreconcilable differences and worked to minimize (rather than resolve) long-standing tensions. They agreed to enlarge the Executive Council and to split the leadership equally. The Williams Department received the office of president and four vice presidents: John Possehl, Richard Gray, Daniel Tracy, and Herbert Rivers. The McDonough Department was given the office of secretary-treasurer and four vice presidents: John Hynes, Lawrence Lindelof, Paul J. Morrin, and William McSorley. Delegates also agreed to adopt a new plan to resolve jurisdictional fights: The Department president would decide disputes as they arose, but international unions could appeal those decisions to an independent referee.[64]

The solution was far from perfect. In fact, the compromise almost fell apart in 1937, when the Carpenters, once again, rejected jurisdictional decisions. By that time, however, the prospect of another split seemed far too dangerous to contemplate. The rise of industrial unionism and the growing popularity of the Congress of Industrial Organizations had already challenged the building trades' claim to exclusive jurisdiction. And New Deal government labor agencies, like the Public Works Administration and the Works Progress Administration, now threatened to undermine labor standards and wage rates that had taken the building trades more than forty years to achieve.

PART TWO

GOVERNMENT MATTERS

Let the slogan go forth that we will stand by our friends and administer a stinging rebuke to men or parties who are either indifferent, negligent, or hostile.

—Samuel Gompers

CHAPTER FIVE

A New Deal for Labor:
Depression, Recovery, and
Government-Labor Relations

The families of the building trades mechanics have been taking it on the chin since the start of the Depression. The wives of the members know what the union means to them and their children in good times and bad. In the end they know that they will benefit far more than if their men gave up the struggle under the pressure of hard times.

—John F. Little, Bricklayers LU 34

U.S. president Franklin Delano Roosevelt may have believed that "the only thing we have to fear is fear itself," but Department president J. William Williams was not so sure. He had no trouble sharing Roosevelt's faith in the nation's "unmistakable march toward recovery." Thanks to government-funded public works programs, unemployment rates were coming down, a sure sign, Williams predicted in 1936, that the construction industry was on its way up. But he had his doubts about the role of organized labor in that recovery. Just where did building trades unions fit in Roosevelt's New Deal plans?[1]

There was no denying the president's support for unionization. Ever since Roosevelt signed the National Industrial Recovery Act in 1933, New Dealers had embraced unions as part of the economic solution and not part of the problem, as open-shop supporters had argued for years. Labor legislation like the NIRA's Section 7(a) and its successor, the National Labor Relations Act of 1935, had proved that "The President Wants You to Join a Union," as organizers proclaimed. But what kind of union, Williams wanted to know. Would President Roosevelt support skilled building trades unions, with high wage rates, established jurisdictions, and closed-shop conditions? Or was he mainly interested in promoting new industrial unions that were springing up every day in mass-production industries like steel, auto making, and electrical manufacturing? When conflicts developed, as they inevitably would, who would decide what constituted "fair" conditions and how work would be assigned? Would it be experienced trade unionists with a history of setting their own standards or political appointees who had their own ideas about labor organization and industrial democracy? Would the government follow the principle established by the Davis-Bacon prevailing wage law and act as a model employer? Or would it join the ranks of construction "chiselers" and try to break down union standards?[2]

These questions reflected some remarkable shifts in government-labor relations that were still taking shape in the mid-1930s. New Deal efforts to "prime the pump" and reemploy the nation's workforce, made government a prime factor in economic affairs, and Washington, D.C., "the center of obtaining and maintaining conditions," as Department secretary Michael J. McDonough reported. Like it or not, there would be no construction work without government support, an economic fact of life that Department leaders could not ignore. With 35 percent of the buildings trades unemployed and another 30 percent working only part-time in May 1936, the building trades needed all the help they could get.[3]

With no real choice but to take politics more seriously, Department leaders now joined the AFL's ongoing campaign to keep legislators apprised of "Labor's Attitude," as AFL president William Green put it. Lobbying, testifying at congressional hearings, and keeping the government supplied with facts and figures to document union standards became full-time jobs. In Washington, D.C., Harry Bates (of the Bricklayers), Michael J. Colleran (of the Plasterers), and John Coefield (of the Plumbers) formed the AFL's Housing Committee, and doggedly drummed up legislative and rank-and-file support for government housing projects. And on the local level regional leaders like plumber George Meany (who was president of the New York State Federation of Labor) kept up the pressure, making it clear to legislators that building trades workers, the best organized workers in any community, needed jobs. "Our objective," as Harry Bates put it, "was to obtain as much Federal funds going into construction" as possible. The strategy apparently paid off: By 1936 government agencies like the Public Works Administration (PWA) and the Works Progress Administration (WPA) had billions of dollars to invest in building, highway, and heavy construction projects.[4]

But federal funds were one thing, as Department leaders were learning every day, and union conditions another. In the first place, government construction projects were designed to employ as many workers as possible, so they were not organized along the same lines as private-sector jobs. The government favored handwork and low technology over skilled workers and heavy equipment, a strategy that allowed New York State, for instance, to use hundreds of unskilled workers wielding picks, shovels, and rollers to build its roads, instead of a smaller number of skilled, well-paid operating engineers who were trained to run steamrollers. Second, government officials could not be counted on to understand, let alone respect, the building trades determined control of jobs, skill, and jurisdiction, or how that control determined "fair" wages, safe working conditions, and a decent standard of living. Early work relief programs, like the Civil Works Administration (CWA) and the Civilian Conservation Corps (CCC), had already raised suspicions. In Massachusetts local leaders complained that CWA administrators had favored "amateurs and unskilled painters" over unemployed union members. CCC policy was even worse, the Plasterers noted, since this relief agency was training workers to do construction jobs, and breaking down building trades standards in the process. If government agencies intended "to start manufacturing journeymen for the different building crafts," as the Plasterers complained, then building trades workers had plenty to fear, especially from well-meaning politicians who had no idea how the construction industry worked.[5]

The Department of Labor was also raising suspicions, especially when an official there attempted to classify standards of work for building trades mechanics. "This is a matter for the building trades to define within their own organizations," President Williams protested in 1936. "The Labor Movement will not tolerate the changing of conditions and methods of doing business that have been in existence since the establishment of Organized Labor." There was no good reason for government interference, as far as the Department could see. Building trades unions were doing the job: No other group of organized workers could match the wage rates and working conditions of the building trades or their history of collective bargaining. And no other method of labor organization had proved more successful, in the construction industry, than the building trades' program of "exclusive" jurisdiction, closed-shop conditions, and high hourly wages. In a dangerous, seasonal, and highly competitive industry, building trades unions had managed to provide a practical measure of security and protection for workers who moved from job to job, with no steady employer. If the government now intended to undermine that security, it could expect a fight.[6]

The Department's message was simple and direct: Because skilled union workers added value to the construction industry, and the economy as a whole, they had earned the right to man the jobs that government was now creating, especially if those jobs would have been handled by union workers in the private sector. And they had a right, as citizens, to expect the government to honor union rates and standards, and not use the current economic crisis to break down those standards. Building tradesmen were worth the high hourly wage rates they had fought so hard to establish, the Department insisted. After all, the skill and experience they brought to the job was crucial to the industry's success. If the government had a long-term interest in promoting a healthy construction industry, it should act now to protect skilled workers, the Department believed, so that when private-sector construction recovered, the workforce would be ready to go. To do otherwise would only ensure shoddy workmanship and labor unrest. "No one with the slightest practical knowledge of building . . . expects as much or as good production. . . . from a man forced by poverty . . . to work for one-half or less than his usual wage," the Bricklayers insisted. And no one who knew anything about building trades workers, George Meany added, could expect union men to violate "the most sacred rule of a trade union—that rule which demands of every union man that he work for not less than the standard wage."[7]

It was a message that made practical sense to building trades unions, which were as much a part of the industry as they were part of the labor movement. But it was a controversial message nonetheless. With so many unemployed workers struggling to survive, union wage rates seemed "unrealistically high" to those outside the trades, and closed-shop conditions seemed "a callous rejection of the nonunion jobless," as one observer put it. Building trades unions were more concerned with their "special" interests than with the nation's interests as a whole, critics charged. And unions that fought to preserve skilled work for members only—over the claims of nonunion veterans or men on relief—became easy political targets, especially when some local unions negotiated six-hour workdays or "boycotted" nonunion materials, practices that would lead to a federal investigation before the decade was over. In fact, it would take the outbreak of the Second World War and the emergency demand for skilled construction workers to demonstrate the real value of building trades unions to the nation at large: Their knowledge, experience, and well-developed labor networks would prove to be invaluable assets when the nation needed their help to win the war.[8]

In the meantime, however, public attention and support would be focused on more vulnerable workers—auto workers, steel workers, packing house workers, textile workers, men and women who were waging a dramatic and dangerous fight to establish their basic industrial rights in the 1930s. Next to these workers, who still suffered ten- and twelve-hour days and often unspeakable conditions, building tradesmen looked like "labor aristocrats" and defensive ones at that: They were fighting to preserve conditions that these new industrial workers had little hope of achieving. Looking at their well-organized unions, it was hard for outsiders to believe that the building trades had fought the same dangerous fights decades earlier and that their victories were based on skill, disciplined organization, and collective bargaining, not selfishness, collusion, or corruption, as critics maintained. But if the building trades' defensive campaign in the 1930s made sense in terms of their own history, it made nothing but a bad impression on the public at large. For in the 1930s another labor campaign was just beginning to take off, one that promised to organize the unorganized and, in the process, reinvent and reinvigorate the American Federation of Labor.

The Rise of the Committee for Industrial Organization

While building trades workers were fighting hard to preserve union standards, another labor story was beginning to unfold, one that proved far more compelling: Unorganized workers were demanding their basic industrial and civil rights, and the nation was standing behind them. Depression conditions had magnified the chronic disparity between "haves" and "have nots," exposing the human costs of "unfair" labor practices. Heartbreaking stories of child laborers in the fields, teenage girls trapped in sweatshops, and adult breadwinners earning only a few cents an hour in open-shop industries were powerful indictments of anti-union employers. Dramatic images of striking textile, steel, and rubber workers, some of the most exploited workers in the country, made the question of social justice front-page news. Graphic reports of mine guards wielding sawed-off shotguns in Harlan County, Kentucky, or policemen firing into a crowd of strikers in Minneapolis and killing two boys, bolstered public support for New Deal labor legislation, as well as the organizing campaign it promised. By 1935 the stage was set for the biggest labor push since the days of the First World War. Production workers at notoriously hostile corporations like General Motors, U.S. Steel, RCA, and Goodyear Tires were desperate to organize, and militant union leaders including John L. Lewis, who helped to establish the Committee for Industrial Organization (CIO), became working-class heroes.[9]

A powerful and dramatic speaker, Lewis was president of the United Mine Workers, an AFL union that had organized on an industrial basis since its founding in the 1890s. A strong opponent of "exclusive jurisdiction" (which, he believed, had undermined all previous attempts to organize mass-production workers), Lewis had urged the AFL's Executive Council to issue industrial charters to unions like the Automobile Workers as early as 1934. The following year he led a more organized campaign. At the AFL's 1935 convention, Lewis and his supporters submitted twenty-one resolutions favoring industrial unionism. Although they lost on every vote, because "craft" supporters outnumbered "industrial" supporters two to one, they generated valuable publicity: Lewis was continually in the spotlight, using everything from the Bible to Shakespeare to prove his point that it was time for a change in AFL policy. In thunderous tones he made it clear that the vote against industrial unionism only proved what AFL critics had been saying for years: that craft unions were out of touch with modern conditions, and that craft leaders like "Big" Bill Hutcheson of the Carpenters, were more concerned with preserving jurisdictional rights than they were with protecting millions of unorganized workers. When Lewis allegedly took a swing at Hutcheson, bloodying his nose to end a debate over jurisdictional rights, most observers already knew that a larger fight was brewing. Within a month AFL industrial union supporters had launched the Committee for Industrial Organization—and within a year the AFL Executive Council would vote to suspend CIO unions. It would be another two years, however, before the CIO officially became the Congress of Industrial Organizations, a rival labor federation.[10]

In the meantime, the fledgling CIO was off to an impressive start: After so many failed attempts to organize workers at Westinghouse, General Electric, and U.S. Steel, CIO industrial unions were finally getting results. Production workers all over the country took up the CIO's banner, taking over company unions, manning picket lines, and demonstrating a militant devotion to the cause of mass organization. But when CIO unions also claimed mechanics (including operating engineers or maintenance workers like electricians, painters, and plumbers) or tried to control new construction at the plants they organized (as CIO Oil Workers did at the Sinclair Refinery in Indiana or as the Auto Workers did at the Fisher Body Plant in Michigan), building trades workers drew the line. CIO leaders may have believed that an industrial union superseded jurisdictional claims; that, after all, was a major part of the CIO's appeal as an organization. But building trades unions were having none of it.[11]

"We of the craft unions have . . . no trouble with industrial unions that attend to their own knitting and respect our jurisdictions," the Bricklayers noted. "But we have a very serious battle with those that trespass." Department leaders were not particularly worried, however. President Williams may have raged against radical, self-aggrandizing "communist" CIO leaders who were trying to build One Big Union to challenge building trades turf, but Secretary McDonough took the rise of the new organization in stride. "It is my opinion that [the CIO] is not going to affect our organization," he noted in 1936, "for the reason that our fellows are not going to permit any encroachment on their jurisdiction."[12] If history was any guide, the building trades would hold on to their work. Just ask the Brotherhood of Maintenance of Way Employees, which had been trying to claim railroad construction work since 1919. Or the International Association of Machinists, which had been fighting the Carpenters over millwright work since 1914. As far as Department leaders were concerned, the CIO offered no credible threat in the mid-1930s, except perhaps on maintenance work and less-skilled jobs like road construction or building demolition. That being the case, it joined forces with the AFL's Metal Trades Department to strengthen craft control in factories, and in 1937 changed its name to the "Building and Construction Trades Department" to better reflect its broad jurisdiction.[13]

But if the CIO posed no immediate threat to the building trades, it did raise some fundamental questions that both the Department and the federal government had to address. Was organizing the unorganized more valuable to the working class as a whole than maintaining established union rights and standards? Did the desperate plight of unskilled workers, the hardest hit during the Depression, negate the building trades' fight for prevailing wage rates and closed-shop conditions? Were skilled workers justified in challenging government labor policies that undermined their standards when so many other workers had no standards worth protecting? Finally, was the federal government an employer like any other, duty-bound to honor union contracts and prevailing rates and conditions? Or did it have a moral obligation to spread relief funds as far as they would go to help those workers least able to help themselves?

Public Works and Prevailing Wage Rates

As far as the Roosevelt administration was concerned, the government's duty was clear: It encouraged collective bargaining and unions standards in private industry as a means of promoting economic recovery, since higher wage rates meant higher consumption. Indeed, the National Labor Relations Act was based on this very premise. And in the public sector it developed employment programs to provide relief work and subsistence wages to the nation's most vulnerable citizens. Yet when it came to government-funded construction projects, like those pioneered by the Public Works Administration, the line between recovery and relief was far less clear. Public works construction projects required skilled building mechanics to see a job through, and these men were not willing to work at nonunion wages or with nonunion relief helpers, regardless of government policies or depression conditions.

At first the problem seemed manageable. The PWA, which employed some three hundred thousand building tradesmen a month between 1933 and 1939, concentrated on heavy construction and large-scale building. New York's Triborough Bridge and Lincoln Tunnel, Oregon's Coastal Highway,

Philadelphia's Thirtieth Street Station, and the wide-ranging Tennessee Valley Authority were all funded through the PWA. In fact, every U.S. county (except three) benefited from PWA construction. Under its original rules, PWA projects were run, for the most part, like any other construction job. The agency relied on private contractors, who were permitted to hire mechanics through building trades unions and who paid prevailing rates. With Department secretary McDonough, as well as Richard Gray (Bricklayers), John Coefield (Plumbers), and Charles Reed (Electrical Workers), serving on the PWA Labor Advisory Board, the Department believed that wage rates and conditions were safe.[14]

But as the New Deal shifted its focus from economic recovery to economic relief, the PWA was forced to change the rules—without consulting the Labor Advisory Board. By 1935 contractors were obliged to hire local labor first, a shift that promised "no little trouble," as President Williams put it. In places like Dover, New Hampshire, and Gainesville, Georgia, where the industry and the trades were not well organized, there were not many unemployed union men available, Williams explained, and that meant contractors would have to abrogate closed-shop contracts to comply with PWA rules. "[These] rules are just the latest move of the long drive to beat down wages on Government work, particularly in the building trades," the Lathers protested. "Men who ought to know better are insisting that building trade wages are so high that they block construction and must come down," one way or another.[15]

It took months of protests to the Department of Labor and meetings with PWA administrators before the rules were "liberalized"; in the fall of 1935, the Department was pleased to report that the local hiring policy was no longer mandatory. But it was still up to local councils to see that PWA directors changed the rules, a move that usually required political and economic strength. For instance, when the state director in Massachusetts insisted that 90 percent of workers employed on eight new projects in and around Boston would have to come off local relief rolls, two thousand union workers threatened to strike, and within a few days building mechanics throughout the state threatened to join them. The PWA's local director seemed unimpressed, especially when only a few hundred men initially walked out. "Men on relief get the preference in employment and the trades resent it," he told the *Boston Globe*. But Governor James Curley took the strike more seriously. It only took a handful of skilled workers to shut a project down, since they were the "key men" who directed the others' work. With $12 million worth of contracts at stake and an election year coming up, Curley did his best to get the unions' side of the story out to the state director and to Harold Ickes, national head of the PWA. By that time, however, federal help was already on the way: Department leaders had used the strike threat to persuade federal officials to investigate the complaint and "iron things out," as Governor Curley put it. The move apparently succeeded. By 1937 union members made up almost the entire PWA workforce in Massachusetts.[16]

The question of relief versus recovery also complicated Works Progress Administration construction projects, largely because the WPA was, first and foremost, a relief agency. Designed to employ unskilled and semiskilled workers who crowded government relief rolls, the WPA handled light construction projects and favored manual over skilled labor. "Our job . . . is to put 3,500,000 people to work," WPA administrator Harry Hopkins made clear, and he was determined to stretch funds as far as they would go—a decision that precluded paying prevailing wage rates for construction projects. Despite the Department's determined lobbying campaign to amend the Emergency Relief Act (which funded both the WPA and the PWA), WPA workers earned what was known as a "security wage" that originally ranged from as low as $19 a month, in the rural south, to $50 in more industrial regions, for 130 hours of work. "Just divide the hours into the monthly wage," the Bricklayers noted, "and what do you get? You get 38 and a half cents an hour [maximum], together with the clear conviction that the Administration is planning a more audacious . . . wage slice than even the boldest of industry's expert wage chiselers would attempt." At a time when building tradesmen averaged about $1.10 an hour (and earned $1.50 an hour in places like New York City), was it any wonder, the Bricklayers wanted to know, "that Organized Labor is having nightmares about the possibility of private employers pointing with pride to the fact that they are paying a penny or two more than the Government's so-called subsistence wage?" President Williams could only agree. "The decision . . . has caused a chaotic condition to exist throughout the Country," he reported, and strikes and protests were erupting wherever building tradesmen were forced to accept such low wage rates.[17]

That the WPA directly hired its own workers, and relied on prefabricated materials (like plaster wallboard on housing construction, for instance), instead of skilled workers, added to the controversy. Building trades unions bitterly complained that government "do-gooders" were undermining quality as well as wage rates, when they hired so-called handymen for skilled construction jobs. Marble setters in Boston refused to work "with incompetents whose tools comprise water pails and sponges," and even nonunion contractors were beginning to back them up. The Associated General Contractors (AGC), an association that represented building, highway, and heavy construction contractors, frankly believed that WPA construction was not only a threat to the free enterprise system but was also a danger to the public at large, since the agency had no apparent regard for experience, knowledge, or skill. "What could be a better way of handling the relief problem," the AGC wanted to know, "than to build projects which will collapse, so that there will be another relief project building a project that will collapse," and so on, so that relief work could go on indefinitely![18]

The unions made a similar argument, using their journals and the labor press to publicize any and all WPA disasters. But the agency was failing at more than construction, they added, since one of the stated goals of the WPA was to keep up worker morale. When a building tradesman takes a low-waged WPA job and sees an unqualified worker getting the same pay, John Little, a New York City bricklayer, told a radio audience in 1935, "he not only knows he is being taken advantage of, but what makes him sore is that he feels that the Federal Government is unconsciously breaking down wage standards under the guise of charity."[19]

Richard Gray, secretary of the Bricklayers, agreed. "[The WPA security wage] has created a very serious situation which threatens to result in a great industrial disturbance. It involves our relation to the entire WPA plan and may lead to strikes throughout the country, unless quick and decisive action is taken." It was not only a question of money, Gray added, it was a question of principle, of morale, and of economy: Not only was the government undermining the building mechanic's standards, Gray contended, it was shattering his faith in fair play and the pride he took in a job well done. Skilled, efficient work still mattered in construction, but skilled, efficient mechanics would not work for security wages. If the government valued a skilled workforce, it would have to pay prevailing rates, whether a worker was on relief or not. After all, Gray added, construction work was not charity, and other government agencies, like the PWA and the Civilian Conservation Corps, had managed to comply with the rules of the Davis-Bacon Act. Even in Canada, where Depression conditions were just as dire, the government paid prevailing rates for relief work. "A man's skill is his individual contribution to the public welfare," Gray added. "We think the public as a whole will benefit because of the higher standards of living that we are trying to maintain."[20]

The argument proved hard to sustain outside the trades. Workers who were still fighting for the eight–hour day and the right to organize, or had been shut out of "closed" local unions, clearly resented the building trades' prevailing wage campaign, and so did social reformers, especially when union wage rates threatened to deplete precious WPA funds. But with strikes erupting to protest security wages, the Department held its ground. By the fall of 1935 Harry Hopkins was ready to compromise: He not only agreed to pay special WPA prevailing rates (to be determined by Hopkins and President Roosevelt, not the Department of Labor), but he also dropped open-shop requirements on WPA construction projects, and authorized local directors to negotiate shorter hour requirements for the skilled workforce, compromises that ultimately brought "security" wages more in line with union rates. In New York, Pennsylvania, and Chicago, for instance, WPA administrators cut skilled workers' hours in half, effectively doubling the hourly wage, the Department's ultimate goal. According to the *Wall Street Journal*, the agreement was "a complete capitulation to the demands of union leaders," but Department members did not agree. "We wish it were 'a complete capitulation.' It is not," the Bricklayers responded. "It is, however, a distinct and definite check to the tendency to break down wages and conditions that 50 years of labor [have] built up."[21]

Jurisdictional Conflicts

If the building trades' defensive strategy did not win public approval, it generally got the job done. The combination of political lobbying and economic "muscle" kept union workers employed on public works projects (under basic union conditions, for the most part) and pushed through new legislation like the Wagner-Steagall "low rent" housing bill, which promised to revitalize slum areas and provide more work for the trades at prevailing rates and union standards. Department leaders also worked to get wages raised and hours shortened on government reclamation projects, like Boulder Dam, and they did whatever it took to ensure that union workers set the standard for predetermined Davis-Bacon wage rates. "In many cases where a determination . . . did not meet with the approval of our organization," Secretary McDonough explained, "I have taken the matter up with Department of Labor officials and have been successful in having the rates modified." All this work on the national level paid off in jobs and better conditions for local building trades workers, as long as local unions continued to "apply the heat" to state and local government officials. If membership rates were any indication, they were facing up to the job: Between 1936 and 1937 the Department grew from 650,566 to 686,985 members (a 6 percent increase, with Iron Workers, Laborers, and Painters leading the way), and between 1937 and 1938 membership reached 789,852 (a 15 percent increase).[22]

But if President Williams and Secretary McDonough expected applause for a job well done, they were quickly disappointed. In fact, after the 1937 Department convention that met that fall in Denver, both men were out of a job. Neither Williams nor McDonough ran for reelection, since it was obvious that they did not have the votes to win. Their failure had nothing to do with New Deal policies, Department political strategies, or even the rise of the CIO. Instead, both Williams and McDonough stumbled over the same rocks that had wrecked the Department before: They were brought down in a fight with the Carpenters' "Big" Bill Hutcheson, who had decided it was time for a change. "The carpenters' president has not forgiven Mr. Williams for standing as a candidate for presidency of the carpenters' union at the last convention," the *New York Times* reported, but that was just the tip of the iceberg. No doubt Hutcheson wanted to remind Williams just who was boss; after all, Williams owed his Department job to Hutcheson's support back in 1934. But he was also determined to protect the Carpenters' jurisdictional rights. John A. Lapp, the Department's newly appointed National Referee on jurisdictional conflicts, had made a decision that Hutcheson could not accept: Lapp had favored the Iron Workers in a hotly contested fight over setting steel bar joists, and Hutcheson wanted to make sure that that mistake did not happen again.[23]

The 1937 jurisdiction case grew out of a PWA project to build a high school in Norwalk, Connecticut, where the carpenters were claiming "almost everything on the job and tell[ing] the contractors to go ahead and do anything . . . with the carpenter," a local iron worker complained. "Most of the contractors do this," he added, since carpenters earned $1.06 an hour and Iron Workers $1.37. But wage competition was not the real issue. Contractors were ready to use carpenters to set steel bar joists because the Iron Workers' local could not, and in fact would not, man the job. Members were busy with other work, and they apparently preferred to hold up construction rather than man the job with "outside" union members, a common contractors' complaint. But even after the international union intervened and sent a crew to Norwalk, the conflict was not solved. At that point the Carpenters walked off the job, leaving it up to President Williams to award jurisdiction. Williams had apparently approved this strategy beforehand, despite the Department's policy against jurisdictional strikes.[24]

Without much delay, President Williams awarded the work to the Carpenters. After all, what was wrong with his union's plan to organize jobs that Iron Workers were leaving for nonunion men? But Lapp, the referee, saw it differently. When the Iron Workers appealed the decision, he promptly reversed it and, in the process, confirmed Hutcheson's well-known distrust of outside "experts." At the same time, Hutcheson was losing what little confidence he had in the Department's ability to further the Carpenters' cause, especially after the Executive Council agreed to revive local jurisdictional boards to settle complaints on the spot. In the late 1920s Hutcheson had led the Carpenters out of the Department over the very same issue: He had no intention of letting local building trades councils determine his union's jurisdiction. And now he was ready to do it again, especially after President Williams and the Executive Council ignored his protest. So when Hutcheson arrived at the 1937 convention, he had a new slate of officers ready to go.[25]

Backed by the Bricklayers, Electrical Workers, Operating Engineers, Laborers, Teamsters, and Marble Polishers—the same unions that had supported the so-called Williams Department in 1934—Hutcheson made it clear that Williams and McDonough had to be replaced, if the Department intended to remain intact. Finding himself in a tight situation, President Williams knew what he had to do. "I am telling you now that I can positively say I haven't an enemy in this room at this minute. I consider that will be the greatest achievement of my life, to realize that I have performed my duties without leaving enmity on the part of any one." And to no one's great surprise he announced, "I am not a candidate for reelection at this convention." Secretary McDonough followed suit, but he had an easier time, largely because his international union was solidly behind him. Addressing the convention on his behalf, Plasterers' president Michael J. Colleran announced that McDonough would not be running for office either, since the Plasterers wanted him back. With these formalities out of the way, the old Tri-Party Alliance and its supporters now claimed both major offices, with Joseph A. McInerney of the Marble Polishers elected president and Herbert Rivers of the Laborers elected secretary-treasurer. They also claimed five out of eight seats on the Executive Council: Hutcheson and Daniel Tobin (Teamsters) now joined Richard Gray (Bricklayers), Daniel Tracy (Electrical Workers), and John Possehl (Engineers) on the Executive Council, which also included John Hynes (Sheet Metal Workers), L. P. Lindelof (Painters), and William J. McSorley (Lathers).[26]

The shift in leadership did little to solve jurisdictional problems, however. "The old time question of jurisdictional disputes," as President Williams put it in 1937, remained "the paramount issue" well after McInerney took office in 1938. The Bricklayers union was fighting the Carpenters over laying wooden block floors, the Roofers over caulking window frames, the Painters over setting opaque glass, and the Plasterers over installing artificial stone and acoustical tile, and the list went on, much to the industry's dismay. "The employer doesn't give a damn who lays the wooden floor blocks, glues the soundproofing slabs to the ceiling, or installs the [metal] chute," a newspaper complained. "But he does want the work done on schedule and within original cost estimates, and it can't be done with union squabbles over jurisdiction holding up construction."[27]

The 1936 jurisdictional plan was supposed to have settled these questions conclusively. But a dispute between the Engineers and Electrical Workers (over operating electric welding sets) made it clear that nothing much had changed regarding the enforcement of jurisdictional awards. When the case went to John Lapp for a final decision, the Plumbers, Sheet Metal Workers, Boilermakers, and Iron Workers all showed up for the hearing, arguing that operation belonged to whichever trade was doing the welding. Lapp apparently agreed with them, but he was unable to persuade the Engineers to go along with his decision, and the union immediately tried to have the case reopened. When Lapp refused, and the Executive Council backed his decision, the Engineers made it clear that members were not going to comply with his ruling. "I am notifying you now that we are not going along with Dr. Lapp's decision," Department vice president John Possehl insisted in December 1937, "and we will strike every job we can wherever we have the power to keep control of the work." The very next month, when Lapp issued another decision against the Engineers—this time awarding the unloading of cement-mixer trucks to the Teamsters—Possehl again refused to comply, seriously undermining the referee's authority. By September 1938 Lapp had already submitted his resignation, and the jurisdictional policy that had seemed so promising back in 1936 was stalled again, at least for the time being.[28]

Engineers, Heavy Construction, and the Associated General Contractors

Whatever his talents and intentions, President McInerney would not be the one to reshape Department policy. Although he was reelected at the 1938 convention, he died only a few months later in 1939, and the Executive Council chose John P. Coyne of the Engineers to succeed him. In a sense, Coyne's appointment was almost accidental: The Engineers' president John Possehl was the more likely candidate, since he served as first vice president of the Department, but that was somewhat accidental, too. Possehl had only recently moved up from second vice president, following the death, in 1938, of first vice president John Hyne. But Possehl decided to resign his Department office so that Coyne, his longtime assistant, could take over as president in August 1939. Addressing convention delegates for the first time a few weeks later, Coyne was still getting accustomed to his unexpected appointment. "I am grieved to relate the circumstances upon which I was selected . . . to fill the unexpired term of our late President," he told the delegates. "It is with deep sorrow that I perform the duties of the office of the President of the Department, due to these circumstances."[29]

But there was nothing accidental about the Engineers' new influence in the Department. Coyne's appointment accurately reflected some important industry shifts. Thanks to government-funded public works projects, including the Grand Coulee Dam, the Golden Gate Bridge, and the Blue Ridge Parkway, highway and heavy construction were becoming the most dynamic sectors of the construction industry. And operating engineers, who manned the power shovels, cranes, and bulldozers that made these projects possible, were becoming the "key trade" for general contractors. As highway and heavy construction developed into major industries, between 1930 and 1940, the number of operating engineers employed in construction grew by almost 50 percent, and the membership of the International Union of Operating Engineers (IUOE) more than doubled. In fact, between 1933 and 1939 the IUOE's construction membership increased more than 300 percent, a change that general contractors in heavy and highway construction could not ignore once the government agreed to pay prevailing rates on public works projects.[30]

Because these general contractors feared that building construction rates and work rules would set the standards in heavy and highway construction, they began to see the value of negotiating with the union: Under a collectively bargained agreement, their industry's particular problems could be addressed. For instance, because highway and heavy construction work was largely unorganized at the time, the IUOE was willing to set a special rate for highway work (since it offered steadier employment than building construction and generated plenty of overtime). By 1936 general contractor associations in thirty U.S. cities had signed agreements with building trades councils, and by 1939 Engineers' president John Possehl was addressing the Associated General Contractors' convention (on behalf of the Department), negotiating state and regional heavy and highway construction agreements, and working with the AGC's newly established Labor Relations Committee in hopes of reaching a national agreement.[31]

Possehl's working relationship with AGC director E. J. Harding opened the door to a joint agreement with the Building and Construction Trades Department. In August 1939 the AGC's Labor Relations Committee presented a plan to the Department's Executive Council to improve labor relations and to protect the contracting system. Seeking an end to costly jurisdictional strikes, skilled labor shortages, and unexpected wage hikes, the AGC was willing to negotiate an industrywide agreement based on uniform, predetermined wage rates and conditions. Basically AGC contractors would accept union wage rates, as long as unions agreed that (1) those rates would prevail for the life of the contract, (2) apprentices would be trained regularly, and (3) jurisdictional conflicts would not interfere with production; the trade controlling the work when a dispute erupted, the AGC insisted, would maintain control until a decision was reached.[32]

Agreeing in principle with the contractors' proposal, Department leaders now met with AGC representatives to work out a plan to settle jurisdictional conflicts on a national basis, without resorting to strikes—"the greatest single achievement in the history of organized labor in the building and construction industry," according to President Coyne. "When we emerged from that room," he reported in 1940, "I was authorized . . . to issue an order that in the future there should be no stoppage of work . . . pending a decision by the president of our department. There were a lot of people who felt that did not mean anything, but I can truthfully testify . . . that a very conservative estimate would be that 80 percent of the stoppages . . . due to disputes over jurisdictional matters has ceased."[33]

At the time, this joint approach made sense. WPA construction policies threatened unions and contractors alike: By 1939, when the Works Progress Administration became the Work Projects Administration, the agency had not only dropped its support for prevailing wage rates, but it was trying to bring its low-wage, day-labor system to large public works projects. "We both have a man-sized job to protect the market we have," E. J. Harding contended, "without any interference from Government." "We have found a common cause to which we both [can] contribute what . . . influence [we have] in behalf of the industry," President Coyne agreed. "The biggest problem that the contractor and the laborer have today," he continued, "is that problem of banding ourselves together—all of us who are engaged in the building and construction industry—for the purpose of preserving that industry, for if we continue to permit legislation [that supports WPA construction] . . . they are robbing our future in the building and construction industry." Adding that "there is nobody who builds on a falling market," Coyne made it clear that "when the building industry does not prosper, neither does the nation. It is up to us to preserve our industry, and if we do that and do it well, we will all prosper—the contractor and the laborer as well."[34]

Although the Department and the AGC (which represented union and nonunion contractors) still had their differences, both agreed that they needed no government help when it came to managing the construction industry. New Deal public works projects may have kept their members employed through some very hard times, but both organizations were becoming increasingly wary of the government's role in manning those projects and setting industry standards. Prevailing wage laws on government projects were one thing, but the Department was not at all sure about new government agencies like the U.S. Bureau of Apprenticeship and Training (which had the potential, critics feared, of undermining skilled wage rates) or the National Labor Relations Board (which was already challenging building trades' claims of exclusive jurisdiction). Government relief work may have been a laudable goal, the AGC agreed, but only as long as it did not interfere with the construction industry's contract system. Nobody knew the industry as well as experienced contractors and building trades unions; that being the case, both the Department and the AGC generally believed that government involvement should end with public works appropriations.

The Rise of the United Construction Workers

The AGC-BCTD fight for government contracts—and against government interference—forged an alliance that made union construction a real power in the heavy construction sector of the industry. AGC contractors and

BCTD unions had the experience, the skill, and the men to complete large-scale construction projects quickly and reliably, even in the most remote areas. The combination proved particularly potent at the time: In the fall of 1939, when the AGC and the BCTD were first coming to terms, world war was erupting in Europe. By mid-September Canada had already entered the fray, and the United States was preparing to launch a national defense campaign that had been in the works since 1936, a campaign that not only required but demanded labor peace. With jurisdictional strikes largely under control, and talks already under way for a national agreement by 1940, the stage was set for union construction to pave the way for an Allied victory. Now it was in the hands of the government to give union construction the job.[35]

There were other contenders, however. In July 1939 the CIO had launched the United Construction Workers Organizing Committee (UCWOC) to unionize construction workers that established trades had ignored. Subsidized by the United Mine Workers and led by A. D. "Denny" Lewis (brother of CIO founder John L. Lewis), the UCWOC promised to organize widely, establish "reasonable wages and working conditions," and eliminate "cut-throat competition and extortionate costs." It also promised employers industrial peace. "The contractor using CIO labor does not worry about having to bargain with 20 separate craft unions," the new union proclaimed. "One single union speaks for every worker on the job. Since there are no jurisdictions he does not have to worry about jurisdictional strikes. There are no regulations against the use of new materials. Hourly rates are calculated on a reasonable basis." CIO construction workers (who paid dues of $1.50 a month and no initiation fee) earned a uniform wage of $9 a day for skilled workers, $6 for helpers, and $5 for laborers, rates well below AFL building trades standards. Although the bulk of the UCWOC's strength was in maintenance and repair work (at CIO-organized factories), road construction (in regions where the CIO was strong), and residential work (which AFL unions largely ignored), the new union had high expectations. "Our particular goal," Denny Lewis proclaimed in 1939, "is to erect CIO-built buildings throughout the United States."[36]

Taking his campaign to Washington, D.C., where two out of three construction workers were unorganized, Lewis and the UCWOC seemed well on their way: The CIO union had negotiated a contract with the Construction Industry Employers, Inc., a brand new organization of builders and contractors. According to the newspapers, the contract "signalized the beginning of a battle with the AFL which ultimately may alter interpretation of the Davis-Bacon act." But the local building trades unions did not agree. "We're not paying any attention to this move," John Lochner, secretary of the Building Trades Council, responded. "All the larger general contractors and master builders have long-term contracts with our organizations." And these contracts paid hourly rates that topped those of the CIO. AFL bricklayers earned about $14 a day, for instance, AFL carpenters earned $12 a day, and AFL painters often worked a six-hour day on private construction. In Lochner's view, the CIO was only doing what small-scale and residential contractors had been trying to do for years: attempting to get union workers to accept less than the AFL union wage.[37]

Leo G. Mitchell, a local mechanic, was far more blunt. "Are you fostering scabs?" he asked CIO leader John L. Lewis. "We cannot picture you as a champion of Labor, union or not. But must view you with contemptible scorn as millions . . . of Christians view Judas Iscariot." George Meany, who had become the AFL's secretary-treasurer in 1939, agreed. "There is no other name for it," Meany told the 1940 BCTD convention. "There is no other possible way to describe a situation where a man, who professes to be a trade unionist, appears before an employer and tells him, 'We will supply you with men, we will work longer hours than the people with whom you have contracts, and we will work for less pay,'" he said. "That is not competition, it is orderly strike breaking."[38]

Whether the CIO truly intended to organize the unorganized or was mainly interested in undermining the AFL's strongest unions did not really matter. For while it was true that AFL building trades rates and conditions were among the best in American industry, there were still plenty of nonunion construction workers who could not join AFL unions, as well as nonunion contractors particularly in small-scale building and highway construction work. "God knows there is plenty of room for organization among the building trades," a state council leader told the 1939 BCTD convention. "As you go around the country you will find [small homes and apartment house jobs] are not organized," another added, "and you cannot sell them organization at the price asked of them to come in." The Engineers had already negotiated a lower highway rate in the hope of organizing that industry. But building mechanics, the highest-paid construction workers, preferred to abandon "rat jobs," leaving them to nonunion workers. The difference in wage rates was obvious: Union rates were 39 percent higher for bricklayers, 34 percent higher for plumbers, 58 percent higher for electrical workers, and 50 percent higher for laborers. But that difference was also dangerous, as Bricklayers' president Harry Bates argued. Local unions that refused to lower rates in order to organize residential jobs were courting disaster. "Unless we control this class of work sooner or later the number of men employed on [it] . . . will exceed the number of members in our organization." And once that was the case, he predicted, nonunion wages would set the standard for prevailing wage rates on Davis-Bacon projects.[39]

At the time, however, no one was particularly worried, especially as the construction industry moved into high gear in 1940. Ever since the German invasion of Poland in the fall of 1939, and the fall of France the following spring, defense construction had become a national priority. Officially the United States remained neutral until the bombing of Pearl Harbor in December 1941. But in 1940 the Roosevelt administration was already making serious preparations for war. By July, Congress had appropriated more than $300 million to construct military housing and training facilities, transport roads, airports, munitions factories, and even recreation centers—war defense projects that would employ 1.3 million workers in 1940. "The civilian army of more than 18,000 building tradesmen and laborers were doing construction work at Fort Meade," a newspaper reported in December, erecting twelve hundred buildings, putting in fifty miles of sewer and water lines, constructing twenty miles of roadbed, and earning weekly wages that totaled $1 million. And that was just one of thousands of similar stories. Within a year total construction employment would reach an all-time high of 2.9 million, and by 1942 the value of new construction would peak at $13.4 billion.[40]

But would union labor and union contractors control the work of national defense? Or would the government employ construction workers directly, as WPA administrators urged. And what about CIO construction workers? President Roosevelt had appointed the CIO's Sidney Hillman to represent organized labor on the Advisory Committee of the Council of National Defense (CND). Did that mean that CIO construction locals would now compete for government work? President Coyne did not think so, especially after Roosevelt appointed Joseph Keenan of the Chicago Federation of Labor (and a longtime member of the IBEW) as Hillman's assistant, and the IBEW's Daniel Tracy as Assistant Secretary of Labor. The Department was also well represented on the CND's Labor Advisory Commission: President Coyne, Harry Bates, and George Masterson (of the Plumbers) had all agreed to serve. By September the CND had adopted a labor policy that recognized the forty-hour week and the principle of overtime payment, and the National Defense Advisory Commission, according to Coyne, had recognized the Building and Construction Trades Department as having exclusive jurisdiction over building and construction work, a claim that Hillman publicly denied but that proved to be more or less true in practice.[41]

Almost as soon as the ink was dry, however, critics were railing against closed-shop defense contracts and union labor "rackets." "That carpenter's wife started something," journalist Drew Pearson reported, "when she told Mrs. Roosevelt that her husband had been unable to get a defense job because of exorbitant union demands for an initiation fee." Fort Meade's workers may have earned $1 million in wages, another paper reported, but they were paying $250,000 in so-called permit fees that would not necessarily buy them a place in the union. Common laborers were being charged $15 to $25, carpenters $55 and up, and "expert" electricians as high as $265 in some places to work on army construction jobs. But what looked like kickbacks to outsiders made economic sense to the leaders of local building trades unions. "It is true that unions expect applicants to pay initiation fees and dues. . . . Members expect service, and it has to be paid for," as one local leader put it. Real union men understood that defense contracts and high wage rates were the results of union organization, he added, and they were willing to pay their share. Nonunion "moaners," on the other hand, wanted "everything handed to [them] on a platter." They wanted union wages and conditions, but they wanted somebody else to pay for it. "If these cry-babies were asked to work on defense jobs at their nonunion wage of $6 or $7 a day—my, my what a howl we would hear." Congressman Clare Hoffman, a Republican from Michigan, however, had a different opinion. "The practice of the unions is just another form of racketeering," he contended. "There would seem to be no reason why those extorting this money should not be indicted for conspiracy to defraud and . . . to interfere with the national defense industry."[42]

Local unions did not help their case when they tied up defense jobs over jurisdictional conflicts (especially roofers, carpenters, and lathers) or demanded travel pay and double-time for overtime and extra shifts (as they did on vital but hard-to-man projects located in isolated areas). When the Washington, D.C., Buildings Trades Council took on the army in a fight to enforce the closed shop, for instance, it won nothing but public disdain: As many as two hundred fifty union members tied up $750,000 worth of defense construction at Walter Reed Hospital in March 1941, when the army hired an open-shop contractor for another hospital job, a contractor who hired nonunion and CIO construction workers alike. "The [Building Trades Council] feels that the strike was justified," a Department of Labor conciliator explained, "because it has always been their policy to refuse to work with nonunion building tradesmen." But neither the Department, the international unions, the army, or the newspapers thought they were right. The fact was that the BTC could neither shut the contractor down (since material drivers were not organized in the area) nor induce the army to persuade the contractor to sign with the union. And that being the case, members had no choice but to return to work, since "the good of the Nation comes first," as the BTC put it. "Of course, the War Department refused to permit any union to dictate its policy in awarding contracts," commented the *Washington Post*. "There could only be one outcome to such an irresponsible flouting of the public interest, and that was to go back to work."[43]

Determined to be recognized as partners in national defense, building trades leaders counseled caution. "Every paper . . . is headlining conditions on jobs," Joseph Keenan reported, "and people who do not understand the make-up of our organization, who do not understand that through the years we have been responsible for the conditions people will enjoy on these jobs, misunderstand us." With civilians being drafted for military service every day, building tradesmen could not afford to look like slackers or thieves. They needed to do a fair day's work for a fair day's pay, and they needed to have responsible men in charge of jobs. "Labor . . . must be on its guard to protect itself against a minority in the ranks who hold positions of trust," Keenan noted, but "who might commit an act that will cause Congress to enact laws . . . that will place us in a position that may take . . . many years to correct." The army was ready to investigate overtime strikes, and there was already talk in Congress about outlawing strikes altogether. Complaints were negligible compared to the number of union men on defense work, Keenan pointed out, and defense agencies generally concurred. "But it is the complaints that are magnified . . . [and] used against union labor," he reminded building trades unionists, "for the purpose of undermining public opinion throughout the country."[44]

Even after Department officers negotiated a stabilization agreement with representatives of the army, the navy, and the U.S. Housing Authority, known as the Office of Production Management (OPM) Agreement, local compliance did not come easily. Eager to reduce friction between the trades, the Department had agreed to standardize shift pay and overtime rates at time and a half, and it had also agreed to outlaw strikes for the duration. In return, the government had agreed to pay more "realistic" area-wide wage rates (a boon for defense workers employed in remote locations), to protect established apprenticeship policies (now threatened by labor shortages), and to require general contractors to employ specialty subcontractors according to customary practice (thus controlling the general contractors' tendency to hire one trade to do another's work). Finally, the OPM Agreement established a government-labor Board of Review (to interpret the agreement and adjust disputes) that basically accepted the Department's nineteen affiliates as the construction workers' "bona fide" representatives, bringing an end to the CIO's quest to man defense construction jobs.[45]

But it did not bring an end to the defense workers' fight for what they perceived to be their rights. Local unions were accustomed to bargaining for their own wage rates and conditions, and they were not about to quietly accept what looked to them like a cut in pay. In fact, just hours after the agreement took effect, in August 1941, some building trades unionists declared a holiday. In St. Louis and Kansas City, Missouri, and in Sandusky and Ravenna, Ohio, thousands of defense construction workers, employed on munitions and ordnance plants, took the weekend off. They had been earning double time for overtime and weekend work, and at this point they were not willing to let the Department, the federal government, or even their international unions interfere with local conditions—not without a fight.[46] It would take more than Department advice, or national agreements, to persuade strong local unions to accept the government's terms. In fact, it would take the bombing of Pearl Harbor, and the entry of the United States into the Second World War, to unite the building trades into the nation's first arm of defense. They still had their differences, and their complaints, but when war came the building trades workers knew which side they were on. They were on their country's side, and that meant production came first.

Although the "trowel trades"—bricklayers, plasterers, and cement masons—were integrated from the start, local unions like the Bricklayers in Jacksonville, Florida, followed the color line when this picture was taken around 1899. Library of Congress, Prints and Photographs Division, LC-USZ62-35754.

Delegates to the 1903 founding convention of the Structural Building Trades Alliance, an independent organization that gave rise in 1908 to the Building Trades Department of the American Federation of Labor. United Brotherhood of Carpenters and Joiners of America Archives, Special Collections Department, University of Maryland Libraries. Reprinted with permission.

"Cowboys of the skies" adjusting a column splice high atop New York City's Singer Machine Building, the tallest building in the world when it was completed in 1908. Robert F. Wagner Labor Archives, New York University, Ornamental & Architectural Workers Local Union No. 580 Photograph Collection. Reprinted with permission.

Building trades leaders John Coefield of the Plumbers (far right), Richard Gray, Bricklayers (third from right), William J. McSorley, Lathers (fourth from right), and Frank Duffy, Carpenters (second from left) take a break from an Executive Council meeting in Florida around 1930. The George Meany Memorial Archives. Reprinted with permission.

Constructing a giant seawall in Guam in 1945, members of the Seventy-sixth Construction Battalion, known as Seabees, haul away a thirty-ton boulder. National Archives and Records Administration, War and Conflict #860.

Delegates to the BCTD's second legislative conference, in 1956, prepare to lobby their representatives in Congress to amend the Taft-Hartley and Davis-Bacon Acts. The George Meany Memorial Archives. Reprinted with permission.

A delegation from the Lathers Union around 1960, including BCTD president Neil Haggerty (front right) and former BTD president William J. McSorley (front left), the Department's last surviving charter member at the time. In 1979 the Lathers Union joined the Carpenters. The George Meany Memorial Archives.
Reprinted with permission.

In July 1964 building trades leaders joined President Lyndon B. Johnson as he signed an amendment to broaden the prevailing wage section of the Davis-Bacon Act to include fringe benefits. LBJ Library Photo by Cecil Stoughton.

Pressured by the civil rights movement and the federal government to open training opportunities to minority workers, building trades unions joined with organizations like the NAACP and the National Urban League in the late 1960s to develop pre-apprenticeship programs. Here apprentice William Harris, a graduate of the Labor Education Advancement Program, known as LEAP, gets on-the-job training from journeyman plumber Bob Schuckman. The George Meany Memorial Archives. Reprinted with permission.

Civil rights legislation also opened opportunities for women in the trades. In 1975 Carpenters Local 61 in Kansas City accepted its first female apprentice, Johnnie Irene Archer. The George Meany Memorial Archives. Reprinted with permission.

BCTD president Robert Georgine (left), along with Earl McDavid (center) from the AFL-CIO's Union Label and Service Trades Department, and Joseph. F. Curtice (right), of the Washington, D.C., Building and Construction Trades Council, launch a joint campaign in 1976 to promote the role of union craftsmen in community development. Steve Yarmola/The George Meany Memorial Archives. Reprinted with permission.

Ironworkers lunching on top of a Marriott Hotel under construction in midtown Manhattan, 1992. Robert F. Wagner Labor Archives, New York University, Stone Derrickmen & Riggers Association, Local 197 Photograph Collection. Reprinted with permission.

Employees of the Willis Roofing Company join forces with Roofers Local 162 in Las Vegas, Nevada, in 1998 to protest the company's unfair labor practices. Building and Construction Trades Department, AFL-CIO. Reprinted with permission.

Painters and Allied Trades District Council No. 9 marching in New York City's Labor Day Parade, 2000. Robert F. Wagner Labor Archives, New York University, International Brotherhood of Painters & Allied Trades Union, District Council 9 Photograph Collection. Reprinted with permission.

President Edward Sullivan addresses the BCTD's 2003 legislative conference as Secretary-Treasurer Joseph Maloney looks on. © 2003 Bill Burke/Page One Photography. Reprinted with permission.

CHAPTER SIX

From Pearl Harbor to Denver: The Building Trades in War and Peace

If it wasn't for the working people of this country, the sacrifices they made, we might have fought for another four or five years, because we delivered the tanks, we delivered the guns, we delivered the battleships, destroyers, and everything else. . . . We didn't expect any credit, but we certainly didn't expect Taft-Hartley.

—Joseph Keenan

"When the nation called for skilled craftsmen, either to build or fight, or to do both," noted Daniel Tracy, U.S. Assistant Secretary of Labor, "the Building and Construction Trades . . . were not only ready and willing but anxious to go 'all out' for victory." Just days after the attack on Pearl Harbor, building tradesmen were enlisting in the armed forces and signing up for shipyard jobs in the Pacific war zone. By January 1942 they were also joining the Seabees, the newly authorized Naval Construction Battalions whose motto was "Construimus, Batuimus" or "We Build, We Fight." Drawn from the same skilled union men who had erected Boulder Dam, the Golden Gate Bridge, and the nation's skyscrapers, Seabees constructed more than four hundred military bases in the Atlantic and Pacific theaters, cleared and paved thousands of miles of airstrips and roadways, constructed warehouses, hospitals, gasoline storage tanks and housing, and repaired ships in the harbor as well as at sea. In the Pacific, where they had the biggest job to do, the Seabees landed right after the Marines. In 1942, when the Japanese attacked Guam, Midway Island, and Wake Island, these construction workers put down their tools, took up rifles, and joined the fight.[1]

Home front defense workers were on the job, too. In Canada, where war had been declared back in 1939, tradesmen revived the shipbuilding industry and launched the aircraft industry in record time. They constructed more than 115 square miles worth of airports and airfields for the Royal Canadian Air Force and enough airplane hangers to equal a twenty-mile-long building, according to reports. Canadian construction workers also erected training schools, military camps, and factories of all kinds: The government had spent some $100 million by 1942 on munitions factories, including a single ammunition plant that occupied 450 separate buildings covering five hundred acres of land. This surge in construction significantly increased the country's industrial capacity and at the same time boosted the war effort. The story of Canadian production since 1939 was amazing, the press boasted. "Canada, a country of 11,500,000 people can compare her war-production record proudly with that of any other country in the world."[2]

In the United States defense construction was hitting its peak in 1942. The federal government had authorized $26 billion worth of urgent military projects, war housing, and community and war industry facilities, and the building trades were getting the job done. Asbestos workers and boilermakers were rebuilding the navy's decimated fleet at Pearl Harbor, and operating engineers were pushing through almost two thousand miles of unmapped wilderness, between British Columbia and Alaska, to construct the Alcan Highway. Thousands of building mechanics were doing secret, hazardous work at Los Alamos, New Mexico, Hanford, Washington, and Oak Ridge, Tennessee. Because they were working on one of the country's top wartime secrets, their unions agreed to forgo any organizing activity at the government's request. "The world knows today that production of the atomic bomb was a race . . . we might have lost . . . if America's labor unions . . . had not pitched in wholeheartedly to recruit needed workers for the 'Manhattan Project,'" Undersecretary of War Robert Patterson later acknowledged. And other government agents agreed. The building trades' control of the skilled workforce proved crucial to staffing defense projects quickly and efficiently, according to John T. Dunlop and Arthur D. Hill, who were both involved in wartime government-labor boards. "The record in this regard for the atomic energy plants was outstanding. No other agency existed," they concluded, "which could have recruited skilled craftsmen for these isolated projects."[3]

And they did it all in record time. Despite long hours, seven-day weeks, and constant friction with military and government agencies, nothing impeded defense work for long. Building trades unions honored their 1941 no-strike agreement, and the work went off without a major hitch, a real tribute, Joseph Keenan pointed out, to the ingenuity and organizational capacity of the building trades. As a director of the War Labor Board's Labor Production Division, a longtime leader of the Chicago Federation of Labor, and a member of the IBEW, Keenan knew what the trades were up against. "I know how many hard won privileges were suspended in order to expedite the job," he said. "I know how successful was the cooperation between your officials, contractors, and government agencies." Daniel Tracy was equally proud of the building trades' achievement. Although critics deplored the hour and wage standards of union labor (some even complaining to President Roosevelt that organized labor was getting "the larger and ever larger share" of money raised by war bonds), Tracy had a different view. "By the skill of your hands and the strength of your spirit you have caused vast war production plants and housing for the workers to rise almost overnight in all parts of the United States, traveling far and wide . . . to make your skills available wherever those skills were needed." "A better record than that in any human activity of such magnitude can hardly be imagined," Undersecretary Patterson agreed. "It is well for the public to know this" he added, "because it presents a picture drastically in variance with that held by the average newspaper reader."[4]

A wireman who had risen through the ranks to lead the Electrical Workers from 1933 to 1940, and a former Department vice president, Daniel Tracy proved to be an essential liaison between the Department and the government for the duration of the war. As the only assistant secretary to Secretary of Labor Frances Perkins from 1940 to 1946, Tracy was second in command in charge of military and war-related construction, and in that capacity he played a crucial role in shaping government-labor relations during the war. Tracy not only understood the demands of labor, as Secretary Perkins put it, he also understood "how labor and employers working together" might move those demands forward. During the Great Depression Tracy had proved to be one of the most knowledgeable and hard-working members of the National Recovery Administration's Labor Advisory Board, able to work with government officials and industry leaders alike. During the war he made an equally good impression, employing "friendship, diplomacy, humor and common sense," along with "effective off-the-record conciliating," as one journalist put it, to persuade building trades workers to accept government demands for continuous production and stable wage rates. But he also ensured that those government demands were fair. When Tracy helped to negotiate the 1941 no-strike agreement that kept defense construction on track, he made sure that the eight-hour day and union-wage standards were included. When he raised the question of stabilizing wage rates in the construction industry later that year, Department leaders were wary at first, but ultimately they followed Tracy's lead. After all, a voluntary, collectively bargained, wage-stabilization agreement was certainly better than government-imposed wage rates, and those were the only available options at the time, Tracy made clear. With wage contracts in cities throughout the nation due to expire in the spring of 1942, fears of inflationary wage hikes were real, and with the bill for defense construction already estimated at $4 billion for 1943, the government was eager to stabilize construction wage rates, one way or another.[5]

To Department leaders who remembered the brutal years following the First World War, Tracy's plan made sense. These leaders feared a postwar backlash if construction wages rose too quickly. Back in the 1920s anti-union contractors and owners had banded together to slash wartime wage rates and launch the open-shop American Plan, and no one wanted to see that history repeated. Nor did anyone want to give government a free hand. Therefore it took months of negotiating with government contracting agencies, and a meeting with President Franklin D. Roosevelt in May 1942, before the BCTD Executive Council was ready to accept a wage-stabilization agreement, one that would provide for a wage adjustment board designed to grant increases in exceptional cases. Both Roosevelt and the contracting agencies were pushing for a May 1 start date, but the Department held out for July 1, since new local agreements would have been finalized by then, allowing wages to be stabilized at the best possible rate. With that obstacle overcome by May 19, the Department's nineteen general presidents signed off on the plan, guaranteeing that after July 1, 1942, "rates paid under collective bargaining agreements" would remain in force for the duration of the war, subject to annual reviews of the plan. Three days later President Roosevelt officially approved the Building and Construction Trades Wage Stabilization Agreement for government war work, the first of its kind in any wartime industry. "The pact virtually blankets the entire Government building construction field for the duration of the war," the *Washington Post* reported, "and provides that any justified wage adjustment shall be handled by a Federal board rather than by individual companies."[6]

The Wage Adjustment Board (WAB), as the government-labor panel was called, had jurisdiction over all employees on government defense construction jobs and would determine whether changing conditions justified an increase over previously bargained rates. Organized through the Department of Labor, and chaired by Daniel Tracy, the WAB originally included one representative each from the War Department, the navy, and the Defense Plant Corporation, and three Department representatives—Harry Bates of the Bricklayers, Robert Byron of the Sheet Metal Workers, and BCTD president John Coyne. Under WAB rules, a local union could present a request for an area-wide increase provided that the request met the standards established by the 1942 stabilization agreement and was approved by both the international union, which tended to screen requests carefully, and the BCTD, which would then submit the request to the Board. Because wage stabilization in the construction industry depended on uniform rates among contractors, requests for increases that were the result of collective bargaining between local unions and local contractors were the most likely to be passed on to the Board.[7]

The WAB was busy from the start. According to its first report to the National War Labor Board (NWLB)—the agency responsible for wartime wage controls by the fall of 1943—the WAB made 113 decisions in December 1942. It denied increases in 76 cases, raised rates up to Davis-Bacon levels in 14 cases, and raised them beyond Davis-Bacon levels in 23 cases. In fact, WAB increases sometimes exceeded rates established by the NWLB's "Little Steel" formula, which capped increases at 15 percent over January 1941 wage rates. But under the circumstances, the WAB stood by these increases since rates tended to go up in areas where skilled labor was in short supply. Bricklayers at a plant in Monessen, Pennsylvania, for instance, were given a 17 percent increase—from $1.62 to $1.90 an hour—to ensure that an adequate supply of skilled men could be imported "from the surrounding areas in which higher rates prevail." And in Danville, Pennsylvania, boilermakers saw wages increase from $1.50 to $1.75—also about 17 percent—and the other crafts also received an increase. "The evidence is clear," the WAB reported, "that a critical situation exists threatening the successful completion of this project and that its correction is imperative to the successful prosecution of the war." Overall, the WAB investigated and settled more than 1,400 cases between July 1942 and September 1943, approving the majority of adjustment requests (and denying about 43 percent) and raising wages above Davis-Bacon rates in about 18 percent of cases.[8]

But even before the Board was a year old, it was evident that some changes had to be made. The National War Labor Board was often in conflict with the Wage Adjustment Board, since both had responsibility for stabilizing construction wages: The WAB handled war-related construction financed by the federal government, while the NWLB handled all private construction, non-war federal construction, and war-related construction performed by nonunion contractors. Friction was inevitable. First of all, NWLB wage standards were designed with steadily employed factory workers in mind, not construction workers who moved from job to job. Second, the regional offices of the NWLB tended to treat construction cases like any other. When these regional offices set wage rates for non-federal construction projects that were either lower or higher than rates established by the WAB or the Davis-Bacon division on nearby government projects, contractors, unions, and the WAB all issued complaints. As relations between the WAB and NWLB became increasingly strained over the question of standardizing wages for all construction workers, a decision was reached to reorganize the WAB under the auspices of the NWLB in the fall of 1943.[9]

Restructured as a tripartite agency, WAB now represented the interests of labor, the public, and specialty and general contractors; as part of the reorganization, government contracting agencies had agreed to withdraw. With Daniel Tracy continuing as chairman, the new Board was expanded to thirteen members, with six representing the public (including John T. Dunlop, an economist with the NWLB), four representing the contractors (including Paul Geary of the National Electrical Contractors Association), and three representing the building trades (Harry Bates of the Bricklayers, Robert Byron of the Sheet Metal Workers, and Herbert Rivers, BCTD secretary-treasurer). With jurisdiction over all construction projects, whether private or public, the new Board would work under somewhat stricter rules: No employees were automatically entitled to 15 percent increases over January 1941 rates, higher-paying trades would generally receive lower percentage increases than lower-paying trades, and wage adjustments could not exceed the Little Steel formula unless they involved "critical needs of war production" and were submitted to the NWLB for approval.[10]

Under its new structure, the wartime stabilization board played a major role in strengthening construction labor-management relations. In fact, the WAB had an impressive record of reaching unanimous decisions, thanks in part to off-the-record meetings, where all sides were free to discuss their problems in very frank terms. "As in all collective bargaining, many a difficult and highly controversial case that might otherwise have caused delay, bitterness, and ill feeling was promptly settled over a drink in a restaurant," board members John Dunlop and Arthur D. Hill later wrote. "These informal sessions promoted harmony and understanding among the three sides of the table that never could have been achieved in the board room." Richard Gray, who was acting BCTD president at the time, apparently agreed. "When that Board was functioning," he later explained, "everybody seemed to think that one good issue would come out it, namely, that employer and public representatives along with labor, sitting . . . across the table from each other, had learned to respect the responsibilities that business and management had placed upon them. We in turn thought that management had observed and learned a better picture of our problems." Changing circumstances would alter that opinion soon after the war was over. But at the time the Wage Adjustment Board seemed to offer a workable model for stable and productive industry—a model that the Department and international union officers accepted as a practical and beneficial compromise.[11]

To be sure, building trades leaders bitterly complained about the WAB, especially when government contracting agencies tried to restrict approved increases to new projects only, creating a double pay standard that unions resented. Local unions also resented government, international union, and Department interference with their bargaining power. But from the Department's point of view, the WAB was a war measure it could live with: The

Board protected union standards, kept aggressive locals in line, and generally kept wage inflation in check. Between 1941 and 1945 wages rose 10 percent (or 13.6 cents an hour), but they rose only 3.7 percent during the period of the wage stabilization agreement, a startling contrast to what transpired in the First World War, when wage rates jumped 35 percent (or about 18 cents an hour) between 1916 and 1919.[12]

According to Dunlop and Hill, the WAB owed its success to its voluntary origins and to the fact that top union leaders played a major role in its proceedings. "There were no 'messenger boys' among the regular labor members," they pointed out. "As a consequence they could make compromises quickly and avoid *pro-forma* dissents." That all members of the Board "knew their industry thoroughly and were not divided by questions regarding fundamentals" also strengthened the operations of the WAB and at the same time improved communications between general and specialty contractors and between basic and specialty trades. As the *New York Times* reported, the war record of the BCTD and contractor associations "in maintaining an amicable relationship was the best in the history of the industry," an experience that would shape industrial relations in union construction for the next thirty years. Although no one could have predicted it at the time, ties forged through the wartime board would lead to a series of postwar national agreements, productivity pacts, and joint labor-management committees that were designed to keep industry decisions in industry hands and to protect building trades unions and their contractors from industrial competition on less-skilled work, a problem that was already causing trouble in the ranks, even before the war was over.[13]

Maintenance versus Construction Work

As long as work was classified as new construction, the building trades had no real trouble maintaining union standards during the war. Nor did they have any real difficulty controlling their work. But once the defense-construction crisis had passed, by 1943, and the demand for large numbers of skilled workers subsided, problems began to multiply. According to one building trades council in the Midwest, maintenance crews were installing equipment at a government-financed aircraft factory. Another council complained that electrical workers and pipe fitters employed on a government-financed explosives factory in upstate New York were terminated before the job was done, so that the chemical company running the plant could finish it with its own men, set its own wage rates, and thereby evade the wage stabilization agreement. In Pocatello, Idaho, building trades workers were ready to strike when the government's Bureau of Ordnance used civil service workers to unload new machinery, paint, build lockers and cabinets, and connect machinery in an armament plant being constructed for the navy. "To put the matter very plainly," the business agent explained, "this is developing into one hell of a situation and I don't know how much longer I can hold the lid down on this keg of dynamite."[14]

Tensions were also mounting in Springfield, Illinois, where commanding officers of the Army Air Force Storage Depot relied on nonunion civil service painters, carpenters, and engineers to do the bulk of the work, contracting out only those parts of a job that the maintenance crew could not handle. "As a result of the inferior work performed by these regular employees," a local council officer complained, "if some work is contemplated at the Depot requiring the skill and ability of mechanics to perform, it has been the practice . . . to let that particular job by contract to some bona fide Union Contractor." When a painting contract was completed by a nonunion crew, however, the local building trades had had enough. The government should work either all union or all nonunion, they insisted, and they were ready to notify union contractors "that no Union men will be allowed to work for them on any project which may be awarded to them at the Government Army Air Force Storage Depot." That these conflicts were less significant than the overall pattern of stable government-labor relations during the war hardly mattered to rank-and-file mechanics who now believed that their long-term security was on the line.[15]

As complaints rose and tempers flared, acting Department president Richard Gray was in a difficult position. The combination of war and the no-strike pledge of the 1941 OPM stabilization agreement made strikes against the government too risky. John L. Lewis and the mine workers might have been willing to call wartime strikes, but as far as Department leaders were concerned, the price was too high, especially after Congress passed the Smith-Connally War Labor Disputes Act in 1943, extending the president's power to seize plants, prohibit strikes, and fine or imprison strike leaders.[16]

At the same time, however, Gray strongly believed that government agencies and hostile industrialists were using wartime agreements to undermine union standards. That they were apparently working together to replace skilled union men with maintenance crews, he noted, had "all the appearances of fitting into a cleverly arranged plan to reduce wage rates in the building and construction industry." A series of meetings with representatives of the Ordnance Bureau, the Army Corps of Engineers, the Office of Services and Supplies, and the War Production Board did little to change his mind. At the meetings, he reported, everyone seemed to agree that the Department's complaints were valid; the War Department even distributed a memorandum restricting maintenance workers to upkeep and repair. But within a short time, Gray complained, "General Robbins sent out another memorandum which gave to the various agencies of the War Department the right to do any new construction work where the material cost would not exceed $25,000 and it further gave the right to do unlimited construction work if and when permission was granted to the Chief of Staff."[17]

Taking his complaint to Assistant Labor Secretary Daniel Tracy, Gray made it clear that the situation was only getting worse. "I could furnish you with at least fifty letters of a similar character in different parts of the Country" to support the Department's claim that the government's decision to use maintenance crews "is merely a subterfuge to reduce the wages of building and construction trades workers at a time when living costs have advanced over 20% and to remove from our legitimate field and turn over to production workers work which has always been performed by the building and construction workers and their employers."[18]

Gray was even more blunt in a complaint to George Meany, AFL secretary-treasurer and a member of the National War Labor Board. Apparently a regional board in Detroit had set up "two classifications for Carpenters, Electrical Workers, Elevator Mechanics, Painters, Engineers, and Plumbers for what is supposed to be maintenance work and further have set up the jurisdiction covered by such work." This work previously had always gone to a union contractor, one who paid prevailing wage rates and hired BCTD union members. "If the National War Labor Board has set up this practice as administrative procedure without consulting the members of the industry, namely, our employers and our representatives of labor," Gray added, "I would like to know on what authority granted to them by Congress or otherwise they take such action." When Gray aired these and other complaints in his report to the Department's convention, James P. Mitchell, who handled labor relations for army construction, severely criticized his actions, but Gray did not back down. "I told him that it was factual," he noted, "and if he cared to refute any of the statements referred to in my report, I would be glad to discuss it with him."[19]

The fact that these maintenance workers were often CIO members increased tensions. In Detroit, for instance, industrial plants that were now doing war work had been organized by CIO unions, and they expected to control both maintenance and production workers. As long as the war raged on, both sides were willing to compromise: The Detroit Building and Construction Trades Council and the maintenance members of the United Automobile Workers (UAW)–CIO had established a joint committee to settle jurisdictional disputes. Determined to keep up their end of defense production, both organizations pledged "full adherence" to the agreement "as part of their contribution to the cause of Victory." And both declared that "they will allow no concern or responsibility to stand in the way of fulfillment of their obligations to the nation in this time of emergency."[20]

As the war drew to a close, however, the fight over maintenance work began to heat up. According to the Detroit council, erecting, installing, and dismantling equipment was construction work, not maintenance work, and local building trades unions would accept nothing less. If AFL building trades workers were needed to set machines on new construction or remodeling jobs, they expected to do the piping and electrical hookups, too: The skilled building trades would not accept "crumbs only," as the Detroit council put it, taking only that part of the work that CIO members could not do. And to make that clear Detroit's building trades unions had already agreed not to furnish men to contractors unless this jurisdiction was clearly spelled out, a move that both the Department's Executive Council and the 1944 BCTD convention supported. In May 1945 representatives of the Department, the local council, and the international unions met in Detroit to notify their employers that unless building trades workers "perform all construction work in its entirety and make all original installations of equipment . . . they will refuse to work on any structures." A committee of contractors also joined the two-day meeting in hopes of working the problem out. "The contractors were assured that the various Industrial Concerns would be notified of the stand taken," a report of the meeting noted, "and . . . that the policy adopted would be a National one." At a dinner party following the meeting, hosted by the local general contractors association, speakers from both sides of the table agreed that "with united action the interests of the Construction Industry would be protected against all hostile encroachments."[21]

But if the building trades expected CIO unions to back down, they were soon disappointed. UAW-CIO maintenance workers were equally determined to fight for their jobs, and they issued an ultimatum of their own: They would not stand for AFL building trades workers to be employed in the automobile industry if that meant displacing CIO workers. Although committees from the BCTD and the UAW-CIO apparently reached an agreement (with the help of Daniel Tracy and Clinton Golden of the Steelworkers-CIO) to establish local and national joint committees to resolve disputes, the plan did not get very far. By the time the BCTD Executive Council approved the draft agreement in August, the fight in Detroit was coming to a head. "We were unable to agree on any propositions in our meetings with . . . the UAW-CIO," reported Ed Thal, the local council secretary. "Many things were brought forth by the [UAW] committee . . . that either [were] impossible to enforce or . . . would put us in the position of being a subordinate organization to the CIO, and possibly jeopardize the position of many Building Trades Councils throughout the Country." The bottom line was that CIO workers intended to control whatever work they could handle—and it looked as if they thought they could handle almost all the construction work in the automobile industry, including the installation of machinery (whether new or old) and all remodeling, decorating, and conversion work, no small matter at a time when defense plants were being converted back to civilian uses.[22]

"Let me say that many . . . propositions were brought forth that indicated to us, that while they would allow us in the plants, it would be predicated on the proposition that their own people would be steadily employed," wrote Thal to Richard Gray. "They also indicated," he added, "that it would be their policy to try to induce the various companies with which they have contracts, to hire enough men that would ultimately lead to the proposition that we would be entirely displaced in doing work, especially for the Automobile Industry." Under the circumstances Thal firmly believed that the building trades had to take a determined stand on the maintenance issue, or they would soon see the rise of a CIO Building Trades Department. "I want to however say . . . that while we totally disagreed with the Representatives of the UAW-CIO," he told Gray, "each and every one of them were very decent people personally and . . . we parted [on] good terms, both sides regretfully admitting that we were too far apart to find a local solution." In fact it would take another ten years, at least—and the merger of the AFL and the CIO in 1955—before any headway could be made on the maintenance issue. And even then it would remain an issue that would not stay settled for long.[23]

Internal Disputes

There were other indications that wartime cooperation was beginning to break down. With victory on the horizon, internal Department disputes were on the rise, a sure sign that conditions were returning to normal. Since taking over as acting president in 1942 (shortly before President Coyne died in 1943), Richard Gray had been well aware of troubling jurisdictional conflicts. But he had not referred any cases to the national referee, contractor Peter Eller, because he believed that war work had to come first. By the spring of 1944, however, Gray was compelled to take action. There were at least ten cases that had "grown to a point where it is necessary for me to refer them to you as required by the Constitution of the Department," he told Eller. "In fact I . . . have been charged by one of the [affiliates] . . . as being derelict to my duty in not making these references. At this time, however, I have no apologies on that score." Too busy with his own war work to give any time to jurisdictional disputes, Eller resigned as referee. Like Gray, he believed that since the country was "engaged in the biggest 'jurisdictional' dispute in all history . . . all of us should lay aside any personal considerations until this dispute [is] settled in our favor."[24]

But that sentiment was beginning to ring hollow, especially after the three-

man Board of Review, which had been established by the 1941 OPM stabilization agreement, claimed authority to settle jurisdictional disputes.
"Slowly, but surely . . . the Board of Review has become bolder and more
brazen," IBEW president Ed Brown complained in April 1945, "first suggesting, later inviting, and now assuming the authority to 'cite' representatives of
[labor] organizations to appear before that august body and defend their
claims for jurisdiction over work." The case in question, a longtime dispute
between Electrical Workers and Iron Workers over erecting steel electrical
towers, had already been decided by the BCTD: "The work as described
above shall be the work of the International Brotherhood of Electrical Workers," the decision read.[25]

Although acting president Richard Gray refused to participate, the Board
of Review proceeded with its hearing anyway. And when it reversed the Department's decision, Brown was livid. "In view of all of this, it can be easily
understood why so many Americans . . . are asking the Sixty-four Dollar
question: 'What are we fighting for?' When organized labor has adhered so
strictly to its no-strike pledge, and when its members have established an all-
time production record in support of our Government, it certainly has a
right to expect that representatives of Government will not be a party to any
encroachment on Labor's rights and privileges." Under the circumstances,
Brown believed, there was no real choice but to sever ties to the government
and "return to the traditional militant Trade Unionism which always characterized the Building Trades Unions, and . . . to have a showdown on the entire question before it is too late."[26]

Department leaders were not persuaded. "Daily we listen to the ranting of
certain members of Congress who have been consistently antagonistic to organized labor," secretary-treasurer Herbert Rivers warned affiliates in an official letter. "This type of [congressman] . . . who at the least provocation is
willing to draft legislation and introduce it, would hamstring organized
labor and restrict its right to strike." Without that right, organized labor was
doomed to failure, he added, and that was why he now urged affiliates to exercise extreme caution. "If this is done . . . we will be able to appear before
the committees in Congress when hearings are held on these proposed anti-
labor bills and show that the building trades do not inconvenience the general public by jurisdictional disputes . . . and, further, that we . . . are continuing to live up to the provisions of our contracts with our employers." Like
many of his colleagues on the Executive Council, Rivers remembered the
"concerted effort that was made to tear down conditions" after the last world
war, and he feared that "corporate and financial interests" were going to try
to do the same thing again, this time aided by Congress. "At no time in the
history of our movement has the above recommended action been so necessary as it is at the present time," Rivers concluded. "This can be easily veri-

fied through the representatives of International Unions who are on the job here in Washington and who have their finger on the pulse of things that affect our interests."[27]

Both men made legitimate points, based on their experience in the labor movement and with the government. In 1945, however, it was too early to predict whether the militant Ed Brown or the cautious Herbert Rivers offered building trades workers the better advice. And it was also too soon to predict whether the building trades' wartime contribution would have any value in the postwar world, although Department leaders had reason to believe that it would. After all, building trades unions had honored their no-strike pledge and worked with government and industry to minimize wage conflicts and rate hikes. Moreover, building trades workers had served in the armed forces, done the groundwork for the nation's defense, and played a vital role in the Allied victory that finally came in the summer of 1945. No one could say that building trades workers had not contributed 100 percent to the war effort or that they, and their families, had not suffered along with everyone else.

"When the history of this war is written," Joseph Keenan said, "a big chapter should be devoted to the engineers and carpenters, electricians and plumbers, iron workers, bricklayers, roofers and laborers, and all the other tradesmen who built America's war plant in record-breaking time."[28] Yet when the fighting was over, and the battles won, the building trades were on their own again. As far as the nation was concerned, it was back to business as usual.

Taft-Hartley and the National Joint Plan

Bells were ringing and people were dancing in the streets on the day the Second World War officially ended. The job was done, the boys were coming home, and it was finally time to celebrate. But once the cheering stopped, and the wartime economy started slowing down, the practical realities of victory began to sink in. Almost two million war workers lost their jobs within ten days of the Japanese surrender, and the expected return of millions of servicemen and servicewomen heightened postwar fears. Without the stimulus of war, would the economy plunge back into depression? Did the end of the war, and the end of nonstop production and overtime pay, mean the end of economic security? Back in 1944 President Roosevelt had promised, once the war was over, to launch an economic bill of rights including the right to a job, adequate wages, a decent home, and a good education. But Roosevelt had died in the spring of 1945, and now people wondered if the dream had died with him. Whether his successor, Harry S.

Truman, would pick up where the New Deal had left off was still anybody's guess.[29]

Pent-up consumer demand and fears of runaway inflation heightened the uncertainty. After more than fifteen years of "making do or doing without," Americans were ready to shop. They had saved some 25 percent of their take-home pay since 1943, and they wanted to enjoy the fruits of victory. "Never was there a greater demand in the history of our country for products of all kinds than there is now," Congressman Carl T. Curtis reported. "The public is eager to buy automobiles, clothing, furniture, equipment, machinery, lumber, and every other commodity." But in the months immediately following victory, supply could not keep up with this enormous demand, leading to shortages, black markets, and an 18.2 percent inflation rate in 1946 that not only threatened labor's wartime gains but fueled a series of nationwide strikes that slowed production down. From the strikers' point of view, their decision was justified: Despite relatively high wage rates, take-home pay had dropped as much as 30 percent when production workers returned to a forty-hour week after the war. At the same time the cost of living had risen 33 percent between 1941 and 1945, and profits were rising by 50 percent between 1945 and 1946. Convinced that they needed a 30 percent wage hike just to stay even, almost five million coal miners, steel workers, auto workers, and electrical manufacturing workers, among many others, walked off their jobs, making 1946 a record year for man hours lost through strikes.[30]

"Labor has gone crazy and management isn't far from insane in selfishness," President Truman proclaimed when the first strike wave erupted in 1945. "There is too much power on each side," he added in 1946, "and I think it is necessary that the government assert the fact that *it* is the power of the people." The nonunion public tended to agree. The number of organized workers had increased during the war from 8.7 million in 1940 to 14.3 million in 1945, according to the U.S. Bureau of Labor Statistics, and union labor now made up about 35 percent of the nonagricultural workforce. The combination of record-high numbers and militant strikes in 1946, as well as an aggressive newspaper campaign against "big labor," generated public fears that unions had grown too powerful for the nation's good. When President Truman decided to show striking workers that he was in charge and seized meat-packing plants, coal mines, oil refineries, and even tugboats in New York City's harbor, he failed to intimidate strikers, but he drew broad support outside union circles. And when Republican legislators blamed strikers for shortages and inflation, they struck a chord with voters. "Got enough houses? . . . Got enough inflation? . . . Got enough strikes?" were the questions asked by Ohio's Congressman John M. Vorys during the 1946 electoral campaign. The answers registered loud and clear. American voters not only elected a Republican majority to both houses of Congress in 1946, but they apparently wanted those congressmen to pass more laws to control labor unions, according to a Gallup poll taken around the same time.[31]

Richard Gray, now officially president of the Building and Construction Trades Department, was not particularly surprised. In fact, at the 1946 BCTD convention earlier that fall, the fifty-nine-year-old bricklayer had predicted the outcome. An officer of the BCTD since the 1930s, when he had led the fight for prevailing wages on WPA projects, Gray had long been wary of government interference in trade union affairs. Reactionary politicians had been trying to gut the Wagner Act since the days of CIO sit-down strikes in the mid-1930s, and Gray hardly expected them to stop trying now. "There are many grave problems confronting organized labor," he told the 1946 convention, "and undoubtedly after the national elections are over . . . we will find a repetition of proposals for restrictive labor legislation." But as long as the building trades avoided jurisdictional strikes, Gray believed, they had nothing to fear from the Eightieth Congress. They had not been part of the sit-down strikes, and they had honored their no-strike pledge during the war. Nor had they been part of the 1945–46 strike wave. On the contrary, building mechanics were still working under wartime wage controls (which had been voluntarily extended late in 1945 and would not be lifted until 1947), and Department leaders were working with the Associated General Contractors and other employer groups on a labor-management agreement to get private industry up and running again. "If we reduce to the minimum any stoppages of work over jurisdictional disputes . . . we will place this Department in a position where we can go before the public and justify any of the claims we may make, because outside of that one point," Gray added, "we have never made an unreasonable claim. We have cooperated with every public program that has been instituted and we have done everything to uphold our position in the social and economic life of this country."[32]

But that "one point" continued to be a dangerous stumbling block. Longstanding but still unresolved disputes between the Carpenters and Laborers, Iron Workers and Sheet Metal Workers, and Electrical Workers and Iron Workers, to name just a few, were heating up even before the votes were counted, and the Department still had no viable plan for finally resolving these conflicts. On the contrary, the "referee system," which had more or less governed decisions since the 1930s, satisfied almost no international union president, and while the Department president had the authority to render "final" decisions, he could rarely make them stick. There were thirty-seven work stoppages between November 1, 1946, and January 1, 1947, each in response to action taken by President Gray.[33]

"It is useless for me to make decisions," Gray told the Executive Council, "because . . . the decisions now create more [strikes] . . . than they prevent,

leaving the Department and its affiliated organizations subject to public criticism . . . which we cannot deny." And that criticism had consequences:
There were already twenty-one anti-union bills before the U.S. Senate and
thirty-seven before the House, and nearly all of these sought to impose the
open shop or to curtail labor's right to strike. Determined to develop a "con-
clusive" method of handling these self-defeating disputes, and thereby avoid
government intervention, Gray appointed a special committee of industrial
relations specialists—William Davis, Sumner Schlicter, and Paul Douglass—
to investigate appropriate jurisdictional dispute machinery and report their
findings to the Executive Council. Daniel Tracy, who had recently been reelected IBEW president, heartily approved the move. The failure to recognize
proper jurisdiction was doing organized labor more damage than all the
newspaper and congressional attacks combined, Tracy maintained. But he
also believed that whatever new machinery the Department adopted to resolve disputes, decisions would have to be governed by predetermined rules
and not by "political expediency or friendship or hostility." And affiliates
would have to honor those rules, Engineers' president William Maloney
added. "Until some of the heads of the organizations in the Building and
Construction Trades Department make up their minds [that] they are going
to live up to decisions after they are made," he told Gray, "we are not going
to get very far with this program."[34]

Meanwhile contractors and Department officers were doing their best to
persuade Congress that "management and labor in the construction industry," as the AGC put it, "are better qualified than anyone else to work out the
problems that will arise in the postwar period." Left to their own devices,
they would get on with the business of building highways, factories, schools,
and houses, all of which were now in great demand. After all, contractors and
unions had been negotiating trade agreements for years, some for more than
forty years! "We meet our employers every day, call them Tom, Dick, and
Harry," bricklayer William Dobson had explained back in 1916. "They understand our troubles and we understand theirs." When Carpenters' president William Hutcheson (an outspoken Republican) addressed a congressional labor committee in February 1947, he made the same point. "Men
engaged in building construction have come to know that they are in the
same category as the building tradesmen. . . . When we sit down around the
table, we realize that they have got just as much interest as we have in it, and
they are just as much entitled to consideration as we are. And the result is
that we have worked up . . . a cooperative understanding," Hutcheson testified, that separated old-line AFL building trades unions from the less experienced and more confrontational CIO unions that were now striking. But if
Congress tried to "hamstring" the building trades, Hutcheson warned, they
would cripple industry, too. Building mechanics had battled the American

Plan in the years after the First World War, and they would do no less now. If the Eightieth Congress were truly interested in rebuilding the nation and promoting labor peace, Hutcheson suggested, it would leave the building and construction industry to work out its own problems as they arose.[35]

But when the Eightieth Congress enacted the Taft-Hartley Act to amend the National Labor Relations Act in June 1947, it was clear that building trades unions could not expect much consideration from current lawmakers. According to the Department, building trades unions had taken the greatest hit: The law practically outlawed their established methods of doing business. The Taft-Hartley Act prohibited the closed shop, and classified secondary boycotts and jurisdictional strikes as "unfair labor practices" and therefore illegal. Apparently the coalition of anti-union Republicans and southern Democrats that passed Taft-Hartley over President Truman's veto were less concerned with CIO strikes than they were with the building trades' high level of organization (up from 65 percent in 1941 to 92 percent in 1947, according to some estimates) and their militant defense of jurisdictional rights. "One of the strongest arguments advanced in Congress in support of the Taft-Hartley Bill was aimed at our very own industry," President Gray complained, "about our squabbles among ourselves. Nothing was said about the squabbles between Government agencies," he added. "They have their jurisdictional disputes just the same as we have." Determined to overturn this legislative disaster, one way or another, Gray now offered a novel strategy. "It is my personal opinion," he told the 1947 BCTD convention, "that there is one and one way only to fight that act and that is as law-abiding citizens . . . trying to comply with it and proving conclusively that parts of it are unworkable."[36]

The Department president had a point. Between 1935 and 1947 the National Labor Relations Board (NLRB) had deliberately chosen not to exercise jurisdiction over construction cases, but under Taft-Hartley it would be required to handle unfair labor practice cases. Yet nobody knew how the NLRB's concept of representation (which had been developed with factories and a stable workforce in mind) would now work in construction. General counsel of the NLRB Robert Denham was determined to find out, however, and President Gray was inclined to let him. In February 1948 Denham decided that every local building trades union would have to win an NLRB election in order to enter into union-shop agreements with employers, a decision that seemed preposterous to anyone experienced in the business. "Before the necessary hearing could be held and preparations made for an election," Bricklayers president Harry Bates explained, "the job might be finished and the employer would be on another job with an entirely new crew."[37] And since closed-shop agreements governed the industry in more than five hundred areas, each involving as many as thirty-four unions and a dozen contractors,

AGC spokesman James Marshall added, it would be a waste of the estimated $1.5 million it would cost to hold union-shop elections, since the vast majority of workers were already union members. In fact, when the NLRB held a pilot election that spring, for Western Pennsylvania's heavy construction industry, it had to assign fifty agents to hold separate elections for engineers, teamsters, carpenters, pile drivers, and laborers employed at various job sites in thirty-three counties, nearly all of whom voted to support their unions. A few months later the NLRB gave up the idea entirely when plans for union shop elections in Detroit fell through after a builders' association refused to participate. "Thus, after 10 months of work and the expenditure of vast sums of public money," *The Laborer* reported, "the administrative machinery of the NLRB has proved unequal to the task."[38]

But the NLRB still had the last word on jurisdictional awards, an unhappy thought, as Harvard economist John Dunlop later put it, since nobody wanted the government deciding jurisdictional disputes in a "helter-skelter" way.[39] Employers may have had the right to make work assignments under the Taft-Hartley Act, but in a well-organized industry like construction, where unions basically controlled skill and training, both sides had to be satisfied for a job to go smoothly. "Maximum speed, economy and efficiency in the industry [depend] on good relations between management and workmen," not government regulations, the AGC contended. With the goal of satisfying Taft-Hartley requirements without engaging the NLRB, an AGC committee now proposed a joint jurisdictional board to the Department's Executive Council, one that would be headed by an impartial chairman.[40] It took four months of intensive negotiations—and John Dunlop's mediation skills—to hammer out a viable labor-management agreement between the Department, the AGC, and specialty and subcontractor organizations. By March 1948 all interested parties, including the BCTD's nineteen affiliates, had approved the National Joint Plan for the Settlement of Jurisdictional Disputes and, by May, the new board was ready to go, with John Dunlop serving as impartial chairman.[41]

Having spent four years getting to know the building trades through his work on the wartime Wage Adjustment Board, Dunlop did not expect the National Joint Plan to eliminate disputes. But he thought it was possible to develop procedures to handle disputes in an "orderly and routine fashion." The first step was to ensure that work was assigned in a reasonable manner, based on a union's experience, skill, and ability to man the job, and not on wage rates alone. Proper work assignments were as vital to the success of a project as the flow of materials, and proper specifications and blue prints, Dunlop maintained. When they were made in a "haphazard manner" trouble inevitably resulted. If contractors and unions could agree that work assignments should be based on the Department's "Green Book" of existing union agreements and decisions of record regarding jurisdiction, and accept decisions rendered by the Plan's Board of Trustees when conflicts erupted, then the National Joint Plan could play a vital role in settling these chronic disputes without government help.[42]

That was a big "if," as Dunlop soon learned. Almost immediately there were complaints that contractors were using the plan to stir up new disputes, that specialty trades were not fairly represented, and that the Board of Trustees took far too long to investigate claims. In fact, before the Plan had celebrated its first anniversary, the BCTD was ready to bail out. Hoping to return to the days when unions alone determined jurisdiction, the Department now wanted to set up its own board and appoint John Dunlop as arbitrator.[43]

But there would be no turning back. Neither Dunlop nor the NLRB would support a union-only board, leaving the Department no practical choice but to renew the National Joint Plan. It did, however, negotiate some changes. The Board of Trustees was replaced by an eight-man National Joint Board (NJB) so that basic and mechanical trades, and general and specialty contractors, would have better representation. The National Joint Board was also empowered to make "job decisions," that is, when a dispute erupted on a job, a decision was rendered for that job only, a change that greatly speeded up the process. But it did not satisfy President Gray, who considered the NJB only a "limited" success. "It is our contention that the machinery should be set up to 'prevent' or at least to keep to an absolute minimum such disputes. There is no sound reason for permitting the recurrence of the same dispute on different jobs in the same city or . . . in any other city." He did agree, however, that the National Joint Plan had overcome some of the difficulties created by the Taft-Hartley Act. "If it were not operating," he told the 1951 convention, "the cases which have come before it would have been taken to the National Labor Relations Board and the unions . . . would have been involved in long and expensive litigation."[44]

"There were always some dissatisfied people," John Dunlop later admitted, "but the reality was, of course, that if they did not have a board, then all of their matters went to the NLRB," and nobody wanted that. In fact, with Dunlop's help, the construction industry successfully bypassed the agency, at least on matters of jurisdiction. Although Richard Gray apparently resented the rise of Harvard-trained "labor experts," it was Dunlop's experience as an NLRB consultant, and the ties he had to the General Counsel's office, that made the National Joint Plan a viable alternative: NLRB agents not only kept Dunlop apprised of cases involving construction unions but they also allowed him the time to work out matters through the industry, not the Board. "So as a matter of fact from 1948 to after 1957," Dunlop later explained, "the NLRB never handled a decision in construction because I was settling it through the jurisdiction board."[45]

At the same time Dunlop was mediating more than thirty-five national agreements that allowed international unions to settle their disputes directly, without resorting to the National Joint Board, a better solution in Dunlop's opinion. "When men make agreements, they have an interest in enforcing them," he noted. "It is only too easy to find loopholes and technicalities in decisions imposed from outside." Reaching those agreements was never easy. Like jurisdictional decisions, national agreements required compromise, "a give and take process," as Dunlop put it, with some localities or branches of a trade gaining work and others necessarily losing work. But he was glad to report, in 1956, that there was "an increasing realization among the general presidents and the International Unions . . . that the responsibilities involved in making national agreements must be courageously accepted."[46]

There were still problems, of course. Some unions and contractors sought court assistance when an NJB decision did not go their way. Others tried to use job decisions as if they set national precedents. And then there were unions that wanted nothing to do with the National Joint Plan. The Electrical Workers and the National Electrical Contractors Association opted out of the plan in the early 1950s, over the question of representation. And the Lathers tried to break their ties, too, after the NJB decided a long-standing dispute in the Carpenters' favor and the Lathers struck in protest. "This dispute grew into a critical issue," the *Engineering News-Record* reported in 1955, "when the 13,000-member lathers union won support for its stand from the powerful AFL plumbers union. . . . Finally, the dispute grew to such proportions that the lathers international union withdrew from the joint board last March." In the meantime the Lathers had appealed the case to the NLRB, in the hope of undermining the authority of the joint board, but the union was disappointed. The NLRB not only agreed that carpenters should do the work but it also ruled that all parties involved in joint board rulings were bound by its decisions, without appeal to the government. "It means that the NLRB recognizes the joint board and is not going to see it upset," Dunlop noted, and it reaffirmed "that jurisdictional disputes are complicated problems and ought to be settled by the people closest to them."[47]

The Denver Decision and Political Action

The National Joint Plan may have kept the government out of Department jurisdictional fights, but NLRB decisions were nevertheless changing the nature of construction unionism. The same policies that had made it possible for building trades workers to man emergency construction jobs in remote areas during the Second World War, including closed-shop contracts, union referrals, and permit systems, were all illegal under the Taft-Hartley Act. And the longtime practice of negotiating agreements before a job began, almost a necessity in contract construction, was no longer strictly legal without an NLRB election first. For instance, when the Atkinson-Jones Company signed an agreement with fourteen building trades unions at the start of a $20-million construction project at the Hanford Atomic Energy Installation in Richmond, Washington, the NLRB nullified the contract. Only a tiny fraction of the eventual ten thousand–man workforce had been employed at the time, and no NLRB elections had been held. That the agency still lacked a viable plan to hold elections did not matter. And neither did the union's claim that the building and construction industry had been working this way for years. "We cannot assume the power to give effect to a custom which is contrary to the statute," the NLRB ruled, thus jeopardizing some five hundred thousand existing contracts all negotiated before work got under way by unions that had not been, and could not be, certified through NLRB elections.[48]

The building trades "customary" organizing tools were on their way out, too. In April 1949 the NLRB found the Denver Building and Construction Trades Council and three affiliates—Carpenters Local 55, Electrical Workers Local 68, and Plumbers Local 3—guilty of a secondary boycott. The Electrical Workers had picketed the general contractor for hiring an "unfair" electrical firm, and union carpenters and plumbers had walked off the job in support. Although the NLRB's decision was reversed on appeal (with the court finding the action to be a legal primary boycott), still that did not settle the matter. In 1950 the NLRB asked the U.S. Supreme Court to decide whether picketing at the job site of a general contractor, to protest the employment of a nonunion subcontractor, violated the secondary boycott provision of the Taft-Hartley Act. The court's reply, a resounding yes, "is a severe blow to building trade unions," the Department reported "and destroys the right they have always had, to refuse to work with non-union men." It also curtailed a union's right to help another union organize a job, the very practice that had given rise to building trades councils in the first place.[49]

The crushing weight of the Denver decision, coupled with the NLRB's refusal to exempt building trades unions from representative elections, shocked the Department into action. Reestablishing the Building Trades Legislative Committee in 1951, the Department also agreed to hold annual regional conferences to keep local, state, and national leaders in touch with one another's problems. At the same time Department officers were working with Senators Hubert Humphrey and Robert Taft on a bill to amend Taft-Hartley: Senate Bill 1973, introduced on August 9, 1951, promised to eliminate the requirement for representative elections in building and construction, and to override state right-to-work laws that legally nullified Taft-Hartley's union security provision. Finally, the Department was also using its monthly *Bulletin* to campaign for a change in Department strategy.

Launched in 1948 to keep local councils apprised of Taft-Hartley's impact, the *Bulletin* now issued emergency calls for political action.[50]

"Let's Look at the Record," a special edition urged building trades workers. "If you have encountered difficulty in getting contractors to sign union-security contracts which have been customary in our industry for over 50 years it is only the beginning. The handwriting is on the wall for all to see—it is no longer secret. Let's not be blind—let's face the bare ugly facts of our present predicament." Fifteen states had already passed right-to-work laws, patterned after Taft-Hartley, but some were even worse. The Texas law, for instance, enacted as an article to the state anti-trust law, had national implications; Texas-based contractors who were parties to the National Constructors Association's national agreement with BCTD unions now contended that, as far as they were concerned, the union security provisions of the agreement were suspended not only in Texas but nationwide. "IS THERE ANYONE WHO STILL DOUBTS THAT THE VERY EXISTENCE OF ALL BUILDING TRADES UNIONS RESTS UPON OUR TAKING PROMPT, CONCERTED AND COLLECTIVE ACTION?" the *Bulletin* wanted to know. "What can we do? In the good old days we could strike but chances are that under the present set-up it would be illegal. Perhaps our only recourse is the 'Ballot Box.' "[51]

It was an issue George Meany had been raising for years. Back in 1947 the AFL secretary-treasurer had made it clear that times had changed and that building trades unions had to change with them. "We have to recognize the fact that we are not fighting the employer on the economic field. If we were fighting him there, there [would be] no question who could win. We are fighting him on the political field," and that required a change in tactics. "Yes, we have built up our organizations and we have raised the wages of the people we represent," Meany acknowledged, "but we have failed somewhere, because we haven't got public opinion with labor in this country, and we might just as well admit it. Labor unions are not in good with the public generally, or the N.A.M. [National Association of Manufacturers], and all the reactionary forces couldn't have passed this legislation." If organized labor expected to reverse Taft-Hartley, it would have to let the public know what unions did for their members. And it would have to let Congress know where union voters stood. "You are not going to remove [the Taft-Hartley law] through strikes here and there," Meany reiterated. "It has to be done in the same fashion as it was put in there." The time had come to take up Samuel Gompers's classic advice to reward labor's friends and defeat its enemies, regardless of political party, a policy that could still bring results, Meany believed, "if you give it a chance to work"[52]

That year the AFL launched Labor's League for Political Education (LLPE) to compile and circulate candidates' records, promote labor's point of view through publications and radio, organize registration drives to get out the vote, and raise the money to finance this political campaign, since, thanks to Taft-Hartley, union funds could not be used. Under the leadership of the IBEW's Joe Keenan, who had earned his political stripes in Chicago's Democratic wards, the LLPE drummed up men and money for the cause, setting up statewide leagues to monitor legislation, organizing local branches in practically every large city in the country, and providing transportation to those who needed it on election day. "You don't get any votes by making speeches . . . or issuing statements. The work must be done at the precinct level," George Meany noted, and Keenan agreed. "It has been proven that a well-established organization functioning with the support of all cooperating groups can elect people to office who will repeal unfavorable legislation. This is much better and less costly," he pointed out, "than . . . expensive and unsure court procedures."[53]

Although Keenan pledged that organized labor would defeat each and every Taft-Hartley supporter even if it took twenty years, the Department could not wait that long. "Daily we hear of the many injustices of Taft-Hartley," President Gray told the AFL Executive Council. "One day it is a court decision requiring one union to ignore another union's picket line—next it is either [an] N.L.R.B. ruling or a court decision declaring a union . . . to be in violation of the secondary boycott prohibitions of the Act—next it is use of the injunction powers of the Act. . . . From many quarters come reports that the N.L.R.B. . . . has assumed the dictatorial position of telling unions and employers what is and what is not proper subject matter for collective bargaining. . . . And so it goes Ad infinitum." Nothing much had changed since 1947, even after both the AFL and the CIO spent $1 million on political activities in 1950. In fact, when President Truman gave his message to the Eighty-second Congress in 1951, "he didn't even bother to go through the motions of asking for repeal," President Gray pointed out. Since organized labor had not mustered the majority needed to overturn Taft-Hartley (or found even three congressmen who understood how the law actually worked, Gray said) it was time to try something new. "It is no longer enough to refer to Taft-Hartley as the 'slave labor law,'" President Gray insisted. "We must come forward with either a new . . . equitable and realistic labor-management relations law or proper amendments to the existing Act."[54]

The National Legislative Conference and Grass-Roots Politics

Amending Taft-Hartley may have been a more practical strategy than holding out for repeal, but there was nothing easy about the process. The Department's original amendment, Senate Bill 1973, never made it out of committee in 1951. And while it did pass the Senate in the spring of 1952, it was killed in the House Education and Labor Committee before the summer was over. Committee chairman Graham Barden, a North Carolina Democrat, not only refused to take action on the bill but also refused to act on three companion bills introduced in the House. "What does it take for us to get the necessary legislation," Gray wanted to know, "which will permit us to carry out our collective bargaining relations on a voluntary democratic basis, free of intervention by Federal Bureaucrats totally unfamiliar with the intricacies of the building industry?" As far as Gray could see, it would take the combined forces of construction labor and management, he told the U.S. Chamber of Commerce Construction Committee, to "put an end to this throttling, choking grip upon our every move by the Federal Government."[55]

But it would also take a united building trades movement, ready and willing to carry out political directives—a task complicated by the fact that some unions strongly opposed amending Taft-Hartley. They wanted repeal or nothing. Indeed, Gray believed that the Department had failed to get its amendment passed, in 1952, because some building trades unions did not support Senate Bill 1973.[56] Internal divisions were nothing new, but at the time they seemed as dangerous as reactionary politicians. Until the Department could prove that it spoke for three million building trades workers, its voice would not be heard in Congress. The building trades movement needed "tightening up," as Gray put it, so that local and state councils, as well as international unions, played a role in Department affairs. There were six hundred local councils in the United States and Canada, and many of these had the organization and the community connections to get the political job done. The UA's Peter T. Schoemann, for instance, who headed the council in Milwaukee, was the kind of active trade unionist that the Department needed on its side. He sat on every community committee that mattered and, to those in Milwaukee, he was "Mr. Everything," as one trade unionist said. Statewide leaders like Cornelius Haggerty, secretary-treasurer of the California state council, were equally valuable. A lather by trade, Haggerty was already well known in the California legislature and the governor's office, and sat on a number of important state boards. Men like these would prove crucial to building a viable political network.[57]

"These are not ordinary times," President Gray told the 1952 BCTD convention. "Day after day we see our long established . . . practices being attacked by the N.L.R.B. and the courts. We also see . . . CIO Industrial Unions and United Mine Workers District 50 attempting to encroach upon our jurisdiction. . . . If we are to effectively combat the forces which are out to destroy building trades unions it must be done at the local level."[58] Both the *Bulletin* and the regional conferences established in 1951 were early attempts to build up a grass-roots political network. But the real breakthrough came in 1955 when the Department held its first national legislative conference.

Called to inform building trades workers about "deficiencies" in federal laws, especially Taft-Hartley and the Davis-Bacon Act (which no longer suited postwar conditions), the conference was designed to bring local, state, and international union representatives together to develop workable strategies. Some eight hundred delegates signed up almost immediately, a hopeful sign that "this grass-roots sentiment will find expression in new and constructive approaches to our many problems," the *Bulletin* noted. When the conference opened in March, there were fourteen hundred delegates from nineteen unions and forty-eight states (as well as Hawaii and the District of Columbia) ready to get to work.[59]

George Meany, now AFL president, did not mince words at the opening session. "Reactionaries are pointing their guns at . . . the building trades . . . [because] if they can destroy the building trades they believe they can destroy the entire labor movement." Senator Patrick V. McNamara, a Michigan Democrat (and past president of Pipe Fitters Local 636) agreed, calling so-called right-to-work laws "sugar-coated hypocrisy." And Representative John E. Fogarty, a Rhode Island Democrat (and union bricklayer), made it clear that "now is the time for action." McNamara and Fogarty had sponsored the Department's most recent attempts to amend Taft-Hartley (by eliminating right-to-work laws) and improve Davis-Bacon coverage, and now labor lawyers stepped up to explain why the Department believed these amendments were crucial. If Davis-Bacon could be extended to cover all federally assisted projects, including roads, Federal Housing Administration–insured houses, and Veterans Administration home building projects, attorney C. R. Gray pointed out, then prevailing rates, the eight-hour day, and the forty-hour week would govern 37 percent of the industry. Louis Sherman, general counsel of the IBEW, and Charles Donahue, attorney for the UA, also provided the kind of technical detail and legislative background that delegates needed to understand and promote the Department's campaign.[60]

For the next two days delegates used this information to lobby congressmen and senators to support the Department's bills, S. 1285 and S. 1269 in the Senate, and H. 4565 and H. 4566, in the House. "The results of the conference were very gratifying," Gray reported. The bills had been referred to the proper committees, the legislative process was under way, and conference delegates had met with almost every committee member involved. But the job was not over yet. Most of the detailed work in Congress was done in committee, Gray pointed out, and busy senators and representatives tended to follow the committee's lead when it came to final votes. "The next step in our legislative program . . . is to insure that the members of the committees . . . realize the backing which organized labor gives to these bills. . . . *They should hear directly from you on how you feel about the proposed bills*," Gray urged the membership. To get them started the *Bulletin* provided the relevant names and addresses, as well as detailed analyses of each bill. "If the Congress knows the situation, it will support our position," the Department contended. "We in the Building Trades do not want the Government in the labor picture.... *We have no wish to change Labor Day into Government Day.*" But since there was no getting around the fact that "the Federal Government is in the construction industry and in a big way," the Department saw no better choice than to push its case in Congress.[61]

Taking his own advice, President Gray let the Senate Public Works Committee know that the Department supported extending Davis-Bacon provisions to the interstate highway bill that was then under consideration. "No doubt there will be loud weeping and wailing ... that a prevailing wage provision in the Highway Bill will greatly increase cost," President Gray wrote. "This is a familiar argument," he knew, but it was also "a smoke screen and a diversion tactic put forth by a minority group of contractors to perpetuate and extend their unfair practice of entering a foreign community ... and underbidding fair local contractors who have based their bids on local prevailing wage rates. Should a highway contractor from Texas, Oklahoma, or South Carolina be permitted to [work in] ... California, Michigan, or New York, and base his bid on the lower wage in his particular State? Do you want to see construction wage rates and economic stability ... upset by out-of-State contractors? Of course not." The effort paid off a few months later when the Senate Public Works Committee agreed that the Davis-Bacon Act should govern employment in the construction of the multi-billion-dollar interstate highway system. But before there was time to celebrate, the provision was knocked out by an amendment from the Senate floor.[62]

It was a learning experience, to be sure: By the time Congress finally adjourned in July 1955, the Department's bills to amend Taft-Hartley and improve Davis-Bacon had not been acted on, and the Highway bill had been defeated as well. Still, the Department did not view the session as a total loss. For one thing, the Federal Housing Authority had adopted a prevailing wage requirement and the Department of Defense had issued a new directive to enforce labor standards on defense construction. Both were "undoubtedly ... the result of the Bills endorsed by the Department ... for amendment of the Davis-Bacon Act. So the effort had results," the *Bulletin* reported. And, second, the building trades' lobbying campaign had demonstrated "that we ... can if we must transfer our strength from our economic and organizational power to the legislative halls. The Department and affiliated internationals do not make a practice of appealing for grass-roots political demonstrations of support unless the issue is of great importance," the *Bulletin* added. "The response to our appeals this year demonstrated that our interpretation of the importance of the Bills which we have endorsed [is] ... shared by our local union members."[63]

Political defeats were disappointing, but they were not unexpected; the building trades were in this fight for the long haul. Nor were they the last word. Department officers, affiliated unions, and local councils kept the pressure up: they continued lobbying, writing letters, and building support for their view of fair labor standards. The effort was rewarded the following July, when U.S. president Dwight D. Eisenhower signed into law the interstate highway construction bill, which included the Davis-Bacon prevailing wage provision. A few months later President Eisenhower granted the Department's request to arrange a labor-management meeting to discuss amending Taft-Hartley. "Out of these deliberations came an administration-backed bill that was introduced in both the House and the Senate," President Gray reported. "This bill was considerably less than what we had hoped for," he admitted, "but it did provide some help," including protection of joint apprenticeship programs and the promise of NLRB certifications without elections. No one expected any immediate relief, especially since the bill did not get out of committee in 1957. Nevertheless, the fact that the federal government was willing to take the building trades' position seriously was a decided improvement.[64]

The outcome, of course, was a far cry from the access to government power that the building trades had experienced during the Second World War, when their skill proved essential to victory. During that critical time a fellow tradesman had been second in command at the Department of Labor, prevailing union wage rates had set the standard for defense construction, and the basic rules of building trades unionism—the closed shop, the union hiring hall, and collectively bargained agreements—had been the keys to meeting wartime production demands. Those days were gone, as the Taft-Hartley Act and the Denver decision demonstrated in no uncertain terms. But that did not mean the fight was over. If building trades workers could not match the political influence their opponents enjoyed, they still had a measure of economic power based on their practical control of skill. And they fully intended to use that power to defend union rights and standards, and the economic security that went along with them.

The Economic Power of Skill: Mechanics, Contractors, and Civil Rights

It is distasteful to bring these things up, I know, and we could all get up here and say everything is hotsy totsy, but at some later day we would be asking ourselves, who is asleep at the switch and how did these things come about?
—BCTD President Richard Gray, 1955

Repressive legislation may have been whittling away "the economic power of our unions," as the BCTD warned in the wake of Taft-Hartley and the Denver decision. But the future had never looked so bright to the men who worked with the tools. Government investment in highway and defense construction was on the rise, especially after the outbreak of war in Korea in 1950. And private construction was back on its feet after a twenty-year hiatus. With residential construction at an all-time high, and a commercial building boom under way in New York City, Chicago, and other urban centers, this was a golden age for the building trades. For the first time in a long while there was more than enough work to go around: Between 1947 and 1954 expenditures for new construction increased by 119 percent nationwide, and set a record high of $47.3 billion in 1957, 3 percent higher than the record set in 1956.[1]

"You just couldn't get enough skilled people," Marvin Boede stated, recalling his early years as a steam fitter. "In those days, there were jobs galore, and guys went around shopping." For young men like Robert Georgine, who was still in high school when he first obtained a permit to work with a rivet gang in Chicago, industry prospects looked good. "The city was really blooming," as far as he could see, and "everything was great." Labor leaders had done "a hell of a job [persuading employers] that the best system was to have a workforce that was skilled and productive," he thought, and he was not alone. In fact, when a labor lawyer encouraged the Chicago Carpenters union to make a legal fight against Taft-Hartley, members did not agree.[2] Like building mechanics throughout the United States and Canada, they were eager to make up for years of lost time and attain a measure of economic security—to buy a house, educate their children, and enjoy some postwar pleasures like a new car, a television, a vacation. More interested in work and overtime pay than legal battles, they focused instead on protecting their greatest industrial asset: their ability to do a job right, the first time. For when it came to erecting skyscrapers and factories, or building atomic plants and military facilities, skill would trump politics every time, or so they believed. As long as union labor controlled the skills that contractors needed, the future would take care of itself.

Skill had always set the building trades apart. It was the key to their early organization and their proven ability to bargain collectively with employers. In a custom industry like building and construction, where almost every job presented new problems that had to be solved on the spot, experienced, creative, and knowledgeable mechanics played a vital role in a contractor's success. Mechanics, or journeymen, had mastered the fundamentals of their craft and performed a wide range of specialized tasks. Supervising their own work, it was up to journeymen to lay out jobs from blueprints and then complete work efficiently so that the next trade could get started. A complex mix of brain, brawn, and competence, construction work required skills that ranged from mathematics and drafting, to stamina and speed, to the safe operation of machinery, skills that took time to develop. "People didn't know how to lay out sheet metal duct work. It was a special skill," as George Andrucki explained. "You couldn't go to a hardware store and buy it like you can buy lumber or a pipe or something." And you could not hire just anyone to operate expensive machinery like cranes or earth-moving equipment, or take on a dangerous job like structural iron work, either, especially in the days when safety was almost an afterthought. "The job was so difficult," Joe Maloney explained, that "not many people wanted to go on top of that iron." Even so-called unskilled labor, like hod carriers or cement mixers, had to know what they were doing on the job: Mixing "mud" in the right proportions for the plasterer or the bricklayer, and then delivering it at the right time and in the right amount so there would be no breaks in the flow of work, took practice.[3]

Whether through formal apprenticeships or work opportunities, building trades unions generally controlled training for construction workers, and that made all the difference in a boom and bust industry. Craft apprentices spent years learning the fundamentals of their trade before they could claim a journeyman's wage, and the better their training, the better able they were to find a job when work was scarce. Neil Haggerty, who had apprenticed as a lather in Boston between 1913 and 1915, had no fear when he moved to Los Angeles in the 1920s, despite an economic depression. "I had no concern about getting a job if there was a job around," he explained, "because I had been trained properly in my apprenticeship in . . . all branches of my particular trade, whether it was wood, wire or metal or anything else of that sort. I could work on a house and build a home or I could work on a cathedral. I was trained that way, so I had enough confidence that I would be all right in finding a job." Twenty-five years later the lesson still held: When Robert Georgine sought a "secure" construction job, to appease his worried family—who had urged him to become a policeman or even a priest to avoid layoffs—he also apprenticed as a lather, largely because a trade with an apprenticeship offered the promise of "guaranteed" work.[4]

But only if you had the aptitude and the discipline to make it through. As sheet metal worker George Andrucki soon discovered, when he started his apprenticeship in 1953, it was one thing to "goof off" in classroom sessions but quite another to try it on the job. Training with men who had come through the Great Depression and the Second World War, he was immediately put in his place. "[The] first thing they taught you was to keep your mouth shut and pay attention and do what you're told. . . . I learned pretty quick that . . . when you start going to work with men that have been working for 25 or 30 years—hard work—you don't fool around with them . . . because . . . they were tough men and they were hard men, and . . . if they had to let you know [that] they would." He stressed that "you didn't talk disrespectful," especially to very skilled mechanics who set high standards on the job. "They would make it a point to say to you that you've got to do a good day's work. . . . That's what a good Union man does. You've got to do a good day's work and you've got to do your work so that it's done right . . . [so that] if you come back and look at it in . . . ten years . . . you'll want to look at it," he said. "That was the way [you could tell they were good union men, that] and how they carried themselves." Impressed by the pride they took in their work, Andrucki followed their advice to quit his job as soon as he obtained his journeyman's card. "I was told . . . that the only way you're ever going to get to . . . know anything or do anything in this trade is . . . to quit where you're serving your time and start to bounce around and see how . . . this trade is worked at in all of the different companies you can go to work for. And that's what I started to do." Although his wife thought that meant he was now unemployed, Andrucki knew better. Work was so plentiful in New York City at the time that the brand-new journeyman was employed the very next day. In fact, over the next ten years he never lost a day of work.[5]

Yet even with so much work available—and rising complaints of skill shortages by employers—it still was not easy to break into the trades. Aptitude and discipline were not always enough. Potential apprentices also needed a father, uncle, or close family friend to sponsor them, and that made the building trades a family affair. BCTD president Richard Gray was a fourth-generation bricklayer, and AFL-CIO president George Meany had followed his father into the Plumbers union. And those were typical stories. "I have to admit that there are many unions that I couldn't get into," said Peter J. Brennan, a painter and president of New York City's Building and Construction Trades Council. But he made no apologies for what he called the "father-son" deal, since it offered working-class sons a start in life and protected competence, too. "When we got a man that came out of a family where he was trained by his father, and his grandfather," Brennan pointed out, "we were sure that we were getting a good mechanic."[6]

The link between family connections and union training would lead to serious criticisms and government action within a few years. But at the time there was nothing unusual about the practice. "If your father was in the building trades, you tried to get in . . . the building trades union," as Andrucki put it. "If your father worked in Con Edison [a local utility] you went into Con Edison." And there were also practical reasons for limiting training opportunities, at least according to building trades workers. "In the building trades there's always this feast or famine thing," Marvin Boede explained. If a local union expanded its membership to suit "peak" employment periods, it would not be able to survive the inevitable "valley." Men who remembered the Great Depression had little interest in opening union doors in the 1950s, as long as the existing membership could handle the work. "You can't protect your members if you indiscriminately give out memberships. That was the mentality that existed," Robert Georgine noted. "It wasn't one that grew up because of maliciousness or selfishness," he added. "It grew up because that was the way they saw things, they had to protect themselves first."[7]

Georgine had a clearer view than most about the costs and benefits of the practice. On the one hand, family connections had secured his place in the Lathers union: Although his father had died when he was still a child, his mother had married a second-generation lather, and with the help of his stepfather and his stepfather's father, who had some "clout" as he put it, Georgine began his apprenticeship. On the other hand, he was the first and only Italian in a basically Irish local, so he was not accepted as a "brother" right away. "Irish and Italian didn't mix too well in Chicago," he pointed out. But since he was also the youngest apprentice in a group of returning war veterans, he soon found a way to break in. The older men had long since forgotten the high school math and geometry they needed to lay out work, but Georgine was fresh out of school, and it all came easily to him. There was a test that apprentice lathers had to take to prove they could read blueprints, lay out work, and then build it, and that was where Georgine's math skills came in handy. Regularly assigned as a partner to test takers over the next three years, he was given the chance not only to improve his skills but also to help the others out. And that made a real difference. "The fact that I was Italian, a skinny little 'black' kid," it got me over some of those humps," he explained, and after that he did "pretty well" in the local. Georgine, who would eventually head the Lathers union—and between 1974 and 2000 the BCTD—had no complaints about his training. "That was a time . . . when . . . people still had that depression mentality," he remembered. "Everybody believed that they had to work hard and unless they worked hard, they wouldn't continue to work, and so it was a good atmosphere to work in, a good atmosphere to learn in, it was a good atmosphere to succeed in," he said. "Success was unlimited without any formal education."[8]

Unions, Contractors, and Productive Industry

Part of that success was directly tied to the decentralized structure of contract construction, and to the fact that collective bargaining was strictly a local affair. Even when international unions signed national agreements with contractor associations, wages, conditions, and benefits were all bargained locally. This policy had its pitfalls: Contractors often resented the local union's power, especially when they were caught in jurisdictional fights or efforts to organize nonunion subcontractors. And contractors and unions did not always agree as to how the customer's dollar should be spent, as Paul Geary of the National Electrical Contractors Association (NECA) put it.[9]

But in an industry dominated by small-scale firms, union contractors benefited from the services local unions provided and the flexibility they ensured: Building trades unions recruited, trained, and delivered a skilled and efficient workforce, when and where it was needed, and they took that workforce off the contractor's hands when the job was done. Even large-scale general contractors, like those that established the National Constructors Association (NCA) in 1947, operated 100 percent union, and they could not have operated any other way at the time. Engaged in building oil refineries and steel and chemical plants in remote areas all over the country, they required a reliable source for the army of skilled workers that they needed to undertake a job, and they benefited from the union's ability to establish area-wide wage rates and working conditions. As long as both sides operated in good faith, and there were no attempts to create artificial skill shortages or impose unfair work rules on either side, many contractors, large and small, general and specialty, accepted union control of the labor market as an efficient way to do business.[10]

But in order for the system to work, contractors and local business agents had to respect each other's interests at the bargaining table, and neither could expect to win everything they wanted, at least not at first. "Don't get impatient," IUOE president John Possehl had warned contractors back in 1939 when he was first trying to forge a relationship with the Associated General Contractors. "Leave something for the future," his successor William Maloney advised local union leaders a few years later. "After you build up confidence with these contractors . . . you will be in a . . . position to sign a better agreement."[11] Like other BCTD leaders, Possehl and Maloney knew that contractors had to make a profit if union members wanted to work, a lesson driven home through daily contact with employers. For instance, after Robert Georgine worked with contractors, architects, and owners in the Lathing and Plastering Foundation of Chicago, in an effort to make the industry more competitive, he was able to see "sides of the industry that I couldn't see just working with the tools. And when I did get elected to office in the local, I tried to . . . convince my own workers, that you've got to work all sides of the story and try to figure out how we can get the most. But at the same time, don't cripple the guy that's giving it to you. I used to try to tell our guys, 'If the contractor doesn't make a fair profit how the hell is he going to pay us what we call a fair wage?' "[12]

Building trades unions and their contractors were in the industry together; one could not prosper without the other, an economic fact of life that the BCTD had been preaching for years. Mutual interests had produced the 1939 agreement with the Associated General Contractors that had kept defense construction on track and preserved the contract system during the wartime emergency. And a mutual desire to cut down on costly jurisdictional fights, and keep the federal government out of industry affairs after the enactment of the Taft-Hartley Act, had led unions and contractor associations to establish the National Joint Board in 1948. Strong, well-organized unions like the Electrical Workers, Bricklayers, and Plumbers had been working with their contractors for years to promote business and jobs, and to guard against open-shop competitors; in fact, when the BCTD began its fight against Taft-Hartley in 1947, the National Electrical Contractors Association had publicly backed the effort. "If a union . . . is to perform effectively the functions which we as employers expect, it needs to have a high degree of security," an NECA spokesman explained. "To us that means a closed shop, the right to the secondary boycott and industry-wide bargaining, at least on an area basis."[13]

Such close cooperation often brought results. When the National Joint Heavy and Highway Construction Committee, an independent joint organizing campaign established in 1954, agreed to forgo building trades rates on highway projects so that union contractors could control the work, the operating engineers, teamsters, carpenters, and laborers who had launched the campaign gained steady jobs. And when BCTD-affiliated unions negotiated national agreements with NCA contractors that traded a no-strike clause for union wage rates and conditions, they bolstered union control of heavy industrial construction. Nevertheless such close cooperation often raised suspicions, especially in cities where organized crime had gained a foothold in the industry. In Joppa, Illinois, for instance, "racketeers" and local union officers had apparently colluded in a series of strikes designed to keep a favored contractor at work on an important government defense job. When Department and international union officers were asked to step in on the new contractor's behalf—the Bechtel Corporation, a prominent NCA member—they did not hesitate. "We have spent sixty years building up our reputation as responsible trade unionists, who stand by our agreements," a Department spokesman told the *New York Times*. "We're not going to let a few fellows who have no real concern for the welfare of their members tear down all we have accomplished."[14]

Department leaders and national contractors also joined forces when industrial unionists—who were often referred to as nonunion workers—challenged building trades control of maintenance, alteration, and mechanical installation work at oil refineries, chemical plants, and steel mills, among many others. As John Dunlop explained, "this work was not new construction on a new or demolished site but rather work assigned by an owner to a contractor employing building tradesmen engaged in the repair, renovation, revamping and upkeep of property, machinery, and equipment. . . . The availability of skilled crews of boilermakers, iron workers, pipefitters, millwrights, and electricians . . . particularly in winter months when outside new construction was down, made such maintenance work attractive to all parties."[15]

The conflict reached back to the rise of the CIO in the 1930s and was still going strong in 1957; in two years of conferences since the AFL-CIO merger in 1955 neither side had been willing to compromise. The fight would continue well into the 1960s, as industrial unions negotiated contract provisions to prohibit employers from contracting work out, and defense manufacturers, such as Martin Marietta, backed them up. But meanwhile construction contractors were lobbying AFL-CIO president George Meany to support the building trades' jurisdictional fight, since they understood, as President Richard Gray pointed out, that "when we lose our work to an industrial union, they lose a construction contract." Contractors were also working with Department leaders to develop the General Presidents' Project Maintenance Agreement, so that building tradesmen and their contractors would continue to have work in the plants they constructed. The first project maintenance agreement, which was implemented at the Tidewater Refinery in

Delaware in 1956, included a no-strike, no-lockout provision and a griev-ance procedure with binding arbitration.[16]

The Sheet Metal Workers and their contractors had also joined forces in a campaign to protect their work by refusing to handle materials produced in shops under contract with the Steelworkers, a policy President Gray heartily endorsed. "What other course is left open for them to follow so that they can protect the work jurisdiction of their membership as granted to them by the American Federation of Labor? How else can they protect the wage scales and working conditions their local unions have fought for and attained throughout the years?" As Gray told delegates to the 1957 convention, "If we lose on this point it will mean that the Steelworkers and other industrial unions will be free to invade the Boilermakers' shops, the Carpenters' mill shops, the Plumbers and Steamfitters' fabrication shops, the Electricians' ju-risdiction . . . at a reduced wage scale and we will be required to handle and install their products to the detriment of our own membership's work juris-diction, wage scales, and working conditions." So determined was Gray to push this fight that he was willing to leave the AFL-CIO if the leadership re-fused to recognize the building trades' "historic" jurisdiction, a strategy that had apparently originated with the Teamsters and had gained the support of many local unions and building trades councils.[17]

Gray's threat never got very far. Building trades unions did not wield the same clout in the AFL-CIO in 1957 as they had back in 1935, when they won their fight for exclusive jurisdiction and CIO unions went off on their own. And AFL-CIO president George Meany, a building trades worker himself, was a far more forceful leader than his AFL predecessor, William Green, had been. Addressing the BCTD convention in 1957, Meany made it clear that he was not going to fall in line. A fight to the finish over exclusive jurisdiction would only benefit anti-union forces, he said, and destroy whatever hopes a united AFL-CIO had of pressing labor's political agenda in Congress. But if the Department was really looking for a fight, Meany added, there were far better targets to aim at. "The right-to-work people are still pretty much alive," Meany told convention delegates, and nonunion contractors, like Brown & Root, were already doing a fair amount of business in the South. "How about a little fight with Brown & Root? What jurisdiction has Brown & Root got? Who gave it to them?" he wanted to know. "They seem to be doing all right. They just finished a job at Seadrift, Texas . . . a one hundred million dollar job," he said. "The estimates are that private industrial and public util-ity construction . . . are up 55 percent in dollar volume since 1954. Is Build-ing Trades employment in this field up 55 percent?" Meany asked, knowing full well that the answer was no. "Maybe a little fight can be developed there."[18]

Meany had a point. Although union control of construction work was unchallenged in well-organized cities like New York, Chicago, and St. Louis, there was plenty of room for organization in the South and Southwest, especially in residential and light commercial construction. Local unions tended to regard these markets as inconsequential, preferring to concentrate on big jobs and Davis-Bacon work, a decision that would prove costly in the long run. And even in safe union cities, industrial relations could not be taken for granted. Collective-bargaining agreements rested on the union's control of skill and the mechanic's reputation for efficiency—a claim that was getting harder to sell in the mid-1950s, thanks to an endless series of short-term strikes between 1952 and 1954. Even U.S. president Dwight D. Eisenhower, who was having a house built in 1954, proved no match for the men on the job. The basic building trades rule that no union worked while another was on strike had cost him an extra $65,000, he complained to his secretary, and consequently he felt "fairly strong about it."[19] He was not alone. For while building trades unions were waging strikes and boycotts to enforce union rules and resist industrial union challengers, the U.S. Congress was contemplating new laws designed to keep "big labor" in check. In fact, at around the same time that President Gray and the Teamsters were urging BCTD affiliates to challenge the industrial unions, a select committee, chaired by Senator John McClellan of Arkansas, was investigating improper activities in the labor movement and focusing directly on the Teamsters and organized crime. By the time President Gray called the BCTD convention to order in December 1957, Teamster president Dave Beck had already resigned as Department vice president, and within a few days the AFL-CIO had revoked the union's charter.[20]

Although Richard Gray believed that it was "un-American" to expel the Teamsters before charges of corruption had been tried in court, support for his position was limited. Few could disagree that rank-and-file members of the Teamsters were "pretty nice guys" as one supporter put it: Many small building trades locals owed their existence to teamsters who refused to deliver building materials when these unions were on strike. But the McClellan committee hearings, which were popularly known as the rackets hearings, had been televised in 1957, and the news had not been good. Along with the Teamsters, the Operating Engineers and the Carpenters were also under public scrutiny for alleged misuse of union funds, and various local building trades unions were cited for rigged elections, bribery, and strike-related violence. Whether or not these allegations were true, serious damage had been done. IBEW president Gordon Freeman may have been right when he reported that "less than *one tenth of one percent*" of union leaders were "ever even *accused* of corrupt practices, let alone convicted." But the fact remained that the public now assumed that "shakedowns" and "sweetheart" contracts were everyday union policies, according to opinion polls, and that it was time for Congress to "do something" about arrogant, dictatorial, corrupt, and strike-happy union leaders. The outcome, namely, the Labor Management Reporting and Disclosure Act of 1959 (better known as Landrum-Griffin), not only imposed extensive reporting requirements and granted the U.S. Secretary of Labor broad powers to investigate unions but it also strengthened restrictions on picketing and boycotts and included a "bill of rights" to protect union members from unscrupulous officers.[21]

This blanket indictment outraged many building trades leaders, since thousands of businessmen and lawyers had also been implicated in the investigation. But they were in no position to protest too loudly. The investigation had publicized widespread complaints of costly union "feather-bedding" policies designed to keep as many union members employed as possible. Critics charged that local contracts often required that a skilled electrical worker be on hand whenever electrical lights were in use or that an operating engineer be employed to turn machinery on and off, even if that meant just flicking a switch. They also complained that skilled, well-paid men, including carpenters and iron workers, were required to unload and carry certain materials, pushing the cost of construction sky high, allegations that were hardly new. But in the context of the McClellan hearings, they provided a golden opportunity for contractors to take the upper hand in industrial relations. AGC president Lester Rogers now encouraged general contractors to drum up opposition to high labor costs, something they had not been able to do before, he told the *Wall Street Journal*. Because building owners generally would not stand for delays on their projects, contractors tended to accept union demands, he explained. But thanks to bad publicity generated by the "rackets" committee, the AGC (which represented union and nonunion contractors) was now determined to "educate these industrial owners" and take a firm stand at the bargaining table. "It seems like the opportune time to go after some of these practices," another contractor added. "We've had a lot of lip service from international leaders," he said, "but no action or accomplishments."[22]

Faced with the prospect of public criticism, on the one hand, and rising prices and government cutbacks in construction, on the other, BCTD president Richard Gray felt compelled to take drastic action at the 1957 convention. He was not particularly worried about the organization itself. The BCTD had broadened the basis of representation that year, by adding two vice presidents to the Executive Council (bringing the number up to ten) and allowing affiliated building and construction councils to cast one vote each at conventions. The Department had also added six regional directors, including one for Canada, to work with local councils on matters of efficiency and organization.[23]

But Gray was worried about the corrosive effects of inflation, the nation's number one problem, he told the delegates. Housing construction had fallen off 30 percent since 1955 because of a shortage of mortgage money he reported, and funds for the federal government's lease-purchase construction program had dried up, too. And that was not all. Plans for erecting schools and public housing had been held up, as had plant construction and major modernization projects. "Up until now, our sole objective . . . has been to get increased wages to compensate for the increased cost of living," Gray noted, but the time had come to reassess that policy since it only meant "more tight money, more inflation, less construction, and more unemployment." Making what he admitted was a "most unorthodox proposal," he now advised building trades unions to "declare a moratorium on wage increases during 1958."[24]

The response was less than he had hoped for. With the exception of fellow bricklayer Harry Bates, nobody backed the plan. It was just bad policy, painter L. M. Rafferty pointed out, since "freezing wages when prices are going up actually cuts wages." And it was not the Department's job to interfere with an international union's collective-bargaining policy, he added, a point that carpenter Maurice Hutcheson heartily endorsed. Gray's proposal "is not going to hold back our fellows if they can negotiate increases," Hutcheson told the *New York Times*. President Gray may have raised a valid point when he later noted a delegate's report that in his area "we have the best wage rate but no work." But almost no one in the BCTD, or the AFL-CIO, for that matter, thought he was on the right track.[25]

If his solution to inflation lacked merit, as his critics charged, Gray's concern for rising construction costs was real. As early as 1954 NCA and AGC representatives had warned Department leaders that high labor costs were limiting work opportunities for AFL construction workers, especially on industrial and housing projects. They put the blame on costly work practices that had apparently developed during the war, when emergency defense construction was done on a cost-plus basis, and every project was a rush job. As BCTD secretary-treasurer Frank Bonadio saw it, the cost-plus system had paid contractors to overman projects, and that in turn had fostered shorter work days and "spread the work" policies. "I doubt very much if the contractors were getting over five hours' work for eight [hours' pay]," Bonadio admitted, but at the time no serious criticism was raised: Projects that would have normally taken three years to complete were erected in record time, with the government picking up the bill. By 1954, however, the volume of government "rush" construction jobs had tapered off, and the days of "easy money," as the *New York Times* put it, were over.[26]

For the next three years joint committees of contractors and building trades leaders would investigate the problem. Their goal was to eliminate specific abuses, including early quitting times, overmanned job sites, and "excessive" rates for fringe benefits like travel pay for out-of-town jobs, without undermining basic wage rates and working standards. But the job proved difficult on both sides. Local contractors, according to Bonadio, were not about to push the issue as long as demand for skilled labor was high. "One thing [contractors] wanted," Bonadio pointed out, and rightly so, he added, was "to have 'eight for eight.' Well, how do you get eight hours' work out of a man for eight [hours' pay]? You have to have good supervision. But, you see, there was still enough work around the country, so that a contractor was afraid to fire people. The minute he did, some other contractor gobbled them up." But by 1957, as Gray had made clear in his convention address, the economic climate had changed, and cut-backs in construction were taking a toll. With 15 percent of the workforce "on the bench," or unemployed, in 1958—the highest proportion since 1949—building trades leaders were ready to take productivity issues and outside competition more seriously.[27]

And just in time, according to the NCA. The number of building trades mechanics employed on NCA projects, including steel mills, atomic energy installations, and oil and chemical plants, had dropped by 27 percent in 1958, and the loss could not be attributed to the recession alone. Union work rules and manpower waste were pricing union contractors out of the market: Some of the largest oil and chemical companies, the NCA warned, were threatening to switch to nonunion contractors, claiming they could save 25 percent on construction costs. The AGC was also alarmed, since industrial unions were apparently winning their fight to do maintenance construction work at industrial plants. Although BCTD affiliates had adopted a productivity code, in 1958, to prohibit slowdowns, forced overtime, and restrictions on power tools and output, change was not easy to achieve. Department-sponsored "traveling teams" were doing their best to persuade local councils to give up what they called "obsolete" area practices, but it was still the responsibility of local unions to enforce the rules. At a time when the majority of building trades workers saw no immediate threats to their livelihood, it was no easy task to get three million workers and six hundred local councils to view local conditions through a long-term, national lens.[28]

Seeing no real choice but to work together in order to protect their economic interests, representatives from the NCA, the AGC, and the BCTD met in January 1959 to establish a joint committee to resolve industrial problems on an industrywide basis. With the help of John Dunlop, who commanded respect in both labor and industry circles, the committee was formally organized as the Construction Industry Joint Conference (CIJC), with Dunlop serving as the impartial chairman of the administrative committee. For the first time, representatives from all segments of the industry would participate in a continuing forum as a group: The BCTD, AGC, and NCA, as well as mechanical and specialty contractor associations, were all represented. Labor and management had common interests in expanding the market for contract construction, supporters agreed, and both sides saw the need to promote the advantages and flexibility of the system. But before the CIJC could "sell" the contract system to industry, Dunlop pointed out, critical problems like skill shortages, rising wage and fringe benefits, and the industry's high number of strikes would have to be addressed, and inefficient practices on the part of unions and contractors would have to be changed. "This is a most difficult problem and one which will require a long time to achieve," Dunlop noted, "but it is fundamental to the industry's future."[29]

Cornelius J. Haggerty and the Missile Sites Labor Commission

Around the same time that the CIJC was getting established, Richard Gray announced his retirement as BCTD president, a position he had held since the Second World War. At age seventy-three, Gray was still an ardent defender of the building trades' jurisdiction, but he had also suffered some serious health problems and his colleagues agreed it was time for a change. His successor, Cornelius J. "Neil" Haggerty, secretary-treasurer of the California State Federation of Labor, seemed to be better suited to the job at hand. Well respected for his political skills, Haggerty had led a successful fight to defeat right-to-work legislation in California. He was also well known as an articulate, persuasive speaker who could hold his own in any court. "Mr. Haggerty speaks with the . . . confidence of a self-educated man," *The Constructor* noted, "and carries an aura of dignity and poise that suggests he is not one to be easily ruffled or flustered." A longtime leader of the Los Angeles Building and Construction Trades Council, Haggerty was proud of his role in negotiating the nation's first regional master labor agreement in 1949, an agreement that "treated the construction industry as an industry," he pointed out, "instead of dealing with it in several segments." Essentially Haggerty believed that labor and management had to live together for the good of the economy and the nation. "This does not mean that we can reach some kind of Utopia," he added, "but much more can be accomplished that way than through any other means."[30]

Almost as soon as Haggerty took office, his leadership was put to the test. Critical delays at national defense construction sites were holding up the government's intercontinental ballistic missile and space programs, and building trades unions were inevitably blamed. The timing could not have been worse given the Soviet Union's successful launch of Sputnik in 1957 and its apparent superiority in the arms race. According to air force officials, more than three hundred work stoppages had disrupted production at missile sites since 1956, many of them due to conflicts between industrial unions and the building trades. "We'll take some of the blame," Haggerty admitted, since he agreed that wildcat strikes were getting out of hand. Missile sites projects were usually located in remote, unpopulated areas, and Haggerty knew from experience that highly skilled, fiercely independent "boomers," the traveling mechanics who manned these projects, were not about to wait for union officers to show up to resolve a grievance.[31]

But management was equally responsible, Haggerty added. Missile technology was still in the experimental stages, and that in itself had invited delays. Because site construction and erection of support equipment began well before missile guidance and fuel systems had been finalized, installations that took weeks to complete were often ripped out and modified in accordance with the latest test results. This practice not only slowed down the missile program but also encouraged workers to believe that time was not of the essence.[32] And that being the case, Haggerty suggested that government representatives get together with contractors and labor leaders to find a workable solution. The Department's eighteen affiliates were trying to curb wildcat strikes, he said, but the situation required a more coordinated effort. In the past he had solved similar problems by advising contractors to employ "coordinators" with authority to settle grievances on the spot, a strategy that he thought might work well on missile site projects. He was also willing to investigate the possibility of a "no-strike" agreement, he told the *New York Times,* and, with the consent of the Executive Council, he began to review World War II–era stabilization agreements that had banned strikes and lockouts, but had given the building trades certain job guarantees. "We want to take a look at these wartime agreements," the EC reported late in 1960, "and then see how far the Defense Department wants to go toward a similar no-strike agreement now."[33]

A few months later the Department was ready to act. U.S. president John F. Kennedy had stressed the urgency of the missile program in his first State of the Union Address in January 1961, and the following month Neil Haggerty announced the Department's newly approved missile sites policy. Noting that the BCTD "has always responded vigorously and wholeheartedly when a President of the United States has sounded the call of national need," the new policy was designed to put an end to wildcat strikes. General presidents would now have to approve any and all plans for strikes, picketing, and work stoppages on missile sites, and state and local councils would be prohibited from aiding local unions on unauthorized strikes. The new policy also made it clear that the rules established by the National Joint Board for the Settlement of Jurisdictional Disputes, and the National Disputes Adjustment Plan (an arbitration plan recently negotiated with the NCA), would be strictly enforced. Reassured by these efforts, U.S. Secretary of Defense Robert McNamara offered his thanks to the Department. "This action reflects responsible leadership," he noted, "and sets forth an example of how free labor meets an urgent problem involving our nation's security. Your response is a tribute to our democratic institutions."[34]

But the Department's promise was not enough for Senator John McClellan, who was investigating missile site problems that spring. Alarmed by reports of skyrocketing payrolls, lax supervision by contractors and government agencies, and bitter jurisdictional disputes—including a walkout at a Denver missile site that got under way just as hearings began—Senator McClellan wanted to outlaw strikes at defense facilities and curb what he called the unions' "public-be-damned" attitude.[35] The Kennedy administration took a more moderate approach. Secretary of Labor Arthur Goldberg now sought and received no-strike, no-lockout pledges from unions and employers, paving the way for President Kennedy to establish, on May 26, 1961, the Missile Sites Labor Commission to devise policies for handling disputes without interrupting work. Chaired by Secretary Goldberg, the commission included representatives from labor, industry, and the public; Neil Haggerty, George Meany, and John Dunlop were all on the team. "This is fully consistent with the no-strike policy adopted February 16, 1961," Haggerty noted. "We are confident that each and every one of our unions will carry out that solemn pledge and do its utmost to promote . . . our nation's program to attain supremacy in space and in missile weapons."[36]

Certainly, there were union leaders and contractors who resented the Missile Sites Commission as an unnecessary government panel.[37] After all, the Department, national contractors, and the CIJC were all working to solve the problem in-house. At the same time, however, the Commission's local on-site committees were achieving remarkable results. "Work stoppages on the nation's missile bases have all but ended during the last two months," the *New York Times* reported in July, "as a result of recent Government, union, and management efforts." In fact, between June and December 1961 only one man-day was lost for every fifteen hundred worked. "This is a good record," Haggerty reported, "but it is not good enough. We must have no work stoppages on Missile Bases." UA president Peter T. Schoemann agreed. "If we do not wish to live out our trade union lives under constant threat of crippling legislation," he told his members, "we had better do some hard rethinking about what labor really does want at the missile and space sites."[38]

The situation was especially tense at Cape Canaveral, an intercontinental ballistic missile (ICBM) and space test center in Florida. Cape Canaveral workers had been involved in more than their share of work stoppages; in fact, they accounted for half of the man-days lost on all missile sites from 1956 to 1961. But the country and the construction industry could no longer stand for delays. Just days prior to establishing the Missile Sites Labor Commission, President Kennedy had challenged NASA to send a man to the moon, and thus work at Cape Canaveral became even more critical. The newly authorized local Missile Sites Labor Committee, which included representatives of the Department of Defense, NASA, the BCTD, and construction contractors—as well as industrial unions and the Federal Mediation and Conciliation Service—was finally able to achieve results. Unions and contractors worked out a project labor agreement that standardized hours of work and overtime premiums (but left it up to local unions to negotiate wages and fringe benefits) and included no-strike, no-slowdown provisions as well as machinery to settle jurisdictional disputes. "Perhaps the most tangible gain," the Department reported, "was the provision which will require all contractors—including those operating nonunion—to pay union standards of fringe benefits, or the equivalent in cash," a provision designed to safeguard job opportunities for building trades unions and their contractors. With a labor coordinator appointed to police the agreement, the BCTD, NASA, and the Department of Defense were satisfied. "This countdown took more than a year, but if the . . . Cape Canaveral Project Agreement goes into orbit successfully," the BCTD *Bulletin* predicted, "an unprecedented era of labor-management peace will help to erase the memory of past strife at this key defense post."[39]

Overall the Missile Sites Labor Commission got the job done; it later endorsed similar project labor agreements at Vandenberg Air Force Base in California, the Mississippi Test Facility at Pearl River, and at test sites in Colorado, Nebraska, and the Dakotas. "Labor-management problems which have received a great deal of publicity in the country," John Dunlop told a congressional committee in 1962, "do not today constitute serious problems." Between 1961 and 1963 more than fifty thousand workers were employed on U.S. missile and test sites, working some 1,176 man-days for every 1 day lost to disputes. In 1963 their work record was almost perfect—99.92 percent free of any work stoppages, according to Secretary of Labor Willard Wirtz.[40]

More important, he added, every single missile site was finished on time. "That is a proud record," Secretary Wirtz told the 1963 BCTD convention. "It did not come from the attack and counter-attack" that opponents waged in Congress and the newspapers, he added. "It came from reasonable, responsible men sitting down quietly together and it came basically through the exercise of private responsibility and with no exercise whatsoever of any government authority." Although neither Wirtz nor Dunlop mentioned it at the time, relationships fostered through the Construction Industry Joint Conference also helped. Thanks to Dunlop's wide sphere of influence, CIJC members were in daily contact with NASA, the U.S. Air Force, the Secretary of Labor, and the Defense Department, among other agencies, making it possible to resolve difficulties quickly. "This association . . . with top officials of Government," the Operating Engineers reported in 1964, "brought about a mutual realization of the desirability and need for project agreements on many of the missile and space sites."[41]

At the same time it strengthened ongoing efforts to promote contract construction to government agencies. For instance, when aerospace manufacturers, including Martin Marietta, lobbied hard to amend the Davis-Bacon Act so that the prevailing wage law would not apply to mechanical installation work—the latest move in the long-running jurisdictional conflict between building tradesmen and industrial workers—the CIJC launched a powerful defense. It coordinated statements presented by the unions, the BCTD, and the contractors associations, and demonstrated the economic value of skilled, all-around building tradesmen on technologically demanding jobs like missile site construction. "We do not believe . . . that companies like Martin Marietta could successfully complete [these] projects . . . without having employees as skilled as those which we employ," the National Electrical Contractors Association testified to Congress in 1962. "The work is difficult and . . . exacting." Contractors also reminded congressmen that it was building trades unions that made that skill available. "These unions serve as a source of qualified and trained individuals in the various skills required for any construction project," according to the NECA, and they "maintain apprenticeship programs under the aegis of government" to replenish their ranks.[42]

These arguments eventually satisfied Congress: The Davis-Bacon Act was not amended, and building trades unions kept control of their work. In fact, they did 95 percent of the work at Cape Canaveral, an impressive percentage particularly in the South.[43] But that very success raised important new criticisms that the Department would have to address: The building trades unions that supplied skilled workers to major government projects like Cape Canaveral tended to be all-white organizations. And the joint-apprenticeship programs that trained those workers could not qualify as equal employment opportunities either, since they recruited along family lines, a situation that was no longer tenable by the mid-1960s, when the civil rights movement was going strong. If building mechanics wanted to do government work, then their unions would have to broaden their membership. If they moved too slowly, as the Department soon learned, the federal government would be ready to step in and show them how.

Equal Opportunity and Affirmative Action

Building trades leaders had their complaints about the federal government; after all, the Department was still pushing Congress, in the 1960s, to pass the Situs Picketing Bill and restore rights lost through Taft-Hartley and the Denver decision. And international unions were still coming to terms with regulations imposed by the Landrum-Griffin Act that, on the one hand, increased expenditures for administrative and legal staff and, on the other, decreased international union influence over local union members.

But building mechanics could not complain about federal funding. Directly or indirectly, the federal government was responsible for the vast majority of heavy construction jobs, jobs that tended to go to union workers. A combination of Cold War defense programs and domestic improvements had bolstered the trades through hard times in the late 1950s and early 1960s. Appropriations for the Interstate Highway System, for instance, had totaled about $2.2 billion a year since 1956, and in 1957 Congress had authorized $352 million for the construction of atomic energy plants for civilian and military use. In 1959 the Housing Act had pumped $650 million into urban renewal projects, and when the law was renewed in 1961, the appropriation reached $2 billion. The 1961 Housing Act also made $500 million available to finance community facilities (including water, gas, and sewage systems), while the Area Redevelopment Act provided another $394 million to improve impoverished cities and rural areas. All these taxpayer-financed public works projects provided good union jobs for construction workers, jobs that only got better as the economy began to revive around 1964.[44]

There was a problem, however, that had been festering for decades, one that came to a head around the same time. Ever since the 1940s federal contracts had included a nondiscrimination clause, to ensure that all Americans, whatever their race or religion, had equal access to government-funded work. And ever since the 1950s the National Association for the Advancement of Colored People (NAACP) had been urging the President's Committee on Government Contracts to enforce that clause on construction work, and especially on apprenticeship programs certified by the U.S. Department of Labor. "These apprenticeship training programs are with very rare exception completely closed to qualified Negroes," noted Herbert Hill, labor secretary of the NAACP. "Because union membership is a condition of employment in the building trades industry," he explained, "the effect of trade union discrimination is to prevent Negro mechanics from working in jobs within the jurisdiction of . . . the Building Trades [Department] of the AFL-CIO."[45] When the President's Committee failed to act, since unions did not sign government contracts, the NAACP did not give up. In the summer of 1961 Congressman Adam Clayton Powell Jr., chairman of the House Committee on Education and Labor, took up the cause. The building trades unions "have repeatedly asked me to report the common situs picketing bill out of my committee," he told an NAACP meeting. But he would not act "until the building trade craft unions start practicing common equality for black workers," he now announced. "I will do every-thing in my power to prevent any legislation favorable to the craft unions from coming out of our committee until these craft unions get in step with democracy."[46]

Stunned by what he called "political blackmail," BCTD president Neil Haggerty vigorously denied Powell's accusation. "There is not a single Inter-national Union affiliated with the Building and Construction Trades Depart-ment which refuses to admit qualified Negro members either by Constitu-tional provision or by national policy." But he could not deny that "some of the affiliated local unions of these . . . international unions, in certain areas of this country, probably do exclude Negroes but they are doing so" in viola-tion of union policy. "The national leadership has made a great deal of progress by persuasion and education . . . to end such discrimination," Hag-gerty insisted, "and they intend to keep on doing so." But he also pointed out that their options were limited. Under the Landrum-Griffin Act, interna-tional unions could not "dictate" to local unions. "We can understand and share your concern over the disappointingly slow pace of integration," he wrote to Congressman Powell, "but it has progressed far more rapidly in the trade union field than at the official level."[47]

To some extent Haggerty had a point. Certain building trades unions, like the Bricklayers, Plasterers, Painters, and Laborers had a long history of ad-mitting black members; in fact, the Laborers had had black leaders from the start. And international union officers consistently opposed drawing the "color line" whenever the subject came up. When bricklayers in Florida wanted to organize segregated locals, in 1928, President Bowen had argued strongly against it. "You may . . . regard the Negro in whatever manner you please, dealing with him in his social relationships. But when the Negro goes on the wall he is a mechanic . . . doing a mechanic's work." A similar case arose in 1941, when twelve black electricians, who had trained at Hampton Institute, tried to join an IBEW local in Norfolk, Virginia. There was no "color bar," International president Ed Brown reminded local union mem-bers, and he hoped that "the local union would not vote against an American citizen applicant" on the basis of race but would make their decision "solely on the basis of competence."[48] Haggerty himself had a good record of trying to break down racial prejudice. As a leader of the California State Federation of Labor, he had sponsored and secured passage of legislation prohibiting discrimination in apprenticeship training in 1951, and had lobbied state leg-islators for years to establish a Fair Employment Practices Commission, which was finally achieved in 1959. So, in his view, there was no point in dis-missing the trades as essentially racist.[49]

But there was also no denying discrimination. Whatever an international officer's advice or action, local union members tended to keep to their own kind, a practice that was hardly unusual before the 1960s, when neighbor-hoods, schools, professions, and even churches were racially segregated. Trades that had developed in the late nineteenth century, like steam fitting, electrical installation, and sheet metal work had been dominated by white workers from the start, so in cities from Milwaukee to St. Louis, and from New York to Washington, D.C., local unions tended to be "lily" white, and the same was true of the Operating Engineers, Lathers, and Elevator Con-structors. Whether this reflected race prejudice or the building trades' gen-eral reluctance to expand their memberships and keep union jobs in the family, the result was the same: Although black Americans constituted 10 percent of the nation's workforce, they accounted for less than 1 percent of building trades apprentices, according to an NAACP study. In fact in Wash-ington, D.C., the nation's capital and headquarters of the AFL-CIO and the BCTD, the Bricklayers, Electrical Workers, Lathers, Plasterers, and Plumbers counted no black apprentices in 1961. And while the Carpenters counted one, it had taken this individual two years, and Congressman Powell's help, to break into the union.[50]

President John F. Kennedy had established the Committee on Equal Em-ployment Opportunity in March 1961, but it took collective action and media coverage to enforce the rules. By 1963 the Congress of Racial Equality (CORE) and the NAACP were picketing all-white construction crews in Cleveland, St. Louis, and Philadelphia, as well as New York City, Newark, New Jersey, and Washington, D.C. When black electricians and iron workers were denied jobs on federal construction sites in the nation's capital, the publicity was devastating. And when no skilled black workers were employed on a federal project at Howard University, a black institution, student pick-eters drew national attention. The crowning blow came when black skilled workers were shut out of a major school construction job in Philadelphia and a mass protest erupted. The following week, on June 4, 1963, President Kennedy pledged the government to end discrimination on federally fi-nanced construction projects, an announcement long overdue according to Herbert Hill. "After more than 20 years of negotiation and protest, the rate of progress for Negroes in the building and construction industry is negli-gible," he told Secretary of Labor Willard Wirtz. "It is less than token and is totally unacceptable."[51]

Strengthening his pledge, President Kennedy issued Executive Order 11114, charging contractors to take "affirmative action" on behalf of black employees and apprentices. At around the same time the BCTD adopted a policy statement on civil rights, but it did not adopt the protesters' point of view, or even the government's. "The daily dialogue in the press and by spokesmen of minority groups," the statement noted, "indicates a serious lack of knowledge of the facts." And so did the government's directive to enroll more black apprentices to make up for past discrimination. Department leaders recognized the government's duty to correct economic injustice, and they now pledged their "good faith to work toward that goal." The new policy urged local unions to accept qualified members and apprentices regardless of race, creed, color, or national origin, and to run hiring halls and referral systems accordingly. But they also pressed their point that economic realities, not discrimination, kept apprenticeship numbers low. The only way to increase opportunities for prospective black journeymen was to increase the number of jobs, the statement noted, since it was "totally unrealistic to train people . . . in greater numbers than can be reasonably employed." Moreover, since skill and craftsmanship were the union worker's stock in trade, potential apprentices would have to demonstrate that they were capable of learning the craft. "Accordingly," the Department concluded, "we do not intend to delegate to outsiders the right to decide the qualifications for entrance into the industry and union membership."[52]

Sharing the Department's fierce opposition to government regulation of apprenticeship training and government selection of apprentices, national contractor associations adopted a similar policy. And in July 1963 they joined with building trades unions in the Construction Industry Joint Conference to establish the Joint Committee on Equal Employment Opportunities. Chaired by BCTD president Neil Haggerty and Robert L. Higgins of the NECA, the joint committee was formed to implement the new civil rights policy and thereby avoid further government action. For instance, the committee urged local joint apprenticeship committees to review their programs and revise their apprenticeship lists to ensure equal opportunity for black applicants. They were also advised to establish an appeals board so that complaints could be reviewed and acted on as soon as they arose. Intending to consult informally with Secretary Wirtz and other government officials, the Equal Employment Opportunities Committee hoped to resolve local difficulties in places like St. Louis, Cleveland, Philadelphia, and New York City before government sanctions were imposed. But they also hoped to have some influence on shaping government policies. "Our problems are very real," President Haggerty had acknowledged from the start, but it would take frank negotiations between men of good-will, and not street demonstrations and executive orders, to effect real change in the building trades.[53]

If the Department expected the government to applaud the new policy, and permit the industry to solve its problems on its own terms, they were soon disappointed. Policy statements and good intentions were no longer enough, Secretary Wirtz told the 1963 BCTD convention, which met in New York City and was being picketed at the time. Wirtz made it clear that whenever he presented the Department's policy "as the honest statement of honorable men" to congressional committees or public meetings, he was universally booed. The Department could not expect much credit for its policy statement, he pointed out, as long as there were large building trades locals with no Negro members and no Negro names on apprenticeship lists, as there were in New York City and elsewhere. And there was no point in arguing, as many locals did, that qualified black applicants had failed to appear, especially if a union had a history of an all-white membership. It was also pointless to complain that the federal government had targeted the building trades unfairly, as President Haggerty and other building trades leaders contended. Of course there were industries and professions with worse records on race than the building trades, Wirtz acknowledged, but that was hardly a persuasive defense. "The only real question is whether prior practices of one kind or another," like the notorious father-son tradition in the building trades, "are to stand in the way of honoring [equal opportunity and fair employment practices]. . . . The judgment of the nation and of the trade union movement, is that this principle is paramount."[54]

Whether local unions and contractors accepted that judgment, however, was another question. Some local leaders, like Harry Van Arsdale Jr., president of New York City's IBEW Local 3, had decided early on that opening union ranks was the only practical action to take. For, as IBEW Secretary-Treasurer Joe Keenan had made clear, local unions had no real choice but to develop plans to recruit and train black workers, if they wanted to have any say in the matter. "You can stall along and stall along," Keenan noted in 1962, "but sooner or later the Government is going to hand out a mandate and then you will take what they give you." That same year Van Arsdale began working with contractors to expand the construction membership of Local 3: The union took in 1,020 new first-year apprentices, including 300 minority candidates. By 1966 minority apprentices accounted for about 15 percent of the local's apprenticeship program. "The significance of this event cannot be stated in strong enough terms," a researcher noted. "Its importance can be gauged by the fact that the U.S. Census of 1960 reported only 79 Negro electrical apprentices in the entire nation."[55]

But other local unions proved far more defensive, especially if members had suffered unemployment over the past few years or had waited a while for their own opportunity to join the union. Members who took it for granted that there was only so much work to go around deeply resented "outsiders"—be they government officials or minority demonstrators—telling them how to run their union. "Do you want to include or do you want to exclude?" that was the question as sheet metal worker George Andrucki saw it. His local union, Sheet Metal Workers Local 28 in New York City, was firmly on the exclusive side. When Congress passed the Civil Rights Act of 1964, which outlawed job discrimination, Local 28, in Andrucki's words, "flat out said that nobody would" comply. The attitude was, "we're going to fight you in every court in the land," he said. "And we did, and we lost in every court of the land. . . . Local 28 is a [legal] textbook case now, and I don't say that with any pride."[56]

The local union fight was strictly reactionary. According to Andrucki, "People that said 'let's follow the directive, let's take in . . . minority people,' they were immediately branded [as] some kind of liberal leftist pinko. . . . They were immediately demeaned. . . . There was no . . . logical debate. There was . . . emotional debate. . . . 'Nobody's going to tell us what to do. . . . This is our Union. . . . They're not taking mine away from me.' " It was unfortunate, he added, that "we didn't have a leadership that could say to us, 'Look, let's approach this in an intelligent way. We can't win with the Federal Government. So let's do it as painlessly as we can and let's get the best people that are out there.' " The membership would have done just that, he believed, had the leadership dealt with the issue directly instead of clouding it in legalities. "We didn't have that good, strong, progressive minded leadership. We suffered because of that."[57]

But by 1965 local options were limited: Keenan's prediction of government mandates had already come to pass. Following President Lyndon B. Johnson's Executive Order 11246, the Department of Labor had established the Office of Federal Contract Compliance which required all contractors and subcontractors on federally financed construction projects to demonstrate that they had taken affirmative action to ensure equal employment opportunities, including opportunities for training. At that point President Haggerty began working with the AFL-CIO's Civil Rights Department and with independent organizations like the A. Phillip Randolph Institute and the Workers' Defense League, to develop a plan to increase minority participation in skilled construction work. The "Outreach" programs that resulted were voluntary joint apprenticeship programs sponsored by the Workers Defense League, the Urban League, or local building trades councils, and funded by the Department of Labor. They were designed to identify promising candidates, persuade them of the benefits of apprenticeship training, and provide whatever tutoring or preparation was necessary for candidates to succeed in the trades. Making an effort to promote the program, local council members visited schools and churches, opened communications with local minority leaders, and used the media to advertise apprenticeships—a real break from the days when it took a family connection to learn how to get into the trades.[58]

These efforts impressed Secretary Wirtz as "an honest, sincere, and effective movement to meet this problem in the building trades." But they were not at all sufficient. "It isn't enough any longer to just not discriminate," he told delegates to the 1967 BCTD convention. Robert C. Weaver, U.S. Secretary of Housing and Urban Development, agreed. "The only criteria that the victims of discrimination have, the criteria by which you and I must judge progress, [are] the figures which show the present degree of minority participation in the Building Trade Unions." And those numbers were not impressive.[59] The Equal Employment Opportunities Commission reported that in 1967 black workers represented less than 1 percent of unionized electricians, plumbers, and elevator constructors; 1.6 percent of carpenters; 3.7 percent of painters; and 4 percent of operating engineers, totals far below the percentage black workers represented in the workforce.[60]

Under those circumstances, the federal government was taking a firmer stand on affirmative action. Racial tensions had exploded in cities throughout the country in the summer of 1967, forcing the federal government to act. Although nobody liked the idea of racial quotas, Secretary Wirtz admitted, there seemed to be no other choice. The Office of Federal Contract Compliance had recently set up numerical "timetables" for construction contractors in Cleveland and Philadelphia, where resistance to integration remained strong. And the Department of Labor was preparing to do the same for apprenticeship training programs, a move that undoubtedly influenced the BCTD's 1967 pledge to support affirmative action and to double international union efforts to recruit qualified minority apprentices and help those less qualified to meet apprenticeship standards. "If we want to remain free, if we want to keep our apprenticeship programs out of the hands of the federal government," UA president Peter T. Schoemann advised, "it is absolutely imperative that we institute affirmative action programs." He made his position clear: "The way to take the castor oil is take it in a big dose now."[61]

By February 1968 the Department had publicly promised to put some teeth into its recruitment policy. The *New York Times* clearly exaggerated when it reported that BCTD affiliates had "ordered" eighty-five hundred local unions to get behind the Outreach programs. But the results were nevertheless encouraging at least to Department leaders, if not to black activists who were taking to the streets in Pittsburgh and Chicago in 1969, demanding a greater presence in the building trades.[62] The number of cities participating in Outreach programs grew from forty-eight in 1967 to fifty-three in 1969, and in that time more than twenty-seven thousand applicants had been recruited and more than thirty-eight hundred had been indentured as apprentices. In Philadelphia, for instance, the Building Trades Council and the Negro Trade Union Leadership Council had used government funds to employ five black recruiters to visit schools, conduct interviews, select trainees, and prepare them to apply for apprenticeships: They conducted a six-week tutoring program with certified instructors, brought in business agents to acquaint recruits with the various crafts, and accompanied recruits to local union interviews and tests, all to ensure that they were treated fairly. As a result, eighty-three minority apprentices were indentured that year.[63]

By that time, however, the situation had changed dramatically. Although President Lyndon Johnson had dropped his program for minority timetables in 1968, after the proposed quota-based Philadelphia Plan was determined to be illegal, in 1969 President Richard M. Nixon had no such qualms. With skilled construction wages at dangerously high levels, and economists suggesting that the civil rights struggle could be used to resolve industry problems, President Nixon saw a good opportunity to kill two birds with one stone. Eager to succeed where his Democratic predecessor had failed, he now revived the Philadelphia Plan to establish quotas for minority hiring on federal construction projects, and the Department of Justice backed him up. Although black workers constituted 30 percent of Philadelphia's building trades workers overall, and 12 percent of the skilled building trades, Nixon's assistant secretary of labor Arthur Fletcher now set strict hiring goals for plumbers, sheet metal workers, electrical workers, iron workers, roofers, and elevator constructors, trades that included almost no black representatives at all. According to Fletcher, there were at least two thousand qualified minority craftsmen ready and willing to work in Philadelphia, and by his calculations contractors could hire one minority for every white craftsman without adversely impacting the existing workforce.[64]

The Philadelphia Building and Construction Trades Council denied Fletcher's assertion, pointing out that when the original Philadelphia Plan had been implemented at the U.S. Mint project the year before, those qualified minority craftsmen had failed to appear. Contractors had followed government rules and hired two electricians, despite their lack of training, but these "instant journeymen" had not been able to do the work. As the Council's business manager testified, "they stood around, basically incapable of participating in the responsibility of the work. The unionized black apprentice electricians who were working at less than the journeyman rate . . . were furious that they . . . knew more than these 'instant journeymen' but were being penalized by virtue of the fact that they were in a unionized program undergoing the necessary training. Financially they would have been temporarily better off had they been nonunion and . . . capitalized on the 'instant journeymen' concept of the Office of Federal Contract Compliance." Ultimately, the black apprentices learned the value of training: Within a few weeks the "instant journeymen" were fired for incompetence, proving to this business manager at least that the Philadelphia Plan, revised or not, "would at best provide for temporary work based on the duration of federal construction projects" but would not "provide the training for permanent careers." And he was certain that this was not what the black community wanted.[65]

But perhaps that was the point. With the postwar building boom approaching its peak in the late 1960s, unemployment rates were dangerously low from a business point of view, making building trades control over skilled manpower an employer's worst nightmare, as one business consultant reported. The sharp rise in wages and construction costs between 1965 and 1970 kept building trades unions and their training programs in the headlines. Apprenticeship systems were archaic, *Fortune* magazine charged in 1968, and their requirements were "rigid and often unnecessary," the *New York Times* added. They not only prevented new men from entering the building trades in numbers sufficient to expand the labor supply, critics noted, but prevented the timely replacement of journeymen who died or retired from the workforce and thus kept wage rates artificially high. "There is overwhelming evidence," *Fortune* asserted, "that if the present practices and trends continue, building contractors may be physically unable to meet the demand, let alone maintain any semblance of price stability."[66]

Government officials apparently agreed, marking a real shift in opinion since 1967. In that year similar complaints against apprenticeship standards had been raised with Secretary of Labor Willard Wirtz when plans were being made to launch the Model Cities urban renewal project. By law, local residents would have to be employed on the project, and Wirtz had been lobbied to create "'short training' programs" for a new category of "rehabilitative craftsmen" who would be paid a special rate and assigned to do "various kinds of things." At the time Wirtz refused to comply, since he thought the building trades did a good job of training. But two years later Assistant Secretary of Labor Arthur Fletcher took a very different stance. A former professional football player, and the highest-ranking black member of the Nixon administration, Fletcher believed that minority workers offered an answer to industry problems and he wanted to put them to work as soon as he possibly could. When he addressed the National Association of Manufacturers' Congress of American Industry in 1969, and presented a plan to cut construction costs, he made it clear that the best place to begin was to eliminate the "nonsense requirements" of apprenticeship. And in 1970 he advocated suspending the Davis-Bacon Act to open up construction jobs to minority workers, putting him firmly on the side of nonunion contractors, as far as union leaders were concerned.[67]

Whatever his motives, Fletcher's plans to increase the number of minority workers, and the building trades workforce overall, reflected the popular belief that demand for skilled workers would increase steadily over the next decade. When Fletcher developed the revised Philadelphia Plan, for instance, he took it for granted that the industry would continue to grow in the 1970s at the same rate that it had been growing since 1965, and he was certainly not alone. "There will be plenty of jobs for everyone," *Fortune* magazine noted late in 1969, when it congratulated black activists for challenging "monopoly power" in building trades unions. After all, the President's Committee on

Urban Housing had recently estimated that the country would need two million more skilled workers by 1975, a number that could only be reached, one
government official noted, by recruiting unemployed black workers, increasing productivity through mass production techniques, and shortening
apprenticeship and training programs.[68]

Building trades leaders were used to hearing such lofty predictions, and
they were also used to seeing them blown apart. Men like President Haggerty, who had been involved with the industry for more than fifty years,
knew from hard experience that booms did not last forever. Some ten thousand minority apprentices had joined the building trades by 1971, a 364 percent increase over six years. But by that time their chances of attaining steady
work and middle-class living standards were slim: The building industry
boom was already going bust, and there was not enough work to go around.
In fact, by 1975 the government's optimistic predictions had fallen flat. That
year there were fewer construction workers employed than there had been in
1969, and fewer good union jobs for skilled construction workers.[69]

PART THREE

REORGANIZING THE FUTURE

For many employers as well as for many workers, closed-shop unionism means compulsion; for one, to negotiate, and the other, to join. It also has a tendency to lose its vital force, to cease activities which in the past gave it life, to forget organization campaigns. . . . As a result of this situation there is undoubtedly much truth in the contention that under the open shop unionism would have to redirect its energies to more constructive ends.

—William Haber, *Industrial Relations in the Building Industry*

From Boom to Bust: Wage Spirals, the Business Roundtable, and Open-Shop Construction

> History can be a great teacher. It can also be a lousy crutch. It is not good enough to say, "But we've always done it that way." The world has changed. It's dynamic. It continues to change and we must change with it.
> —BCTD President Robert Georgine, 1983

When Neil Haggerty first took over as BCTD president, in the early 1960s, the nation was on a postwar high. Progress seemed inevitable. President John F. Kennedy embodied the confidence of a new generation; the Reverend Martin Luther King Jr., the promise of equal opportunity and racial equality; and astronaut John Glenn, the power and possibilities of American ingenuity and national resolve. But by the time Haggerty announced his retirement, in the spring of 1971, confidence had given way to despair. Kennedy and King had been brutally murdered. The United States was embroiled in a controversial and costly war in Vietnam. And racial, class, and generational tensions were exploding in the streets, on college campuses, and on picket lines. Even the remarkable achievement of landing a man on the moon, in 1969, could not counter the impression that the country was out of control.[1]

Caught up in the chaos and conflicts of the times, building trades unions were mired in controversy. If their members performed high-quality work that made projects like the Kennedy Space Center and the moon landing possible, their history of protecting their own at all costs overshadowed the value of skill. Stereotyped as overpaid, underworked, racist "hardhats" whose main goal was to keep their numbers small, construction workers were dismissed as "the rudest, crudest, and most sexist of all workers," one historian reported. And despite the fact that working-class sons did much of the fighting in Vietnam, construction workers were also portrayed as mindless patriots and warmongers, especially after a violent clash with antiwar demonstrators in the spring of 1970. That New York City's Building and Construction Trades Council publicly supported the invasion of Cambodia, encouraging a grateful President Richard M. Nixon to later name Council president Peter J. Brennan as U.S. Secretary of Labor, further strengthened the militantly conservative image of the building trades.[2]

On the job site, however, they were radicals. Representing about 55 percent of full-time construction workers in the mid-1960s, building trades unions were "fat and sassy," according to one government official: Construction was booming, unemployment was at a record low, and the government had not imposed wage-price controls because the war in Vietnam was an undeclared war. These circumstances were tailor-made to boost construction wages and benefits. In fact, when the President's Council of Economic Advisors suggested a voluntary wage cap in the mid-1960s, limiting annual increases to 3.2 percent, there were no union volunteers. "It was turned down cold," a BCTD spokesman reported. "It's suicide," another added, "for any national union officer to tell any local union official he can't ask for more than a certain amount," and the record bore him out: Average wage settlements (including benefits) rose steadily from 6.4 percent in 1966 to 14 percent in 1969, alarming figures to contractors, industrialists, and potential home buyers alike.[3]

Although BCTD officers blamed sky-high inflation and a rising cost of living for the sharp rise in union wage rates, President Nixon took the opposite view. Elected in 1968 to bring the nation back on track, he blamed "monopolistic" local unions and strike-happy construction workers for the wage-price spiral that now threatened the nation's economy. To make his point, in the fall of 1969 he ordered a 75 percent cutback in federal construction, a move that was inevitable according to the *New York Times*. "High interest rates and profiteering in land have contributed to pushing up the cost of highways, post offices and other public projects," the paper conceded. "But the biggest push has come from new labor agreements" that not only called for three-year increases in wages and fringe benefits, on top of already healthy rates, but kept "intact the archaic rules limiting productivity in the building trades and the rigid admissions tests through which the unions maintain a permanent artificial scarcity of skilled manpower, and thus feast on high-premium overtime rates."[4]

With the construction industry averaging 932 work stoppages a year between 1966 and 1969, according to the Bureau of Labor Statistics, President Nixon was determined to stablize wages and cut down on strikes. In 1969 he established the Construction Industry Collective Bargaining Commission (CICBC), a tripartite board to address ongoing problems (including training, productivity, and localized bargaining) and to devise voluntary procedures to settle contract disputes. Based on a plan developed by John Dunlop, at the request of Secretary of Labor George Schultz, the twelve-man CICBC included representatives from labor, industry, and the public: Neil Haggerty, Peter Schoemann (UA), Maurice Hutcheson (UBCJA), and Hunter Wharton (IUOE) were all members, as was Dunlop, who represented the public.[5]

The CICBC plan was to increase the size and quality of the construction workforce, extend the working season, involve national unions and contractor associations in local contract negotiations and in strike and lockout decisions, and encourage the development of wide-area, multi-employer bargaining units to keep strong local unions in line and put an end to what critics called "whipsawing," the tendency of the trades to strike one after another. "If one [trade] got a raise for so much, the other would say, 'Well we're better than they are, so we want double,'" iron worker Joseph Maloney recalled. And sheet metal worker George Andrucki agreed. "One of the most important things, in our eyes," Andrucki explained, "was keeping up with the steam fitters instead of thinking about the . . . industry as a whole." At the same time, national "no-strike" agreements tended to bolster local strike activity, an unintended consequence to be sure: Because union members could usually find work with large NCA contractors, they did not hesitate to strike local contractors. "The mere fact that a national [no-strike] agreement holder is working in an area where negotiations are taking place," as one specialty contractor explained, "can transform a normally reasonable business agent into a demanding and belligerent negotiator."[6]

The CICBC intended to change that outlook, but it was always easier to set goals and outline policies than it was to achieve results, especially since the Commission had no enforcement powers and there was no consensus on how to proceed. While CICBC members argued the pros and cons of establishing a voluntary wage board, the construction industry counted more than one thousand strikes in 1970, and negotiated wage increases averaged 17 percent—a rise that struck even longtime union supporters as outrageous. "Rank-and-file union members have been willing to support lengthy strikes, and to sustain them until their demands are met," economist Daniel Quinn Mills reported, and union leadership "facing reelection and a militant membership . . . have been unwilling to counsel moderation." But that strategy was doomed to fail, President Haggerty warned the trades. If these "devastating" strikes continued, he noted in his Labor Day address, "our employers will soon turn to other sources for their labor supply." The handwriting was on the wall, he added. "Hundreds of millions of dollars of work" had already been lost to nonunion contractors that year.[7]

With more than a thousand construction agreements due to expire in the spring of 1971, it was time for drastic action. In February President Nixon suspended the Davis-Bacon Act as well as state prevailing wage laws. According to Secretary of Labor James D. Hodgson, the suspension was designed to attract union attention "the way a two-by-four gets the attention of a mule." But the president's action came as no surprise to the BCTD. In fact, in a joint meeting of contractors and major building trades presidents, John Dunlop had brokered an agreement to suspend the Davis-Bacon Act and then institute government controls. Thus, on March 29, President Nixon not only reinstated the prevailing wage law, but he also replaced the moribund CICBC with the Construction Industry Stabilization Commission (CISC), a twelve-man tripartite board authorized to establish national craft disputes boards that would review locally negotiated contract settlements, link wage increases to productivity, and, ideally, hold increases to around 6 percent. "As good Americans, we will abide by [the order]," President Haggerty noted. "We have no choice but to obey." Like other building trades leaders, however, he believed that the construction industry was being targeted unfairly. As sheet metal worker Edward J. Carlough told the *Wall Street Journal,* the plan was intolerable and unacceptable. "I say in all candor," he added, "that we will not buy 6 percent."[8]

Despite initial objections, which did not let up until other industries were also subject to controls a few months later, the CISC proved largely successful according to Department leaders and union contractors. "The stabilization program has benefited our industry," an AGC spokesman attested, "in that it has eliminated most of the inequities between crafts in various areas of the country, and has brought more realistic collective bargaining than has been present in a long time." The craft boards (which were funded by unions and contractor associations, not the government) improved communications between local and national entities, cut the percentage of time lost to strikes by 60 percent in 1971, and kept wage increases to an average of 11 percent that year and 6.5 percent in 1972. In the process, both labor and management in various industry branches—building, highway, and heavy construction—got a broader sense of how the industry worked as a whole, and how work rules that suited commercial building, for instance, wreaked economic havoc on industrial or highway projects. To be sure, neither contractors nor BCTD officers welcomed government interference. "To say that . . . we dislike the burden of wage controls and our required expenditure of money and manpower," as carpenter and CISC member William Siddell put it, "is a drastic understatement."[9]

But, like the Wage Adjustment Board during the Second World War, the government-imposed wage board now strengthened the power of national officers to rein in local union demands and clean up costly "area practices," power they deemed essential to preserve collective bargaining. For while the Nixon administration was strengthening its hand in the construction industry, contractors and industrialists were joining forces to shore up their power: Large corporations like U.S. Steel and Dow Chemical had already demonstrated the effectiveness of "taking a strike," or shutting down production, when local unions struck local contractors, and the idea was catching on. Nor was the timing coincidental. In fact, some of Nixon's strongest supporters on construction issues were founding members of the Construction Users Anti-Inflation Roundtable. This powerful group of contractors and industrialists initially organized in order to reform the collective-bargaining system so that owners would get more for their construction dollars, but it ended up trying to subvert that system entirely.[10]

The Rise of the Roundtable

As construction wages and benefits escalated rapidly between 1968 and 1970, putting pressure on manufacturing workers to increase their wages accordingly, a group of contractors, construction executives, and industrialists were ready for a showdown. Fed up with construction labor relations that were "chaotic at best" if not "despotic or unbelievable," they began meeting in 1968 first under the auspices of the Associated General Contractors and then the U.S. Chamber of Commerce—which was headed by construction executive Winton Blount, soon to join the Nixon administration as postmaster general. Union and nonunion contractors, as well as representatives of major construction users including U.S. Steel, Monsanto, and the Ford Motor Company, debated the value of hiring halls, national agreements, and protective labor laws like Davis-Bacon and Norris-LaGuardia (which had restricted the use of injunctions in labor disputes since the 1930s). "Various proposals to bring about a radical reduction in the power of organized labor are being put forward," *The Constructor* reported. "Fundamental in all of them is a conviction that the right of the employer to run his own business must be reaffirmed."[11]

Organized as the Construction Users Anti-Inflation Roundtable (CUAIR) in 1969, the group was determined to forge an alliance between contractors and owners to strengthen the contractors' bargaining power. "Our objectives are clear and reasonably easy to define," noted Robert Gunness, president of Standard Oil, Indiana. "Specifically, we intend to fight forcefully against unreasonable construction costs, particularly as created by spiraling labor wage rates. Broadly we want to provide a forum . . . to keep construction users well informed about the labor problems that contractors face daily, and as a result to make the users a more effective influence in resolving conflicts." Once users understood that it was worthwhile, in the long run, to shut down production if necessary to undermine local power, contractors could increase productivity, control wage rates, and thereby preserve the collective-bargaining process. For after all, as AGC contractor John Healy put it, the point was to "save the unions from themselves."[12]

But was that the point? M. R. Lefkoe, a business reporter, did not think so. Hired by some Roundtable supporters to analyze construction labor problems, he favored restructuring the industry entirely. His 1970 book, *The Crisis in Construction,* was subtitled "There *Is* an Answer," and the answer was to abolish the craft system. Small-sized firms unable or unwilling to train employees were the key to union strength in the industry, he argued, and conflicting interests between general and specialty contractors also boosted union power. But if those firms were willing to merge to form strong, well-capitalized corporations able to hire and train their own workforce, he countered, they would be in a stronger position to make the kind of changes profitable industry required. Once craft unions lost control of skilled manpower, contractors could abolish jurisdictional rules and the apprenticeship programs that supported them. "If all the restrictions were removed," Lefkoe advised, "there is no question but that undreamed-of methods, materials, and equipment would be discovered and put into use very quickly." No doubt union leaders would protest, he added, but there would be nothing much they could do, once contractors had all the men they needed on their payrolls, including truck drivers to deliver materials. And because these contractors would be offering year-round employment, Lefkoe predicted, complaints would soon subside. "It . . . is likely that a great many skilled craftsmen who carry union cards would be willing to renounce their union membership," he insisted, "in return for year-round employment at union wage rates."[13]

Lefkoe's analysis caused quite a stir. But it was considered more of a wake-up call for the building trades than a practical plan for industrial action. Frank Bonadio, who replaced Neil Haggerty as BCTD president in the spring of 1971, heard that call loud and clear. Department secretary-treasurer since 1954, and a man well versed in all sides of the industry, he was fully aware that union construction and union apprenticeship training were under fire. His own hometown, Baltimore, was the birthplace of the rabidly anti-union Associated Builders and Contractors (ABC), and its influence was growing: By 1971 nonunion firms were doing 32 percent of nonresidential industrial construction, twice the percentage they had claimed in 1969. "There has always been nonunion competition," Bonadio told the 1973 BCTD convention, "but it now appears to be of increasing proportions. Companies like

Brown & Root and Daniels Construction appear to be in a position to outbid some of our union contractors no matter how well established."[14]

But in 1973 Bonadio was still confident that the BCTD and the Construction Industry Stabilization Commission could meet the challenge head on. Craft boards, project labor agreements, a new national productivity pact with NCA contractors, and a new jurisdictional disputes board—which had taken eighteen months to negotiate and imposed financial penalties on unions violating board decisions—all promised to strengthen union construction. But only as long as local unions agreed to change their ways, Bonadio warned. "The relationship between the union contractor and the union should not be the same as that between a bull and a toreador," he insisted. "Labor and management have a mutual interest in securing job opportunities, and appropriate action must be taken to place the union contractor in a position to compete effectively," a lesson he believed that building trades unions should have learned by now.[15]

John Dunlop, addressing the same convention, seemed to share his conviction. "Two [or] three years ago I would have said to you that collective bargaining was in extremely deep trouble in this industry," Dunlop told the delegates, but "today the industry is better off, collective bargaining is better off." Working together on the CISC craft boards, contractors and union leaders had learned the value of coordinated bargaining, acknowledging that "the settlements of one branch of the industry have an effect upon the settlements of another, and that one branch of the industry, while . . . it has a right to maintain its autonomy . . . cannot but recognize that we live in an interdependent industry." As long as the building trades acted with this interdependence in mind, forgoing the "whipsawing" and "me, too" bargaining that priced union labor out of the market, the economic health of union construction would improve, he believed. "There are many in our country who would like to see the dismantling of [union construction] . . . who would like to see the industry become one in which collective bargaining did not play anywhere near the role that it has historically," he added frankly. That being the case, Dunlop impressed upon the delegates the importance of working cooperatively "with the employers and the government" to expand the workforce, improve dispute settlement plans, and modernize the bargaining process to reflect the practical economics of the industry.[16]

At the time conditions seemed promising. With wage increases averaging 5.5 percent in 1973, and the number of strikes down significantly, the Construction Industry Stabilization Commission had apparently redeemed the industry. Even President Nixon agreed that construction was no longer "sick," as he told the BCTD legislative conference that year. When the Commission expired in April 1974, however—just a few months before President Nixon resigned his office in the wake of the Watergate scandal—relapse seemed imminent. Local unions picked up where they had left off in 1971, engaging in what *Business Week* called "unusually militant negotiating." The number of strikes increased 60 percent over the 1973 total, and union wage rates began to rise, too. Settlements, including wages and fringe benefits, rose an average of 9.2 percent over the life of the contract, and union construction was once again at the center of a public storm. That the cost of living rose a full 12 percent that year, as BCTD officers pointed out, did little to alter public opinion.[17]

Significant as these increases were, they were not the Department's biggest problem. For by the time the CISC had expired, the construction boom had gone bust. Between 1973 and 1974 the housing industry had collapsed, electric utilities had curtailed expansion, heavy and highway construction had dried up, and commercial building had dropped dramatically. The only thing going up in construction was the unemployment rate, which reached 22 percent by 1975. And that proved to be the real crisis in construction for the building trades.[18]

The Georgine Administration

Although Frank Bonadio served as BCTD secretary-treasurer for more than sixteen years, "Bonnie," as he was known to his friends, served only three years as BCTD president. On his brief watch the Department established the Impartial Jurisdictional Disputes Board, negotiated an important project labor agreement to construct the Trans-Alaska Pipeline, and laid the groundwork for the BCTD's Research Department which began hiring staff in 1974 to work on issues like pension reform, occupational health and safety, and common situs picketing. But as president, Bonadio had also witnessed the increasing political influence of the Construction Users Roundtable (which had merged with the Business Roundtable in 1972), the alarming rise of "double-breasted" union/nonunion firms (which had been sanctioned by the NLRB in 1973 and allowed contractors to use building trades' hiring halls when they needed skilled men to meet a tight deadline, and to subcontract work out to nonunion shops when they did not), and the imminent threat of economic recession in 1974. Convinced that it was time to pass the torch to a younger generation of construction leaders better able to handle the stress, Bonadio resigned his post in the spring of 1974, and the Executive Council tapped secretary-treasurer Robert A. Georgine to succeed him. The following year Joseph F. Maloney, general organizer for the Iron Workers—and a veteran of some very tough fights to modernize collective-bargaining agreements and open local union doors to minority members—was elected secretary-treasurer.[19]

Just forty-one years old when he took over as president, Georgine was already well known in the industry. He had first drawn attention at the national level in the 1960s, when he represented the Lathers in a long-running jurisdictional dispute with the Carpenters; although the Lathers ultimately lost the case, Georgine had distinguished himself as a forceful speaker with an agile mind who could marshal evidence skillfully and argue his case diplomatically. And he was just as impressive on the job site. A colleague remembered a particular case, in Washington, D.C., in the early 1960s, when a jurisdictional fight became personal. "The other guy towered over him. He came from a much larger union. And the contractor didn't appreciate Bob barging in. But Bob wouldn't back down. He used cool logic and his firm diplomatic skills to win his point." A union activist with an open mind, as one journalist described him, Georgine had the ability to "get people to get along," another colleague pointed out. He could be tough, if that's what the situation called for, or tactful, whatever it took to bring people around to his point of view. The Department would put this skill to good use for almost thirty years.[20]

Georgine had learned the practical arts of compromise and coalition building in his early years with the Chicago Lathers. "People don't realize it but a labor union, particularly a construction union, really is the embodiment of democracy, people speaking for what they want and believe whether it's right or wrong. If it's what they want they don't hesitate they just say it." But he learned early on that "like anything else, one voice can't do anything. The ability to get guys to see things your way determined whether or not you were going to be successful. . . . [But] how do you convince the majority? . . . By getting around talking to everybody, and getting enough groups, making a few compromises here and there." As he explained, "It all boils down to just good common sense and the ability to . . . suppress your own ego so that you . . . understand what the objections are to whatever it is you want, analyze [those objections] and see what it takes to either modify what you want, or what you have to do to get [others] to see it as in their own best interest. You have to do that, but you can't do it alone. You have to convince others to feel that way. And when you get that, when you get a few to become apostles . . . and you keep doing that . . . then nobody can stop you."[21]

Georgine got a chance to test those skills on the national stage almost as soon as he took office. Construction activity had dropped 13 percent between 1973 and 1974, and construction unemployment rates were twice as high as the national average; in fact, in some major cities more than half the available carpenters, bricklayers, iron workers, and laborers could not find jobs. "The plain, simple, unvarnished fact is that we are fighting for our lives—our economic and social existence," Georgine told Department members in 1975. "Not even in the darkest depression days of the early nineteen-thirties has the construction industry been in the condition of disaster that it is today." Although he blamed the Federal Reserve Board's tight money policy for the collapse of the industry, he was not looking for scapegoats. "The main issue . . . is not to recount the woes we have or who or what brought them on us," he told delegates to the 1975 BCTD convention. "Our task is to . . . devise means of escape from the economic swamp in which we are expiring." And in his estimation one of the quickest routes out of the mire was through labor legislation; namely, passage of the Equal Treatment of Craft and Industrial Workers Bill, also known as the Common Situs Picketing Bill.[22]

The BCTD had been trying to enact situs picketing legislation ever since the U.S. Supreme Court's 1951 Denver decision had ruled that contractors on a construction site were entirely separate entities with separate labor policies, a ruling that prohibited unions from picketing general contractors who hired nonunion subcontractors. From the Department's point of view, the Denver decision discriminated against construction workers, since industrial workers were permitted by law to picket factory sites. Situs picketing legislation, therefore, would give building trades unions the same rights that other unions enjoyed, a sentiment endorsed by every president since Harry Truman, according to the *New York Times*. Although the Denver decision had never been a pressing issue in highly organized cities like New York and Chicago, Georgine explained, "the building trades had made it their 'cause celebre.' Every year they'd make a really big push to get it changed [but] in all that period of time . . . they never got it out of committee. And every congressman, particularly Democrats, used it," he added. "The Democrats would say, 'We're for situs. That's the first thing we're going to do.' " But the issue was basically a fund raiser as far as politicians were concerned: Candidates would make a speech at a union meaning, collect their campaign contributions, and then let the issue die until the next election cycle.[23]

The situation was looking up in 1975 because President Gerald Ford seemed genuinely interested in getting situs picketing legislation passed. "I had made a deal with Jerry Ford, we were pretty good friends," Georgine remembered. "He agreed that if we passed [situs picketing], he would sign it." Observers took it for granted that Ford's newly appointed secretary of labor, John Dunlop, had initiated the legislation, making good use of his "disarmingly low-key, almost professorial" demeanor, as the papers put it, to slip it by the president. But that was not the case. In fact, it was Ford who told Dunlop that he was prepared to support the legislation, as he wanted the building trades' vote in the upcoming presidential election, a decision that took Secretary Dunlop by surprise. "President Ford had told me that he had served in the House for 25 years and knew the legislation well. He asked me to support it," Dunlop recalled. "The issue was not my idea."[24]

With the help of a host of labor lawyers, committee staffers, and fellow union leaders, Georgine worked overtime to build up congressional support while Secretary Dunlop focused on crafting legislation that White House policy makers could endorse. "John was supersensitive to the needs of labor on the one side and the needs of the community on the other side," Georgine pointed out, "and wasn't a big fan of situs picketing . . . [except perhaps] in a philosophical way." So in order to make the bill more acceptable, "we had to do a lot of cleaning up in the legislation," Georgine noted. Because employers feared that local unions would use situs picketing as a license to strike and drive up costs, Dunlop added an amendment that required national union approval of situs picketing action. And at the request of President Ford, who knew that the legislation was controversial, Dunlop also drew up a companion bill (which eventually became Title II of the situs bill) to restructure collective bargaining in the construction industry. "I revised the legislation to provide for a national machinery, analogous to the jurisdictional machinery, which would handle all disputes in the industry, contract disputes as well as secondary boycott issues. . . . The effect would be to make the industry strike free," Dunlop explained. But even that was not enough for opponents. The Associated General Contractors (whose membership was split between union and nonunion contractors and faced some serious internal problems of its own) thought that the plan did not go far enough to eliminate strikes, while the Business Roundtable thought that it threatened the very basis of free enterprise. "You're looking at a piece of the new philosophy of national planning," the Roundtable's Roger Blough complained, "no question about it."[25]

In the end, all that work and all that compromise came to nothing. "We had passed it in the House, we had passed it in the Senate, and then they had to go back and forth in the two labor committees, and we had a fight in the Senate on the report, we had a filibuster that lasted forever and we beat it," Georgine recalled. "We were there till the wee hours of the morning every night, but we did our job and we got it done, and Jerry [Ford] helped." But when the legislation finally got to the president's desk, the deal had fallen through. The National Right to Work Committee, which took credit for the two-week filibuster that almost killed situs picketing in the Senate, had not given up. With the help of Senator Paul Fannin, who had mobilized two hundred thousand major Republican contributors, Right-to-Work supporters flooded the White House with seven hundred thousand postcards and letters urging Ford to veto the bill.[26]

When the president called Georgine to his office, a few nights before Christmas, the BCTD president was not particularly worried. "In my life, you give your word, you keep it," he explained. But as soon as he shook the president's hand, "I knew I was dead. He was like a wet fish." A group of state party chairman had told Ford that day that they would support Ronald Reagan for president if Ford signed the legislation. "So we talked," Georgine remembered. "I said, 'Mr. President . . . if you don't sign situs, you're not going to be the next president of the United States,' and he said, 'Bobby, if I do sign it I won't get nominated.' We talked some more. I ended up, I shook his hand, I said, 'Jerry I know in the final analysis you're going to do the right thing'—I was trying to hang a guilt trip on him—so I left, he went to Vail, and he vetoed it in Vail. Unfortunately, it was just the system, you know. But we survived."[27]

Angered by the president's double cross, building trades leaders quickly resigned from the administration's voluntary Collective Bargaining Committee in Construction that President Ford had established in April to facilitate coordinated bargaining. And Secretary of Labor Dunlop, who had chaired and championed the committee, resigned his office as well, citing fears that government, labor, and management no longer shared "the confidence and trust" necessary to move forward.[28]

But the Department did not give up hope for passing situs picketing legislation. In fact, after organized labor helped to defeat Ford in the 1976 election and President Jimmy Carter pledged to sign the legislation if it passed, Georgine and his troops were back at work. Focusing full attention on the Senate, and presuming that past pledges from the House still held, Georgine was confident that he had the votes in 1977, and Capitol Hill observers agreed, according to the *New York Times*. But if Georgine believed that the Department had persuaded a majority that situs picketing legislation would merely restore equal rights to construction workers, many employers vehemently disagreed. The point of situs picketing was to "unionize all construction," an AGC spokesman attested. The trades "would rather liquidate competition than . . . assert real leadership to end restrictive work practices and unrealistic wage demands that have . . . caused the general contractor and the American public to seek [nonunion] economic alternatives." Representative Mickey Edwards, a Republican from Oklahoma, agreed. "Calling this a bill for equal treatment of workers," he told the *New York Times*, "is like calling a pork chop a salami in order to sell it at a delicatessen."[29]

Apparently he was not alone. When the bill came to a vote in the House of Representatives in March, a coalition of anti-union Republicans and Democrats soundly defeated it. "With the entire labor movement dutifully marching lockstep behind the building trades," the *New Republic* reported, "common situs came to the floor and labor found itself outlobbied, outorganized, outsmarted and outnumbered." Critics inside and outside the labor movement now chided the Department's arrogance. "The building trades didn't do their homework," charged Sol Chaikin, president of the International Ladies' Garment Workers' Union. "They didn't touch base with the people whose votes they were counting on. The Right to Work Committee and the

Associated General Contractors did the job of arousing public sentiment that we of labor should have been doing." Worse yet, the *New Republic* added, the defeat had further undermined the credibility of the labor movement, confirming the growing impression that "big labor" had lost its "clout" in the nation's capital.[30]

Well aware of the criticism, Georgine made it clear that "I am not going to alibi," as he told the 1977 BCTD convention. "But I want to tell you, quite frankly, that much of that criticism is . . . hogwash. . . . The Building and Construction Trades Department and its affiliated unions were never overconfident." If they were guilty of anything, he said, it was taking politicians at their word: Eighty-eight Democrats had ignored their party's platform and their personal pledges to support situs picketing. "It is true," he conceded, that "we spent more time and energy talking with Congressmen who were either undecided or opposed to situs picketing than we did with those who had assured us, as they accepted our campaign support, that they were with us all the way." But no matter how the newspapers tried to spin the political story, there was no good reason to count the building trades out yet. In fact, nearly all the recommendations made by the Department's 1977 legislative conference, concerning energy, housing, public works, transportation, and pensions, he pointed out, had been adopted. "If organized labor in general— and the building trades in particular—are just paper tigers," Georgine wanted to know, "how do you account for the fact that the Building and Construction Trades Department helped shape the Employment Retirement Income Security Act of 1974, so that it would recognize the special needs of collectively-bargained multi-employer funds?"[31]

Urging delegates to adopt a new political strategy to defeat opponents in Congress, particularly so-called friends who "took but never gave," Georgine also proposed a new organizing strategy: a department division "staffed by trained, knowledgeable building tradesmen" to coordinate local campaigns to organize the unorganized. If construction unions could not effectively picket open-shop contractors, then they would have to organize nonunion workers, many of whom, he pointed out, were union men in search of a job.[32]

"Do you think that we would be faced with the growth of the open shop if it were not for the lack of jobs in the construction industry?" Georgine asked the delegates. "Not on your life. Because of the depression, a nonunion contractor, not restricted by collective bargaining has a competitive edge. He can offer less than union wages, he can work people at different wages, he can attract highly skilled union craftsmen, if that craftsman has been out of work long enough and his family is suffering. When times are tough, as they are now in construction, union men who haven't worked for months and months . . . put their cards in their pockets or in their shoes, and they go to work nonunion." And once that occurred, Georgine noted, "the worker deals a devastating blow to the economic well-being of all workers. . . . He must then work under whatever conditions and wages or benefits that his boss unilaterally decides to give him." Persuading delegates to raise the per capita tax to fund a multi-craft organizing campaign, he made it clear that it was time to "educate the construction workers concerning the benefits of belonging to a union. We have to show them that their own long-term best interests lie with organized labor."[33]

The task would prove monumental. For as one former business agent noted in 1977, "Zero growth is still the philosophy of the average local union member." Experience had taught him that "the quickest way for a nonunion contractor to get rid of a B.A. today if approached to 'go union' is to say 'OK if you'll take my 10 (or my 15) men into your local.' Any B.A. who will show up at a local union meeting with 10 or 15 prospective new members, would certainly not survive the next union election." "We liked our little haven of happiness," as another business agent explained, "and didn't care to share it with too many people."[34]

By that time, however, those local "havens of happiness" were limited to midwestern or northeastern city centers. In the suburbs outside those well-organized cities, nonunion residential and small commercial construction flourished. And in the South and Southwest where industry was moving, nonunion contractors also controlled the work. They usually manned their jobs with experienced "permit men," who had initially trained in the military or in vocational schools and then honed their skill on union jobs. Permit men paid a fee to work on these jobs when business was booming, but they had no opportunity to join the union whether or not they were qualified. By essentially leasing union work to permit men, and letting permit men go when work slowed down, local unions took it for granted that they were protecting their members' jobs in the long run.[35]

However, by the 1970s the opposite was proving true: Closed, protective unions that had manned small-scale jobs with permit men had created a trained workforce that owed no loyalty to the union. "The mistake we made was . . . [that] we basically taught them the trade and then we said, 'we don't have any use for you,'" a business agent later admitted, a point that was not lost on the Associated General Contractors, which was becoming a vital force in open-shop construction. When contractors in Nebraska sought an alternative to union labor for commercial and industrial projects, for instance, the local AGC chapter highly recommended the home building industry. "These workers are open-shop, trained, and have an attitude that is attuned to free enterprise thinking," an official noted. "We have talked to some employees of framing crews . . . who are making $6.50 to $7.50 per hour even when they are doing piecework. Our question to them was, would you be interested in . . . doing such jobs as building forms, pouring and finishing concrete, tying re-bar and other commercial-type work? We mentioned a wage of $9.00 per hour for experienced men. The reaction [was] very enthusiastic."[36]

If the BCTD expected to slow the tide of nonunion construction, it would have to organize residential jobs, and thus cut the supply of nonunion workers at the source. And it would have to prove to union members and contractors alike that the trades were serious about organizing. Taking the first step, Robert Georgine hired Tom Owens, director of the Teamsters' Construction Division, to head the Department's campaign. Although the AFL-CIO had expelled the Teamsters back in 1957, the building trades had never severed ties completely. Because teamsters delivered essential building materials, they could make or break a strike, so close relations on the job site were critical. Teamsters sat on local building trades councils and on the Department-related (but technically independent) National Joint Heavy and Highway Committee, and their union had proved to be, as President Georgine told the 1977 convention, a reliable friend to building and construction workers. Apparently Georgine and Andy Anderson, who headed the Teamsters' Western Conference, had made an agreement a few years back to help each other out, and so far the agreement was working. "He has never let me down," Georgine noted. "Every time I call him and I need him he is there," which was certainly more than the BCTD president could say for his friends in Congress.[37]

"There's a lot of muscle in the BCTD-Teamsters coalition," noted Victor Riesel, a well-known newspaper columnist and outspoken critic of labor racketeering. "There's 'youth,' too," a reference to "Bobby" Georgine, the Department's forty-three-year-old president. "There is also an administrative committee . . . made up of some of the nation's most powerful union chiefs—the laborers' Angelo Fosco, the plumbers' Marty Ward, the carpenters' Bill Siddell, the electrical workers' Charley Pillard, the iron workers' Jack Lyons and the operating engineers' Jay Turner. . . . So the talk of the building trades' demise and of their loss of control of the industry is as exaggerated as Mark Twain's death." It may have been true, Riesel added, that some local unions were making concessions at the bargaining table, taking pay cuts (as some trades did in New York and St. Louis), or giving up perks like paid travel time (as some did in Florida), but that was only a natural reaction to a "soft" labor market, he said, not proof positive that the trades were on their way out. "Thus prediction No. 1 for 1978: watch this front," Riesel advised readers. "It will crackle. And don't bury the building trades until roosters lay eggs. They're a very tough crowd of unionists."[38]

"If We Don't Change, It's Good-bye"

There was no denying that the support of the Teamsters was crucial to the BCTD's organizing plans. In residential and apartment construction, as one organizer noted, controlling the delivery of ready-mixed concrete "is the fastest and most practical way to get a job stopped," a tactic that quickly increased the cost of nonunion construction. But it was by no means enough. If the Department expected to turn the tide of nonunion construction, all the trades would have to cooperate. "The job has to be done on the local level," Georgine insisted. "It has to be done by the local unions, and the internationals to which they belong, and the Department can direct that effort." But that presumed a level of local commitment, industrywide solidarity, and institutional trust and cooperation that simply did not exist. "Believe me, fellows, they are gobbling us up," warned James Lee, president of California's State Building Trades Council. "While we are fighting amongst ourselves like a dog and cat, the open shop contractor is walking off with all the meat."[39]

The California leader had a point. Jurisdictional conflicts were still going strong in the late 1970s, despite the machinery provided by the Impartial Jurisdictional Disputes Board; in fact within a few years, the Board would cease functioning. And local building trades councils still complained that too many unions refused to join. Even after the Department sponsored regional conferences to promote affiliation, local fights over politics, jurisdiction, per capita taxes, and past policy continued to keep the trades apart. There were also conflicts within the Department that got in the way of unified action. A coalition of smaller unions led by the Sheet Metal Workers and including the Asbestos Workers, Elevator Constructors, Granite Cutters, Lathers, Marble Polishers, and Roofers had been trying to expand the Executive Council since 1975, so that every union, no matter what size, would have a voice in making Department policy. At around the same time Canadian members were looking for better representation, too; they wanted the right to hold their own conventions and shape policy to suit their particular needs.[40] These situations were eventually resolved behind the scenes through compromises and concessions on both sides: In 1977 the Canadians held their first regional conference (but President Georgine appointed members of the new Canadian Executive Board of the BCTD). And in 1979 a fifteen-member Governing Board of Presidents replaced the ten-member Executive Council. However, no changes were made to the Department's administrative committee, which included representatives from the six largest affiliates and met once a month to handle policy matters.[41]

"It's not an easy thing" to reach consensus, Georgine later explained, "and I don't say this in a derogatory sense, I say this in a real sense, people are people. If you've got seventeen organizations trying to work together, you've got the leaders of each one of those organizations who feels like a king in his own right. . . . Personalities get involved, . . . [and] jealousies—not only jealousies of the individual himself but jealousies of the strength of his union. And the damages they've done at one time or another to your union and jurisdictional problems that you've had and so forth. . . . This guy doesn't like that guy, or that union, so now to get them all to try and forget all of that stuff and look at the big picture, is no small task."[42]

Whether it was his diplomatic skills or the stark circumstances that some building trades unions faced in the late 1970s and early 1980s, Georgine apparently brought the trades together. By April 1978 the organizing campaign was ready to go. Each affiliate had appointed a Director of Organization who now took a seat on the Department's Organizing Committee. Meeting regularly that spring, the committee decided to finance only those campaigns that had the full support of all trades in an area. And that meant that the trades had agreed, at least in principle, to provide full-time organizers, standardize union initiation fees, and welcome newly organized members into the ranks. By May the committee had voted to support the National Joint Heavy and Highway Committee's bottom-up campaign to organize workers at a Daniel Construction Company project in Bath County, Virginia—a campaign that could cost as much as $1,000 a day, organizers estimated. It was also screening requests for organizing programs in Arizona, North and South Carolina, Erie, Pennsylvania, Baltimore, and Washington, D.C., among many others.[43]

The major focus, however, was on Los Angeles County, where nonunion contractors were growing fast. Back in the 1960s, as one drywall contractor remembered, "If you weren't union, you didn't work" on large residential projects. "It was unheard of." But all that was changing by the mid-1970s: The ABC had targeted Los Angeles as the "proving ground" for the nonunion movement, as President Georgine put it. Almost three hundred contractors had withdrawn from collective-bargaining agreements, declaring their intention to subcontract work to nonunion contractors. "We have to get together, band together," a state building trades leader warned, "and we are going to have to develop a program."[44]

With the Department behind him, Tom Owens launched an ambitious pilot organizing campaign in the spring of 1978. As he told the Los Angeles committee, the BCTD was not "interested in picking up the tab for erratic picketing of non-union contractors or lawsuits caused by such picketing." The idea was to develop new organizing techniques (which included improving the building trades' reputation and standing in the community), to train organizers (who would also work with minority groups and community leaders), and to develop plans for future funding (since the Department was already spending more than $1.5 million, and requests for organizing programs were coming in fast). With an immediate goal of reversing the nonunion trend, Owens and the organizing committee also intended to stabilize local bargaining and conditions, put an end to job-wide "economic" strikes, standardize starting times, holidays, and shift provisions, and develop what he called "model jobs," that is, all-union projects manned by qualified mechanics who took pride in their work and their high productivity.[45]

With cement mason Con O'Shea heading up the Los Angeles campaign, construction workers shut down seven residential projects by June; over the next eighteen months they would picket thirty-eight nonunion projects. In O'Shea's opinion, that was a real accomplishment. "There is still a great lack of aggressiveness on the part of our Local unions," he complained. "The large majority . . . will not consider any move whatsoever without a meeting with their respective attorneys."[46] Meanwhile organizers were developing new strategies. Since nonunion contractors often paid employees in cash, organizers were working with state and federal agencies to make sure that taxes were being paid so that union and nonunion contractors had equal costs and tax evaders could be prosecuted. They were also investigating lenders who made construction loans for nonunion projects. If union funds were deposited with these lenders, O'Shea explained, "we are going . . . to use this position to get their help in straightening the job out."[47]

Bottom-up organizing was also on the agenda. The Los Angeles team was trying to get local union members hired on nonunion projects with the goal of organizing the workforce and then signing the contractor to a union agreement. If these rank-and-file organizers happened to get fired for union activities, so much the better. "In general we want our local unions to go on the offensive as relates to the filing of charges for one reason or another. . . . We have also made connections with the F[air] E[mployment] P[ractices] C[ommittee] regarding the matter of discrimination in employment," O'Shea reported, "with the hope that we can successfully prosecute [nonunion] employers who might discriminate against the hiring of minority members. . . . What we are talking about and doing is new to most of our leaders in the area, but we . . . realize that our former methods were not getting the desired results."[48]

Although local enthusiasm for the campaign proved strong, there was still too much talk and not enough action, as far as Tom Owens was concerned. For one thing, only a few international unions had assigned representatives to work on the campaign, at least at first. And many local unions were still unwilling to grant the flexibility that organizers needed to sign up new contractors and their employees. Bottom-up efforts fell flat, for instance, when local unions refused to lower initiation fees or waive past fines against former members. "Every Local Union has a different program in going after the nonunion Tradesman," O'Shea explained, "and we have been unable to come up with any blanket program due to the self autonomy of each and every Local Union."[49]

Autonomy was getting in the way of traditional top-down organizing, too. Although the Los Angeles committee was convinced that a multi-trade agreement, negotiated through the Building Trades Council, would strengthen union labor's overall position, getting local unions to agree to standardized contract provisions was proving impossible. According to O'Shea, 60 percent of the unions, including the Bricklayers, Carpenters, Electricians, Laborers, Lathers, Painters, Plumbers, Cement Masons, Sheet Metal Workers, and Roofers, had a "favored nation clause" in their collective-bargaining agreements that limited local residential and commercial work to local contractors. So under these rules a union contractor in one part of the region could not move workers to a job in another part, a restriction that kept many firms from agreeing to sign with the union.[50]

"These problems are extremely political at the local level," Owens reported to President Georgine early on in the campaign, and that being the case he wanted the general presidents to issue "a directive to their respective local unions alleviating these restrictions." But given the policy of local autonomy, that was easier said than done. A few months later O'Shea had given up hope that existing agreements would be amended, even though "this restriction . . . is the biggest argument given by a nonunion contractor against signing a Union Agreement," he told Georgine. "I have attempted to point out to [the trades] that the crafts such as the Operating Engineers and the Iron Workers are in much better shape, organizational wise, than the average Building Trades Union, and they have had the free movement of men for many years and have prospered under those conditions." But he was getting nowhere. "There seems to be a deep feeling . . . in the neighboring counties of Ventura, Santa Barbara . . . and Orange, that if the contractors were given free portability of employees that the Local Unions in those outlying areas would be gobbled up by the Local Unions in the L.A. Metropolitan area."[51]

Certainly these circumstances frustrated O'Shea, who was not convinced that local unions understood the long-term value of organization. "As you know," he reported early in 1979, "our Building Trades Local Unions in the Southern California area are enjoying full . . . employment for their membership. It is my gut feeling that as long as this . . . situation continues, that . . . the leadership of those Local Unions will not push themselves into a full blown organizing effort with all of the sacrifices and concessions that go along with such an effort. . . . You can have the most hardworking men on the Organizing Committee, willing to do anything you might ask them to do, but . . . it is the leader of that Local Union who is the one who calls the final shot on establishing picket lines, assisting other local unions . . . removing men from picketed jobs, sending mailings concerning the organizing effort [and] making the concessions that we have discussed so many times." But frustrated or not, he was also convinced that the organizing campaign was making a real difference. "If we had not established the program," he told Georgine, "things would be a lot worse in L.A. County today. I am certain from things that I see and hear that we have got the Industry's eye and they know that we are going to give them a battle." It was a shame, he added, that "we could not convince the Crafts to make [the necessary] . . . concessions, but it is no use . . . wishing for something and we just have to get to the business at hand."[52]

Although O'Shea's gut feeling would eventually prove true, at the time the BCTD was greatly encouraged by the outcome. The Los Angeles County campaign "gave us a chance to try all three techniques of organizing workers, the work and convincing owners they should build with union labor," Owens reported. And the effort had been worthwhile: Building trades unions counted ten thousand new members in eighteen months' time, and about 95 percent of the work in and around Los Angeles was going to union contractors in 1979. Better yet, the numbers had gone up despite the ABC's offer of free legal services to contractors willing to go nonunion, proving to building trades workers and employers alike that construction unions could still win a fight. "The whole idea is to impede growth of the open shop . . . and we've shown we can do that. . . . We've accomplished that in L.A.," President Georgine was quoted in the *Washington Post*. "Now this effort must be duplicated all over the country," he urged the BCTD's 1979 convention. Bolstered by the apparent victory in Southern California, the BCTD began sponsoring organizer training sessions at the George Meany Center for Labor Studies, in Silver Spring, Maryland, and launched five new multi-craft campaigns in Maine, central Pennsylvania, Phoenix, Orange County, California, and Washington, D.C. And since Canadian workers were hardly immune to the nonunion threat, in 1980 the BCTD's Canadian office was also developing a multi-craft organizing program.[53]

Neither Georgine nor anyone else at the BCTD thought that the battle had been won. In fact, at around the same time that the Los Angeles campaign was taking off, ABC members were using the press, the courts, and the NLRB to denounce the Department and its seventeen affiliates as a "national conspiracy" to derail free competition, and to prove that union construction was just too expensive for the nation's good. "There are no economic or jurisdictional strikes" on a merit shop project, the ABC boasted through advertising supplements in newspapers like the *Washington Post* and the *New York Times*. Merit shop contractors bring "productive practices and efficiency back to construction," waging campaigns "against featherbedding, jurisdictional disputes, restrictive hiring rules, and bans on modern technology," campaigns that were usually met with "union violence," they alleged. At the same time, the Business Roundtable and the Chamber of Commerce, along with the Associated General Contractors, were stepping up efforts to repeal, or at least weaken, state and federal prevailing wage laws, to eliminate union hiring halls and subcontracting clauses, to undermine multi-employer pension plans, and generally to "attack union rights in courts and in the Congress," as President Georgine reported. "We are under attack from . . . all sides," he told the 1979 convention. "It is no exaggeration to say that the corporate community is waging war on the construction worker. . . . If these corporations can destroy the Building Trades, none of our democratic institutions will be safe."[54]

Research and Market Recovery

The new organizing program was only one of the changes the Department made to combat the open shop. It also instituted new procedures to approve project labor agreements which were becoming an essential tool in the fight to retain work: Because project agreements prohibited jurisdictional disputes, reduced overtime rates, and basically standardized working conditions among the trades, they allowed union contractors to compete more effectively. By 1981 some eighty-three thousand union members were working under ninety-two project labor agreements, including the General Presidents' Project Maintenance Agreement that dated back to 1956, and the National Power Construction Stabilization Agreement that went into effect in April 1978. Without these agreements, Georgine noted, this work would have gone open shop.[55]

At the same time the Department was developing a national Pension Investment Education Program to encourage union and management trustees to invest in job-creating construction projects. It was stepping up political efforts, too, launching a weekly legislative bulletin, *The Builders,* to highlight issues like prevailing wage laws, pension reform, and health and safety standards on the job site. Finally, the Department was investing in improved communications with local councils and an extensive public relations program. "We had to," Georgine reported in 1981. "The massive attempt to destroy the prevailing wage system—to say nothing of collective bargaining and the very existence of unions currently being executed by certain contractors, business interests, and their government supporters—forces the Department to spend an enormous amount of time and money defending the Davis-Bacon, Walsh-Healey, and Contract Work Hours and Safety Standards acts," among many others.[56]

Part of that money was used to fund the Center to Protect Workers' Rights (CPWR), a nonprofit research organization established in 1979 to collect and analyze the hard data Department leaders needed to counteract allegations of widespread union featherbedding, restrictive work rules, and the inflationary impact of Davis-Bacon wage rates. With three researchers and a lobbyist at work full-time and a number of part-time consultants, including attorneys, public relations specialists and economists, the CPWR prepared congressional testimony and analyzed the impact of proposed budget cuts and regulatory changes on construction workers. It also worked with local councils and union legislative representatives to monitor and defend protective legislation, particularly Davis-Bacon and the Occupational Safety and Health Administration (OSHA). Producing a variety of educational materials, fact sheets, and opinion pieces for major newspapers, the CPWR also supported solidly researched scholarly studies, including economist Steven G. Allen's "Unionized Construction Workers Are More Productive" and "Prevailing Wage Laws Are Not Inflationary: A Case Study of Public School Construction Costs." "The top priority of the trades right now is to expose the truth, to scrape away the myth that nonunion is less expensive," Georgine explained. "Our strategy is to educate the policy-making people about the construction industry."[57]

The CPWR was also researching the network that linked corporate leaders in the Business Roundtable to some of the largest and most aggressive nonunion construction firms, including Brown & Root and Daniel International. The Business Roundtable had paved the way for the growth of open-shop construction, a CPWR researcher reported, by getting its members to break their ties to unionized construction firms in favor of open-shop contractors. At the same time established union contractors were making the most of the situation, demanding project labor agreements and economic concessions, and going double-breasted in order to operate on a nonunion basis whenever it suited them. "Building trades unions were led to believe that these [phenomena] were taking place on the basis of the economics involved, and [that] union contractors needed to be competitive with the open shop contractor," the CPWR reported. "It is our conclusion that the occurrence of these phenomena are more likely a direct result of the activities of the Business Roundtable . . . to bring about a union free environment." President Georgine wholeheartedly agreed. After all, as he told a congressional committee in 1979, the Roundtable was nothing more than "a guerilla army dressed in three piece suits" bent on annihilating the building trades. "They are the real opponent and if we are to successfully fight them they must be exposed," he warned convention delegates that year. "They have spent hundreds of thousands [of dollars] in legal fees to attack union rights in courts and in Congress. And they have made the ABC and the open-shop movement what it is today."[58]

Because the Business Roundtable was out to slash "the wages of construction workers . . . [lower] their own construction costs . . . [and] take over labor-management relations in the construction industry," as Georgine noted in 1979, it was a force that had to be reckoned with, especially after the Roundtable initiated the Construction Industry Cost Effectiveness Project (CICEP) in the late 1970s. "The most concerted effort ever made to stream-line construction of the country's industrial and commercial future," according to the *Engineering News-Record,* the CICEP brought together some two hundred fifty contractors, owners, and analysts to identify and resolve persistent productivity problems. "The researchers are showing an ability to let the chips fall where they may," the journal reported. "In many instances, that means placing blame on themselves. They know that such an even-handed approach is crucial if those not involved in the study—especially labor—are to find the project's analyses credible and join the effort to work out solutions." Thomas Dailey, AGC president and a member of the CICEP, agreed. "This project is the most important study of construction industry cost-effectiveness ever undertaken," he told the 1981 BCTD convention. "It represents a means to bring back the construction market in America's in-dustrial sector. It will require a joint venture between users, contractors and labor in order to be successful," he added, making it clear to the Department that "you need to work with us in its implementation."[59]

Although Department leaders shared an interest in productivity, they were reluctant to sign on, since the CICEP had not involved them from the start. They were willing to listen, however: In the fall of 1981 representatives from nine affiliates and the BCTD met with CICEP officials to learn more about the project. The fact that CICEP leader Charles Brown was willing to concede the value of a strong union sector—but not at any cost—helped the situation. After all, as the *Engineering News-Record* pointed out, "if the union sector continues to weaken appreciably, the country's largest industry will lose its principal systems for training workers and ensuring their availability when and where they are needed." When the committee published its first set of recommendations in 1982 and called for improved supervision and safety standards, strict enforcement of building codes, and the increased use of semiskilled "subjourneymen," Department leaders offered a measured re-sponse. "Generally speaking, there are some things we're in agreement on with them," Georgine conceded. "But there are some things where we think they missed the boat. I think we'll be able to work things out with the Busi-ness Roundtable. We might be a lot closer than a lot of people think."[60]

Offering their own plan for a healthy construction industry, the BCTD and the National Construction Employers Council (NCEC) (which repre-sented union contractors in all branches of the industry) developed a joint Market Recovery Program (MRP) for Union Construction late in 1982. Im-proving relations between contractors and unions, they believed, would increase work opportunities for both sides. The program grew out of local efforts, like the five-year-old Operation Most, in Columbus, Ohio, that traded contractor pledges to improve management and to avoid controversial work assignments for union pledges to prohibit make-work practices and work stoppages, a bargain that seemed to work. Under Operation Most, union construction had completed $700 million worth of work without losing time to jurisdictional disputes. At the same time unions in Nevada and Utah, where the nonunion push was particularly strong, had held on to highway construction work by agreeing to hold wage rates to the level prevailing at the time the contract was bid. And in Utah, Nevada, and California, a number of trades had agreed to reduce fringe-benefit payments, permit flexible work hours (including the four ten-hour-day schedule favored by nonunion contractors), and eliminate strict apprenticeship ratios (to bring on more semiskilled "subjourneymen").[61]

Like it or not, union concessions were part of the Market Recovery Program. Given the strength of nonunion construction in growing areas like the South and Southwest, the sluggish economy in the 1980s, and the sizable gap between union and nonunion wage rates, the building trades' options were limited. But concessions would have to go both ways, Georgine insisted, in order for the program to succeed. "We must be responsible in our relationships with [contractors]," he told the 1983 BCTD convention. "But, in return, we must demand that our contractors be responsible with us. That means no double-breasted dodges to avoid their legal and moral responsibilities. And no phony bankruptcies. That means a clear recognition that the wages of workers are not the only area for cost savings. Profit gouging is as unacceptable as featherbedding. Exorbitant executive salaries and benefits are as harmful to competitiveness as leapfrogging wages. This mutual responsibility is the cornerstone of our Market Recovery Program. It holds out the promise of a more efficient, a more productive, a more competitive construction industry. And more union construction work."[62]

In many ways there was nothing particularly new about the Market Recovery Program. It was the logical extension of the joint-labor management "eight-for-eight" philosophy that BCTD presidents and economist John Dunlop had been promoting since the time of the Second World War. The national productivity pact first negotiated with the National Constructors Association in the 1950s, to address restrictive union practices and inefficient work rules, for instance, covered much of the same ground. What was different this time was the Department's commitment to make the program work and to persuade rank-and-file craftsmen that local goals would have to change to preserve union construction. And that would be no easy job. "Any business manager who will agree to drastic change won't be business manager for long," one union leader noted. In most cases, another added, "you can get local and state leaders of unions to agree to what the general presidents think is good policy, but there is the potential for accusations of 'sellout' in every election, local or international." Georgine was inclined to agree. "Some of our members don't know there is a problem," he admitted, a complaint echoed by a local business agent. "Some members don't even know that contractors have to be the low bidder to get jobs," he said, making it clear that union leaders would have to become educators for the program to succeed. "You don't have to have a degree in economics to understand what is happening," this business agent insisted. "This is basic."[63]

The job fell to BCTD Secretary-Treasurer Joseph F. Maloney, a structural iron worker from Boston who knew both sides of the industry. Using "straight-forward" language, as the *Engineering News-Record* put it, to sell the program to wary local unions, Maloney brought a good deal of talent to the job. On the one hand, he was a tough negotiator who could not be easily intimidated. On the other, he had broad experience in labor-industrial relations: Maloney had worked with John Dunlop in Harvard's Trade Union Leadership program, he had served on the Construction Industry Joint Conference and various stabilization committees, and he had assisted Frank Bonadio in the 1960s and 1970s, negotiating project labor agreements (PLAs). "These were good to the extent that [PLAs] stabilized . . . particular jobs," he explained, and they also proved very useful in establishing standard conditions such as uniform holidays and working hours. "While chairing many of these meetings," Maloney remembered, "I'd be accused of concessionary bargaining and I'd defend that by saying . . . we were making adjustments in our agreements that should be [there]." Working with NCEC president James Baxter on the Market Recovery Program, Maloney now focused on cleaning up collective-bargaining agreements to make sure that current contract provisions reflected current realities. For instance, double time for overtime work dated back to the Second World War, and it was put in "not to enrich the individual," Maloney explained, "but to stop the abuse of overtime [during the war] so that more people could work without working excessive hours." Benefits such as travel pay, which had been developed to ensure that smaller unions like the Asbestos Workers would be able to man large construction projects in out-of-the-way areas, had also gotten out of hand; in some areas travel pay had become a general fringe benefit, one that contractors were no longer willing to pay.[64]

Although critics inside and outside the building trades dismissed market recovery efforts as just another "sweetheart deal" to benefit labor leaders at the expense of the rank and file, Maloney did not agree. The Market Recovery Program's advice to set overtime rates at time and a half for the first two hours daily (and the first eight hours on Saturday), to standardize hours and holidays, to limit pay for travel and shift work, and to eliminate restrictions on tools were not concessions, Maloney insisted, "they just make common sense." "When you stop and think of a construction job with so many diverse entities on it," he later explained, "unless you get some kind of stability in how that job operates, you're going to have a dysfunctional job. And that was what we tried to do." The strategy was controversial, especially when multi-craft agreements cut wage rates and benefits, or increased the number of apprentices (or subjourneymen) on a job, as an agreement did in Mobile, Alabama, where open-shop construction was growing fast. But it did garner local support when local contractors won jobs that they might otherwise have lost. For instance, in the twenty areas targeted by the Market Recovery Program a majority of union contractors reported "positive" changes: Local MRP committees were meeting regularly in 78 percent of the areas, 71 percent of these had established task forces to measure open-shop activity, and another 43 percent had committees to identify nonproductive practices and work rules. "We . . . are determined to make the union contractor more competitive," UBCJA organizer Bob Ozinga reported, "by removing anachronisms from agreements and adding flexibility."[65]

Joe Maloney echoed the same message when he addressed the Business Roundtable's National Users Conference late in 1984. Two years ago, he pointed out, when the CICEP issued its first report, the Roundtable had portrayed the building trades as being "only aroused enough to rearrange the deck chairs on the Titanic. . . . I submit . . . that we responded . . . by making more changes in local labor agreements than were made in the prior 82 years." Thanks to the joint Market Recovery Program, almost all the inefficient labor practices identified by the CICEP had been corrected, he noted, and union contractors "were seeing results," according to NCEC president William E. Besl. Building trades unions were also pushing hard for project labor agreements to make union contractors more competitive, Maloney added. More than two hundred agreements were already in effect, and a "sweeping new" national agreement was in the works that promised to ease work rules and enforce uniform work hours on all major construction projects. But so far the effort had been one-sided, according to Maloney. Business Roundtable users were still working for a "union-free business environment," effectively boycotting union contractors, a strategy, Maloney suggested, that might backfire in the long run.[66]

The Market Recovery Program by no means solved the building trades' problems. On the contrary, the joint BCTD-NCEC project was more of a tourniquet than a cure: Throughout the 1980s the Business Roundtable and the National Right to Work Committee were still trying to repeal state and federal prevailing wage laws, and the open-shop trend in construction continued to grow. In fact, by the mid-1980s twenty out of the nation's top twenty-five construction firms were double-breasted, including longtime union firms like Bechtel. But the Market Recovery Program did allow union construction to survive some hard economic and political times, and it did improve the overall standing of union labor in the industry. When the economy began to revive around 1985, for instance, the BCTD used a combination of concessions, demonstrations, and political influence to negotiate important project labor agreements at the new billion-dollar General Motors Saturn manufacturing complex in Spring Hill, Tennessee (in a region where 95 percent of construction work was done open shop) and at the $800-million Toyota assembly plant in Georgetown, Kentucky.[67]

"Local unions in recent years had lost 10 percent of their membership," the *Washington Post* reported late in 1985, "but they have recovered those losses and expanded because unionized construction firms that employ them are booming, company and union officials say. They add that cost-cutting union contracts, which include 'no-strike' guarantees, enable the construction firms to win some jobs that previously only went to nonunion companies." As one contractor told the *Post,* "My costs are now compatible with an open-shop firm. It may cost me $120,000 more to use union labor, [but] I can finish the job two months earlier." His partner agreed. "With the nonunion, we never made a dime. The work force was inexperienced. . . . They didn't show up. You would pay them on Wednesday and not see them Thursday or Friday, and I could not find enough qualified people for some jobs." The surge in union construction also benefited nonunion workers who now had a reason to join the union. "On the nonunion side I got no training," explained a rodman with fifteen years' experience. "You go out on the job and learn by mistakes . . . and accidents." The union training classes he now attended were "more professional," he said. "You don't go out with untrained and unskilled people, and I found out what I'd been missing for 15 years."[68]

But if Department affiliates hoped to regain the ground they had lost over the last thirty years, they would have to do more than just make concessions. "Wage givebacks," as economist Steven Allen noted, "are not likely to help restore much of the market share lost in recent years to the open shop." For instance, after building trades workers in Houston agreed to a wage freeze in 1983, and took a 15 percent wage cut in 1984, contractors came back the very next year looking to cut another 15 percent. "We've done everything but give them our shoes and socks," a carpenter complained, and it still was not enough. Indeed, when no work materialized after the BCTD negotiated an area agreement in Houston that cut union wages by 20 percent and increased the number of apprentices and subjourneymen permitted on a job, Georgine was forced to admit that "we may have been used as a tool to force down the bids of the open shop contractors."[69]

Mike Lucas, the IBEW's Director of Organizing, was more blunt. "Top-down market recovery efforts without bottom-up organizing is not only ignorance, it is suicide," he maintained. As long as construction companies were able to meet their labor demands without calling a union hiring hall, market recovery plans only promised a race to the bottom. "It does little good to make concessions in a market recovery program unless something is done to organize the craftsmen who are competing against their union brothers," he insisted, since "nonunion employers can lower their wages and fringes in response to union concessions at a much more rapid pace than union employers can." Employers first signed union agreements, he added, "because we had something that was necessary to their continued operation—i.e., skilled manpower. When we regain control of that manpower, when we rebuild a working monopoly, we will be able to raise wages and regain those concessions we have already made, and not until."[70]

It was still an open question whether the building trades were finally ready to heed this message and organize the unorganized, which meant, in very practical terms, eliminating local barriers like high initiation fees, restrictive membership policies, and referral systems that benefited longtime members over new recruits. But it was a question that the Department and its member unions would have to take seriously, if they hoped to do more than merely survive.

CHAPTER NINE

Back to Basics: The COMET Program, Internal Tensions, and the Las Vegas Campaign

> Successfully rebuilding market share is not a matter of simply devoting enough resources to organizing. Instead, it requires a more careful understanding of the dynamics of competition in a market, an understanding of who the players are, and a careful effort to use limited resources to organize new contractors that can become the sustainable core of a larger union sector in the long run.
>
> —David Weil, 2003

Nobody knew if the worst was over. After all, construction unions controlled less than 20 percent of the workforce by 1990, an ominous drop from the mid-1960s when they controlled almost 50 percent and a serious indictment of building trades' policy since then. But if President Georgine's assessment held any weight, things were looking up. "We have taken some real shots in the past 10 years," he admitted. "An anti-union president and an open shop movement had us on the ropes for a while." Yet there had been no collapse, as critics predicted. Instead, he told the 1990 BCTD convention, the building trades had met the threat "head on," adapting strategies to meet changing demands, and demonstrating over and over again that "we are the best: the best trained and most highly skilled building tradesmen in the world."[1]

The Department president was putting the best face on a bad situation, but his point was essentially true: Thanks in part to the open shop's successful campaign to lower wages and benefits, the industry was facing a serious manpower shortage and building trades unions had a real opportunity to grow. In fact, according to a 1990 report in the *Engineering News-Record,* they were well positioned to become "the supplier of skilled, cost-effective labor that everyone wants to use," since they offered potential workers "a well-paying career that also provides adequate health-care benefits and retirement," something nonunion employers could not match at the time. So while current conditions were discouraging, to say the least, the game was not over yet. If the leadership was ready to seize the moment and make up for years of lost time and lost opportunities to broaden union membership, then the building trades could look forward to a promising future. However, that remained a very big "if" in the minds of building trades leaders, including Georgine.[2]

But there were signs of revival nevertheless. While the Department had lost a fierce legislative battle to outlaw double-breasted companies, it continued to stave off significant attacks on the Davis-Bacon prevailing wage law, including repeated attempts to enforce regulations to increase the use of semiskilled "helpers" on federal job sites. And Department affiliates in Massachusetts had defeated a referendum sponsored by the Associated Builders and Contractors to repeal the state's prevailing wage law in 1988: Building trades unions had joined forces with other AFL-CIO unions, senior citizens groups, and civil rights and women's rights organizations to wage a grassroots, community-based defense of fair wages, stable industry, and decent living standards, and their campaign had attracted widespread attention and support. The following year the BCTD negotiated a ten-year no-strike project labor agreement with the Massachusetts Water Resources Authority (MWRA) to clean up Boston Harbor, a $6.1-billion public works job that would be manned through union hiring halls. The ABC immediately challenged it in court and initially won the case. But in 1993 the U.S. Supreme Court upheld the agreement, a crucial decision that permitted the Department to show what labor agreements could accomplish on major public works projects. According to Douglas B. MacDonald, director of the MWRA, the project agreement had "greatly benefited taxpayers," since the cleanup was not only on schedule so far but was also $428 million under budget.[3]

There were also changes within the Department that seemed promising. The Lathers had joined the Carpenters in 1979, and in 1983 the Tile, Marble, and Terrazzo Finishers International Union had absorbed the Granite Cutters before merging with the Carpenters in 1988. The Teamsters had also returned to the AFL-CIO and the BCTD in 1987, bringing the total number of Department affiliates to fifteen. At the same time the Department was becoming a real force on construction health and safety issues. In 1990 the Center to Protect Workers Rights had forged a partnership with the National Institute for Occupational Safety and Health (NIOSH) to research and document major risks in this all-too-hazardous industry and to develop industrywide strategies to improve performance. Four years later the Construction Industry Partnership (a joint BCTD-contractor committee) was working with the National Resource Center for OSHA Training to develop Smart Mark, an industrywide health and safety training program available to all affiliates by 1997. Citing the Business Roundtable's advice that "owners should only do business with contractors who invest in training and maintain the skills of their workforce," the BCTD promoted Smart Mark training as a benefit to union members and employers alike.[4]

Department leaders were also beginning to pay more attention to public relations and community concerns. In 1985 the Governing Board of Presidents voted to support the University of Miami's Diabetes Research Institute, and the following year the Department launched its "Blueprint for Cure" campaign, pledging to raise $10 million to help fund the construction of a first-class research and treatment facility. Local and international unions began hosting walkathons and golf and tennis tournaments, and thirty thousand rank-and-file construction workers solicited funds on street corners, bus stops, and shopping malls in cities throughout the United States (and Canada by the 1990s), making the Department's annual Dollars Against Diabetes—or DAD's—Day the largest single-day fund-raising campaign for diabetes research. After the first $1 million DAD's Day in 1989, U.S. president George Bush recognized the Department's program as a "shining example of volunteerism in action" and one of the top private-sector initiatives in the nation. And by 1990 the Department was able to present a check for $7 million to the president of the University of Miami, a sizable down payment on the new Diabetes Research Institute which opened for business in February 1994. In fact, over the next ten years the Department's Blueprint for Cure campaign would raise more than $30 million for the institute.[5]

The most promising sign of revival, however, was the renewed interest in organizing, a shift that was not without controversy. With the exception of the organizing campaign in the 1980s, the Department had generally steered clear of the issue. And even though an organizing director had been employed since that campaign, there was no consensus on how far the Department should go: Some general presidents strongly believed that workforce organizing was the key to long-term survival and urged Georgine to play a leadership role, whereas others thought that organizing was best left to the affiliates. But at least one affiliate, the International Brotherhood of Electrical Workers, was pushing the program forward. One of the first to recognize the limitations of market recovery programs, as long as nonunion contractors dominated the market, the Electrical Workers had launched an organizing program in 1987, and in 1988 the international union made it mandatory for local unions to establish organizing goals and committees. "We had to do something," President John J. Barry pointed out, "because we could see the slippage in the numbers and in the control of work. . . . Construction locals were in horrendous shape, for the most part, and organizing was a word that was [still] foreign to their vocabularies."[6]

Determined to reverse the trend, President Barry launched a program in the Brotherhood's construction branch. He directed Mike Lucas, an energetic organizer who had been conducting successful campaigns for IBEW utility, manufacturing, and maintenance locals since the 1960s, to work with construction locals one at a time to persuade business managers and staff that organizing was their last chance for survival. IBEW local unions began to pass "salting" resolutions that permitted the membership to work for nonunion contractors, a move designed to give union "salts"—or rank and file organizers—access to nonunion workers.[7]

Salting was a strategy as old as the labor movement. The term dated back to nineteenth-century mine owners who would "salt" their mines with gold dust to make them appear more valuable. It was picked up by union organizers who "salted" nonunion jobs with union activists, a strategy that the IBEW's first president and general organizer, Henry Miller, pioneered in the 1890s. But a century later the strategy was still controversial, and not just with employers. The whole point of salting a nonunion workplace was to bring in new members and new contractors, and that was still easier said than done. Established union contractors did not necessarily welcome the competition, and union members raised on an exclusionary philosophy still believed that if they opened the doors, "they'd run all over us," as one IBEW organizer put it. In fact, when a local organizer in Albuquerque, New Mexico, initiated his first recruit—a former union member employed by one of the largest nonunion contractors in the area—tensions ran so high at the local union meeting that the police had to be called to restore order. "I just kept organizing. I was going to do it or we were going to die," the organizer remembered, but in the meantime the membership voted his boss, the business manager, out of office.[8]

This dog-in-the-manger attitude astounded President Barry, who knew full well that there were more than five hundred thousand construction electricians working in 1989, yet the IBEW claimed only about 28 percent of them. "Even though they were driving by three or four nonunion jobs on their way to work, the need to organize was still not apparent," he remembered. "I'd start on organizing and they thought . . . I was a little off my rocker. 'We don't bother with that because we have an apprentice program,' they'd say." But his answer was always the same: "We are going to organize. . . . Every damn time I saw them, going around the country, or in Canada: 'We're in the organizing mode and we're going to stay in it, otherwise we'll be extinct.' That was it, over and over. I thought maybe I'd just be a one-term president." But what Barry called his "redundancy" was just the beginning of the campaign. For there were "political obstacles" that had to be overcome first, according to Jeff Grabelsky, director of Cornell University's Construction Industry Program and a longtime IBEW member. "Even if we had local business managers who bought into the notion that we needed to organize, they were either unwilling or unable to overcome the resistance that their members had." So with Grabelsky's help the IBEW launched COMET (Construction Organizing Membership Education Training) in 1990 to demonstrate to local union leaders and rank-and-file workers alike the overall value of increasing union ranks. "The COMET program," Grabelsky pointed out, "arose out of a very real and obvious need, that you've got to engage your members in the same conversation that their leaders are having."[9]

Developed by a team of IBEW leaders assisted by Cornell University's Construction Industry Program, COMET was designed to answer the question "Why Organize?" In intensive, four-day "Train the Trainer" courses, union representatives analyzed the rise of nonunion construction since the 1960s, probed the connection between unionization rates, bargaining strength, and wage standards, and aired their fears about taking in new members. Some took it for granted that organizing would only lengthen the out-of-work list or undermine conditions on the job. Others dismissed nonunion workers as unskilled, unqualified "scabs" and "rats" who would have "no commitment or loyalty to the union." All these issues were addressed straightforwardly. There were sessions that shed light on the union's early history of aggressive organizing, on industry dynamics that linked wide-scale organizing to the survival of union construction, and on the similarities and differences between union and nonunion construction workers. And in the process COMET participants discovered for themselves "that the common bonds of craft and trade and the shared experience and aspirations of all construction workers are much more powerful than the differences that separate the organized and the unorganized," program leaders reported. "This is one of the profound moments of realization in the COMET program."[10]

Armed with the knowledge they needed and a detailed trainer's manual, COMET-trained local leaders now spread the gospel of organizing to rank-and-file workers. In a four-hour training class, they did their best to persuade local members that a union had two choices when it came to competing with nonunion workers: It could either cut wages in a "race to the bottom," or raise the standards of nonunion workers and level the playing field. Because organizing inevitably raised the costs of nonunion construction, trainers maintained, it made union contractors more competitive, and thereby expanded job opportunities. So, contrary to conventional building trades wisdom, organizing made union members more secure, not less, and protected union conditions against the threat of nonunion standards. When the program was delivered effectively by well-prepared trainers, the members "got it," organizers noted, since it was not that hard for members to understand why the trades needed to organize. The business manager in Albuquerque agreed. "COMET dramatically changed attitudes," he said. With the membership on board, the local was able to hire full-time organizers, inaugurate an active salting campaign, and eliminate long-standing barriers to new membership. In fact, after adopting the COMET philosophy, the local not only recruited three hundred new members but also organized fifteen electrical contractors, including the largest nonunion contractor in the area.[11]

It did not take long for COMET to take off. The Carpenters union adopted the program early on, customizing it to suit trade needs. Then word began to spread. COMET-trained electricians and carpenters would talk up the program on the job site, and iron workers and sheet metal workers would say to their business managers, "Why don't we have this program?" And before too long they did, and so did the Painters, Asbestos Workers, Plumbers, and Roofers, each affiliate making its own innovations along the way. For instance, the IBEW required all business managers to take the four-day "train the trainer" course, but the Painters and the Asbestos Workers put their entire national leadership through it. Tim Nichols, a leader of the Michigan State Building Trades Council, introduced another important change. Convinced that the trades needed to get together to talk about their common and unique problems, he sponsored the first multi-trade COMET program. But if organizers agreed that the multi-trade program was "a great dynamic and a precondition for multi-trade organizing," they were not satisfied yet. By the 1990s there was training about the need to organize, and training on how to organize that went along with it, through an additional program known as COMET II. But there was almost no actual, sustained organizing activity at the time. As economist David Weil put it, the COMET approach proved successful in building support for the concept of organizing, but local initiatives lacked "clear guidance on how to proceed once support had been built." Indeed, union leaders were mastering the rhetoric but not the reality of organizing, COMET proponents admitted, tending to believe that the job was done as long as the majority of members had been trained.[12]

By this time both the Carpenters and the Painters, among other international unions, were demanding that President Georgine and the Department step up to the plate. They wanted organizing to become a Department priority, and they would not take no for an answer—they saw no point in paying Department per capita taxes unless the Department was willing to take action. Although organizing proponents were apparently successful in 1991, when the Governing Board of Presidents officially approved the COMET program, that vote did not carry much weight until 1993, when Bob Ozinga was hired as the BCTD's COMET coordinator. A former business manager and organizing director for the Colorado Building and Construction Trades Council, Ozinga had also run a statewide construction organizing program for the Carpenters. He knew from experience that "organizing is a tough thing for the building trades to do." As the Department had learned in the Los Angeles campaign ten years earlier, wide-scale organizing not only threatened political stability at the local and sometimes even the international union level, but it also had a tendency to expose all the flaws and weaknesses in any organization. And in an industry as complex as construction, with branches ranging from residential to commercial to heavy and highway construction, organizing strategies that benefited carpenters, ironworkers, laborers, and electricians in commercial building construction, for instance, would not increase work for boilermakers on industrial construction projects. But since COMET was an educational and motivational program, not an organizing campaign in itself, it provided a good opportunity for the BCTD to get behind construction organizing. "It may be a way of bringing the building trades back together," Carpenters' organizer Jim Sala noted, "so we don't fight each other over a smaller and smaller part of the pie."[13]

With the Department now sponsoring multi-trade COMET programs in Georgia, Massachusetts, Michigan, Indiana, Washington, and West Virginia, building trades' hopes were on the rise. As Ozinga remembered, the IBEW's construction organizing director, Jim Rudicil, "was all over North America, meeting with groups of building trades members and leaders . . . and he was very, very effective. It was exciting. It created something that the building trades hadn't seen or felt . . . in many generations, because there was a sense of 'Wow, we've got hope. There's something here we can change in what we perceived to be a diminishing movement, a diminishing way of life and work.' And that spread. It was contagious. It was a veritable prairie fire of its own because it didn't come from the top down. It came more from the bottom up." And that led to some very intense and exciting discussions at the highest level of the building trades, discussions that were bringing results. Multi-trade organizing campaigns were already under way in Branson, Missouri, and Washington, D.C., making 1994 a "watershed year," Ozinga reported to the general presidents. At that point President Georgine began to boost the project, advocating multi-trade organizing at the legislative conference, for example, an indication that a change in building trades policy was finally under way.[14]

The press was beginning to pay attention, too: Journalists portrayed the COMET program as a giant organizing campaign, with battle plans to salt and then strip nonunion contractors of their most skilled workers and to use the National Labor Relations Board to press unfair labor practice charges whenever employers discriminated against union activists. Before COMET, as the *Wall Street Journal* pointed out, contractors had not worried about "union infiltration for more than a generation mainly because . . . the construction unions hadn't done much organizing. . . . But COMET is changing the face of a growing number of individual markets." The *Engineering News-Record* also weighed in on the program. "Nonunion contractors are about to be hit with a double-barreled blast of union activism," and the "all-out bottom-up organizing blitz aimed at nonunion craftsmen" would no doubt prove to be "an excruciating experience for nonunion firms." But the editors were willing to approve the COMET campaign—as long as no violence erupted—largely because "the 15 member unions of the AFL-CIO's Building and Construction Trades Department remain just about the sole bulwark protecting the wages, benefits and working conditions of construction workers in the U.S. . . . There is no arguing with any program that supports workers' rights to organize themselves," they added. "Workers' rights to self determination and better wages and working conditions cannot be quarreled with."[15]

The Associated Builders and Contractors did not agree. "The name COMET is perfect. It is just a flash in the pan," an ABC spokesman countered, adding (with some exaggeration) that there had been "at least 40 nationally announced organizing programs over the past four decades and none have been successful." In the meantime, however, the ABC was taking no chances. In 1993 it published "Coping with COMET," a detailed guide on how to avoid "unwanted organizing campaigns" that included a checklist for fair hiring policies, suggested answers to workers' questions about union representation, and offered recommendations for maintaining good employee relations. At the same time the ABC sponsored a series of labor law seminars for chapters across the country designed to prepare nonunion employers to withstand the union "assault." "I cannot stress enough the gravity of this new union program," ABC president Joe Ivey warned his members. "The success or failure of your business is directly related to ABC's ability to 'shoot down COMET.'" The Associated General Contractors took the same approach, distributing a video called "Preparing for COMET" to advise its nonunion members on how to defeat the plan. Overall, COMET organizers were pleased that opponents were obviously alarmed, since that "legitimized our efforts in the eyes of some leaders and many members," as Jim Rudicil put it. But they were taking nothing for granted. "If we start totally believing our adversaries' statements, we are in trouble," organizer Jim Sala warned. And President Georgine agreed, pointing out that the building trades still had a long, long way to go. "Unless and until every construction worker belongs to a union, we can't rest," he told the 1994 building trades' legislative conference. "Universal membership is our goal."[16]

Two Steps Forward, One Step Back

While the COMET program was invigorating the building trades movement, promoting the kind of multi-craft cooperation that was crucial to success, tensions within the Department were coming to a head—a pattern that had stymied industrywide organizing efforts before. Jurisdictional disputes, for instance, remained an ongoing problem. As one industry analyst explained, preassembled materials and modular components had "gradually transformed the traditional skilled fabricator into a less skilled installer," which meant, in effect, that there was plenty of construction work that any number of trades could perform. Although the Department had revised the Plan for the Settlement of Jurisdictional Disputes in 1984 (requiring contractors to be "stipulated" to the plan in order for disputes to be processed) and amended it again in 1994 (to allow Canadian disputes to be processed in Canada), neither change made it easier to enforce unpopular awards. Worse yet, as Georgine reported, "unstipulated" contractors were stirring up trouble by offering unions "jurisdiction they never had." There were complaints that in Virginia the Carpenters union was claiming the work of the Laborers, Operating Engineers, and Iron Workers; that in California the Iron Workers union was training members to weld pipe; that in Indiana the Laborers union was taking over work belonging to the Cement Masons; and that in British Columbia, Canada, the Teamsters union was raiding the Boilermakers. "What I am seeing," the Boilermakers' vice president attested, "is cannibalism within the Trade Union movement beyond imagination." Policy-related conflicts also kept tensions high. Around 1991 the Carpenters stopped paying per capita taxes for a little more than a year, apparently to protest the Department's spending priorities. And in 1995 the Teamsters stopped paying on fifty-five thousand members employed in ready-mix concrete and supply to demonstrate the union's dissatisfaction with the way project agreements and the National Construction Stabilization Agreement had been negotiated.[17]

There were also problems stemming from the construction industry's "men only" culture. The Department had hired Mary Ellen Boyd to work on apprenticeship-related programs late in 1993, a move that seemed radical at the time. Women had been entering the trades in greater numbers ever since the federal government set hiring goals in 1977, and they accounted for 9 percent of apprenticeships in 1994, the Department reported. But they were a long way from becoming "brothers" in the trade union sense, something Boyd had learned on the job. An operating engineer who received her training at home (her father owned a small pipeline company, so she started out working summers as a "swamper"), she had worked two years on the pipeline before deciding to go to college. She had also worked on apprenticeship training for New York's State Labor Commissioner and had helped to establish Nontraditional Employment for Women, a nonprofit organization designed to help women enter the trades. "In New York we made significant inroads; I don't think we changed the ideas or the culture or even the predisposition of the men who ran the construction industry, contractors as well as unions, but we did reduce their fear level. . . . Every single morning we would shape up at construction sites, sometimes we'd have ten women sometimes we'd have thirty and we would present ourselves for work." Systematically documenting the unsuccessful efforts of women to be hired as laborers on the $1.5–billion Battery Park City construction project in the mid-1980s (which employed about twenty women and twenty-two hundred men overall), they filed a class action discrimination suit that was settled for more than $1 million in 1987. "We did not want to hurt the unions; we did not want to hurt the construction industry; we wanted only our equal rights," Boyd explained.[18]

Deciding to work for the changes she sought within the unions themselves, Boyd then took a job with the Carpenters District Council in New York City, as assistant director of the apprenticeship school. In fact, it was her boss, Paschal McGuinness, who later helped her get the job with the BCTD, arranging for an interview with President Georgine. In a three-hour session, she frankly told Georgine what she thought was wrong with the building trades and the industry. "I didn't hold anything back," she said. "I just wanted him to know who I was." It took a while, but with Secretary-Treasurer Joe Maloney's help, she finally landed a job. When she arrived in Washington, D.C., however, Boyd wasn't sure if the move had been worth it. She did not have an office, she did not have a title, and she was basically left alone. "For about the first two weeks I thought I had made a terrible mistake," Boyd admitted. But when Congress took up the issue of changing apprenticeship training rules— an issue she had worked on in New York—she proved her value to Leo Zeferetti, the Department's legislative director. He was impressed not only with the statistics she marshaled but also with the fact that she could write. After she successfully worked with President Georgine on some congressional testimony, Boyd gradually gained more responsibility as well as credibility. A stickler for developing "coherent, consistent policy," she encouraged Georgine to meet with staff members regularly to discuss broad issues of interest, including organizing, project labor agreements, and labor legislation. The idea was to generate policies and position papers that could then be presented to the Governing Board of Presidents, a new approach for the Department. Outspoken and versatile, Boyd was becoming a real player in Department affairs, a change that some Department leaders welcomed as a breath of fresh air and others dismissed as a serious error on Bob Georgine's part.[19]

But Georgine was facing bigger problems by 1995. After more than twenty years as BCTD president he was rapidly losing the support of a majority on the Governing Board. Some attributed the change in attitude to Georgine's failure to push the situs picketing bill after the Department lost its fight in the late 1970s. Others thought that the Department had grown stale because it had waited too long to promote organizing, thus failing to serve the practical needs of affiliated unions and state and local councils. There was also a very strong feeling that money was at the root of Georgine's problems. In 1991 he had been appointed chairman and chief executive officer of ULLICO, the Union Labor Life Insurance Company, which had been founded back in 1925 to provide affordable coverage for union members but now managed pension trust portfolios. Although the Governing Board of Presidents had originally approved the move, members were having second thoughts. Speculation on how much money Georgine was earning from his two jobs fueled serious opposition to his leadership. By February it was clear that painter A. L. "Mike" Monroe was going to challenge Georgine at the upcoming convention that summer, and that the Carpenters, Laborers, Operating Engineers, Painters, Plasterers, Sheet Metal Workers, and Teamsters were planning to support him. "Mike took Bob on," former UA president Marvin Boede remembered, "and the way things were set up he looked like a real goner."[20]

At the time, the news was stunning. After all, Georgine and his partner Joe Maloney had never had to fight to keep their jobs: There had not been a contested election since the 1930s, when the Department had split in two, or a serious squabble at a BCTD convention since the mid-1970s, when delegates had hotly debated the pros and cons of expanding the Executive Council. Now there were letters back and forth challenging the Department's use of money. Questions were raised about the jet plane the Department had purchased in the mid-1980s, how it was used, and whether a labor organization should enjoy such a luxury (although in 1986 the Governing Board had found the plane to be a cost-efficient solution to the Department's frequent need for short-term, last-minute travel). There were also questions about whether rank-and-file members even knew how per capita taxes were being spent, since Georgine and Maloney had failed to provide the general presidents with copies of annual audits since 1991, as the constitution required (a complaint that may have been related to the BCTD's 1985 decision to hold conventions every five years—previously audits had been presented to the convention every other year, a policy that no one had questioned at the time). But whether these complaints reflected real structural problems, personal animosity, or both, did not matter. The fact remained that affiliates were stirred up, and that, as one carpenter told the *Engineering News-Record,* was not necessarily bad. Controversy, he pointed out, could have a positive outcome, "since a lot of people . . . [get] activated."[21]

Although Monroe's supporters believed the BCTD needed a president with "more hands-on involvement," as Laborers' president Arthur A. Coia put it, Georgine's supporters countered that he was the right man for the job. Georgine not only had the political and industrial contacts that the job required, Bricklayers' president Jack Joyce pointed out, but also the "ability to motivate a fractious, and not entirely egoless, group of union presidents," a rare quality in the trades. And that being the case, Georgine's supporters took Monroe's challenge seriously. Before too much time had passed, the word was out that Georgine was donating his BCTD salary to fund scholarships for Cornell's Construction Industry Program, thereby blunting the "two job" issue. There were also meetings between Georgine supporters and some Carpenters officials. Eight affiliates were backing Georgine: the Asbestos Workers, Boilermakers, Bricklayers, Electrical Workers, Elevator Constructors, Iron Workers, Plumbers, and Roofers. But he needed the votes of a large union, like the Carpenters, to defeat Monroe and his running mate, Larry McDonald, who headed the Teamsters' construction division. Conflicts within the Carpenters union worked to Georgine's advantage; although President Sigurd Lucassen steadfastly opposed Georgine on a number of issues (including the Department's failure to take organizing seriously), up and coming leaders like Douglas McCarron (who was second in line for Lucassen's job, according to the union's electoral policy) were eager to challenge him, or so it seemed to observers. So if Paschal McGuinness, who was first in line, were to run with Georgine, the door would not only be open for McCarron to make his challenge but the Carpenters would also likely back Georgine, or so the theory went. Apparently Joe Maloney agreed. Early in August Maloney announced his plans to retire, and Paschal McGuinness was named to succeed him as a candidate for secretary-treasurer, a decision that tipped the scales in Georgine's favor.[22]

In the end there was no contested election. "The stage was set for a potentially nasty contest for the presidency of the AFL-CIO's Building and Construction Trades Department," the *Engineering News-Record* reported. "But the script was changed at the last moment." At a meeting of the Governing Board of Presidents, just one day before the convention opened, Monroe and McDonald announced that they would not be candidates for office, allowing the affiliates "to close ranks" behind Georgine, as the trade journal put it, "and present at least the appearance of solidarity." There had been some important compromises. The Governing Board of Presidents had agreed to support a constitutional amendment, to go into effect in the year 2000, that would restrict executive officers from holding any other salaried job. The Board also agreed to withdraw controversial resolutions challenging Georgine's and Maloney's handling of Department finances. Finally, the Board decided not to challenge the fact that up until McGuinness announced his candidacy, both he and Georgine had been members of the Carpenters union because the Carpenters had absorbed Georgine's original union, the Lathers. But since metal lathers in New York City had joined the Iron Workers, Georgine was able to switch his membership and comply with the BCTD's constitutional requirement that no two executive officers belong to the same union, a point his opponents had earlier planned to press.[23]

When Georgine addressed the convention the next day he seemed gratified that affiliates had managed to reach a consensus. "It was no secret that we were headed for a conflict at this Convention," he told the delegates. "But like the family that we are, we took those issues that divided us into a board meeting yesterday, and we came to a meeting of minds. Now, I won't kid you, it wasn't easy for us. We had a few harsh words," he admitted. "Both sides of the issue had some very strong convictions. But, in the end, we acted for what we believe is in the best interests of the building trades. . . . Like all families, we have very strong attachments. And sometimes regrettable conflicts. But we don't hesitate to voice our gripes, [and] make our suggestions about what should be done. . . . But in the final analysis, we are still brothers and sisters. We confine our complaints and our criticisms to and within that family circle. We resolve our problems inside our own house. . . . And that was how we approached our meeting yesterday."[24]

"So, okay. . . . That was yesterday. Today is today," he continued. "So let's talk about where we are headed." Addressing the general criticism that the Department was out of touch with rank-and-file realities, Georgine staked out four important goals. Restructuring the Department was first on the list, so that it could better respond "to the pressures . . . of today and tomorrow." Next he wanted to expand the organizing committee (to include rank-and-file, local council, and international staff representation) and hammer out a multi-trades organizing plan. Then he wanted to finish a project that the Department was already working on: the establishment of a grass-roots political lobbying campaign in every local council, to create an army of voters "that will be more powerful than any . . . political action committee." Finally, a committee of local council leaders was already working on a plan to develop a leadership training program to be offered through the George Meany Center. "We have an exhilarating future ahead of us," he promised the delegates. "We have it in our grasp to reorganize this industry. We know how to turn the increasing skills shortage to our advantage," he added. "We have all these opportunities ahead and all we need is the will to make them happen."[25]

The Building Trades Organizing Project

That will would be tested more than once during the next five years, a period that would prove to be both exciting and disappointing. Within three months after the close of the convention President Georgine had hired Professor Lois Gray, a specialist in union structure and government from Cornell University, to study the Department's structure and function and to analyze the possibilities for change. Before the year was over she was interviewing Department staff, international presidents, and state and local council officers to determine how the Department operated and whether it served their needs. Overall, constituents seemed to be satisfied with BCTD efforts in areas like political lobbying, national and project agreements, research, and safety and health promotion, Gray reported. But when it came to public relations, education, organizing, and especially communication between the Department and state and local councils, there was plenty of room for improvement. State and local officers were looking for more than representation: They wanted information and training on issues like bargaining trends and legislative action. "The councils felt like they were unattached," explained Mary Ellen Boyd, Georgine's new chief of staff (a job that had her running day-to-day operations by 1997, after Secretary-Treasurer McGuinness stepped down). "They were out there kind of floating, without any line of communication to them."[26]

Taking his cue from the report, Georgine created two new divisions in 1996 and appointed two veteran council leaders to head them. Tim Nichols, an iron worker from Michigan's State Building Trades Council, was named Director of External Relations, charged with overseeing legislation, apprenticeship and training, health and safety issues, and government relations. And Bill "Giz" Kaczorowski, a steam fitter from Baltimore's Building Trades Council, was named Director of Field Services, responsible for handling matters related to state and local councils. By 1997 the Field Services Division was sponsoring regional meetings (which included open forums with Georgine), and department staff members were conducting week-long leadership training sessions at the George Meany Center (which emphasized organizing and communication skills). The new division also surveyed local councils in 1997 to get a handle on how these councils were staffed and financed, whether their geographical jurisdiction coincided with actual construction markets, and how successful they were in maintaining membership of all the trades. In Georgine's view, strengthening these councils had to be a Department priority. "Everything we're doing depends on our members in the field," he explained, so "we're changing our focus from Washington, D.C., to the grassroots where our members live and work."[27]

Endorsing these efforts, and approving the expenses that went along with them, the general presidents backed the expansion of field operations. But they also made it clear that restructuring would not solve all the Department's problems. Without unity among the affiliates, as Carpenters' president Douglas McCarron pointed out, restructuring would not matter. And at the moment, chances for unity looked slim: Department leaders may have reached a political consensus at the 1995 convention, but in 1996 they were still fighting over some very thorny jurisdictional matters, including the development of so-called vertical or wall-to-wall agreements, whereby one trade manned all the jobs it could handle, regardless of established jurisdiction. "The conflicts go beyond 'the age-old problem of jurisdictional friction between crafts' and concern an 'expansionist program,'" the *Engineering News-Record* reported. Bricklayers' president Jack Joyce, for instance, was particularly enraged by what he called "predatory objectives and behavior" on the part of the Laborers, alleging that the union was negotiating with contractors to "include the definition of other crafts into their own collective bargaining agreements." Although Laborers' president Arthur Coia strongly disagreed, pointing out that "jurisdictional boundaries are changing" and that he was just trying to put people to work, Joyce urged the general presidents to support a resolution of censure in February 1996. Failing to persuade his colleagues, he then called on President Georgine to broker a truce that came to be known as the Solidarity Compact: an agreement among all the affiliates to recognize basic craft jurisdictions, prohibit raiding between affiliates, ban vertical agreements (and enforce that ban on local unions), and resolve all questions of jurisdiction through the Plan for the Settlement of Jurisdictional Disputes.[28]

Whether affiliates would actually honor the compact (which was never signed by all the general presidents) remained to be seen. And even if they all complied, there was also a question of whether such a compact suited industry realities. For there were some general presidents who privately thought that fifteen trades were just a little "archaic," in light of industry practices, and that mergers promised a better solution to jurisdictional disputes. In fact, there were those who favored a single construction union with autonomous self-governing divisions for each trade as the best defense against open-shop competition; however, they never explained how they thought this might be accomplished. Although the idea of mergers periodically captured the attention of the press, it was so controversial, one union leader wisecracked, that it would probably take a pistol to the head to get some presidents to consider it, and even that might fail to penetrate. Under the circumstances, then, the Solidarity Compact seemed to be a step in the right direction: If the building trades hoped to make any progress on organizing the unorganized, they first had to agree to stop fighting among themselves.[29]

And that was becoming a top priority: By 1996 it was clear that local councils were looking to the Department to take the lead on industrywide organizing. Experience with the COMET program had demonstrated the value of using rank-and-file workers to spread the organizing gospel, but it had also underscored the need for a coordinated campaign. "COMET is . . . the best tool I have seen in my ten years of working for a local Building Trades Council," an officer from Cincinnati explained, but it was not working as well as it could, since "the Operating Engineers 'COMET' one job, and the Electricians 'COMET' another job, and the Pipefitters 'COMET' a third job." The effort was sincere, but it was not enough to save unionized construction in places like Cincinnati, where the open shop flourished, he said. That would require "a concentrated action of all the trades," a position that President Georgine had finally come to endorse. In fact, the whole point of restructuring the Department and improving relations with state and local councils, he pointed out, was to develop the infrastructure necessary to launch successful, locally based, multi-trade organizing campaigns. A fiercely competitive, complex industry like construction required a comprehensive, market-wide response, organizers noted, since organizing individual contractors had proved to be "an exercise in futility," as one economist put it. "Multi-trade organizing reflects what our industry looks like in the field," Georgine later noted. "It allows us to organize on a scale to win." Although it would prove to be far more complicated, demanding, and expensive than anyone expected, at the time multi-trade, market-wide organizing offered building trades unions real hope for the future.[30]

The plan was becoming a reality, thanks in part to a 1995 U.S. Supreme Court decision upholding the rights of union salts to organize nonunion employers. The Town and Country decision, as it was called, "puts a legal foundation under our organizing efforts," Georgine reported. It marked a "major milestone" that enabled the Department to move beyond COMET training and develop a comprehensive organizing campaign. "The impetus came from all that excitement . . . in the field," Bob Ozinga remembered, "but it took some very hard work by some individuals at the highest level to have that translate into a real program." By July a team of building trades and AFL organizers—including Jeff Grabelsky, Adam Pagnucco, Steve Lerner, and Ozinga—had a proposal ready to go: the Construction Organizing Training and Action Project (COTAP), a joint undertaking by the BCTD, its affiliates, and the AFL-CIO's Organizing Department. Designed to integrate training with organizing, the project's long-range goal was to develop the capacity to unionize entire construction markets, devise a system to identify, train, and place construction organizers, and launch a model campaign within eighteen months.[31]

When the committee presented the proposal to the Governing Board of Presidents, members were encouraged by the reception. There were still a number of general presidents who saw no need to organize, as long as local unions had members on the bench. But this governing board meeting marked a major turning point, nevertheless. Committee members not only demonstrated that union density had dropped from 42 percent in 1970 to 18 percent in 1995, but they also made it clear that "if we were really going to make a difference in construction organizing, if we were really going to turn the tide from a decline in unionization of the construction industry to a more vibrant growing dynamic, then we would have to do so together," as Bob Ozinga recalled. "We'd have to do it on a very large scale and we'd have to have some very ambitious strategies, the likes of which we haven't seen since perhaps our unions were founded—organizing large numbers, not just 2 or 3 or 5 or 20 workers at a time," he said. Construction unions would have to organize around eight thousand workers a year, the committee informed the general presidents, just to maintain the current 18 percent rate, and one hundred sixteen thousand workers a year to reach 37 percent in ten years' time, the percentage they had held in the mid-1970s. "We . . . talked about organizing," recalled Jeff Grabelsky, who made the presentation, "and then laid out [the COTAP] proposal that said there's really something that we can do and the Department has a role to play, and affiliates can work together on this project."[32]

With the Board's approval, Georgine appointed a committee to work out the specifics. The team proved to be "a good combination of people," organizers agreed, and the process itself was exciting, since it brought together a cross-section of the building trades: Committee members included international union organizing directors, local council leaders, and local union business managers who worked out the structure, staffing, and principles of the plan. The committee also worked with the BCTD's Research Department, analyzing some three hundred labor markets to select a target area with "a vibrant construction market, excellent economic projections, . . . a strong and united Building Trades Council," and a local union membership ready and willing to take on the monumental task of talking one-on-one to hundreds of unrepresented workers.[33]

By September, when the committee presented the pilot program to the Governing Board, the original Construction Organizing Training and Action Program had evolved into the Building Trades Organizing Project (BTOP): a multi-craft, market-wide organizing campaign set to begin in Las Vegas, Nevada. Casinos, hotels, houses, and shopping centers were going up all over the city, and demand for skilled labor was high. In fact, construction employment had increased some 47 percent since 1996, making Las Vegas the "hottest city in the country for building," according to one union spokesman. Although organizers would later express second thoughts, at the time Las Vegas seemed a promising choice. On the one hand, President Georgine enjoyed good relations with the building trades leadership, the Carpenters union was building a major training center there, and the Hotel and Restaurant Employees union was about to embark on a campaign to organize casino and hotel workers with AFL-CIO support. On the other hand,

Las Vegas was a strong union town, despite Nevada's right-to-work laws, and about 40 percent of the construction workforce was unionized. In Las Vegas the difference between working union on the "Strip" (where the building trades controlled almost all the work) and working nonunion on residential and light commercial projects was obvious. Workers on the Strip could expect fresh water, overtime pay, and relatively safe working conditions. Workers off the Strip, especially Latinos who did not speak English, could not.[34]

With the Board's approval secured by October, the Las Vegas campaign began to gear up. Jim Rudicil, the IBEW's construction organizing director, was hired to head the project, and the BCTD put up $1 million toward the $6 million that a two-year project was expected to cost. AFL-CIO president John Sweeney provided another $1.2 million, as well as the services of the Federation's organizing and strategic research staff, and the affiliates contributed the rest. But a successful campaign would require more than money and organizers. It would also require a level of practical solidarity that so far had not been easy to achieve: The general presidents would have to enforce, as well as endorse, the Solidarity Compact. They would also have to ensure that "internal obstacles," including high local initiation fees and referral lists favoring the existing membership, would be removed. Although some trades would ultimately refuse to comply, increasing tensions on the Governing Board and on the ground in Las Vegas, in the fall of 1996 the future looked bright. "We intend to organize every construction worker in our target area," Georgine promised. "We intend to regain America's construction market. We intend to keep union contractors in business."[35]

When it was launched in January 1997, the Las Vegas BTOP campaign energized the labor movement. The AFL-CIO, the BCTD, and the Southern Nevada Building and Construction Trades Council were all working together, rallying union and nonunion workers, setting up a media campaign, and filing numerous complaints with the National Labor Relations Board against open-shop contractors. During the first three months almost six hundred union members had completed the COMET I training class, taking the first important step toward opening union doors. And one hundred twenty-five of these had honed their organizing skills through COMET II and were ready to salt nonunion job sites. Their goal was to help unrepresented workers "understand their rights and demand fairness, better pay and working conditions," as a BTOP manual put it. With the BTOP staff compiling a database of likely union prospects, union salts encouraged their nonunion colleagues to organize worker committees and protest unfair labor practices on the job. The point, as Jim Rudicil explained, was for nonunion workers to see the union "as their friend and not their enemy," and for union members to support, not criticize, nonunion workers.[36]

There were also forty full-time organizers on board in Las Vegas by September and their numbers were rising: There would be more than sixty in a few months' time, drawn from the BCTD and international and local unions. Some were more effective than others; there were complaints early on that some unions refused to put their best men on the job. But those who took the campaign seriously were busy all the time. Organizers reported that unrepresented workers would tell them, "Yeah our employers are horrible, they totally rip us off, they don't treat us with any respect, etc., etc. but I don't intend to be working for this employer three months from now, so I'm not going to get involved in a campaign." So the first step, as one organizer explained, "was to get those workers to understand that their next employer would not be any better as long as nonunion standards prevailed in that sector of the market."[37]

BTOP organizers visited numerous residential and light commercial job sites, dropping off leaflets in both English and Spanish and talking with workers until management forced them to leave. They also hosted weekly get-togethers, complete with translators, so that workers could meet with union representatives from all fifteen trades. And they were doing house calls, as Rudicil reported, a strategy that nonunion employers called "harassment" and "intimidation" but that seemed to be working well, according to union leaders. The effort not only improved the buildings trades' reputation among workers who had expected to be shut out, but it also helped organizers document cases of unfair labor practices on nonunion jobs. For instance, after visiting a group of Latino workers employed by a nonunion roofing company, BTOP organizers learned that the company did not pay overtime rates, illegally charged workers for safety equipment, and routinely cheated non–English speakers out of their pay.[38]

Certainly the work was demanding. The best organizers regularly worked fifteen-hour days. But before the year was over they were beginning to see results. By the fall of 1997 local unions counted some three thousand new members—a 14 percent increase—and 255 contractors had joined union ranks. If these gains had as much to do with the expanding market in Las Vegas as BTOP itself, the result seemed amazing nonetheless to local leaders like Stan Smith, executive secretary of the San Francisco Building & Construction Trades Council. "It reminds me of what I have read and heard from such giants as Harry Bridges of the Longshoremen's union and Joe O'Sullivan and Dan Del Carlo of the Building Trades, in the 1930's, when the unions reorganized. BTOP is using all the tried and true methods, such as one-on-one visits, that were successful in the '30s, plus all the high technology of the 1990s"—a reference, perhaps, to the television infomercial that BTOP began broadcasting that fall. "The biggest difference?" he asked. "In the '30s, unions organized under pro-worker laws, while BTOP operates under the most anti-worker laws of any nation in the industrialized world. However they both have the same agenda; a decent living and a job with dignity. Most of us workers don't ask for much more." But not everyone shared his enthusiasm, since BTOP was a very costly proposition: By 1998 the campaign had spent more than $4 million and the Department was looking for $3 million more. As one union contractor noted, the trades would have been better off had they offered nonunion workers "a $500 signing bonus."[39]

Anti-union opponents had bigger complaints: They were especially enraged by the BTOP strategy of filing unfair labor practice charges with the National Labor Relations Board. "Whatever the violation, however minor, we're going to file charges on it," Jim Rudicil explained, "because it's ultimately a violation of workers' rights." During the first nine months of the campaign, charges were filed against twenty-three construction companies, including Precision Concrete, an ABC "merit shop" company that was employed on a high-profile, high-rise hotel project in downtown Las Vegas. According to lawyers employed by BTOP, union supporters were spied on, transferred to less desirable jobs, denied raises, threatened with discharge and bodily injury, and fired for union organizational activities protected under the law, charges the company president dismissed as "100 percent baseless." BTOP's charges were merely an organizing ploy, he said, designed to pressure him to sign with the union without holding an NLRB election.[40]

The charges were "frivolous," a local ABC spokesman agreed, an attempt to put "open-shop contractors out of business by forcing them to spend money in legal fees." And that was not fair, the national president of ABC added. "We believe that union membership should be a matter of choice. Free choice." But so did the NLRB: The federal agency issued complaints against Precision Concrete in August, indicating that examiners believed that the company had violated the National Labor Relations Act, according to an NLRB representative. In order to avoid a trial, Precision Concrete agreed to settle the case in October, rehiring eight union supporters and paying out more than $20,000 in back wages. This BTOP victory did not result in a contract; in fact, concrete workers would wage a series of strikes and demonstrations in the summer of 1998 demanding higher wages, paid benefits and vacation time, water breaks, and the right to organize. Yet the effort was worthwhile nonetheless. "It's about making the contractor follow the rules," Rudicil noted, "and elevating the conditions of the worker."[41]

But that was proving to be more difficult than the Department had expected, President Georgine admitted in 1998. Membership numbers were up, he was pleased to report, but market share had not increased substantially, so it was time to make some serious changes at all levels of BTOP. As the campaign was demonstrating, it was one thing to develop a strategy for organizing hundreds of thousands of workers, and another to test that strategy on the ground. In the first place, the original BTOP plan had called for training large numbers of competent workforce organizers, and so far that had not taken place: At times of heightened organizing activity, as one BTOP veteran put it, lead organizers are just too busy to devote much time to training.[42]

Second, the campaign seemed to lack the kind of disciplined, strategic direction that many believed was necessary. Organizing targets appeared to be chosen haphazardly, some complained, and what had started out as a workforce organizing campaign was rapidly becoming a salting program, leaving thousands of workers unorganized. Worse yet, those workers who were taking great risks to organize their shops still had trouble joining the union: Although BTOP staff regularly met with local union leaders to pinpoint obstacles to admitting new members, those obstacles still existed in far too many cases, and that was a real setback. If newly organized workers could not count on the safety net provided by union membership, then BTOP's workforce organizing plan and the chance of sustained market recovery were doomed. With the stakes so high, it was time to get BTOP back on track. "This is a different type of organizing campaign," Georgine told the Governing Board, one that required "a more effective over-arching strategy" as well as better trained staff, more experienced organizers, and stronger support from local building trades unions. "If we don't win here," he added, "we all lose."[43]

With a new director in place—Bob Ozinga, the Department's COMET director and a thirteen-year veteran of multi-trade organizing—the Department was ready to launch BTOP "Phase 2." Making a real effort to streamline the staff and cut down on expenses, Ozinga also wanted to test the premise that was at the root of the original BTOP plan: that unrepresented workers will stand up and take chances and take risks if they believe there's a better thing coming. The concrete industry in light commercial and residential construction seemed to be a good place to begin. The workforce was huge and almost entirely Latino—carpenters, laborers, and cement masons, primarily, who worked for a discrete number of employers, did the same kind of work, and had expressed significant interest in organizing and moving into action.[44]

"I felt that we could really do it, that we could begin to demonstrate the viability of this strategic concept we had brought to the table when this whole thing started," Ozinga explained. "So over a period of time, several months in fact, more and more of our effort was concentrated on those workers, and more and more action began to take place." With the backing of some of the most talented organizers in the building trades and the AFL-CIO, and the support of the Carpenters, Laborers, and Cement Masons, these unorganized workers began to take direct action. They held strikes, prayer vigils, sit-down demonstrations, and other forms of civil disobedience. And they intended to continue until conditions changed. "If the employers don't respond with decent treatment and working conditions," organizer Tony Valdez (from Laborers Local 872) told the press, "we'll see mounting job actions and public demonstrations by . . . workers who are sacrificing so much to obtain their right to have unions." And that really shook up the industry, Ozinga reported. "Traditionally, companies associated strikes with unions," he explained, "and here you have unorganized workers walking out."[45]

At around the same time nonunion employees of the Willis Roofing Company were joining forces with Roofers Local 162 in a comprehensive organizing campaign that would prove to be one of BTOP's genuine successes. The Roofers counted only about eighty members in Las Vegas when BTOP began and had almost no presence in residential or light commercial work, so Willis Roofing was a valuable target. The company controlled about 60 percent of the residential market, and it had strong business ties to major builders including Lewis Homes (the largest developer in Las Vegas) and Kaufman and Broad Homes (one of the largest homebuilders in the country). Willis Roofing also had a long history of OSHA and wage and hour violations, making it vulnerable to a public campaign and one that the vast majority of Willis workers would support. "On average, these roofers work 60 to 70 hours a week at straight time, but they are told to put 40 hours on their time card," organizer Tony Diaz explained. So they were ready and willing to take a risk and demand union protection.[46]

With research and legal help from the BCTD and the Roofers international union, Local 162 filed a class action wage and hour suit against the company in May 1998, demanding that Willis Roofing refund money illegally deducted from workers' paychecks for mandatory safety equipment. The local also helped Willis workers distribute leaflets to prospective customers at a Lewis Homes open house to let them know just how these houses were being constructed. "Workers who put roofs on Lewis Homes homes are organizing to fight against unfair treatment by Lewis'[s] roofer, Willis Roofing," one leaflet read. "Lewis Homes has been added to the lawsuit that charges its subcontractor, Willis Roofing, with: Cheating workers on piece rates; Improperly charging workers for safety equipment . . . Failing to pay overtime; [and] Retaliating against workers." Urging customers to call Lewis Homes, the leaflet advised them to "Tell Lewis Homes to use fair Subcontractors." As a result, the company president met with union leaders and agreed to provide information to support the lawsuit against Willis Roofing.[47]

The Roofers and BTOP waged a similar campaign against Kaufman and Broad, letting the public know that the company rejected Latino mortgage seekers twice as often as white applicants, that it was under a Federal Trade Commission consent decree for making "false, misleading and deceptive statements" in marketing its houses, and that the company was unfair to workers and home buyers alike. The Roofers developed a website to spread the message, spotlighting conditions faced by Willis workers such as Victor Griego. "I wanted a guarantee instead of a promise [about] clean water, breaks, and better wages. The promises were broken," he said.[48]

BTOP also sent the company's board of directors detailed information on Willis Roofing's labor practices and on the strikes and public demonstrations that were slowing down production of Kaufman and Broad houses. Taking their case to Kaufman and Broad's shareholders meeting in Los Angeles, organizers made their presentation while Willis workers, union members, and supporters from the community demonstrated across the street. By the summer of 1999 Kaufman and Broad had had enough. After thousands of union members throughout the country sent personal messages to the company's CEO to "Stop Willis from dragging your name through the dirt"—along with dirt-filled containers to make the point clear—Kaufman and Broad persuaded Willis Roofing to negotiate with the union. "Developers wanted the lawsuits dropped," the *Engineering News-Record* reported, "and were instrumental in encouraging talks with the union." As a result, Roofers Local 162 not only welcomed more than two hundred new members but Willis workers also won $400,000 in back wages (to settle the suit), and a four-year agreement that included employer-paid health benefits and annual wage increases of fifty cents an hour.[49]

By that time, however, the Las Vegas BTOP campaign had officially closed up shop; after two and a half active, eventful years, responsibility for the organizing drive reverted to the local movement in May 1999. The campaign was just too expensive to continue, unless there was widespread support for aggressive workforce organizing, and that simply was not the case at the time. As organizing tactics crossed into civil disobedience in the concrete and roofers campaign, local unions tended to step back. Given their long history of working closely with their contractors, as well as the fact that all their members were working at the time, they tended to shy away from fierce economic battles. At the same time there was no indication so far that the Department's experiment in multi-trade organizing had produced the kind of trade solidarity necessary for success. The BCTD's 1998 motto "15 Unions, 1 Voice" was still more of a goal than a reality: Long-standing trade rivalries, the belief that BTOP benefited some unions at the expense of others, and the failure of some international presidents to push locals unions to open their doors all contributed to an underlying sense of dissatisfaction that hastened the end of the Las Vegas campaign.[50]

The BTOP experience nevertheless raised important questions. What role should the Department play when it comes to organizing? How essential is market-wide, multi-trade organizing to the long-term survival of the building trades? And if it is essential, what steps would the trades and the Department have to take to execute an ambitious plan like BTOP? Is bottom-up organizing sufficient to revive union construction, or does market recovery also require more traditional top-down organizing in order to sign up new contractors and help them win work? That these questions failed to stimulate a critical review to ascertain what had worked and what had not worked in Las Vegas disappointed BTOP organizers. But they did take justifiable pride in the fact that when building trades unions honored the commitments they made when they signed on to the campaign, the strategy had worked.[51] For if BTOP never reached its highest goals, it did have some lasting, positive effects nonetheless.

"We did a lot of very good things," Mary Ellen Boyd later noted. "There was a significant increase in membership." By 1999 the Las Vegas market boasted the fastest-growing union sector in the industry: Some three hundred new contractors and subcontractors had signed collective-bargaining agreements, and local unions had signed up around seven thousand new members, a 35 percent increase. The Laborers union grew by 50 percent, the Carpenters added two thousand new members, the Bricklayers tripled its membership from five hundred to fifteen hundred, and the Roofers multiplied its by ten—the once marginal local of eighty members was now a viable organization eight hundred–strong. Thanks to BTOP, as organizer Steve Lerner pointed out, local unions had increased the size of their apprenticeship programs and their organizing budgets, as well as the number of trained organizers who lived and worked around Las Vegas. And if membership had not increased at the rates organizers had originally hoped for, construction unions had strengthened their power at the bargaining table and the ballot box. In fact Bob Ozinga credited the 1998 reelection of Nevada's Democratic senator, Harry Reid, to the resurgence of the building trades.[52]

The End of One Era and the Beginning of Another

Building trades prospects outside Las Vegas were also looking up. Between 1996 and 1998 construction unions had added more than one hundred fifty thousand new members nationwide. "After 25 years of lower wages, no benefits, inferior training, and unsafe and unhealthy conditions, unrepresented workers have had enough," Georgine said. "We welcome them." But the Department's plan to organize the unorganized was still a work in progress. "While we've grown from having 250 full-time organizers in the mid-1980s to more than 1,000 today," Georgine told delegates to the 1998 legislative conference, "we are learning that we need to do much more work to meet the challenge of full-scale organizing." Sharing those lessons through a new campaign called Milestones to Organizing, the Department developed a systematic guide for local councils that laid out the rationale for multi-craft, market-wide workforce campaigns; explained the organizing process in detail; and identified, milestone by milestone, what local councils needed to do and what kind of legal, research, and training support they could expect from the BCTD when they did so—a partnership that made Milestones a "well-conceived" and "smart response to the limitations of the Las Vegas campaign," according to one of the organizers.[53]

Because the first milestone was to ensure that all local unions were council members, the Department declared a six-month amnesty period: Between June and December 1998 unions did not have to pay more than a year's delinquent dues to rejoin councils, no matter how long they had been gone. Another crucial milestone was the financing of an adequate war chest, since Las Vegas had made it clear that the BCTD could not afford to subsidize multiple campaigns for long: Organizing funds had to equal at least 30 percent of a council's total income. Other milestones included building membership support and eliminating obstacles like high initiation fees, restrictive referral policies, and inadequate training opportunities to upgrade the skills of nonunion workers—all problems that BTOP organizers had encountered repeatedly in Las Vegas. "Make no mistake about it," Georgine said. "There is no way our voice can stay strong if our members decline. Either we lift the living standards of unrepresented workers, or they will eventually drag us all down. Through COMET we've trained over 1,000 instructors and over 100,000 members," and the investment seemed to be paying off. "After decades of decline, union density is up by 1 percent," Georgine reported; an incremental increase but an increase all the same. "Let's keep up this momentum."[54]

By March 1999 it looked as if all systems were go. According to the *Engineering News-Record,* the BCTD was taking its Las Vegas show on the road, with the first stop scheduled for Seattle. That assessment proved to be overly optimistic: The Seattle Building Trades Council would eventually decide not to go ahead with the project. At the time, however, conditions for success seemed promising. The Plumbers and Pipefitters union was also starting an organizing campaign in Texas, which UA President Martin Maddaloni urged affiliates to support. And the Department had begun targeting temporary employment agencies, including Tradesmen International, Contractors Labor Pool, and Labor Ready, which were on their way to becoming hiring halls for nonunion contractors. The steady pace of organizing activity together with the Department's ongoing political, educational, health and safety, and project labor agreement programs, all seemed to support the belief that the building trades had finally turned an important corner. "From organizing unrepresented workers to mobilizing and motivating our members in the political process, to reaching out to our communities, we have become the new Building Trades," President Georgine told the 1999 legislative conference.[55]

Whether this shift would prove to be more apparent than real, no one knew at the time. And whether affiliates were truly committed to building bridges to civic and community groups, as Georgine suggested, as a means of organizing the new immigrant workforce, remained to be seen. But it would not be Georgine who would lead the campaign. Satisfied that he had kept his 1995 promise that by the year 2000 the building trades "will be on as strong a roll as we were when this century began," he was ready to take his leave. In January 2000 the U.S. Bureau of Labor Statistics announced the largest increase in construction union membership in decades; 131,000 workers had signed union cards the previous year, bringing union density up to 19.1 percent. At around the same time President Robert A. Georgine announced his plans to retire from the BCTD, effective April 15, and devote full attention to building up ULLICO, which he still served as CEO, an announcement that caught many of the general presidents by surprise. "I'm leaving the building trades at a time when membership is increasing," he noted, "and the goals that I set at our 1995 convention have been achieved." "It's a good time to leave and get some younger blood in there," he told the *Engineering News-Record*. But others were not so sure. "Bob was able to keep [the building trades] together most of the time," a colleague pointed out: He provided leadership when the various unions disagreed on policies and goals. "Georgine is one of those leaders that you don't replace," another added. "You succeed him, but you don't replace him."[56]

His "topping out" party, held on the eve of the BCTD's annual legislative conference, was a great celebration of Georgine's achievements. ("Topping out" referred to the building trades' tradition of marking the pinnacle of a construction project with an evergreen tree, a flag, and a party.) It would also prove to be his last hurrah: Georgine's career at ULLICO would blow up a few years later over questionable business ethics, seriously tarnishing his reputation. But in April 2000 the future was looking better than it had in a while, and Georgine's supporters had plenty to cheer about. The White House chief of staff, John Podesta, a fellow Chicago native, set the tone for the evening as master of ceremonies. Speakers including Senators Ted Kennedy and Ted Stevens, Congressman David Bonior, and former secretary of labor John T. Dunlop all attested to Georgine's political, professional, and social strengths, as did former secretary-treasurer Joseph F. Maloney and president-elect Edward C. Sullivan.

A wide range of sponsors from international unions, to state councils, to the Associated General Contractors, the Bechtel Corporation, and the Diabetes Research Institute also testified to Georgine's wide sphere of influence.

Even Nontraditional Employment for Women tipped their "Hard Hats to Bob Georgine, a leading supporter of opening the trades to women," and the Italian American Democratic Leadership Council saluted him as "A Great Italian, A Great Democrat, and A Great American." When a video captured the highlights of his career, accompanied by the Frank Sinatra hit "My Way," however, Georgine offered a friendly correction. He had not done things his way, he told supporters. He had done things the union way, and that had made all the difference. But if he was pleased by the tribute, Georgine made it clear the next day, when he addressed the legislative conference, that the Department had no time for nostalgia. Praising the fifteen affiliates for their recent progress in organizing, Georgine warned them not to become complacent. Union leaders must "change whatever it is that needs changing," he insisted, "even if it means changing the configuration of the unions," a reference to a subject that had come up many times before, namely, that some of the affiliates should merge to increase their own strength in the industry as well as the strength of the Department as a whole.[57]

Certainly Georgine took no risks when he voiced this controversial opinion. But his farewell advice, nevertheless, harkened backed to his days coming up through the Lathers. When he was still making his mark with the building trades, Georgine had been a reformer, boldly staking out the high ground whether he thought he could reach it or not, and then doing whatever he could to move others toward it. But over time he had learned that that was not the way to get things done at the national level. For better or worse, common ground and consensus ruled the Building and Construction Trades Department. It had been Georgine's particular talent to assess how far the majority of general presidents was willing to go and then move the others along, a strategy that had ultimately preserved the Department as an institution but did not necessarily address the critical issues facing the trades. Now that internal politics were no longer his concern, Georgine was free to offer this unpopular advice, for he certainly knew in April 2000 that the majority on the Governing Board of Presidents did not favor mergers. The subject was so "touchy," the newly installed president Ed Sullivan told the *Engineering News-Record*, that he did not intend to push it.[58]

His instincts were correct. President Sullivan, an elevator constructor who had started out as a helper in Boston, and his new partner, Secretary-Treasurer Joseph Maloney, a boilermaker from Toronto who had served the Department as Director for Canadian Affairs, already had enough on their plates. (Maloney, a graduate of Harvard's Trade Union Leadership program, was no relation to former secretary-treasurer Joseph F. Maloney.) Despite the show of good-will and optimism that had marked Georgine's topping out party, an undercurrent of dissatisfaction dating back to divisions in 1995, if not before, was beginning to resurface. There was already talk that

Sullivan would face a challenger at the convention scheduled for July, when he and Maloney would stand for election in their own right. "There are a lot of sharks out there and if he is not politically savvy," an unnamed observer told the *Engineering News-Record,* "he'll be shark bait."[59]

Although the challenge did not materialize, and both men were elected unanimously, convention debate made it clear that the new leadership team would face serious difficulties: Longtime conflicts over vertical agreements, organizing strategies, voluntary membership on local building trades councils, and the structure of the BCTD's administrative committee were all coming to a head. And outright hostility between the Painters and the Carpenters left many wondering what would happen next. Acknowledging that the Department was at a crossroads, President Emeritus Georgine reminded the delegates that the building trades had survived worse crises in the past. "We revived our industry and preserved our unions. . . . We won more funding for housing, highways, mass transit, clean water, and all other programs that created new jobs and met our nation's needs. . . . And together we held our own against the nonunion sector, and held off every one of their attacks against Davis-Bacon, our pay scales, and our very survival. . . . Our future is in great hands," he now told the delegates, echoing a phrase that President Sullivan had coined at the legislative conference that spring. "There's nothing that an elevator constructor and a boilermaker can't fix." However, if the past was prologue in the building trades, and the Department's history any indication of its future, then delegates could only hope that this assessment was right.[60]

Epilogue: Challenge
and Change

Times have never been easy for the Building and Construction Trades Department. Ever since the rise of the skyscraper revolutionized the industry around the turn of the twentieth century—encouraging the development of national general contracting firms, introducing new materials and building practices, and intensifying inter-union competition to control less-skilled parts of the work—jurisdictional conflicts have undermined efforts to promote industrywide solidarity. And ever since the Structural Building Trades Alliance first tried to resolve those conflicts, by limiting membership back in 1903 to "primary" trades only, fierce debates have raged over the Department's structure, function, and basis of representation. To a large extent these debates stem from a very mixed constituency: With a membership ranging from large amalgamated unions like the Carpenters and Laborers to smaller trades like the Asbestos Workers and Roofers, and from state, provincial, and local councils throughout the United States and Canada (some much better organized than others), achieving a fair balance of power in the organization has proved to be no easy task. Whether affiliates should have an equal vote on local and national policy-making boards, regardless of membership or per capita taxes paid, and whether mergers would ultimately strengthen the Department's structure and cut down on jurisdictional battles are questions as old as the Department itself.

These recurring debates are also rooted in the industry's structure, a structure that has changed significantly since the Department was chartered in 1908. The rapid proliferation of prefabricated building materials after the Second World War, the expansion of a competitive nonunion workforce since the 1950s, and the success of open-shop contractors and double-breasted firms since the 1970s have all undermined union control of construction work: Although construction remains one of the best-organized private industries in the United States, second only to transportation, according to the U.S. Bureau of Labor Statistics, in 2002 building trades unions represented only 17.8 percent of almost seven million workers.[1]

But in an industry employing highly skilled mechanics, semiskilled installers, and less-skilled laborers, this drop in union density is more complicated than a mere loss of market share. Whether workers are primarily employed in commercial, highway, or heavy construction makes a real difference in how they experience and perceive industry trends. Union construction workers as a group may have lost significant work opportunities over the last thirty years, but basic trades like the carpenters, painters, and laborers, for instance, face circumstances very different from those facing skilled mechanical trades like the electrical workers, elevator constructors, and plumbers and steam fitters. With a range of market strengths and weaknesses, and a strong tradition of craft autonomy, Department members do not necessarily agree on how to turn the situation around. Policies that some leaders deem essential to the survival of union construction, including area-wide agreements, standardized work rules, and more liberal membership policies, seem more like unwarranted interference with local bargaining power to others. And efforts by some trades to work with contractors to improve productivity, ease jurisdictional rules, and promote "common sense" practices to keep members employed are dismissed by others as "selling out" and "piracy" pure and simple.

That being the case, reaching consensus on policy issues like workforce organizing, jurisdictional boards, multi-craft bargaining, and project labor agreements can be difficult. "You can pull but you can't push," as one international union leader put it: The general presidents ultimately decide how far the Department can go and whether they will press local unions to cooperate, a process that is usually complicated by internal union politics. No wonder past president Robert Georgine was hailed as a master diplomat; keeping the trades together for twenty-six years and enacting real changes in the process took finesse. But his achievement also rested on compromise, too much compromise according to critics who argue that consensus politics are not enough. After all, keeping all the trades at the table hardly matters when nonunion firms dominate the industry.

However, as the last few years have demonstrated, the lack of consensus can prove equally dangerous. When the Governing Board of Presidents voted to abolish the six-member administrative committee soon after President Ed Sullivan took office, they undermined a long-term political compromise between large and small affiliates that had held the trades together throughout Georgine's administration. And when the Carpenters broke with the AFL-CIO in the spring of 2001 over organizing, spending, and jurisdictional policies and the decision forced them out of the BCTD, many questioned whether the Department could or even should survive.[2]

Indeed, the first few years of the twenty-first century proved harrowing. With rumors that a rival building trades federation was in the works and a jurisdictional battle about to explode, President Sullivan and Secretary-Treasurer Joe Maloney were caught in the crossfire. On the one hand, the AFL-CIO had initially prohibited the Carpenters from participating in local councils, jurisdictional boards, and the Heavy and Highway Division, a decision immediately embraced by Department hard-liners who now used the opportunity to claim previously contested work. On the other hand, union leaders could not ignore practical industrial conditions. Because carpenters generally made up about 20 percent of the workforce on any job site, an all-out war had the potential of destroying what was left of unionized construction. "While we are busy tearing our house asunder," as the Operating Engineers pointed out, "the non-union and anti-union will be laughing all the way to virtual full market share in the construction industry." So it made more sense for the Carpenters to participate in local councils, unofficially, and for President Sullivan to appoint a committee to keep the lines of communication open, Department decisions that minimized hostilities on the job. "There is no impact in day-to-day work," reported a council leader from Seattle. "The relationships on the jobsite, they don't change. Carpenters and plumbers and electricians continue to build buildings." And that was as it should be, others agreed. "Local unions and their councils have their hands full dealing with nonunion competition," as one leader later explained. "These kind of pressures and distractions don't do the members we work for or the industry we depend on any good."[3]

Worse yet, these "pressures and distractions" developed at a very inopportune time. Just a month before the Carpenters left the AFL-CIO, U.S. President George W. Bush had issued an executive order prohibiting project labor agreements on federal construction projects, an issue that the Associated Builders and Contractors' political action committee had targeted during the 2000 election campaign. And in April he revoked contractor responsibility rules intended to deny federal contracts to firms violating labor, employment, and environmental laws. "George W. Bush didn't hesitate for a second before going to war against unions and union members," President Sullivan pointed out, and apparently the ABC agreed. When a White House deputy assistant addressed the organization's convention the following year, "the bond between Bush and ABC was clear," the *Engineering News-Record* reported. In fact, "one contractor expressed his feelings succinctly: 'We expect results.'" That the labor movement was suffering some bad publicity at around the same time did not help matters: An unfolding financial scandal that would eventually involve Robert Georgine and the board of directors at ULLICO only strengthened the anti-union cause. And rising tensions on the Department's Governing Board of Presidents did not help either. One Department leader feared that the Board was ready to implode, an opinion that gained credence when the BCTD's 2002 legislative conference opened with an unexpected and fierce attack on President Sullivan's leadership. "It was anything but dull," reported the *Engineering News-Record*.[4]

No one knew what caused the outburst, but observers generally linked it to a failed effort to reunite the building trades. An attempted reunion with the Carpenters in February 2002 had fallen apart when neither side could agree to conditions, a disappointment that not only escalated tensions but also underscored the serious nature of the fight. "This is not a bunch of crusty old building trade guys versus a bunch of impulsive young building trade guys," a Department spokesman told the press. "There is a divergence of views over what it will take for unions not just to survive but prosper." The question of restructuring the Department "to meet our responsibilities to our employers and our members," he added, was "challenging how we have thought and acted in the past."[5]

But since the building trades' ability to protect basic standards, including Davis-Bacon prevailing wage rates, depended on solidarity in the ranks, both sides recognized the value of a united Building and Construction Trades Department. "If any of the 15 unions whose members are involved [in construction] are not part of the building trades, it obviously hurts us all," a Department member acknowledged, since "our mission is to increase union market share and union density throughout North America and that certainly includes the carpenters and the trades that it represents." "It's bad for our industry if we're not all together," President Sullivan agreed. "It's tough enough with us all together!"[6]

As industrial and political pressures continued to mount, building trades leaders finally reached a meeting of minds in December 2002. The Governing Board of Presidents agreed to reinstate the Department's administrative committee and to modernize the Plan for the Settlement of Jurisdictional Disputes by providing a mechanism to consider "area practice" as a major factor in conflict resolution. And the Carpenters agreed to rejoin the BCTD. "We need all our craft members to be successful," a Department leader noted, a fact of industrial life that the Carpenters appreciated. For although the union still had its differences with the AFL-CIO, it was "delighted" to return to the BCTD, according to Carpenters' president Douglas McCarron. And that was good news for building trades workers. "For the past 20 months, our relationship with the Carpenters has been operations as usual," a local council leader noted. "I'm proud that the Building Trades have held together, and continued to respect each other and not divide." Now, another leader added, "we can go on to worry about more important issues facing unions."[7]

By the following spring, when President Sullivan called the BCTD's 2003 legislative conference to order, the air had apparently cleared. Whatever differences building trades leaders still had on issues like jurisdiction and organizational structure, they were willing to present a united front and concentrate on the business at hand: securing the future of union construction. Success in the current political climate, President Sullivan noted, depended on "employing new strategies, building new coalitions, and offering new initiatives" designed to strengthen the building trades' value to the industry as a whole. For instance, the Department's expanded Smart Card safety and security credentialing system was proving to be an industrial asset, particularly in light of increased security concerns following the attacks of September 11, 2001. And the newly established Helmets to Hardhats program, which gave returning veterans an opportunity for jobs and training, offered a promising new solution to one of the industry's biggest complaints: a critical shortage of skilled workers. According to estimates, the construction industry needed to recruit 1.6 million skilled workers over the next five years, and that would be no easy task, President Sullivan acknowledged, since the job was demanding, conditions were rough, and qualified applicants of high school age were far more likely to go on to college than to work in the trades. "No vacation, the work is hard, it's dirty, it's cold, it's hot, you're subject to layoffs and we're not going to give you health care for the first six months"—with an advertisement like that, he said, "it's pretty hard to entice them." But returning veterans, who often had families to support, were more likely prospects, Sullivan added, since "they know how to go to work every day . . . and they've got some training that . . . may relate to building trades. They make good candidates, especially if we can link them up, give them apprentice credits for what they've learned in the service. So we're excited about that."[8]

The Department president was also excited about a new "tripartite collaboration" between representatives of the Construction Users Roundtable, national contractors' associations, and building trades unions to address the issue of construction cost-effectiveness on an industrywide level. Although contractors and owners, and contractors and building trades unions, had forged ties in the past—usually at the third partner's expense—they now apparently agreed that each had an industrial role to play. Aiming to eliminate jurisdictional disputes, increase productivity, and improve workplace safety, owners, contractors, and the Department's general presidents were now planning regular meetings and forming working committees to find "attainable, measurable, and meaningful" ways to improve the construction industry, a reversal of Roundtable policy that seemed promising to Sullivan. "I think that they've realized . . . that [supporters of the old Business Round-table] went too far," he said. "They were [originally] just trying to create more competition and have a better voice in bargaining. They accomplished that," he noted. But in the process they also supported the growth of so-called merit shop construction firms that basically ignored the issue of training, a failing that grows more costly as parts of the industry grow more technologically demanding. "All of our unions today have continuing education," Sullivan pointed out. "That's what tweaked the interest of these other groups. . . . Owners of petrochemical plants, refineries, the electrical plants, the nuclear industry are realizing that we're the only ones that do the true training."[9]

Certainly, there is no guarantee that the Helmets to Hardhats program or the Construction Users Roundtable collaboration will revitalize union construction. Whether rank-and-file workers will concur in the Department's view of a skill shortage and the need to recruit new members or accept new plans for "cost-effective" construction remains to be seen. But as President Sullivan told the delegates to the legislative conference in the spring of 2003, he is confident that "together we can and will prevail." After all, "we stand on the shoulders of the strong men who founded our unions over 100 years ago," unions that had represented "over 80 percent of all the construction workers in the United States" just fifty years earlier. Times had changed, and changed significantly, Sullivan acknowledged, but what had not changed was "the need for expanded organizing efforts, strong leadership and united action . . . at the national, state and local levels." Satisfied that the building trades were changing with the times to address new pressures, Sullivan made it clear that there was no other choice. "There is so much to accomplish, so much to protect, and so much to lose if we fail to meet the challenges before us."[10]

Whether the Department can meet those challenges, and forge the kind of solidarity the building trades need to reclaim their industrial position, no one can predict: The building trades may have lost the dominance they once enjoyed in construction work, but they have not lost the skill or vitality that made them a real force in the industry and the labor movement. If it is too soon to tell if the recent shakeup in the trades marks the end of one era or the beginning of another, one thing is sure. The outcome will depend on the future, not the past, for it is up to the new generation of building trades workers and their leaders to decide how far they are willing to go to push an agenda for change.

NOTES

Introduction

1. "New York's Men of Steel: Hard Hats, Soft Hearts," *Washington Post,* Sept. 15, 2001, C1; "Building Trades Lend Hand and Heart to WTC Site Recovery and Cleanup," *Engineering News-Record* (Dec. 17, 2001): 31 (LexisNexis); "UBC Members at the World Trade Center: The Missing, The Workers," from the official website of the United Brotherhood of Carpenters and Joiners of America, www.carpenters.org/common/hotnews_content.html; Robert P. Mader, "The Heart of America Can Never Be Questioned Again," *Contractor Magazine* (Oct. 2001): 47.

2. "New York's Men of Steel," C1; "Women at Work," *Long Island Newsday,* Oct. 21, 2001 (online).

3. "New York's Men of Steel," C1; "A Nation Challenged: The Workers; As Dig Goes On, Emotions Are Buried Deep," *New York Times,* Nov. 18, 2001, B1; "Building Trades Lend Hand and Heart," 31.

4. "End of Puny Wage Hikes Had Better Be Here Soon," *Engineering News-Record* (Sept. 29, 1997): 134 (LexisNexis). Estimates of union density vary widely for the 1940–60 period, some reaching as high as 87 percent in the 1950s. See Daniel Quinn Mills, *Industrial Relations and Manpower in Construction* (Cambridge, Mass.: MIT Press, 1972), 16–17, for a discussion of the confusion surrounding these figures. The over 50 percent estimate is from Michael Goldfield, *The Decline of Organized Labor in the United States* (Chicago: University of Chicago Press, 1987), 192.

5. "New York's Men of Steel," C1; Mark Arezzi to Grace Palladino, May 8, 2003.

6. Mark Erlich, "Who Will Build the Future," *Labor Research Review* 7 (fall 1988): 3.

7. For a general overview of the early history of the industry and the trades, see William Haber, *Industrial Relations in the Building Industry* (Cambridge, Mass.: Harvard University Press, 1930). Union journals and the local labor press tend to offer the most detailed views of the building trades workers' experience for the late nineteenth and early twentieth centuries.

8. Report, Local 1 St. Louis, *Electrical Worker* (June 1899): 9. Local 1 charged a $35 fee.

9. Robert A. Christie, *Empire in Wood: A History of the Carpenters' Union* (Ithaca, N.Y.: New York State School of Industrial and Labor Relations, Cornell University, 1956), 124; Haber, *Industrial Relations,* 176, 334–35.

Chapter 1

1. Thomas E. Tallmadge, ed., *The Origin of the Skyscraper: Report of the Committee Appointed by the Trustees of the Estate of Marshall Field for the Examination of the Home Insurance Building* (Chicago: Alderbrink, 1939), 5–11; the report was dated Nov. 22, 1931; William Aiken Starrett, *Skyscrapers and the Men Who Build Them* (New York: Scribner's, 1928), 27; "Terra-Cotta," *Chicago Tribune,* May 4, 1884, 14.

2. George H. Douglas, *Skyscrapers: A Social History of the Very Tall Building in America* (Jefferson, N.C.: McFarland, 1996), 20–21; *Chicago Tribune,* Aug. 2, 1885, 19; William Haber, *Industrial Relations in the Building Industry* (Cambridge, Mass.: Harvard University Press, 1930), 15–16, 19; Starrett, *Skyscrapers,* 1, 35; Spencer Klaw, "The World's Tallest Building," in *A Sense of History: The Best Writing from the Pages of "American Heritage"* (New York: Smithmark, 1996), 589.

3. Haber, *Industrial Relations,* 4–5, 36–37, 57–61; Royal E. Montgomery, *Industrial Relations in the Chicago Building Trades* (New York: Arno, 1971 [1927]), 5–7; Michael Kazin, *Barons of Labor: The San Francisco Building Trades and Union Power in the Progressive Era* (Urbana: University of Illinois Press, 1987), 89–93; Andrew Wender Cohen, "The Building Trades, Violence, and the Law in Chicago, 1900–1920," Research Seminar Paper #72 (May 11, 2000), Center for the History of Business, Technology, and Society, Hagley Museum and Library, Wilmington, Del., 6–7. For a broader discussion on Chicago, see Cohen, *The Racketeer's Progress: Chicago and the Struggle for the Modern American Economy, 1900–1940* (New York: Cambridge University Press, 2004). The quotation is from Haber, *Industrial Relations,* 5.

4. Haber, *Industrial Relations,* 4–5, 57–61; Cohen, "Building Trades," 6–9; Richard Schneirov and Thomas J. Suhrbur, *Union Brotherhood, Union Town: The History of the Carpenters' Union of Chicago, 1863–1987* (Carbondale: Southern Illinois University Press, 1988), 28.

5. For subcontracting, and for examples of ethnic and religious unions, see Schneirov and Suhrbur, *Union Brotherhood,* 5–6, 13–26, respectively; Raymond J. Robertson, *Iron Workers 100th Anniversary: A History of the Iron Workers Union* (Washington, D.C.: IAB-SOIW, 1996), 17.

6. For examples of the differences between working people and their organizations in this period, see Stuart B. Kaufman et al., *The Samuel Gompers Papers,* vol. 1 (Urbana: University of Illinois Press, 1986); Richard Oestreicher, *Solidarity and Fragmentation* (Urbana: University of Illinois Press, 1986); Robert E. Weir, *Beyond Labor's Veil: The Culture of the Knights of Labor* (University Park: Pennsylvania State University Press, 1996); Bruce C. Nelson, *Beyond the Martyrs: A Social History of Chicago's Anarchists, 1870–1900* (New Brunswick, N.J.: Rutgers University Press, 1988).

7. For the carpenters' strike see Schneirov and Suhrbur, *Union Brotherhood,* 24–28; Richard Schneirov, *Labor and Urban Politics* (Urbana: University of Illinois Press, 1998), 152–53.

8. For brief histories of these and other building trades unions, see *The Builders: The Seventy-five-Year History of the Building and Construction Trades Department, AFL-CIO* (Washington, D.C.: BCTD, 1983); *Chicago Tribune,* May 11, 1884, 17.

9. The labor correspondent of the *Chicago Tribune* is quoted in Schneirov and Suhrbur, *Union Brotherhood,* 35.

10. For business agents, see Haber, *Industrial Relations*, 318–20, 346–47; for the Bricklayers' arbitration agreement, see Harry C. Bates, *Bricklayers' Century of Craftsmanship: A History of the Bricklayers, Masons, and Plasterers' International Union of America* (Washington, D.C.: BMPIUA, 1955), 58, 65; *Chicago Tribune*, May 18, 1884, for the Bricklayers' donation. The quotation is from Schneirov and Suhrbur, *Union Brotherhood*, 36.

11. Cohen, "Building Trades," 19–20; Schneirov and Suhrbur, *Union Brotherhood*, 41; the quotations are from Montgomery, *Industrial Relations*, 18.

12. For the eight-hour movement, see John R. Commons et al., *History of Labour in the United States*, vol. 2 (New York: Macmillan, 1936), 375–94; Starrett, *Skyscrapers*, 81–84; the quotation is from Douglas, *Skyscrapers*, 127.

13. Douglas, *Skyscrapers*, 118–19, 123–27; Ernest Poole, "Cowboys of the Skies," *Everybody's Magazine* 19 (Nov. 1908): 641–53; Martin Segal, *The Rise of the United Association: National Unionism in the Pipe Trades, 1884–1924* (Cambridge, Mass.: Harvard University Press, 1970), 4–5; Grace Palladino, *Dreams of Dignity, Workers of Vision: A History of the International Brotherhood of Electrical Workers* (Washington, D.C.: IBEW, 1991), 10, 26–29 (quotation at 10); William English Walling, "The Building Trades and the Unions," *World's Work* 6 (Aug. 1903): 3793.

14. Haber, *Industrial Relations*, 278; Starrett, *Skyscrapers*, 32–33, 87; quotation from Walling, "The Building Trades and the Unions," 3790.

15. Haber, *Industrial Relations*, 36–43, 161–69; Garth L. Mangum, *The Operating Engineers: The Economic History of a Trade Union* (Cambridge, Mass.: Harvard University Press, 1964), 10–12; "The First Concrete Skyscraper," *Architectural Record* 15 (June 1904): 531–44.

16. For the Bricklayers' aversion to joining councils, see Bates, *Century of Craftsmanship*, 108–10; for the carpenters, see Robert A. Christie, *Empire in Wood: A History of the Carpenters' Union* (Ithaca, N.Y.: New York State School of Industrial and Labor Relations, Cornell University, 1956), 106–8,158–59; for the steam fitters, see Segal, *Rise of the United Association*, 108–33; for the painters' split, see Elizabeth and Kenneth Fones-Wolf, "Voluntarism and Factionalism Disputes in the AFL: The Painters Split in 1894–1900," *Industrial and Labor Relations Review* 35 (1982): 58–69.

17. "Against the Federation," *Nashville American*, Dec. 22, 1897, in *Samuel Gompers Papers*, vol. 4 (1991): 416–17; Haber, *Industrial Relations*, 332–33 (parts of the constitution are cited on 561–62 n. 2). Steinbiss's quotations are from a retrospective on the founding convention of the NBTC, "Origin of the International Building Trades Council," *The Labor Compendium* (Aug. 1906): 4.

18. William J. Spencer, "The Building Trades as Organized Prior to the Formation of the Building Trades Department," *American Federationist* (1916): 560.

19. Christie, *Empire in Wood*, 131; the information on "specialist" unions is from "Rule or Ruin Policy," *The Labor Compendium* (Apr. 1906): 1; Bates, *Century of Craftsmanship*, 110; Haber, *Industrial Relations*, 333.

20. "Against the Federation," *Samuel Gompers Papers*, 4:416–17; Haber, *Industrial Relations*, 332–33. For building trades sections, see the May 8, 1901, AFL circular published in the *American Federationist* (June 1901): 231–32; AFL *Proceedings*, 1899, 8–9, 147.

21. For interesting discussions of BTCs in New York, Chicago, and San Francisco, see Haber, *Industrial Relations*, 346–68, 370–96, 400–424; Montgomery, *Industrial Relations*; and Kazin, *Barons of Labor*. The quotations are from Cohen, "Building Trades," 26, 34.

22. Cohen, "Building Trades," 34–37; Montgomery, *Industrial Relations*, 28–35.

23. George Perkins to Samuel Gompers, Apr. 2, 1900, *Samuel Gompers Papers*, vol. 5 (1996): 214–15. Perkins was a resident of Chicago and president of the Cigar Makers International Union.

24. Montgomery, *Industrial Relations*, 28–32, 34–35; Schneirov and Suhrbur, *Union*

Brotherhood, 77–82; quotations are from Walling, "The Building Trades and the Unions," 3794.

25. The quotation is from Haber, *Industrial Relations,* 349–50 (BTEA quotation at 350). Other quotations are from Walling, "The Building Trades and the Unions," 3790, 3793.

26. Haber, *Industrial Relations,* 351–56; quotations are from Walling, "The Building Trades and the Unions," 3793–94.

27. Haber, *Industrial Relations,* 357–58; Sidney Fine, *"Without Blare of Trumpets": Walter Drew, the National Erectors' Association, and the Open Shop Movement, 1903–57* (Ann Arbor: University of Michigan Press, 1995), 18–21; for an example of the term *Parksism,* see "An Address at Fort Edward, New York," Aug. 24, 1904, *Samuel Gompers Papers,* vol. 6 (1997), 328. Samuel Gompers tells the crowd that when Daniel Davenport, an open-shop proponent, testified against the AFL's anti-injunction bill, he referred to it as "legalized Parksism" or, in other words, as Gompers noted, "extortion and robbery."

28. Starrett, *Skyscrapers,* 84–86; Haber, *Industrial Relations,* 354–57, 564; Fine, *"Without Blare of Trumpets",* 18–21 (quotation at 18). For the Iron Workers' view of Parks, see Robertson, *Ironworkers 100th Anniversary,* 32–33. The quotation is from Walling, "The Building Trades and the Unions," 3794.

29. Christie, *Empire in Wood,* 110–19, 129–33.

30. Michael P. Carrick to Samuel Gompers, Aug. 28, 1903, enclosed in Gompers to Executive Council, Sept. 3, 1903, in *Samuel Gompers Papers,* 6:173–74. Although William J. Spencer later remembered that the meeting was held in Lafayette, Indiana, Carrick's letter notes that they met in Indianapolis.

31. Carrick to Gompers, Aug. 28, 1903; Gompers to Executive Council, Sept. 3, 1903, *Samuel Gompers Papers,* 6:174.

32. Coverage of the founding meeting of the SBTA from *Chicago Tribune,* Oct. 8, 1903, 2; Oct. 9, 1903, 7; Oct. 10, 1903, 4; and Oct. 11, 1903, 6.

33. *Chicago Tribune,* Oct. 11, 1903, 6. Spencer, Michael Carrick (Painters), and T. M. Guerin (Carpenters) constituted the committee (Christie, *Empire in Wood,* 132).

34. "Plan Control of Building Trades," *Chicago Tribune,* Oct. 10, 1903, 4.

Chapter 2

1. Local citizens' alliances organized throughout the country in 1903 to oppose strikes and boycotts and looked to the courts and other government agencies to prevent trade unions from interfering with business. The quotations are from William J. Spencer, "The Structural Building Trades Alliance," *The Carpenter* (Feb. 1904): 4–5; and Spencer, "The Building Trades as Organized Prior to the Formation of the Building Trades Department," *American Federationist* (July 1916): 562.

2. Martin Segal, *The Rise of the United Association: National Unionism in the Pipe Trades, 1884–1924* (Cambridge, Mass.: Harvard University Press, 1970), 45, 49, 66–67; glossary entry, *The Samuel Gompers Papers,* vol. 6 (Urbana: University of Illinois Press, 1997), 586.

3. Spencer, "Structural Building Trades Alliance," 5; Spencer, "Building Trades," 561–62.

4. Spencer to Whom It May Concern, n.d., *The Carpenter* (Mar. 1904): 9; Spencer, "Building Trades," 562; Spencer to the Building Trades, n.d., *The Carpenter* (Mar. 1905): 5; T. M. Guerin, "The Need of an Alliance of Building Trades," BPDA *Official Journal* (Nov. 1903): 744. Guerin was general organizer for the United Brotherhood of Carpenters and Joiners.

5. Spencer, "Building Trades," 562; Spencer to Whom It May Concern, 9.

6. "Report of Committee Representing the United Brotherhood at Convention of

Structural Building Trades Alliance," *The Carpenter* (Sept. 1904): 9. The officers present were vice presidents Frank Buchanan (Iron Workers), Frank Duffy (Carpenters), Alexander Bainbridge (Painters), Herman Lillien (Laborers); James Hannahan (Engineers), and Secretary-Treasurer Spencer (Plumbers). For a complete list of delegates, see "Proceedings of the Convention of the Structural Building Trades Alliance," *Plumbers', Gas and Steam Fitters' Official Journal* (Sept. 1904): 13.

7. "Rule or Ruin Policy," *Labor Compendium* (Apr. 1906): 1.

8. For a brief sketch of Gubbins's career, see Andrew Wender Cohen, "The Building Trades, Violence, and the Law in Chicago, 1900–1920," Research Seminar Paper #72 (May 11, 2000), Center for the History of Business, Technology, and Society, Hagley Museum and Library, Wilmington, Del., 8, 13, 27–28; and his glossary entry in *Samuel Gompers Papers*, 6:562; Spencer, "Building Trades," 562.

9. Although Gubbins's circular was not reprinted in BMIU officers' reports, 1903, it was mentioned on page 5 of the president's report. Dobson's comments were included in his secretary's report for 1903, on page 429. For a report of Frank Buchanan's address, see BMIU, *Report of Convention Proceedings*, 1904, 57–58. See also Harry C. Bates, *Bricklayers' Century of Craftsmanship: A History of the Bricklayers, Masons, and Plasterers' International Union of America* (Washington, D.C.: BMPIUA, 1955), 135–36.

10. Duffy to Frank Morrison, Sept. 4, 1907, series I:2, box 3, United Brotherhood of Carpenters and Joiners Papers, Special Collections, University of Maryland, College Park (hereafter, UBCJA Papers, UMCP).

11. For a thumbnail sketch of Duffy's career, see his glossary entry in *Samuel Gompers Papers*, 6:556; for his role in founding the SBTA, see Robert A. Christie, *Empire in Wood: A History of the Carpenters' Union* (Ithaca, N.Y.: New York State School of Industrial and Labor Relations, Cornell University, 1956), 134.

12. "Proceedings of the Convention of the Structural Building Trades Alliance," 13–16.

13. Spencer to Board of Governors, Jan. 13, 1905, SBTA Minutes Book, vol. 1 (1904–1908), 26, Executive Council Files, box 1, George Meany Memorial Archives, Silver Spring, Md. (hereafter, SBTA Minutes Book, GMMA).

14. Carrick died on May 8, 1904, and an obituary appeared in *The Carpenter* (June 1904): 5; for the BPDA's support of a broad organization see Board of Governors Minutes, Oct. 10, 1904, SBTA Minutes Book, 1:6, GMMA; and "Editorial," *Labor Compendium* (June 1905): 8. For the Iron Workers' position, see "Editorial," *The Bridgemen's Magazine* (June 1905): 19.

15. Frank Buchanan to William J. Spencer, Mar. 6, 1905, in *The Bridgemen's Magazine* (Apr. 1905): 6; and "Extracts from the Proceedings of the Board of Governors," ibid., 7; "Call for Referendum Vote on Continued Affiliation with the Structural Building Trades Alliance," ibid., 9.

16. Spencer to the Basic Building Trades, n.d., *The Carpenter* (Mar. 1905): 6; BMIU, *Report of Convention Proceedings*, 1904, 88; "Report of the Proceedings of the Structural Iron Workers Convention," *The Bridgemen's Magazine* (Oct. 1905): 67.

17. L. W. Tilden, "Report of Meeting," *Plumbers', Gas and Steam Fitters' Official Journal* (Sept. 1906): 2; Dave Farley to Editor, *The Carpenter* (July 1904): 4; Duffy is quoted in Walter Galenson, *The United Brotherhood of Carpenters* (Cambridge, Mass.: Harvard University Press, 1983), 177; Spencer, "Building Trades," 563.

18. "Structural BTA Proves a Dismal Failure," *Labor Compendium* (Mar. 1905): 3.

19. "Rule or Ruin Policy," *Labor Compendium* (Apr. 1906): 1; and "Editorial," ibid. (June 1905): 6; for the open-shop connection, see "An Unjust Labor War," ibid. (Mar. 1906): 13.

20. Alfred Prince to Gompers, Apr. 13, 1905, *Samuel Gompers Papers*, 6:413–14; the percentage is based on building trades voting strength, AFL *Proceedings*, 1905, 41–42.

21. Minutes, Oct. 10, 1904, SBTA Minutes Book, 1:6, GMMA. Unfortunately the debate over Lennon's request was not recorded. However, both the Carpenters and the Laborers voted to deny it.

22. Minutes, Mar. 6, 1905, 50–51; Gompers to Spencer, Mar. 8, 1905, SBTA Minutes Book, 1:56, GMMA.

23. James Kirby's career is outlined in his glossary entry, *Samuel Gompers Papers,* vol. 8 (2001), 540.

24. Kirby to the Board of Governors, Aug. 23, 1906, "Report," *The Carpenter* (Oct. 1906): 27.

25. Kirby's report, Aug. 21, 1905, SBTA Minutes Book, 1:87, GMMA.

26. Minutes, Feb. 11, 1907, 297, SBTA Minutes Book, 1:297, GMMA.

27. Harry Stemburgh to Spencer, Aug. 14, 1905, 86; Spencer to Board of Governors, Aug. 18, 1905, 85; Kirby's report, Aug. 21, 1905, SBTA Minutes Book, 1:88, GMMA.

28. Jacob Tazelaar to delegates, International Hod Carriers and Building Laborers Unions, *Proceedings,* 1907, 41–42.

29. Kirby to Board of Governors, Mar. 1, 1906, 153, and Mar. 29, 1907, SBTA Minutes Book, 1:332, GMMA; James Kirby, "Building Trades of the South," *The Carpenter* (May 1907): 2.

30. "A Member of Old 75" to Editor, *The Carpenter* (Sept. 1907): 26–27.

31. Ibid., 27; Spencer, "Building Trades," 558.

32. Walter R. Kee's report on conditions in Spokane is included in Spencer to Board of Governors, Mar. 2, 1906, SBTA Minutes Book, 1:150, GMMA.

33. W. J. Bushnell to Spencer, Nov. 14, 1906, SBTA Minutes Book, 1:262, GMMA; for Duffy's and Merrick's comments, see Minutes, Nov. 21–23, 1905, ibid., 118–20; for Kirby's comments, see president's report to Board of Governors, Oct. 29, 1906, ibid., 224. The decision not to enforce the rule was passed as a resolution (223–24).

34. Duffy to Spencer, Mar. 20, 1907, SBTA Minutes Book, 1:324–25, GMMA.

35. The application was signed by representative of the Plumbers local, the Painters local, the Stone Cutters Society, and the Plasterers Tenders Union 36 and 87; Spencer to Board of Governors, Jan. 21, 1907, SBTA Minutes Book, 1:288, GMMA; Duffy to Spencer, Mar. 20, 1907, ibid., 324–25; Board of Governors meeting, Feb. 15, 1907, ibid., 329–30.

36. Report on the SBTA 1907 Convention, *Plumbers', Gas and Steam Fitters' Official Journal* (July 1907): 6; Skemp to Spencer, June 11, 1907, SBTA Minutes Book, 1:361–62, GMMA; Spencer to Skemp, June 20, 1907, ibid., 363–64; Balhorn and other painters are quoted in the *Labor Compendium* (Mar. 1907): 5; (Aug. 1907): 4.

37. Spencer to Board of Governors, June 22, 1907, SBTA Minutes Book, 1:364–65, GMMA; *Labor Compendium* (Mar. 1907): 5; Spencer, "Building Trades," 563.

38. Kirby to Board of Governors, Aug. 26, 1907, SBTA Minutes Book, 1:385, GMMA; Spencer to Board of Governors, Nov. 8, 1907, ibid., 392.

39. The report of the AFL Building Trades Committee is included in "A New Organization Forming," *Amalgamated Sheet Metal Workers' Journal* (Feb. 1908): 48–50. The committee also included John Alpine (Plumbers), Alex Crinkshank (Granite Cutters), Matthew Comerford (Engineers), Frank Feeney (Elevator Constructors), Charles Leps (Tile Layers), Michael O'Sullivan (Sheet Metal Workers), Benjamin Russell (Slate and Tile Roofers), Frank Ryan (Iron Workers), and Henry Sands (Composition Roofers).

40. "Report of the Committee on Building Trades, 1907," in *Samuel Gompers Papers,* vol. 7 (1999), 257; the McNulty quotation is from "Discussion on Report of Building Trades Committee," ibid., 7:276; "Report of James Kirby to the Board of Governors," *The Carpenter* (Jan. 1908): 13.

41. "Discussion on Report of Building Trades Committee," 278.

42. Ibid., 279.

43. "A New Organization Forming," *Amalgamated Sheet Metal Workers' Journal* (Feb. 1908): 48–50 (quotation at 50).

44. Kirby to Board of Governors, Dec. 28, 1907, SBTA Minutes Book, 1:407–8, GMMA; James Duncan et al. to AFL Building Trades, Dec. 28, 1907, *The Carpenter* (Jan. 1908): 11–12. Although Duncan, Huber, Kirby, and Spencer signed the call, the text notes that the "six trades that now compose the Structural Building Trades Alliance" had called the meeting with AFL approval.

45. Founding convention, Building Trades Department (BTD) *Proceedings,* Feb. 10, 1908, 10–12. There were forty-eight delegates representing nineteen unions. The Asbestos Workers were inadvertently omitted from the list, but after they were informed about the meeting by telegram they sent a delegate. For an example of the Carpenters' complaints, see Duffy to Spencer, Dec. 30, 1906, and Kirby to Spencer, Feb. 5, 1908, series I:2, box 3, UBCJA Papers, UMCP.

46. Founding convention, BTD *Proceedings,* Feb. 10, 1908, 8–10 (quotations at 8, 10).

47. "Report of Delegates to the Convention of Building Trades Organizations Affiliated with the AFL," *The Carpenter* (Mar. 1908): 23–25.

48. Gompers to Spencer, Mar. 26, 1908, in BTD *Proceedings,* 1908, 14–15 (quotation at 15).

49. Ibid., 15.

Chapter 3

1. Frank Duffy to William Spencer, June 4, 1908, series I:2, box 2, United Brotherhood of Carpenters and Joiners Papers, Special Collections, University of Maryland, College Park (hereafter, UBCJA Papers, UMCP).

2. Martin Segal, *The Rise of the United Association: National Unionism in the Pipe Trades, 1884–1924* (Cambridge, Mass.: Harvard University Press, 1970), 63; William Haber, *Industrial Relations in the Building Industry* (Cambridge, Mass.: Harvard University Press, 1930), 336, 340; Garth L. Mangum, *The Operating Engineers: The Economic History of a Trade Union* (Cambridge, Mass.: Harvard University Press, 1964), 35; BTD *Proceedings,* 1911, 54. For per capita taxes, see Receipts, Apr.–May 1908, BTD Executive Council Minutes Book, vol. 2 (1908–10), 40–42, Executive Council Files, George Meany Memorial Archives, Silver Spring, Md. (hereafter, EC Minutes Book, GMMA).

3. W. C. Gridley (UB 667 Cincinnati) to Ed Zint (Cincinnati SBTA), Aug. 14, 1907, series I:2, box 3, UBCJA Papers, UMCP; Frank Duffy to William Spencer, Dec. 26, 1906, and Duffy to Spencer, Dec. 30, 1906, box 2, ibid.; Duffy to Thomas M. Dooley, Jan. 9, 1907, box 3, ibid.

4. James Kirby to William Spencer, Feb. 5, 1908, series I:2, box 3, UBCJA Papers, UMCP.

5. F. A. Canfield et al. to EC, Aug. 8, 1908, 60–61; Kirby's report, May 21, 1909, EC Minutes Book 2:253, GMMA.

6. Patrick Reddington to Duffy, Aug. 10, 1908, Kirby to Duffy, May 25, 1908, series I:2, box 3, UBCJA Papers, UMCP.

7. Kirby's report, BTD *Proceedings,* 1909, 15; Spencer to Alexander Rosenthal, n.d., *Official Journal of International Hod Carriers' and Building Laborers' Union of America* (May 1909): 84–85, 86 (comment).

8. Duffy to Spencer, July 15, 1909, and Spencer to Duffy, July 19, 1909, series I:2, box 2, UBCJA Papers, UMCP.

9. BTD *Proceedings,* 1909, 120.

10. Robert A. Christie, *Empire in Wood: A History of the Carpenters' Union* (Ithaca, N.Y.: New York State School of Industrial and Labor Relations, Cornell University, 1956), 173–174; BTD *Proceedings,* 1909, 118–19.

11. BTD *Proceedings,* 1909, 107; "Wholesome Advice," *Amalgamated Sheet Metal Workers' Journal* (Dec. 1909): 503.

12. Haber, *Industrial Relations,* 154–56 (quotation at 154).

13. H. M. Taylor to Editor, *The Carpenter* (Apr. 1904): 6, cited in Christie, *Empire in Wood,* 109; *The Carpenter* (June 1908), cited in Haber, *Industrial Relations,* 36; Royal Montgomery, *Industrial Relations in the Chicago Building Trades* (New York: Arno, 1971 [1927]), 132–33. "The Controversy with the Carpenters in New York," *Amalgamated Sheet Metal Workers' Journal* (June 1909): 214–19.

14. Christie, *Empire in Wood,* 171–72; quotation is from Daniel Featherston, BTD *Proceedings,* 1910, 118.

15. "The Controversy with the Carpenters in New York," *Amalgamated Sheet Metal Workers' Journal* (June 1909): 214–19 (quotation at 218); "Piracy Will Meet with Resistance," *Amalgamated Sheet Metal Workers' Journal* (Oct. 1910): 372–73; "Report of Delegates to BTD Convention," *Amalgamated Sheet Metal Workers' Journal* (Nov. 1909): 456–60; (Dec. 1909): 496–503 (quotation at 503).

16. The declaration is cited in BTD *Proceedings,* 1910, 109; Redding quoted at 110. Michael O'Sullivan, "Report," *Amalgamated Sheet Metal Workers' Journal* (Oct. 1910): 362. For evidence of the architects' and contractors' support, see Duffy to Kirby, Feb. 8, 1910, EC Minutes Book, 2:466, GMMA.

17. BTD *Proceedings,* 1910, 120, 136, 138.

18. James Duncan to Samuel Gompers, Dec. 7, 1910, *The Samuel Gompers Papers,* vol. 8 (Urbana: University of Illinois Press, 2001), 149–50; Gompers to Duncan, Dec. 10, 1910, quoted in ibid., 151 n. 12.

19. Spencer to Samuel Gompers, June 13, 1911, 312–13; Gompers et al. to Spencer, June 17, 1911, EC Minutes Book, vol. 3 (1910–12), 341–47, GMMA; See also Christie, *Empire in Wood,* 175–76.

20. Gompers et al. to Spencer, June 17, 1911, EC Minutes Book, 3:341–47, GMMA; for organizers, see Samuel Gompers to Spencer, Feb. 18, 1911, ibid., 223; and Samuel Gompers to Spencer, Jan. 24, 1912, ibid., 430; for local councils, see *Painter and Decorator* (Oct. 1913): 547.

21. Duffy to Spencer, Feb. 15, 1911; Aug. 22, 1911; Feb. 5, 12, 1912 (enclosing the General Executive Board motion of Jan. 30, 1912); and Feb. 7, 1912; Short and Spencer to Huber and Duffy, Feb. 28, 1912, series I:2, box 2, UBCJA Papers, UMCP.

22. Duffy to Spencer, Mar. 15, 1912; May 27, 1912 (the vote was 32,077 in favor, 15,490 against), series I:2, box 2, UBCJA Papers, UMCP; BTD *Proceedings,* 1912, 31, 83, 120–25; 1913, AFL *Proceedings,* 1913, 100; Walter Galenson, *The United Brotherhood of Carpenters: The First Hundred Years* (Cambridge, Mass.: Harvard University Press, 1983), 175.

23. BTD *Proceedings,* 1913, 137.

24. Ibid., 88, 135–41, 157; Duffy to Spencer, Aug. 7, 1913; Aug. 28, 1913, series I:2, box 2, UBCJA Papers, UMCP; Galenson, *United Brotherhood of Carpenters,* 175.

25. BTD *Proceedings,* 1911, 30.

26. Ibid., 1910, 137; 1911, 103.

27. Spencer to EC, July 29, 1911, EC Minutes Book, 3:352, GMMA; Spencer to Scully, July 27, 1911, ibid., 352; Scully to Spencer Aug. 2, 1911, ibid., 358; BTD *Proceedings,* 1912, 38–39; D'Allesandro to Spencer, Mar. 12, 1913, EC Minutes Book, vol. 4 (1912–16), 106, GMMA.

28. Spencer to George Fuller Company, Dec. 23, 1911, EC Minutes Book, 3:395–96, GMMA. A similar letter went to Mark Eidlitz & Son, Heddon Construction, Norcross Bros., James Stewart & Co., Thompson-Starrett Co., Wells Bros. Co., and Whitney Steen. This correspondence, along with some responses, can also be found in BTD *Proceedings,* 1912, 70–72.

29. BTD *Proceedings,* 1913, 85–86, 120, 169–70 (amalgamation quotation at 86; restructuring the Executive Council quotation at 169).

30. Mangum, *Operating Engineers,* 301–2; Christie, *Empire in Wood,* 178–80; Spencer to Executive Council, Aug. 14, 1914, n.p.; Oct. 28, 1914, EC Minutes Book, 4:301, GMMA; President Williams's report to Executive Council meeting, June 7, 1915, ibid., 341–42, 350–52 (quotations at 342, 352).

31. Duffy to Gompers, June 8, 1914, cited in Christie, *Empire in Wood,* 179.

32. Christie, *Empire in Wood,* 179–81; BTD *Proceedings,* 1915, 95, 114–17, 120. The Carpenters' referendum on reaffiliation was not completed until April 1916, when it passed by a vote of 36,621 to 5,378 (Hutcheson to Spencer, Apr. 4, 1916, EC Minutes Book, 4:445, GMMA).

33. "Report of Conference Committee of O.P.I.A. and B.M.&P.I.U.," *The Plasterer* (Aug. 1913): 1–2; Haber, *Industrial Relations,* 46, 99.

34. "Report of BTD Convention," *The Plasterer* (Dec. 1913): 5–6 (contractors' quotation at 6); editorial on P. H. McCarthy, ibid. (Jan. 1914): 12–13; Sol Slyter (SF #66) to Editor, ibid. (July 1913): 10; McGivern's report, ibid. (Feb. 1914): 1 (quotation); "Report of BTD Convention," ibid. (Dec. 1914): 7.

35. Jason Hosea to Spencer, June 19, 1920, EC Minutes Book, vol. 5 (1916–23), 262–63, GMMA.

36. President Williams's report, BTD *Proceedings,* 1916, 58; *The Builders: The Seventy-five-Year History of the Building and Construction Trades Department, AFL-CIO* (Washington, D.C.: BCTD, 1983), 92.

37. President Williams's report, BTD *Proceedings,* 1916, 37–38.

38. "American Labor's Position in Peace or in War," AFL *Proceedings,* 1917, 75, 76.

39. AFL *Proceedings,* 1917, 3.

40. BTD *Proceedings,* 1917, 31.

41. Melvyn Dubofsky, *The State and Labor in Modern America* (Chapel Hill: University of North Carolina Press), 66; Christie, *Empire in Wood,* 219–22. See also Frank L. Grubbs Jr., *Samuel Gompers and the Great War: Protecting Labor's Standards* (Wake Forest, N.C,; Meridional, 1982). For the evolution of the War Labor Board, see Valerie Jean Conner, *The National War Labor Board: Stability, Social Justice, and the Voluntary State in World War I* (Chapel Hill: University of North Carolina Press, 1983).

42. President Donlin's report, BTD *Proceedings,* 1919, 35–36 (quotations at 36).

43. Ibid., 36–38 (quotations at 37).

44. BTD *Proceedings,* 1919, 58–62 (quotation at 61); 80–81.

45. Ibid., 79–81 (quotations at 80–81).

46. Miller is quoted in Haber, *Industrial Relations,* 182.

Chapter 4

1. The quotations are from Joseph A. McCartin, *Labor's Great War: The Struggle for Industrial Democracy and the Origins of Modern American Labor Relations, 1912–21* (Chapel Hill: University of North Carolina Press, 1997), 173, 200.

2. President Donlin's report, BTD *Proceedings,* 1919, 34; Sidney Fine, *"Without Blare of Trumpets": Walter Drew, the National Erectors' Association, and the Open Shop Movement, 1903–57* (Ann Arbor: University of Michigan Press, 1995), 203; Lewis Lorwin, *The American Federation of Labor: History, Politics, and Prospects* (Washington, D.C.: Brookings Institute, 1933), 476–79.

3. President Donlin's report, BTD *Proceedings,* 1922, 61 (quotation); 1919, 34–35.

4. Ibid., 1919, 34–35 (quotation at 35); 1920, 73. For the IWW, see Melvyn Dubofsky,

We Shall Be All: A History of the Industrial Workers of the World (Urbana: University of Illinois Press, 1988); for Canada, see Craig Heron, ed., *The Workers' Revolt in Canada, 1917–1925* (Toronto: University of Toronto Press, 1998).

5. McCartin, *Labor's Great War,* 174–76, 191–93, 220–23; Philip Taft, *The A. F. of L. in the Time of Gompers* (New York: Harper and Brothers, 1957), 362, 394–400.

6. For the 1919 strike wave, see Foster Rhea Dulles and Melvyn Dubofsky, *Labor in America: A History* (Arlington Heights, Ill.: Harlan Davidson, 1984), 223–29; Francis Russell, *A City in Terror: 1919, the Boston Police Strike* (New York: Viking, 1975); Dana Frank, *Purchasing Power: Consumer Organizing, Gender, and the Seattle Labor Movement, 1919–29* (New York: Cambridge University Press, 1994), 34–39, 45–46, 99; David Jay Bercuson, *Confrontation at Winnipeg: Labour, Industrial Relations, and the General Strike* (Montreal: McGill-Queen's University Press, 1990 [1974]); President Donlin's report, BTD *Proceedings,* 1922, 59.

7. Fine, *"Without Blare of Trumpets,"* 201–3; Frank, *Purchasing Power,* 97–101; BTD conference, Dec. 12, 1919, BTD Executive Council Minutes Book, vol. 5 (1916–23), 225–26, Executive Council Files, George Meany Memorial Archives, Silver Spring, Md. (hereafter, EC Minutes Book, GMMA) (Detroit); BTD *Proceedings,* 1921, 138 (Boston).

8. BTD *Proceedings,* 1921, 41 (Bulger), 123 (Hynes); *Journal of Electrical Workers and Operators* (Apr. 1920): 516–17.

9. Tom Moore, "The Building Trades Industrial Conference Issued by the Provincial Council of Carpenters" [ca. May 1920], series 1:2, Clippings, United Brotherhood of Carpenters and Joiners Papers, Special Collections, University of Maryland, College Park.

10. BTD *Proceedings,* 1920, 156–58 (quotation at 156); International Officers Meeting, Montreal, June 8, 1920, EC Minutes Book, 5:258, GMMA; Skemp to Gompers, July 30, 1921, reel 105, frame (fr.) 284–85, *American Federation of Labor Records: The Samuel Gompers Era* (microfilm edition, 1979), Microfilming Corporation of America.

11. The phrase comes from "Building Trades" to Editor, Jacksonville *Artisan* (Dec. 30, 1916). For racially exclusive locals, see George W. Sanders to Samuel Gompers (hereafter, SG), Mar. 2, 1920, reel 251, p. 146; A. W. Hammett to SG, Oct. 1, 1921, reel 271, p. 60; for local unions unwilling to join one another's strikes, see SG to Hutcheson, May 6, 1920, reel 253, p. 755; W. D. Highfield to SG, Apr. 7, 1920, reel 253, p. 70; S. C. Harshfield et al. to SG, June 12, 1922, reel 281, p. 62; Letterbooks of the Presidents of the American Federation of Labor, Manuscripts Division, Library of Congress, Washington, D.C. (hereafter, SGLB, LC).

12. For the Omaha case, see Meeting, July 29, 1920, EC Minutes Book, 5:283, GMMA; Duncan is quoted in BTD *Proceedings,* 1920, 56–57. The Granite Cutters did pay the assessment but under protest (Duncan to Spencer, July 7, 1920, BTD *Proceedings,* 1921, 80). For the AFL assessment request, which was turned down, see Duncan to SG, Apr. 13, 1922, reel 279, p. 578; SG to Duncan, Apr. 25, 1922, reel 279, p. 573; SG to EC, Apr. 25, 1922, reel 279, p. 577; and EC to Duncan, May 13, 1922, reel 280, p. 131, SGLB, LC.

13. A. F. Eageles to SG, July 27, 1922, reel 281, p. 997 (Portland); Noonan to SG, cited in SG to Spencer, July 19, 1921, reel 267, pp. 581–82 (Norfolk); Jack Prather to SG, n.d., reel 253, p. 293 (Wichita Falls), SGLB, LC.

14. Garth L. Mangum, *The Operating Engineers: The Economic History of a Trade Union* (Cambridge, Mass.: Harvard University Press, 1964), 111. For the origins of the permit system, see ibid., 82–86; BTD *Proceedings,* 1911, 37; William Haber, *Industrial Relations in the Building Industry* (Cambridge, Mass.: Harvard University Press, 1930), 203–4. For an example of a threat, see Mrs. Postlewait (of Postlewait Glass and Paint Co., Inc., Kansas City, Mo.) to SG, Aug. 10, 1922, reel 282, pp. 598–99, SGLB, LC.

15. Haber, *Industrial Relations,* 207–8. For newspaper coverage, see, for example, "Plasterers' Rule Holds Up Building," *New York Times,* June 12, 1920, 13 (hereafter, *NYT*);

"Trade Unionism and Crime," *NYT*, Oct. 1, 1922, 5; " 'Incalculable Benefits' of Union Labor; Devices Employed by Labor Unions in Building Trades to Limit Output and Make More Jobs," *Wall Street Journal*, Dec. 5, 1922, 7.

16. SG to Mrs. Cynthia Parmalee (Sacramento), Sept. 28, 1922, reel 283, pp. 847–48, SGLB, LC. Parmalee's letter is quoted on page 850.

17. SG to Chas. A Sherman, May 25, 1920, reel 254, p. 511, SGLB, LC.

18. SG to W. A. James, Mar. 3, 1920, reel 250, p. 554, SGLB, LC.

19. Testimony and conclusions of the Dailey Commission are cited in Royal E. Montgomery, *Industrial Relations in the Chicago Building Trades* (New York: Arno, 1971 [1927]), 209–10.

20. Haber, *Industrial Relations*, 368; Robert Christie, *Empire in Wood: A History of the Carpenters' Union* (Ithaca, N.Y.: New York State School of Industrial and Labor Relations, Cornell University, 1956), 214–15.

21. Michael Kazin, *Barons of Labor: The San Francisco Building Trades and Union Power in the Progressive Era* (Urbana: University of Illinois Press, 1987), 257–59 (quotation at 259); Haber, *Industrial Relations*, 570–71 n. 8.

22. Montgomery, *Industrial Relations*, 275–301, Citizens' Committee's "Statement of Policy" quoted at 291–92; Richard Schneirov and Thomas Suhrbur, *Union Brotherhood, Union Town: The History of the Carpenters' Union of Chicago, 1863–1987* (Carbondale: Southern Illinois University Press, 1988), 102–8.

23. President Donlin's report, BTD *Proceedings*, 1922, 41, 47, 58; the NAM claim is in Christie, *Empire in Wood*, 244. For the volume of construction business, see Raymond J. Robertson, *A History of the Iron Workers Union* (Washington, D.C.: IABSOIW, 1996), 79. The exact figure is $5.75 billion.

24. President Donlin's report, BTD *Proceedings*, 1922, 58; Montgomery, *Industrial Relations*, 288; C. W. Lakey to SG, Aug. 11, 1922, reel 282, p. 754, SGLB, LC.

25. President Donlin's report, BTD *Proceedings*, 1921, 55; Fine, *"Without Blare of Trumpets,"* 202; Schneirov and Suhrbur, *Union Brotherhood, Union Town*, 106–8.

26. President Donlin's report, BTD *Proceedings*, 1922, 58–62 (quotations at 58, 60).

27. Haber, *Industrial Relations*, 182; Hutcheson to Spencer, Apr. 1, 1920, included in NBJA Minutes, Apr. 26, 1920, 3; NBJA Minutes, Aug. 2, 1920, 1; E. J. Russell to Spencer, Oct. 22, 1920, included in NBJA Minutes, Nov. 29, 1920, 14–16, box 43, BTD Executive Council Files, GMMA.

28. Hutcheson to Spencer, Nov. 30, 1920, NBJA Minutes, 23; NBJA Minutes, Mar. 7, 1921, 4–7; Mar. 8, 1921, 14, box 43, BTD Executive Council Files, GMMA.

29. President Donlin's report, BTD *Proceedings*, 1921, 57.

30. Walter Galenson, *The United Brotherhood of Carpenters: The First Hundred Years* (Cambridge, Mass.: Harvard University Press, 1983), 242; BTD *Proceedings*, 1921, 108–24 (quotations at 109–10).

31. Secretary-Treasurer Spencer's report, BTD *Proceedings*, 1922, 68.

32. SG to Donlin, Mar. 24, 1922, reel 278, p. 444; Duffy to SG, Mar. 16, 1922, reel 278, p. 468, SGLB, LC.

33. SG to Duffy, Aug. 26, 1922, reel 282, p. 876; Duffy to SG, Aug. 9, 1922, reel 282, p. 878 (quotation); SG to Duffy, Aug. 31, 1922, reel 283, p. 14; SG to William Collins, Oct. 3, 1922, reel 283, p. 945, SGLB, LC.

34. SG to Donlin, Sept. 20, 1922, reel 283, p. 434, SGLB, LC; Christie, *Empire in Wood*, 243–45.

35. BTD *Proceedings*, 1923, 96; Tracy to Green, May 13, 1925, cited in *Proceedings*, 1925, 79.

36. Galenson, *United Brotherhood of Carpenters*, 211. The agreement was finalized on March 21, 1928 (Christie, *Empire in Wood*, 246). It was published in the 1928, 1929, and 1930 BTD *Proceedings*, and also appears in the 1936 BTD *Proceedings*, 150.

37. BTD *Proceedings*, 1927, 89 (NBJA), 97 (Noonan quotation); Secretary Treasurer Spencer's report, BTD *Proceedings*, 1928, 51 (UB membership).

38. Christie, *Empire in Wood*, 248; William Green's address, BTD *Proceedings*, 1928, 92.

39. BTD *Proceedings*, 1927, 68–69; "Building Trades Department Tries the Impossible and Must Fail in the Attempt," *Bricklayer, Mason and Plasterer* (Jan. 1928): 28; "Report of President Bowen," *Bricklayer, Mason and Plasterer* (Aug. 1928): 182–83.

40. BTD *Proceedings*, 1928, 103; President McSorley's report, BTD *Proceedings*, 1929, 51; 1930, 54. For a sketch of Broach's approach to leadership, see Grace Palladino, *Dreams of Dignity, Workers of Vision: A History of the International Brotherhood of Electrical Workers* (Washington, D.C.: IBEW, 1991), 129–34.

41. For the Carpenters, see Galenson, *United Brotherhood of Carpenters*, 96–122; for the IBEW, see Palladino, *Dreams of Dignity*, 23–66; for the Bricklayers, see "Report of President Bowen," 180.

42. For craft-industrial unionism, see Christie, *Empire in Wood*, 124–25, 167, 182; and Christopher Tomlins, "AFL Unions in the 1930s: Their Performance in Historical Perspective," *Journal of American History* (1979): 1027–31. BTD *Proceedings*, 1932, 102–4 (International Association of Machinists fight).

43. BTD *Proceedings*, 1931, 99–102 (quotations at 100, 102).

44. BTD *Proceedings*, 1931, 102–3.

45. Mary Beth Norton et al., *A People and a Nation*, 2 vols. (Boston: Houghton Mifflin, 1982), 2:706; Desmond Morton, *A Short History of Canada* (Toronto: McClelland and Stewart, 2001), 166.

46. Mangum, *Operating Engineers*, 134–35; Palladino, *Dreams of Dignity*, 143; Christie, *Empire in Wood*, 271; Galenson, *The United Brotherhood of Carpenters*, 230.

47. Robertson, *History of the Iron Workers Union*, 84; Mangum, *Operating Engineers*, 134; *The Builders: The Seventy-five-Year History of the Building and Construction Trades Department, AFL-CIO* (Washington, D.C.: BCTD, 1983), 137, 184, 218, 236, 248, 266, 283.

48. EC Meeting, Jan. 1931, 173; Spencer to President Herbert Hoover, Jan. 24, 1931, 175 (prevailing wage), EC Minutes Book, vol. 7 (1928–34), GMMA; president's report, BTD *Proceedings*, 1931, 63–68; 1932, 54, 59.

49. Huddell was apparently murdered in Washington, D.C., but the case was never closed. For the circumstances, see Mangum, *Operating Engineers*, 129–30.

50. Christie, *Empire in Wood*, 271; Franklin D. Roosevelt, "The Task Ahead for Building," in President Donlin's report, BTD *Proceedings*, 1923, 51–52; Galenson, *United Brotherhood of Carpenters*, 240–41.

51. McDonough served in the California legislature from 1925 to 1929 (*The Builders*, 300); Michael McDonough to Bricklayers' Convention, BMIU *Proceedings* 1936, 33–34; BTD *Proceedings*, 1933, 61–67 (quotation at 64).

52. McDonough discussed the importance of this first agreement in an address to the Bricklayers' 1936 convention; BMIU *Proceedings*, 1936, 33–34. See also Christie, *Empire in Wood*, 273; BTD *Proceedings*, 1934, 60–79, 85 (this report was also issued as Solomon Barkin and BTD, "Negotiating the Construction Code").

53. President McDonough's report, BTD *Proceedings*, 1934, 85; EC Meeting, Sept. 6, 1934, EC Minutes Book, 7:359–60, GMMA.

54. EC Meeting, June 23, 1933, EC Minutes Book, 7:306, GMMA; President McDonough's report, BTD *Proceedings*, 1934, 85.

55. Joint Meeting, Executive Council and General Presidents and Representatives, June 14, 1934, EC Minutes Book, 7:347–48, GMMA; "Labor Opens Parley Here Monday," *San Francisco Chronicle*, Sept. 30, 1934, 10; "Building Union Bloc Spurns Green Plea," *NYT*, Sept. 29, 1934, 5; BTC report, *Stone Cutters Journal* (Jan. 1935): 8.

56. " 'Secession' Hinted by Building Unions," *NYT*, Oct. 7, 1934, 30; BCTD *Proceedings*, 1934, 82, 99 (quotation), 104 (quotation).

57. For the "double vote," see "Important Facts concerning San Francisco BTD Convention," *Bridgemen's Magazine* (November 1934): 643; BTD *Proceedings*, 1934, 105–7, 122–26.

58. "Supplementary Report and Decision of the Executive Council of the American Federation of Labor," *Bricklayer, Mason and Plasterer* (Oct. 1934): 165–66; "Building Trades Convention Called," *Bricklayer, Mason and Plasterer* (Nov. 1934): 186–87; "Building Trades Department Holds Convention, Elects New Officers and Opens Headquarters," *Bricklayer, Mason and Plasterer* (Dec. 1934): 199–200.

59. "Rift Widens in Building Trades Union," *Washington Post*, Nov. 27, 1934, 19.

60. BTD EC to All Affiliated Unions, Dec. 12, 1934, *Journeymen Plumbers and Steam Fitters' Journal* (Jan. 1935): 36–38 (quotation at 38).

61. "Unions Map Fight in Building Trades," *NYT*, Oct. 3, 1935, 26. Before the Williams Department could move into AFL headquarters, it operated temporarily out of the Bowen Building ("Building Trades Department Holds Convention, Elects New Officers and Opens Headquarters," *Bricklayer, Mason and Plasterer* [Dec. 1934]: 199).

62. President Williams's report, BTD *Proceedings*, 1935, 47, 61.

63. President McDonough's report, BTD *Proceedings*, 1935, 63–67; for the case itself, see *In the Supreme Court of the District of Columbia Holding an Equity Court, James W. Williams et al. v. Michael J. McDonough et al., Equity #58248.*

64. "Building Trades Move to End Jurisdictional Controversies," *The Lather* (Sept. 1936): 5; "Plan for Settlement of Jurisdictional Disputes Approved by Executive Council," *The Lather* (Apr. 1937): 8. John A. Lapp, an experienced arbitrator and director of labor relations for the Public Works Administration, was appointed referee.

Chapter 5

1. The phrases are from President Roosevelt's first inaugural address and his April 28, 1935, radio address (or fireside chat).

2. President Williams's report, BTD *Proceedings*, 1936, 64. For a discussion of the National Labor Relations Act and its effect on AFL policy, see Christopher Tomlins, *The State and the Unions: Labor Relations, Law, and the Organized Labor Movement in America, 1880–1960* (New York: Cambridge University Press, 1985), 142–51.

3. McDonough speech, BMIU *Proceedings*, 1936, 33; AFL Unemployment Report, May 1936, reel 57, fr. 2645, *American Federation of Labor Records: The Samuel Gompers Era* (microfilm edition, 1979), Microfilming Corporation of America (hereafter, *AFL Records*).

4. Bates, Colleran, Coefield, to CLUs and SFLs, May 6, 1936, reel 57, fr. 2640, *AFL Records;* Harry C. Bates, *Bricklayers' Century of Craftsmanship: A History of the Bricklayers, Masons, and Plasterers' International Union of America* (Washington, D.C.: BMPIUA, 1955), 232; Theodore Liazos, "Big Labor: George Meany and the Making of the AFL-CIO" (Ph.D. dissertation, Yale University, 1999), 138–39.

5. Bates, *Bricklayers' Century of Craftsmanship*, 232; Andrew Burt to W.G., Dec. 6, 1933, reel 40, fr. 2520, and Jan. 1, 1934, fr. 2532; T. A. Scully to Frank Morrison, Mar. 19, 1934 (Civilian Conservation Corps, Camp Kessuque, Iowa), reel 42, fr. 2249, *AFL Records.* For similar complaints, see Charles Trout, *Boston, the Great Depression, and the New Deal* (New York: Oxford University Press, 1977), 207–8. See also Bonnie Fox Schwartz, "New Deal Work Relief and Organized Labor: The CWA and the AFL Building Trades," *Labor History* 17 (1976): 38–57.

6. Williams to Frances Perkins, Jan. 1, 1936, in President Williams's report, BTD *Proceedings*, 1936, 96. For exclusive jurisdiction, see Philip Taft, *The A. F. of L. in the Time of Gompers* (New York: Harper and Brothers, 1957), 185–86.

7. "New Works Progress Rules Make Possible the Prevailing Rate and the Closed Shop on WPA Jobs," *The Bricklayer, Mason, and Plasterer* (Oct. 1935): 164. George Meany radio speech, Aug. 9, 1935, cited in Liazos, "Big Labor," 151.

8. Trout, *Boston*, 209, 224. For the Department of Justice investigation, see Robert A. Christie, *Empire in Wood: A History of the Carpenters' Union* (Ithaca, N.Y.: New York State School of Industrial and Labor Relations, Cornell University, 1956), 307–16.

9. John Dos Passos, "Harlan: Working under the Gun," *The New Republic*, Dec. 2, 1931; Paul Comly French, "Children on Strike," *The Nation*, May 31, 1933; Carlos Hudson, "Minneapolis—One Year Later," *The Nation*, Oct. 30, 1935; Margaret Marshall, "Waiting for Lewis," *The Nation*, May 20, 1936, all republished online on *New Deal Network* (http://newdealferi.org/texts/index/htm).

10. Walter Galenson, *The United Brotherhood of Carpenters: The First Hundred Years* (Cambridge, Mass.: Harvard University Press, 1983), 254–55; Benjamin Stolberg, *The Story of the CIO* (New York: Arno, 1971), 23–26. See also Melvyn Dubofsky and Warren Van Tine, "John L. Lewis and the Triumph of Mass-Production Unionism," in Dubofsky and Van Tine, eds., *Labor Leaders in America* (Urbana: University of Illinois Press, 1987), 185–206; Robert H. Zieger, *The CIO, 1935–1955* (Chapel Hill: University of North Carolina Press, 1995; Walter Galenson, *The CIO Challenge to the AFL: A History of the American Labor Movement, 1935–1941* (Cambridge, Mass.: Harvard University Press, 1960).

11. For efforts to organize General Electric and Westinghouse workers before the rise of the CIO, see Grace Palladino, *Dreams of Dignity, Workers of Vision: A History of the International Brotherhood of Electrical Workers* (Washington, D.C.: IBEW, 1991), 34, 51–54; Joseph McCartin, *Labor's Great War: The Struggle for Industrial Democracy and the Origins of Modern Labor Relations, 1912–1921* (Chapel Hill: University of North Carolina Press, 1997), 128–36; Ronald Schatz, *The Electrical Workers: A History of Labor at General Electric and Westinghouse, 1923–60* (Urbana: University of Illinois Press, 1983), 3–80. For competition with industrial unions, see BTD *Proceedings*, 1936, 188–89. Lake County Indiana building trades workers, for example, were trying to get the CIO out of the Sinclair Oil Refining Company "so the building trades mechanics could get the work that rightfully belongs to them." For complaints about the Fisher Body plant in Flint, see BCTD *Proceedings*, 1937, 72.

12. The quotations are from "Craft Unions Must Carry the Fight to the Industrial Unionists," *The Bricklayer, Mason, and Plasterer* (Nov. 1935): 185; J. W. Williams address, BTD *Proceedings*, 1936, 58; and Bricklayers *Proceedings*, 1936, 30–31; Michael McDonough address, Bricklayers *Proceedings*, 1936, 34.

13. For Maintenance of Way, see Herbert Rivers to William Green, Aug. 6, 1945, Executive Council (EC) Case, Box 44, BCTD Records, George Meany Memorial Archives, Silver Spring, Md. (hereafter, GMMA). For CIO competition suggestion, see Galenson, *CIO Challenge to the AFL*, 529. For millwright fight, see Galenson, *United Brotherhood of Carpenters*, 174–75, 246–48. For change in Department title, see M. J. McDonough to Frank Morrison, Nov. 15, 1936; and BCTD report in AFL *Proceedings*, 1937, 133–34.

14. William E. Leuchtenburg, *Franklin D. Roosevelt and the New Deal, 1932–1940* (New York: Harper and Row, 1963), 133–35; Garth L. Mangum, *The Operating Engineers: The Economic History of a Trade Union* (Cambridge, Mass.: Harvard University Press, 1964), 140; Ickes to Williams, Sept. 17, 1935, in BTD *Proceedings*, 1935, 43.

15. Mr. Wyzanski to Frances Perkins, Jan. 23, 1935; Williams to Perkins, Dec. 20, 1934; Lubin Memo to Perkins, Dec. 22, 1934; Perkins [actually Lubin ghostwriter] to Ickes, Dec. 22, 1934, box 90, RG 174, U.S. National Archives, Washington, D.C.; "Whacking the Building Trades," *The Lather* (Feb. 1935): 11.

16. "Eight Projects Face Walkout," *Boston Globe,* Jan. 9, 1936, 1, 24 (quotation); "Claims Vary on PWA Strikers," *Boston Globe,* Jan. 10, 1936, 1; "Inquiry into PWA Strikes," *Boston Globe,* Jan. 11, 1936, 2; Trout, *Boston,* 223.

17. Searle F. Charles, *Minister of Relief: Harry Hopkins and the Depression* (Syracuse, N.Y.: University of Syracuse Press, 1963), 131. For the $19 rate, see "The Economically Damned," *The Elevator Constructor* (July 1935): 24; "Government Proposes to Increase Morale by Decreasing Wages," *The Bricklayer, Mason, and Plasterer* (Feb. 1935): 24–25 (quotation); President Williams's report, BTD *Proceedings,* 1935 (Williams's Convention), 42.

18. Trout, *Boston,* 223; BCTD *Proceedings,* 1936, 181–82; "We Told You So," *The Constructor* (Oct. 1937): 16.

19. "Treasurer Richard J. Gray Broadcasts Labors' Position on 'Security Wage,'" *The Bricklayer, Mason, and Plasterer* (Dec. 1935): 202–3.

20. Ibid.

21. Charles, *Minister of Relief,* 155; BCTD *Proceedings,* 1936, 124; "The Great Game of Politics: The Surrender," *Wall Street Journal,* Sept. 24, 1935, 4; "New Works Progress Rules Make Possible the Prevailing Rate and the Closed Shop on WPA Jobs," *The Bricklayer, Mason, and Plasterer* (Oct. 1935): 163; "State Administrators Who Demand Heat Must Get Heat," The *Bricklayer, Mason, and Plasterer* (Nov. 1935): 185

22. BCTD *Proceedings,* 1937, 87–88 (quotation at 87), 96–97 (membership).

23. Ibid., 126, 164; Carpenters *Proceedings,* 1936, 285; "AFL Urged to Cut Last Ties with CIO," *New York Times,* Sept. 28, 1937, 9 (hereafter, *NYT*); "Wider Rift Fought in Building Trades," *NYT,* Oct. 1, 1937, 8 (quotation); "Decision of the National Referee in the Case of the IABS&OIW vs. UBCJA on the Question of Jurisdiction in the Setting of Steel Bar Joists," Apr. 23, 1937, box 43, EC Case Files, BCTD Records, GMMA.

24. John R. Thompson, BA Iron Workers 424, New Haven to Morin, Apr. 7, 1936; Thompson to J. W. McCain, n.d.; M. J. Louden, general organizer, to Morin, Oct. 16, 1936; Louden to Morin, Oct. 23, 1936, box 43, EC Case Files, BCTD Records, GMMA.

25. "Decision of the National Referee," box 43, EC Case Files, BCTD Records, GMMA; Galenson, *United Brotherhood of Carpenters,* 250; BCTD *Proceedings,* 1937, 110.

26. BCTD *Proceedings,* 1937, 126 (quotation), 164.

27. President Williams's report, BCTD *Proceedings,* 1937, 67; unidentified newspaper clipping, "Carpenters vs. Bricklayers," Dec. 28, 1937, Scrapbook, courtesy of Mike Dorsey. I am grateful to Mr. Dorsey for making this scrapbook available to me.

28. BCTD *Proceedings,* 1938, 135, 146; Mangum, *Operating Engineers,* 291, 301 (quotation); Galenson, *CIO Challenge to the AFL,* 516 (Lapp's resignation).

29. BCTD *Proceedings,* 1939, 74 (quotation). In Possehl's obituary, Sept. 17, 1940, Scrapbook, Coyne notes that Possehl sponsored his nomination and selection as BCTD president.

30. Mangum, *Operating Engineers,* 12, 15, 134–35, 155. According to Mangum, the number of operating engineers employed in 1930 was 69,882, and in 1940 it was 101,870 (*Operating Engineers,* 12). IUOE membership totaled 33,705 in 1930 and 53,969 in 1939 (135). About 43 percent of the total are hoisting and portable members, and their numbers increased from 6,537 in 1933 to 23,467 in 1939 (135).

31. Mangum, *Operating Engineers,* 253–55; "Labor Relations," *The Constructor* (Nov. 1937): 18; E. J. Harding, "AGC Labor Relations Activities," *Constructor* (Nov. 1937): 18–19.

32. Associated General Contractors' 1939 Resolution "To Improve Labor Relations," in Executive Council report, BCTD *Proceedings,* 1939, 110–11; John P. Coyne, "Labor and Contractors," *The Constructor* (Feb. 1940): 21–22, 48.

33. Coyne, "Labor and Contractors," 21.

34. Harding's remarks, BCTD *Proceedings,* 1939, 144; Coyne, "Labor and Contractors," 21, 48–49.

35. Booth Mooney, *Builders for Progress: The Story of the Associated General Contractors of America* (New York: McGraw-Hill, 1965), 88.

36. Galenson, *CIO Challenge to the AFL,* 521–22; "Lewis Puts C.I.O. in Building Field," *NYT,* July 26, 1939, 1; "C.I.O. Built Buildings Goal of A. D. Lewis," unidentified clipping (Nov. 24, 1939), Scrapbook (quotations); "C.I.O. Signs First Building Contract Here," *Washington Post,* Nov. 23, 1939, 21. See also Thaddeus Russell, " 'Restore Teamster Power': Militancy, Democracy, and the IBT," *New Labor Forum* (spring/summer 1999): 111–22.

37. The two-thirds figure comes from U.S. Bureau of Labor Statistics, cited in unidentified clipping, "No Solidarity Forever," Mar. 7, 1941; clippings, "C.I.O. Built Buildings Goal of A. D. Lewis," (Nov. 24, 1939), "CIO Building Pact called 'Stunt' by AFL," n.d., Scrapbook (quotations).

38. Leo G. Mitchell to John L. Lewis, Feb. 22, 1940, Scrapbook; Meany's address, BCTD *Proceedings,* 1940, 204.

39. Delegate Case and Delegate Knout, BCTD *Proceedings,* 1939, 189; Galenson, *CIO Challenge to the AFL,* 522–24; Bates is quoted at 524.

40. Marybeth Norton et al., *A People and a Nation: A History of the United States,* 2 vols. (Boston: Houghton Mifflin, 1982), 2:771–72; *The Builders: The Seventy-five-Year History of the Building and Construction Trades Department, AFL-CIO* (Washington, D.C.: BCTD, 1983), 19; John T. Dunlop and Arthur D. Hill, *The Wage Adjustment Board: Wartime Stabilization in the Building and Construction Industry* (Cambridge, Mass.: Harvard University Press, 1950), 4–5; "Construction for National Defense," *The Constructor* (June 1940): 18; Clipping, "18,000 Civilians Get $1,000,000 Pay at Fort Meade in Week," Dec. 30, 1940, Scrapbook (quotation).

41. BCTD *Proceedings,* 1940, 91–97. For Hillman's denial, see Galenson, *CIO Challenge to the AFL,* 525.

42. Clippings, Drew Pearson and Robert S. Allen, "Washington Daily Merry-Go-Round," Dec. 31, 1940; "Union Initiation Fee Survey," Jan. 15, 1941; "Coyne's Absence Balks Union Fee Racket Quiz," Jan. 30, 1941; "Wail of Nonunion Building Mechanics Tickles Ears of Some Congressmen," Dec. 7, 1940, "Hoffman Flays Defense Job Fee 'Extortion,' " Dec. 9, 1940, Scrapbook.

43. "Strike Ties Up Work on $750,000 Job at Walter Reed," *Washington Evening Star,* Mar. 6, 1941, A2; "Strike Called for Today at Walter Reed," *Washington Post,* Mar. 6, 1941, 1; "Building Workers Decide to End Strike at Walter Reed," *Washington Evening Star,* Mar. 14, 1941, 1 (quotation); "Fiasco at Walter Reed," *Washington Post,* Mar. 15, 1941, 6 (quotation).

44. BCTD *Proceedings,* 1940, 24, 25, 26 (quotations are taken out of order).

45. The text of the agreement can be found in Dunlop and Hill, *Wage Adjustment Board,* 138–40.

46. BCTD *Proceedings,* 1941, 99–103; Galenson, *CIO Challenge to the AFL,* 525; " 'Holiday' of Unions Tie Up Building at Munitions Projects," Aug. 3 1941, Scrapbook.

Chapter 6

1. Daniel Tracy's address, BCTD *Proceedings,* 1943, 139; *The Builders: The Seventy-five-Year History of the Building and Construction Trades Department, AFL-CIO* (Washington, D.C.: BCTD, 1983), 20–21; "Seabee History: Formation of the Seabees and World War II," published on the website of the Department of the Navy, Naval Historical Center, www.history.navy.mil/faq/faq67–3.htm; "20th Anniversary of Seabees Reminder of Role of Craftsmen," *The Construction Craftsman* (June 1962): 10–11.

2. "Canada 'Drafts' All Nation's Workers," *Washington Post,* Sept. 27, 1942, B4; "Canadian Munitions," *Washington Post,* Aug. 22, 1942, X9 (quotation).

3. *Builders,* 21, 61, 71, 267; Garth Mangum, *The Operating Engineers: The Economic History of a Trade Union* (Cambridge, Mass.: Harvard University Press, 1964), 162; Robert Patterson's address, IBEW *Proceedings,* 1946, 13 (quotation); John T. Dunlop and Arthur D. Hill, *The Wage Adjustment Board: Wartime Stabilization in the Building and Construction Industry* (Cambridge, Mass.: Harvard University Press, 1950), 14 (quotation); Dunlop, "Project Labor Agreements," Joint Center for Housing Studies, Harvard University, Sept. 2002, 3 (online).

4. Keenan's address, BCTD *Proceedings,* 1943, 124–26 (quotation at 125); Tracy's address, BCTD *Proceedings,* 1943, 138 (Patterson also quoted); A. B. Carter to Roosevelt, Apr. 30, 1942, in Lawrence Levine and Cornelia Levine, *The People and the President: America's Conversation with FDR* (Boston: Beacon, 2002), 446.

5. Grace Palladino, *Dreams of Dignity, Workers of Dignity: A History of the International Brotherhood of Electrical Workers* (Washington, D.C.: IBEW, 1991), 173–75, 192 (quotations at 175); "Study Ways to Peg Wages in Building," *New York Times,* Apr. 10, 1942, 26 (hereafter, *NYT*); "Pay Stabilization Up to President," *Washington Post,* May 19, 1942, 1, 16.

6. Dunlop and Hill, *Wage Adjustment Board,* 26–27 (the agreement appears in Appendix 3, 141–42); "Industry Wage Pacts Backed by Roosevelt," *Washington Post,* May 23, 1942, 4.

7. Dunlop and Hill, *Wage Adjustment Board,* 30–33.

8. "15% Wage Formula Exceeded by Board," *NYT,* Apr. 5, 1943, 1, 11 (quotation at 11); the figures are from Daniel Tracy's address, BCTD *Proceedings,* 1943, 139–40.

9. Dunlop and Hill, *Wage Adjustment Board,* 35–39.

10. Ibid., 39–41, 117 (quotation at 41); "WLB Limits Building Trade Wage Changes," *Washington Post,* Oct. 15, 1943, 13.

11. Dunlop and Hill, *Wage Adjustment Board,* 108–9 (quotation at 109); Theodore Liazos, "Big Labor: George Meany and the Making of the AFL-CIO" (Ph.D dissertation, Yale University, 1999), 205; BCTD *Proceedings,* 1947, 161 (quotation); Marc Linder, *Wars of Attrition: Vietnam, the Business Roundtable, and the Decline of Construction Unions* (Iowa City: Fanpihua, 1999), 419.

12. Dunlop and Hill, *Wage Adjustment Board,* 117–18.

13. Ibid., 108–9, 128 (quotation; order is reversed); "AFL and Builders Make a Pact to Handle Post-War Disputes," *NYT,* May 11, 1945, 13.

14. Robert P. Patterson memorandum, "Decision of Board of Review Established under Building Trades Stabilization Agreement," Mar. 19, 1942; Gray to Tracy, May 22, 1944 (Wright Curtiss); Neil Cunningham to Gray, Mar. 20, 1943 (Lewiston, Maine); W. C. Wright (BA, Pocatello BTC) to Coyne, Apr. 16, 1943, box 44, Executive Council (EC) Case Files, BCTD Records, George Meany Memorial Archives, Silver Spring, Md. (hereafter, GMMA).

15. J. Earl Welch to Gray, Oct. 29, 1943 (Springfield, Ill. Army Air Force Storage Depot), box 44, EC Case Files, BCTD Records, GMMA.

16. James B. Atleson, *Labor and the Wartime State: Labor Relations and Law during World War II* (Urbana: University of Illinois Press, 1998), 194–97; for reactions to the coal strike, see Levine and Levine, *The People and the President,* 476–89.

17. Gray's memo, Mar. 23, 1943; Memorandum, Mar. 26, 1943, Conference with Colonel O'Gara (office of Services of Supply), Major Jacobs and Mr. Flaherty (Army Engineers), Brennan (Ordnance), Keenan (War Production Board), Bieretz (IBEW), and Gray, acting president; Gray to Tracy, May 22, 1944, box 44, EC Case Files, BCTD Records, GMMA (quotation).

18. Gray to Tracy, May 22, 1944, box 44, EC Case Files, BCTD Records, GMMA.

19. Gray to Meany, Dec. 4, 1943; C. H. Petersen to Gray, Dec. 3, 1943; Gray to Petersen, Dec. 15, 1943, box 44, EC Case Files, BCTD Records, GMMA (quotation).

20. Joint Agreement, Apr. 3, 1943, box 44, EC Case Files, BCTD Records, GMMA.

21. Detroit BTC proposal, July 2, 1945, enclosed in Ed Thal to Herbert Rivers, July 6, 1945 (quotation); report of Detroit Conference, May 16, 17, 1945, box 44, EC Case Files, BCTD Records, GMMA (quotation); "AFL Building Unions Demand Every Job," *NYT*, May, 19, 1945, 9.

22. Minutes of the joint committee representing CIO–Automobile Workers and AFL BCTD, June 26, 1945; Gray to Tracy, Aug. 4, 1945; Thal to Gray, July 16, 1945 (quotation); Detroit BTC proposal, July 2, 1945, enclosed in Thal to Rivers, July 6, 1945, box 44, EC Case Files, BCTD Records, GMMA; "Map Plan to Avert AFL-CIO Disputes," *NYT*, July 4, 1945, 14.

23. Thal to Gray, July 16, 1945 (quotation); Detroit BTC proposal, July 2, 1945, enclosed in Thal to Gray, July 6, 1945, box 44, EC Case Files, BCTD Records, GMMA.

24. Gray to Peter Eller, Mar. 29, 1944; Eller replies, Mar. 31, 1944, box 44, EC Case Files, BCTD Records, GMMA. On April 28, 1944, William Hutcheson replaced Eller as national referee.

25. Brown to All Local Unions and All Members of the International Staff, Apr. 10, 1945, box 44, EC Case Files, BCTD Records, GMMA.

26. Ibid.

27. Rivers to International Presidents and State and Local BCTCs, Nov. 29, 1945, box 44, EC Case Files, BCTD Records, GMMA (quotations are out of order). Rivers sent this letter by order of the BCTD Executive Council.

28. "Joseph Keenan, Vice Chairman for Labor Production, War Production Board," *The Bricklayer, Mason, and Plasterer* (July 1943): 115.

29. Mary Beth Norton et al., *A People and a Nation: A History of the United States,* 2 vols. (Boston: Houghton Mifflin Co., 1982), 2:842–43; Levine and Levine, *The People and the President,* 522.

30. Norton, *A People and a Nation,* 2:843–45; "Construction Workers—How Many and at What Wages?" *Engineering News-Record* (Feb. 7, 1946): 123–24; Atleson, *Labor and the Wartime State,* 207–9 (quotation at 207–8); Walter Galenson, *The United Brotherhood of Carpenters: The First Hundred Years* (Cambridge, Mass.: Harvard University Press, 1989), 287; William O'Neill, *American High: The Years of Confidence, 1945–1960* (New York: Free Press, 1986), 84–87.

31. Atleson, *Labor and the Wartime State,* 209 (quotation); Robert Zieger, *American Workers, American Unions, 1920–1985* (Baltimore, Md.: Johns Hopkins University Press, 1986), 100; O'Neill, *American High,* 87; Norton, *A People and a Nation,* 2:844–46 (quotation at 846); Joshua B. Freeman, *Working-Class New York: Life and Labor since World War II* (New York: New Press, 2000), 3–7; Michael Goldfield, *The Decline of Organized Labor in the United States* (Chicago: University of Chicago Press, 1987), 10 (includes Bureau of Labor Statistics figures that put the percentage of the unionized workforce at 23.6 in 1946, and the percentage of the unionized nonagricultural workforce at 34.5).

32. "Groundwork Laid by AGC and AFL for Settling Postwar Disputes," *Engineering News-Record* (May 17, 1945): 71; BCTD *Proceedings,* 1946, 239 (quotation).

33. Gray to [all EC members], Feb. 7, 1947, box 44, EC Case Files, BCTD Records, GMMA.

34. Gray to [all EC members], Feb. 7, 1947; Tracy to Gray, Feb. 14, 1947, Maloney to Gray, Feb. 10, 1947, box 44, EC Case Files, BCTD Records, GMMA. The special committee of industrial relations specialists reported to the Executive Council in April 1947; Christopher Tomlins, *The State and the Unions: Law and the Organized Labor Movement, 1880–1960* (New York: Cambridge University Press, 1985), 282.

35. The Wage Adjustment Board was officially terminated on February 24, 1947. Dunlop and Hill, *War Adjustment Board,* 48; "Groundwork Laid by A.G.C. and A.F.L. for Set-

tling Postwar Disputes, "*Engineering News-Record* (May 17, 1945): 71; Dobson is quoted in Linder, *Wars of Attrition,* 147; "Bill Tells 'em," *The Carpenter* (Apr. 1947): 9–12 (quotation at 11–12).

36. Atleson, *Labor and the Wartime State,* 18 n. 81; "Construction Workers—How Many and at What Wages?" 123. According to economist Steven Allen, the 92 percent estimate is undoubtedly high; he states that the employment share of unionized contractors was between 50 and 55 percent from 1939 to 1970 (Steven Allen, "Declining Unionization in Construction: The Facts and the Reasons," *Industrial and Labor Relations Review* 41 [Apr. 1988]: 347). "1948: Looking Forward," BCTD *Bulletin* (Apr. 1948): 2; BCTD *Proceedings,* 1947, 161 (quotation); R. Alton Lee, *Truman and Taft-Hartley: A Question of Mandate* (Lexington: University of Kentucky Press, 1966), 75–77; Melvyn Dubofsky, *The State and Labor in Modern America* (Chapel Hill: University of North Carolina Press, 1994), 201–5.

37. Dunlop and Hill, *War Adjustment Board,* viii; Minutes, July 1947, box 44, EC Case Files, BCTD Records, GMMA; "AFL Building Trades Unions to Fight Taft-Hartley on Construction," *Engineering News-Record* (July 31, 1947): 15; Harry C. Bates, *Bricklayers' Century of Craftsmanship: A History of the Bricklayers, Masons and Plasterers' International Union of America* (Washington, D.C.: BMPIUA, 1955), 260.

38. "NLRB to Rule over Construction Trades," BCTD *Bulletin* (Feb. 1948): 1; "What Employers Say of Taft-Hartley Act," BCTD *Bulletin* (June 1948): 3; "Denham Gives Up Plan to Hold Union Shop Elections," BCTD *Bulletin* (Oct. 1948): 3; "NLRB Plan to Poll Nation's Builders Proves to Be a Dud," *The Laborer* (Nov. 1948): 14.

39. John T. Dunlop interview, June 18, 2002.

40. J. D. Marshall, "Labor Relations for General Contractors," *The Constructor* (July 1947): 142 (quotation); EC report, BCTD *Proceedings,* 1947, 170. This report included a telegram from the AGC urging BCTD to act on the joint jurisdiction board plan submitted on Sept. 5, 1947.

41. EC report, BCTD *Proceedings,* 1948, 125–26.

42. "National Joint Plan for the Settlement of Jurisdictional Disputes," Draft Copy, Oct. 15, 1948; John T. Dunlop, "The Settlement of Jurisdictional Disputes," clipping, *New Jersey Building Contractor* (ca. May 1956), box 3, Jurisdiction Files, BCTD Records, GMMA (quotations).

43. "National Joint Plan for Settlement of Jurisdictional Disputes Terminated by Unions," BCTD *Bulletin* (June 1949): 3; "Old Plan of Ending Disputes on Jurisdiction Is Restored," *The Laborer* (June 1949): 13.

44. "National Joint Plan for Settlement of Jurisdictional Disputes to Continue," BCTD *Bulletin* (Aug. 1949): 4; "Department Annual Report to AFL," BCTD *Bulletin* (Sept. 1953): 1 (quotation); President Gray's report, BCTD *Proceedings,* 1950, 123–25; 1951, 126 (quotation).

45. Dunlop interview; "Let's Look at the Record," BCTD *Bulletin* (Oct. 1951): 7

46. Dunlop interview; "The Settlement of Jurisdictional Disputes: Summary of Remarks for Painters Conference," draft, Dec. 10, 1956 (quotation), box 3, Jurisdiction Files, BCTD Records, GMMA.

47. Charles MacGowan to Gray, July 3, 1951; J. H. Lyons to Dunlop, Aug. 24, 1950; Joseph D. Keenan to Dunlop, May 21, 1953; McSorley to Dunlop, Mar. 16, 1955; draft article, *Architectural Forum* (Oct. 1955): 4 (quotation); "Jurisdictional Disputes Board Upheld," clipping, *Engineering News-Record* (Sept. 1, 1955): 106 (quotation); "Another Storm Subsides," clipping, *Engineering News-Record* (Sept. 1, 1955), box 3, Jurisdiction Files, BCTD Records, GMMA. BCTD *Proceedings,* 1953, 146, notes that the IBEW was not affiliated with the NJB.

48. "NLRB Outlaws Hiring Practices in the Building Trades," BCTD *Bulletin* (July 1949): 1; "Text of President Gray's TH Testimony before Senate Labor Committee," BCTD

Bulletin (Apr. 1953): 2; "NLRB Outlaws Building Trades Contracts," BCTD *Bulletin* (June 1950): 1 (quotation); "NLRB Rules on Work Permits," BCTD *Bulletin* (Jan. 1951): 1, BCTD *Proceedings,* 1951, 125.

49. "NLRB Trial Examiner Finds Small Building Construction under TH Act," BCTD *Bulletin* (Aug. 1948): 1; "Unions Appeal from NLRB Decision," BCTD *Bulletin* (July 1949): 4; "NLRB Asks Supreme Court to Rule on Denver Building Trades Case," BCTD *Bulletin* (Nov. 1950): 1, 4; "Supreme Court Rules against Labor on Secondary Boycott," BCTD *Bulletin* (June 1951): 1 (quotation).

50. "Sectional Building Trades Conferences," BCTD *Bulletin* (July 1951): 1; "Let's Look at the Record," BCTD *Bulletin* (Oct. 1951): 1–8.

51. "Let's Look at the Record," BCTD *Bulletin* (Oct. 1951): 4, 6, 8.

52. George Meany's address, BCTD *Proceedings,* 1947, 193–95 (quotations taken out of order).

53. Philip Taft, *The A. F. of L. from the Death of Gompers to the Merger* (New York: Harper and Brothers, 1959), 311–13; Meany's address, BCTD *Proceedings,* 1948, 183 (quotation); Palladino, *Dreams of Dignity,* 212 (quotation).

54. "AFL Executive Council Adopts President Gray's Taft-Hartley Recommendations," BCTD *Bulletin* (Sept. 1952): 1, 2, 3 (quotations); Lee, *Truman and Taft-Hartley,* 206–10.

55. President Gray's report, BCTD *Proceedings,* 1952, 113; "Labor's Stake in Construction," BCTD *Bulletin* (Feb. 1952): 4 (quotation). Gray was addressing the Construction Industry Council of the U.S. Chamber of Commerce.

56. President Gray's report, BCTD *Proceedings,* 1952, 114.

57. Marvin Boede interview, Feb. 5, 2002; Cornelius J. Haggerty, "Labor, Los Angeles, and the Legislature," an oral history conducted in 1969 by Amelia Fry, in *Labor Leaders View the Warren Era,* Regional Oral History Office, the Bancroft Library, University of California, Berkeley, 1976 (online).

58. "Open Letter to Phil Murray," BCTD *Bulletin* (Mar. 1952): 1; President Gray's report, BCTD *Proceedings,* 1952, 116–17 (quotation).

59. "National Building Trades Conference," BCTD *Bulletin* (Feb. 1955): 1 (quotation); "National Legislative Conference of Building Trades," BCTD *Bulletin* (Mar. 1955): 1.

60. "National Legislative Conference of Building Trades," 1–2.

61. Ibid., quotation at 2; "Prevailing Wage for Highway Construction," BCTD *Bulletin* (June 1955): 1 (quotation). Emphasis in original.

62. "Highway Bill Contains Prevailing Wage Provision," BCTD *Bulletin* (May 1955): 2; "National Legislative Conference of the Building Trades," BCTD *Bulletin* (Jan. 1956): 2.

63. "Legislative Review," BCTD *Bulletin* (July 1955): 1 (quotation); "Highway Bill Defeated," BCTD *Bulletin* (Aug. 1955): 1.

64. "Department Report to AFL-CIO," BCTD *Bulletin* (Oct. 1957): 1–2.

Chapter 7

1. "Apprentices Bureau Weakened," BCTD *Bulletin* (Sept. 1954): 1; "Labor's Stake in Construction," BCTD *Bulletin* (Feb. 1952): 1; "Construction in the South," BCTD *Bulletin* (Sept. 1955): 1; "Construction Activity in 1957," BCTD *Bulletin* (Jan. 1957): 2; Marvin Boede interview, Feb. 5, 2002.

2. Boede interview; Robert Georgine interview, Aug. 28, 2002; Richard Schneirov and Thomas J. Suhrbur, *Union Brotherhood, Union Town: The History of the Carpenters' Union of Chicago, 1863–1987* (Carbondale: Southern Illinois University Press, 1988), 138–39.

3. Joshua B. Freeman, *Working-Class New York: Life and Labor since World War II* (New York: New Press, 2000), 17; Daniel Quinn Mills, *Industrial Relations and Manpower in Con-*

struction (Cambridge, Mass.: MIT Press, 1972), 183–84; George Andrucki interview, conducted by Janet Wells Greene, Dec. 2, 1998, Robert F. Wagner Labor Archives, Tamiment Library, New York University (hereafter, Andrucki interview); Joseph F. Maloney interview, Sept. 6, 2002.

4. Cornelius J. Haggerty, "Labor, Los Angeles, and the Legislature," an oral history conducted in 1969 by Amelia Fry, in *Labor Leaders View the Warren Era,* Regional Oral History Office, Bancroft Library, University of California, Berkeley, 1976 (online); Mills, *Industrial Relations,* 185.

5. Andrucki interview.

6. Ibid.; Brennan made these remarks at the 1963 BCTD convention, *Proceedings,* 1963, 181.

7. Andrucki interview; Boede interview; Georgine interview.

8. Georgine interview.

9. Geary's address, BCTD *Proceedings,* 1957, 194.

10. Marc Linder, *Wars of Attrition: Vietnam, the Business Roundtable, and the Decline of Construction Unions* (Iowa City: Fanpihua, 1999), 116–20, 158; Garth L. Mangum, *The Operating Engineers: The Economic History of a Trade Union* (Cambridge, Mass.: Harvard University Press, 1964), 261–70; Mills, *Industrial Relations,* 27–28; Geary's address, BCTD *Proceedings,* 1957, 194.

11. Mangum, *Operating Engineers,* 255.

12. Georgine interview; quotations inverted for clarity.

13. Geary's address, BCTD *Proceedings,* 1957, 194.

14. Mangum, *Operating Engineers,* 256–57; "19 AFL Unions Join to Combat Tie-ups at Big Atom Jobs," *New York Times,* Sept. 20, 1953, 1, 55 (quotation) (hereafter, *NYT*).

15. "An Open Letter to Phil Murray," BCTD *Bulletin* (Mar. 1952): 1–4; BCTD *Proceedings,* 1957, 141; John T. Dunlop, "Project Labor Agreements," Joint Center for Housing Studies, Harvard University, Sept. 2002, 5–6.

16. "An Open Letter to Phil Murray," BCTD *Bulletin* (Mar. 1952): 1–4; BCTD *Proceedings,* 1957, 56–61, 136–37, 141 (quotation); BCTD *Proceedings,* 1975, 38–39.

17. BCTD *Proceedings,* 1957, 136, 137 (quotations); "Building Crafts Try to Bar Labor's Regional Mergers," *NYT,* Apr. 28, 1956, 1, 38; "Big Labor Unions Renew Battles," *NYT,* Feb. 3, 1957, 155; "Midwest Delegates Ask Building Trades [to] Weigh Quitting AFL-CIO," *Wall Street Journal,* Sept. 27, 1957, 2; "Building Unions Sift Peace Plan," *NYT,* Aug. 5, 1957, 15; "AFL-CIO Building Trades Unit to Challenge Meany Plan for Ending Craft-Industrial Union Disputes," *Wall Street Journal,* Aug. 5, 1957, 2; "Hoffa Makes No Move to Spur Building Trades Unions Revolt," *Wall Street Journal,* Aug. 6, 1957, 2.

18. Meany's address, BCTD *Proceedings,* 1957, 187–88 (quotations at 188).

19. Linder, *Wars of Attrition,* 138. According to Linder's figures, which are based on U.S. Bureau of Labor Statistics reports, there were 794 strikes in 1952, involving 24 percent of construction employment; 1,039 strikes in 1953, involving 22 percent; and 804 strikes in 1954, involving 17 percent. R. Alton Lee, *Eisenhower and Landrum-Griffin: A Study in Labor-Management Politics* (Lexington: University of Kentucky Press, 1990), 19.

20. Dave Beck to Executive Council, Nov. 27, 1957, BCTD *Proceedings,* 1957, 147–48.

21. BCTD *Proceedings,* 1957, 139, 225 (quotations); "Other Convention Action," BCTD *Bulletin* (Dec. 1957), 3; Gray and delegates from the Carpenters, Elevator Constructors, Laborers, Lathers, Sheet Metal Workers, and Stone Cutters voted against expelling the Teamsters from the AFL-CIO; Grace Palladino, *Dreams of Dignity, Workers of Vision: A History of the International Brotherhood of Electrical Workers* (Washington, D.C.: IBEW, 1991), 225 (quotation); Lee, *Eisenhower and Landrum-Griffin,* 45–47, 62–63, 72.

22. "Contractors' Group Is Skeptical of Effort to Cut Featherbedding," *Wall Street Journal,* Feb. 11, 1958, 2.

23. "Rooney to Building Trades Board," *Plasterer and Cement Mason* (Aug. 1957): 4. These changes were the result of a special convention that met in August 1957 to revise the Department's constitution. The convention also raised per capita taxes for international unions, established annual affiliation fees for state and local councils, and eliminated the "double vote" clause that benefited large unions. "Regional Directors Appointed," BCTD *Bulletin* (Dec. 1957): 3.

24. President Gray's address, BCTD *Proceedings,* 1957, 134–38 (quotations at 135, 138).

25. "Union Chief Bids Labor Freeze Pay to Curb Inflation," *NYT,* Dec. 3, 1957, 1, 38; "President Gray's Opening Address," BCTD *Bulletin* (Dec. 1957): 3.

26. Institute of Labor and Industrial Relations, *The Resolution of Jurisdictional Disputes in the Building Trades and Economic Prospects for the Industry, 1957–1958* (Ann Arbor: University of Michigan-Wayne State, 1958), 50–51 (quotation at 51); "AFL Building Units Fight Cost-Inflating Job Practices," *NYT,* Feb. 1, 1954, 1, 16.

27. Institute of Labor and Industrial Relations, *Resolution of Jurisdictional Disputes,* 51 (quotation); Linder, *Wars of Attrition,* 69.

28. "Building Unions to Fight Waste," *NYT,* Jan. 28, 1959, 20; "A Look at Building Trades' New Chief," *The Constructor* (Aug. 1960): 25

29. Draft statement, "Some Basic Problems in the Construction Industry," Aug. 27, 1959, Construction Industry Joint Conference Files (hereafter, CIJC), box 1, BCTD Records, George Meany Memorial Archives, Silver Spring, Md. (hereafter, GMMA) (quotation); "Council Is Set Up in Building Field," *NYT,* Jan. 29, 1959, 14; "Need for Construction Unity Stressed by Labor Committee," *The Constructor* (Feb. 1959): 69.

30. "Chief of Building Union Resigns," *NYT,* Feb. 5, 1960, 19; "Coast Man Heads Building Trades," *NYT,* Feb. 25, 1960, 21; "A Look at Building Trades' New Chief," *The Constructor* (Aug. 1960): 24–26 (quotation at 24).

31. "U.S. Acts to Halt ICBM-Base Waste," *NYT,* May 8, 1961, 1; "Building of Missile Bases Lags," *NYT,* Sept. 18, 1960, 1, 68 (quotation); Howard E. Wayne, *The Missile Sites Labor Commission, 1961–1967* (Washington, D.C.: U.S. Government Printing Office, 1969), 3.

32. "Missile Unions Held Unfairly Accused," *NYT,* June 11, 1961, 21; Wayne, *Missile Sites Labor Commission,* 1–2.

33. "Building of Missile Bases Lags," *NYT,* Sept. 18, 1960, 68; "A Look at Building Trades' New Chief," *The Constructor* (Aug. 1960): 26; "Labor Is Seeking Missile Harmony," *NYT,* Dec. 1, 1960, 21 (quotation).

34. "Policy on Missile Sites," BCTD *Bulletin* (Mar. 1961): 1; Robert S. McNamara to Haggerty, Feb. 17, 1961, published in BCTD *Bulletin* (Mar. 1961): 3.

35. "U.S. Acts to Halt ICBM-Base Waste," *NYT,* May 8, 1961, 29; John McClellan, "Sen. McClellan Hits H.R. 100," *The Constructor* (June 1967): 26.

36. "JFK Names Top Board for Missile Base Peace," BCTD *Bulletin,* special edition (May 26, 1961): 1 (quotation); "Board to Prevent Strikes at Missile Sites Is Created," *Wall Street Journal,* May 29, 1961, 4.

37. See, for example, *The Builders: The Seventy-five-Year History of the Building and Construction Trades Department, AFL-CIO* (Washington, D.C.: BCTD, 1983), 28; and H. E. Lore's address, BCTD *Proceedings,* 1961, 227. Lore represented the NCA.

38. "Cape Canaveral," BCTD *Bulletin* (Dec. 1962): 2; "Missile Bases Ending Job Delays as Joint Peace Effort Pays Off," *NYT,* July 15, 1961, 9 (quotation); "Labor Aims to Avoid Missile Site Strikes," *NYT,* May 1, 1962, 26 (quotations).

39. Wayne, *Missile Sites Labor Commission,* 37–39, 74; U.S. Acts to Halt ICBM-Base Waste," *NYT,* May 8, 1961, 1, 29; "Cape Canaveral," BCTD *Bulletin* (Dec. 1962): 2 (quotations taken out of order).

40. Dunlop's testimony before House Special Subcommittee on Labor, July 25, 1962,

box 1, CIJC Files, BCTD Records, GMMA; Willard Wirtz's address, BCTD *Proceedings,* 1963, 249.

41. Wirtz's address, BCTD *Proceedings,* 1963, 249; report of the General President, *Official Record of the IUOE* (Apr. 1960–Apr. 1964), 320 (quotation).

42. NCA press release, June 21, 1962; NECA statement, Special Committee on Labor of the Committee on Education and Labor, June 15, 1962, box 1, CIJC Files, BCTD Records, GMMA.

43. IUOE officers report, 1964, 31–34, box 4, CIJC Files, BCTD Records, GMMA.

44. President Haggerty's report, BCTD *Proceedings,* 1965, 4; National Interstate and Defense Highways Act, transcript (online, http://ourdocuments.gov); "Consequences of the Development of the Interstate Highway System for Transit," *Research Results Digest* (Aug. 1997): 3 (online); "Two Houses Pass Atomic Power Bills," *Washington Post,* Aug. 21, 1957, A10; "The 'Hill' Did Pretty Well Despite Ike's Plaint," *Washington Post,* Sept. 1, 1957, E1. Representative Morris K. Udall, "Report on the 87th Congress," *Arizona Frontiers* 1 (Dec. 1961): 16–17 (online); "Congress Votes Kennedy Housing Program," *Wall Street Journal,* June 29, 1961, 4; "'3rd Try' Housing Bill Signed by President," *Washington Post,* Sept. 24, 1959, A2.

45. Herbert Hill to Roy Wilkins, Oct. 23, 1956, pt. 13 supplement, reel 2, fr. 299, NAACP Papers, Library of Congress (hereafter, LC); press release, "Chicago Engineering Union Admits First Negro after NAACP Protest," May 31, 1956, ibid., fr. 502.

46. Jacob Seidenberg to Wilkins, Oct. 31, 1956, pt. 13 supplement, reel 13, fr. 117–19, NAACP Papers, LC; "Powell Assails Craft Unionists," *NYT,* July 15, 1961, reprinted in BCTD *Bulletin* (July 1961): 1.

47. Haggerty to Powell, July 18, 1961, reprinted in "The Building Trades Replies," BCTD *Bulletin* (July 1961): 1.

48. Bowen to J. W. Potter et al., Local Union 25, Sarasota, Fla., Apr. 13, 1928, included in president's report, *Bricklayer, Mason and Plasterer* (Aug. 1928): 180–81 (quotation at 181); Herbert R. Northrup, *Organized Labor and the Negro* (New York: Krause Reprint, 1971 [1944]), 26.

49. "President Haggerty Testifies on Apprentice-Discrimination Bill," BCTD *Bulletin* (Aug. 1961): 4.

50. A. Philip Randolph to Meany, June 14, 1961, pt. 13 supplement, reel 1, fr. 795, NAACP Papers, LC; "First D.C. Negro Gets Union Carpenter Card," *Washington Post,* Oct. 29, 1961, A2.

51. Press Release, June 7, 1963, "Action to Ban Construction Job Bias Welcomed by NAACP," pt. 13 supplement, reel 13, fr. 421–22, NAACP Papers, LC (quotation); Dean J. Kotlowski, "Richard Nixon and the Origins of Affirmative Action," *Historian* (spring 1998): 523 (EBSCO).

52. "Civil Rights," *Construction Craftsman* (July 1963): 1 (quotations taken out of order).

53. Statement, CIJC: Joint Committee on Equal Employment Opportunities, Aug. 9, 1963, box 1, Subject Files, BCTD Records, GMMA (quotation); "Building Trades Press Equality," *NYT,* July 31, 1963, 1, 13. Labor representatives on the joint committee were Neil Haggerty, Maurice Hutcheson (Carpenters), Gordon Freeman (IBEW), Peter T. Schoemann (UA), and Peter Fosco (Laborers). Peter J. Brennan's address, BCTD *Proceedings,* 1963, 181, 183.

54. Wirtz's address, BCTD *Proceedings,* 1963, 250–52 (quotations at 251 and 252).

55. Keenan is cited in Palladino, *Dreams of Dignity,* 255; F. Roy Marshall and Vernon M. Briggs, *The Negro and Apprenticeship* (Baltimore, Md.: Johns Hopkins University Press, 1967), 61, cited in George Santiago, "Power and Affiliation within a Local Trade Union:

Local 3 of the International Brotherhood of Electrical Workers" (Ph.D. dissertation, City University of New York, 1987), 112.

56. Andrucki interview.

57. Ibid.

58. Wirtz's address, BCTD *Proceedings,* 1967, 205; Carrie G. Donald et al., "Creating Bridges of Cooperation: A Local Building Trades Council's Approach to Expanding Minority Business Participation and Training Opportunities," draft paper, 13–14 (online; http://www.louisville.edu/cbpa/lmc/research/creatingbridges); President Haggerty's report, BCTD *Proceedings,* 1967, 29.

59. Wirtz is quoted in President Haggerty's report, BCTD *Proceedings,* 1967, 29; Wirtz's address, BCTD *Proceedings,* 1967, 201; Weaver's address, BCTD *Proceedings,* 1967, 267–68.

60. Linder, *Wars of Attrition,* 254–55.

61. Haggerty to Wirtz, Feb. 1, 1968, box 1, Subject Files, BCTD Records, GMMA; Linder, *Wars of Attrition,* 249.

62. "18 Unions Pledge to Seek Negroes for Building Jobs," *NYT,* Feb. 14, 1968, 1; "Unions and Blacks," *Wall Street Journal,* Feb. 26, 1969, 16.

63. James Loughlin, business manager, BCTC of Philadelphia, Aug. 27, 1969, box 4, CIJC Files, BCTD Records, GMMA.

64. Linder, *Wars of Attrition,* 256–57; Loughlin, Aug. 27, 1969, box 4, CIJC Files, BCTD Records, GMMA.

65. Loughlin, Aug. 27, 1969, box 4, CIJC Files, BCTD Records, GMMA.

66. For a business critique of union control of skill, see M. R. Lefkoe, *The Crisis in Construction: There Is an Answer* (Washington, D.C.: Bureau of National Affairs, 1970), 13, 56–58, 80–84. Quotations from *Fortune* are included in "Union 'Stranglehold' Is Charged," *NYT,* Dec. 15, 1968, R1.

67. Wirtz's address, BCTD *Proceedings,* 1967, 204; Linder, *Wars of Attrition,* 252–54 (quotation at 252).

68. Quotations from *Fortune* are cited in Linder, *Wars of Attrition,* 251; "Unions Are Urged to Spur New Housing," *NYT,* Sept. 24, 1969, 18.

69. BCTD *Proceedings,* 1971, 23, 27; Linder, *Wars of Attrition,* 252.

Chapter 8

1. See, for example, William L. O'Neill, *American High: The Years of Confidence, 1945–60* (New York: Free Press, 1986); James Miller, *"Democracy Is in the Streets": From Port Huron to the Siege of Chicago* (New York: Simon and Schuster, 1987); Grace Palladino, *Teenagers: An American History* (New York: Basic Books, 1996).

2. Joshua B. Freeman, *Working Class New York: Life and Labor since World War II* (New York: New Press, 2000), 237–40 (quotation at 239); for a discussion of the media's role in creating the "hard-hat" image, see Peter Levy, *The New Left and Labor in the 1960s* (Urbana: University of Illinois Press, 1994); and Christian Appy, *Working-Class War: American Combat Soldiers and Vietnam* (Chapel Hill: University of North Carolina Press, 1993). For working-class youth and the war in Vietnam, see Lawrence M. Baskir and William A. Strauss, *Chance and Circumstance: The Draft, the War, and the Vietnam Generation* (New York: Knopf, 1978); "Construction Union Chief in New York Is Chosen to Succeed Hodgson," *New York Times,* Nov. 30, 1972, 1, 37 (hereafter, *NYT*).

3. The 55 percent figure is from U.S. Bureau of the Census, "Labor Union Membership in 1966," as reported in Marc Linder, *Wars of Attrition: Vietnam, the Business Roundtable, and the Decline of Construction Unions* (Iowa City: Fanpihua, 1999), 100; Linder, *Wars of Attrition,* 18–19, 60–67 (quotation at 18); "Building Unions Said to Spurn Wage Plea," *NYT,* Feb. 6,

1966, 36 (quotations); "Labor Notes," *The Constructor* (Aug. 1966): 54–55; "'Running Scared' Building Unions Hunt for Recruits," *U.S. News & World Report,* Dec. 12, 1977, 81–82.

4. Linder, *Wars of Attrition,* 32; "Crackdown on Construction," *NYT,* Sept. 5, 1969, 36 (quotation).

5. Linder, *Wars of Attrition,* 138–39 (for the number of strikes), 290; "President Forms a Panel to Solve Building Disputes," *NYT,* Sept. 23, 1969, 1, 56.

6. "Should Management Take a Strike?" *The Constructor* (Nov. 1968): 36–37; Joseph F. Maloney interview, Sept. 6, 2002; George Andrucki interview conducted by Janet Wells Greene, Dec. 2, 1998, Robert F. Wagner Labor Archives, Tamiment Library, New York University; Linder, *Wars of Attrition,* 185 (contractor quotation).

7. Linder, *Wars of Attrition,* 305, 309–11; Garth L. Mangum and John Walsh, *Union Resilience in Troubled Times: The Story of the Operating Engineers, 1960–1993* (Armonk, N.Y.: M.E. Sharpe, 1994), 70–72; Daniel Quinn Mills, "Wage Determination in Contract Construction," *Industrial Relations* 10 (Feb. 1971): 75, quoted in Linder, *Wars of Attrition,* 291; "Honor Pacts or Lose Jobs," *NYT,* Sept. 4, 1970, 9 (quotation).

8. Mangum and Walsh, *Union Resilience,* 71; Hodgson is quoted in Jefferson Cowie, "Nixon's Class Struggle: Romancing the New Right Worker, 1969–1973," *Labor History* 43 (Aug. 2002): 274; John T. Dunlop to Grace Palladino, Mar. 26, 2003, in my possession; "Building Trades Unions Must Heed Nixon Fiat on Wages, Leader Says," *Wall Street Journal,* Mar. 31, 1971, 2; Daniel Quinn Mills, "Construction Wage Stabilization: A Historic Perspective," *Industrial Relations* 11 (Oct. 1972): 353–54; President Bonadio's report, BCTD *Proceedings,* 1971, 28–29, 38.

9. John Healy's address, BCTD *Proceedings,* 1973, 248 (quotation); Walter Galenson, *The United Brotherhood of Carpenters: The First Hundred Years* (Cambridge, Mass.: Harvard University Press, 1983), 353–54 (quotation at 354).

10. Linder, *Wars of Attrition,* 24, 182–84; "Should Management Take a Strike?" *The Constructor* (Nov. 1968): 36–37; Georgine's address, BCTD *Proceedings,* 1977, 177.

11. Linder, *Wars of Attrition,* 184–86 (quotations at 184); Booth Mooney, "Labor Law: Time for New Reforms," *The Constructor* (Dec. 1968): 36–37 (quotation at 37).

12. Linder, *Wars of Attrition,* 182–86 (Healy quoted at 182); "Checklist for Roger Blough's Construction Roundtable," *Dodge Construction News,* Nov. 13, 1970, 11; Robert Gunness, "Inflation and the Construction Industry," Board of Directors Meeting, Chicago Association of Commerce and Industry, Aug. 6, 1970, box 6, Project Agreement Files, BCTD Records, George Meany Memorial Archives, Silver Spring, Md. (hereafter, GMMA) (quotation; Gunness represented the Chicago Contractors Users Council, a CUAIR affiliate); "Industry Quietly Forms Group to Curb Spiral of Construction Costs," *Wall Street Journal,* Aug. 14, 1969, 1.

13. Linder, *Wars of Attrition,* 223–24; M. R. Lefkoe, *The Crisis in Construction: There Is an Answer* (Washington, D.C.: Bureau of National Affairs, 1970), 138 (quotation), 140–43, 158–65 (quotation at 162).

14. President Bonadio's address, BCTD *Proceedings,* 1973, 140 (quotation); Linder, *Wars of Attrition,* 171–72.

15. Linder, *Wars of Attrition,* 42, 132, 160; President Bonadio's report, BCTD *Proceedings,* 1973, 42–43; address to convention, BCTD *Proceedings,* 1973, 141 (quotation).

16. Dunlop's address, BCTD *Proceedings,* 1973, 196–200 (quotations at 197 and 200).

17. Mangum and Walsh, *Union Resilience in Troubled Times,* 73; Nixon is quoted in Linder, *Wars of Attrition,* 325, and *Business Week* is quoted at 326; "Federal Pay Curbs Ruled Out on Work Done after April 30," *Wall Street Journal,* May 14, 1974, 4.

18. President Georgine's report, BCTD *Proceedings,* 1975, 21–22; Linder, *Wars of Attrition,* 331; "Hard-Hat Havoc," *Wall Street Journal,* Apr. 10, 1975, 1; "Hard-Hat Unions Fight Back," *Washington Post,* June 19, 1978, A1, A5.

19. *The Builders: The Seventy-five Year History of the Building and Construction Trades Department, AFL-CIO* (Washington, D.C.: BCTD, 1983), 34–37; President Georgine's report, BCTD *Proceedings*, 1975, 37; Executive Council report, BCTD *Proceedings*, 1975, 80–81; Linder, *Wars of Attrition*, 197, 220; Richard Schneirov, *Pride and Solidarity: A History of the Plumbers and Pipefitters of Columbus, Ohio, 1889–1989* (Ithaca, N.Y.: Cornell University Press, 1993), 130–31. The NLRB case sanctioning double-breasting was Peter Kiewit Sons' Co., 206 NLRB 562(1973); the Supreme Court would uphold the decision in a 1976 case, *South Prairie Construction Co. v. Operating Engineers Local 627*, 425 U.S. 800 (1976).

20. John T. Dunlop interview, June 18, 2002; "Twenty-nine Years of Dedicated Labor Leadership: A Tribute to Bob Georgine," souvenir program, April 2000, 6 (quotation); Marvin Boede interview, Feb. 5, 2002.

21. Robert Georgine interview, Aug. 28, 2002.

22. "Hard-Hat Havoc," *Wall Street Journal*, Apr. 10, 1975, 1; "Construction Workers Mass in Capital to Demand Jobs," *NYT*, Apr. 22, 1975, 19 (quotation); BCTD *Proceedings*, 1975, 172–73 (quotation at 172).

23. Georgine interview; "Common Situs Picket Rights for the Building Unions," *NYT*, Nov. 6, 1975, 42.

24. Georgine interview; "Paul Fannin's Legacy: Hard Hats' Freedom," *National Right to Work Newsletter* (Feb. 2002): 6 (online); "Picketing Bill Vetoed by Ford in Dunlop Defeat," *Wall Street Journal*, Dec. 23, 1975, 3 (quotation); Dunlop interview, June 18, 2002; Bruce Kaufman, "Reflections on Six Decades in Industrial Relations: An Interview with John Dunlop," *Industrial and Labor Relations Review* 55 (Jan. 2002): 341–42 (quotation at 342).

25. Georgine interview; "Common Situs Picketing Rights for the Building Unions," *NYT*, Nov. 6, 1975, 1; Dunlop interview; Linder, *Wars of Attrition*, 334–35 (quotation at 334).

26. Georgine interview; "Paul Fannin's Legacy: Hard Hats' Freedom," 6.

27. Georgine interview.

28. "Replacing Dunlop Isn't the Most Serious of Ford's Labor-Management Problems," *Wall Street Journal*, Jan. 15, 1976, 7 (quotation); "9 Labor Leaders Quit Ford Panel," *NYT*, Jan. 9, 1976, 1.

29. Georgine interview; "Picketing the Issue in Construction Fight," *NYT*, Mar. 13, 1977, 110. The AGC spokesman was James Sprouse, executive vice president; "House Rejects Bill on Picketing Sites by Building Unions," *NYT*, Mar. 24, 1977, D16.

30. "House Rejects Bill on Picketing Sites by Building Unions," A1, D16; Georgine interview; Ken Bode, "The George and Jimmy Show," *New Republic*, May 21, 1977, 30–33 (quotation at 30); "Labor Losses: Pressure for Changes in Leadership," *NYT*, Mar. 26, 1977, 19.

31. Georgine's address, BCTD *Proceedings*, 1977, 179, 181 (quotations); "Carter Signs Bills for Public Works and the Creation of a Million Jobs," *NYT*, May 14, 1977, 49.

32. Georgine's address, BCTD *Proceedings*, 1977, 176, 183 (quotations).

33. Ibid., 175–76 (quotation); "Building Unions Plan Organizing Campaign," *NYT*, Dec. 1, 1977, 18. The convention approved a three cent a month per capita assessment intended to raise about $650,000 a year; "'Running Scared' Building Unions Hunt for Recruits," *U.S. News & World Report*, Dec. 12, 1977, 81–82.

34. Frederick E. Wendell to Robert A. Georgine (hereafter, RAG), Nov. 28, 1977, box 6, Project Agreement Files, BCTD Records, GMMA (quotation); former B.A. David Foree of IBEW Local 309 is quoted in Louis Baczewski, "International Brotherhood of Electrical Workers Local 309 and the Fate of American Construction Trade Unions, 1965–2002," unpublished paper, Eastern Illinois University, 2001, 10.

35. Baczewski, "International Brotherhood," 1, 6, 9; Jeffrey Grabelsky, "Bottom-Up Organizing in the Trades: An Interview with Mike Lucas," *Labor Research Review* 7 (fall 1988): 23, 29–32.

36. The quotation is from Foree in Baczewski, "International Brotherhood," 3; Cal Solem to Omaha and Lincoln Contractors, May 30, 1979, enclosed in William Siddell to RAG, Aug. 30, 1979, box 9, Organizing Files, BCTD Records, GMMA.

37. Georgine is cited in Riesel, "Lively Muscled Corpse," clipping, Dec. 14, 1978, box 1, General Files, BCTD Records, GMMA.

38. Riesel, "Lively Muscled Corpse."

39. Con O'Shea to RAG, June 1, 1978, box 9, Organizing Files, BCTD Records, GMMA; BCTD *Proceedings*, 1977, 165, 177 (quotations).

40. For jurisdiction, BCTD *Proceedings*, 1977, 327–28; BCTD *Proceedings*, 1981, 327–28; "Jurisdictional Plan Set to Go," *Engineering News-Record* (May 10, 1984): 57; for local councils, BCTD *Proceedings*, 1977, 202; for Canada, BCTD *Proceedings*, 1975, 79, 320–23; BCTD *Proceedings*, 1977, 85, 264–65, 393–94. For an overview of the Canadian situation, see Roy J. Adams, "Canada-U.S. Labour Link under Stress," *Industrial Relations* 15 (fall 1976): 295–312; Joseph B. Rose, "A Canadian View of Labor Relations in Construction," *Industrial Relations* 18 (spring 1979): 156–72; Joseph B. Rose, "Some Notes on the Building-Trades Canadian Labour Congress Dispute," *Industrial Relations* 22 (winter 1983): 87–93.

41. For Executive Council expansion, BCTD *Proceedings*, 1975, 209–11, 450–85; 1977, 221, 291–302; 1979, 360–61; "Americans Didn't Control Convention of Canadian Unionists, Labor Leader Says," clipping, n.d, box 1, General Files, BCTD Records, GMMA.

42. Georgine interview.

43. For the Daniel Construction campaign in Bath, see Thomas H. Owens to Director of Organization, International Unions, Apr. 14, 1978; J. L. Trauba to Employees, RE: Bath County Pumped Storage Project, July 18, 1977; RAG to General Presidents, Aug. 30, 1978, box 9, Organizing Files, BCTD Records, GMMA. For committee activities, see Owens, Organizational Report, May 8, 1978, and May 15, 1978; William Siddell to RAG, Apr. 27, 1978, box 9, Organizing Files.

44. Ruth Milkman, ed., *Organizing Immigrants: The Challenge for Unions in Contemporary California* (Ithaca, N.Y.: Cornell University Press, 2002), 173–74 (quotation at 173); Georgine's address, BCTD *Proceedings*, 1979, 272; James Lee's address, BCTD *Proceedings*, 1977, 165.

45. Owens to RAG, May 15, 1978 (quotation); Owens, handwritten notes, LA County Pilot Program, n.d., box 9, Organizing Records, BCTD Records, GMMA.

46. O'Shea to RAG, Jan. 8, 1979, box 9, Organizing Files, BCTD Records, GMMA.

47. O'Shea report, Apr. 1, 1978, box 9, Organizing Files, BCTD Records, GMMA.

48. Owens, handwritten notes, "LA, Con O'Shea, Jake West, 17 months," n.d.; O'Shea report, Apr. 1, 1978, box 9, Organizing Files, BCTD Records, GMMA (quotation).

49. O'Shea report, Jan. 8, 1979, box 9, Organizing Files, BCTD Records, GMMA.

50. Ibid., Apr. 1, 1978.

51. Owens to RAG, June 14, 1978; O'Shea report, January 8, 1979, box 9, Organizing Files, BCTD Records, GMMA.

52. O'Shea report, Jan. 8, 1979, box 9, Organizing Files, BCTD Records, GMMA.

53. Owens to RAG, June 14, 1978; Owens report, Aug. 12, 1980; Timothy Catherwood to Owens, Apr. 16, 1980, box 9, Organizing Files, BCTD Records, GMMA; "L.A. Drive Boosts Building-Union Rolls," *Washington Post*, Nov. 26, 1978, A7; "Union Construction in Trouble," *Engineering News-Record* (Nov. 5, 1981): 26 (LexisNexis); Georgine's address, BCTD *Proceedings*, 1979, 272.

54. Fred Driscoll's address, BCTD *Proceedings*, 1977, 327; "[Merit Shops] Have Turned the Tide in Construction's Economic Revolution," advertising supplement, *Washington Post*, n.d., ca. Jan. 1978, 2, 10, box 1, General Files, BCTD Records, GMMA (quotations); Georgine's address, BCTD *Proceedings*, 1979, 267–75 (quotations at 267 and 275).

55. President Georgine's report, BCTD *Proceedings*, 1981, 95–96; Garth L. Mangum and

John Walsh, *Union Resilience in Troubled Times: The Story of the Operating Engineers, AFL-CIO, 1960–1993* (Armonk, N.Y.: M.E. Sharpe, 1994), 180–83.

56. President Georgine's report, BCTD *Proceedings*, 1981, 95–96 (quotation at 95).

57. Ibid., 103–4; "Building Research" *Southern Exposure*, ca. 1980, clipping, box 9, Organizing Files, BCTD Records, GMMA; "Prevailing-Wage Study Finds No Link to Costs," *Engineering News-Record* (Jan. 22, 1981): 167 (LexisNexis); "Union Construction in Trouble," *Engineering News-Record* (Nov. 5, 1981): 26 (LexisNexis; quotation).

58. "Roundtable Research Report," David Solomon to RAG et al., Sept. 25, 1979; "Open Shop Construction," Solomon to RAG et al., n.d., box 9, Organizing Records, BCTD Records, GMMA (quotation); Michael Goldfield, *The Decline of Organized Labor in the United States* (Chicago: University of Chicago Press, 1987), 110 (quotation); Georgine's address, BCTD *Proceedings*, 1979, 268 (sentences reversed for clarity).

59. Linder, *Wars of Attrition*, 357; "Man of the Year; Charles D. Brown," *Engineering News-Record* (Jan. 27, 1983): 58 (LexisNexis); "Moving Ahead on Productivity," *Engineering News-Record* (Feb. 26, 1981): 80 (LexisNexis; quotation); Thomas Dailey's address, BCTD *Proceedings*, 1981, 263 (sentences reversed for clarity).

60. "Roundtable Issues First Reports on Cost-Efficiency," *Engineering News-Record* (Mar. 25, 1982): 65 (LexisNexis); "Man of the Year: Charles D. Brown," *Engineering News-Record* (Jan. 27, 1983): 58 (LexisNexis); Georgine is quoted in "Plan for Construction Productivity Stirs Industry, Takes Aim at Unions," *Wall Street Journal*, Apr. 21, 1983, 35; "Union Construction Needs Help," *Engineering News-Record* (Nov. 5, 1981): 104 (LexisNexis).

61. Linder, *Wars of Attrition*, 361; President Georgine's report, BCTD *Proceedings*, 1983, 82–83; "Committees Help Union Management and Labor Help Themselves," *Engineering News-Record* (Nov. 5, 1981): 33 (LexisNexis); "Union Construction in Trouble," *Engineering News-Record* (Nov. 5, 1981): 26 (LexisNexis).

62. President Georgine's report, BCTD *Proceedings*, 1983, 82–83; Georgine's address, BCTD *Proceedings*, 1983, 206–7 (quotation); "Committees Help Union Management and Labor Help Themselves," 33.

63. "Union Sector Weighs Its Future," *Engineering News-Record* (Aug. 26, 1982): 118; "Union Construction in Trouble," *Engineering News-Record* (Nov. 5, 1981): 26 (LexisNexis; quotations).

64. BCTD *Proceedings*, 1983, 262; "Making Market Recovery Work," *Engineering News-Record* (Aug. 2, 1984): 88; Maloney interview.

65. For an example of such criticism, see Professor David Montgomery's comment in "Construction Jobs," *NYT*, June 10, 1984, C16; "NCEC, Trades to Issue Bargaining Guidelines," *Engineering News-Record* (Feb. 23, 1984): 56 (LexisNexis) "Market Recovery Gaining," *Engineering News-Record* (Mar. 22, 1984): 52 (LexisNexis); Bob Ozinga to Editor, *Engineering News-Record* (Oct. 18, 1984): 9 (LexisNexis); Maloney interview.

66. "Roundtable Study Shaving Costs," *Engineering News-Record* (Dec. 13, 1984): 58 (LexisNexis; quotation); Linder, *Wars of Attrition*, 362–63.

67. Linder, *Wars of Attrition*, 382; "Situs Picketing Threat Surfaces," *Engineering News-Record* (May 1, 1986): 10–11; "Saturn Project Pact Infuriates Open Shop," *Engineering News-Record* (Dec. 12, 1985): 56

68. "Construction Unions Try to Shore Up a Crumbling Foundation," *Engineering News-Record* (Feb. 4, 1985): 52 (LexisNexis); "After Years of Decline, Construction Unions Rebuild Their Ranks," *Washington Post*, Dec. 2, 1985, B1, B4 (quotations).

69. Steven Allen, "Declining Unionization in Construction: The Facts and the Reasons," *Industrial and Labor Relations Review* 41 (Apr. 1988): 359; Mark Erlich, "Who Will Build the Future," *Labor Research Review* 7 (fall 1988): 6, 11 (quotations).

70. Grabelsky, "Bottom-Up Organizing in the Trades," 23, 36 (quotations are taken out of order).

Chapter 9

1. David Weil, "Building Comprehensive Market Recovery Strategies for the Construction Industry: Obstacles and Opportunities," *WorkingUSA* (summer 2003): 26; Steven Allen, "Declining Unionization in Construction: The Facts and the Reasons," *Industrial and Labor Relations Review* 41 (Apr. 1988): 343–59; President Georgine's report, BCTD *Proceedings,* 1990, 15 (quotation); Georgine's address, BCTD *Proceedings,* 1990, 335–36 (quotation).

2. "The New Deal for Unions Should Be Four Aces," *Engineering News-Record* (Apr. 26, 1990): 92.

3. "Trades Facing Dual Threat," *Engineering News-Record* (Aug. 15, 1985): 51; "Building Trades Fighting Back," *Engineering News-Record* (Apr. 24, 1986): 63; President Georgine's report, BCTD *Proceedings,* 1990, 80–81 (double-breasting), 85 (Massachusetts Campaign); BCTD *Proceedings,* 1995, 69–70 (helpers' regulation). "Court Washes Out Boston Pact," *Engineering News-Record* (May 27, 1991): 8; "High Court OKs Boston Labor Pact," *Engineering News-Record* (Mar. 15, 1993): 8 (quotation). The fourteen-year project, which was completed in 2000, eventually cost $3.9 billion, $2.2 billion less than estimated. "Boston Harbor: $3.9 Billion Cleanup Nears Completion," *Greenwire,* Mar. 15, 2000 (LexisNexis). See also Mark Erlich, *Labor at the Ballot Box: The Massachusetts Prevailing Wage Campaign of 1988* (Philadelphia: Temple University Press, 1990).

4. The Tile Setters eventually joined the Bricklayers in the late 1990s. President Georgine's report, BCTD *Proceedings,* 1995, 49–51 (CPWR-NIOSH agreement); BCTD *Proceedings,* 1990, 36–37; 1995, 109–10 (Construction Industry Partnership, originally called the 1990s Committee); "Coalition Formed for Union Manpower Needs," *Engineering News-Record* (Oct. 26, 1989): 5; President Sullivan's report, BCTD *Proceedings,* 2000, 28; "Safety: Building Trades Will Market Training Card," *Engineering News-Record* (Apr. 28, 1997): 7 (Smart Mark); "Look for the Smart Mark," advertisement, *The Builders* (July 1998): 4 (quotation).

5. President Georgine's report, BCTD *Proceedings,* 1990, 25–26 (quotation at 26); BCTD *Proceedings,* 1995, 51–52; Georgine's comments, BCTD *Proceedings,* 1990, 457; "Seeking a Cure," *Engineering News-Record* (March 27, 1986): 19; "The Industry with a Heart," *Engineering News-Record* (Dec. 24, 1987): 58; President Sullivan's report, BCTD *Proceedings,* 2000, 25.

6. John J. Barry interview, Oct. 1990.

7. Mike Lucas conversation, Apr. 7, 2003; Jeffrey Grabelsky, "Lighting the Spark: COMET Program Mobilizes the Ranks for Construction Organizing," *Labor Studies Journal* 20 (summer 1995): 8–10.

8. Victor J. Van Bourg and Ellyn Moscowitz, "Salting the Mines: The Legal and Political Implications of Placing Paid Union Organizers in the Employer's Workplace," *Hofstra Labor and Employment Law Journal* 16 (fall 1998): 2–3 (LexisNexis). I am grateful to Mark T. Robbins for directing me to this article. Mike Lucas conversation; Brian Condit et al., "Construction Organizing: A Case Study of Success," in Kate Bronfenbrenner et al., *Organizing to Win: New Research on Union Strategies* (Ithaca, N.Y.: Cornell University Press, 1998), 312–13 (quotation at 312); Weil, "Market Recovery Strategies," 44–45.

9. John Barry interviews, Oct. 1990 and July 26, 2001; Jeffrey Grabelsky interview, June 24, 2002; Grabelsky, "Lighting the Spark," 4–21; Jane Lewis and Bill Mirand, "Creating an

Organizing Culture in Today's Building and Construction Trades: A Case Study of IBEW Local 46," in Bronfenbrenner et al., *Organizing to Win*, 297–300.

10. Grabelsky, "Lighting the Spark," 6–7, 10–14 (quotation at 13); Weil, "Market Recovery Strategies," 29.

11. Grabelsky, "Lighting the Spark," 13–15; Condit et al., "Construction Organizing," 309–13 (quotation at 313); Lewis and Mirand, "Creating an Organizing Culture," 297–308.

12. Grabelsky interview; Weil, "Market Recovery Strategies," 29 (quotation).

13. Although I found no documentation of the debate surrounding the Department's decision to endorse the COMET program, my analysis is based on conversations with Department members and on evidence that the Carpenters did withhold per capita taxes at around this time, although no link to the organizing policy (or lack of one) was clear. Governing Board of Presidents report, BCTD *Proceedings*, 1995, 469–71; Robert Ozinga interview, Mar. 31, 2003. Sala is quoted in "Building Trades Plan Big Organizing Drive," *Engineering News-Record* (May 3, 1993): 6 (LexisNexis). For different strategies suiting different trades, see Charles W. Jones to Georgine, Sept. 12, 1996, and Georgine to Jones, Sept. 25, 1996, box 34, General Presidents' Correspondence, Robert A. Georgine (hereafter, RAG) Files, BCTD Records, George Meany Memorial Archives, Silver Spring, Md. (hereafter, GMMA).

14. Robert Ozinga interview; "Building Trades Plan Big Organizing Drive," *Engineering News-Record* (May 3, 1993): 6 (LexisNexis); Grabelsky interview; "Law of the Jungle Is Gaining Strength," *Engineering News-Record* (Jan. 31, 1994): 70 (LexisNexis); Governing Board of Presidents report, BCTD *Proceedings*, 1995, 469–71 (organizing).

15. "Union 'Salts' Infiltrate Construction Industry," *Wall Street Journal*, Nov. 18, 1993, B1, cited in Grabelsky, "Lighting the Spark," 17; "Building Trades Plan Big Organizing Drive," *Engineering News-Record* (May 3, 1993): 6 (LexisNexis); "Building Trades Organizing Plan Goes to the Roots of Unionism," *Engineering News-Record* (May 3, 1993): 136 (LexisNexis; quotation).

16. "Nonunion Firms on Alert as Unions Start Organizing," *Engineering News-Record* (June 14, 1993): 10 (LexisNexis); Georgine, Ivey, Sala, and Rudicil are quoted in Grabelsky, "Lighting the Spark," 6, 17, 18.

17. Marc Linder, *Wars of Attrition: Vietnam, the Business Roundtable, and the Decline of Construction Unions* (Iowa City: Fanpihua, 1999), 395–96 (quotation at 396); "Trades Facing Dual Threat," *Engineering News-Record* (Aug. 15, 1985): 51 (quotation); BCTD *Proceedings*, 2000, 428–29; D. L. Shamblin to RAG, March 28, 1994; Richard C. Albright to Larry McDonald, Sept. 21, 1994 (quotation); RAG to Sigurd Lucassen, Dec. 12, 1992, box 34, General Presidents' Correspondence, and Aaron Belk to RAG, Sept. 15, 1995, box 22, Administrative Committee Meetings, RAG Files, BCTD Records, GMMA.

18. "The Women on the Job—In Construction," *New York Times*, Aug. 28, 1977, IV, 6 (hereafter, *NYT*); BCTD *Proceedings*, 1995, 31; Mary Ellen Boyd interview, June 24, 2002; "Battery Park City and Developer Settle $500,000 Sex Bias Case," *Engineering News-Record* (Aug. 20, 1987): 123 (LexisNexis). The $500,000 referred to back wages.

19. Boyd interview.

20. Georgine discussed some of the roots of the conflict in his address to the convention, BCTD *Proceedings*, 1995, 320–24; "Georgine Faces Challenge," *Engineering News-Record* (July 10, 1995): 12. Marvin Boede interview, Feb. 5, 2002.

21. A. L. "Mike" Monroe to Joseph F. Maloney, June 2, 1995; RAG to A. L. Monroe, June 8, 1995; RAG to Ron Carey, Aug. 7, 1995, box 33, General Presidents' Correspondence, RAG Files, BCTD Records, GMMA; Georgine's address, BCTD *Proceedings*, 1995, 323–24; "Georgine Faces Challenge," 12.

22. "Georgine Faces Challenge," 12; "Trades Election Shaping Up," *Engineering News-Record* (Aug. 7, 1995): 13 (LexisNexis).

23. "Trades Pulling Together," *Engineering News-Record* (Sept. 11, 1995): 9 (LexisNexis;

quotations); Pre-Convention Governing Board Meeting, Aug. 28–31, 1995, BCTD *Proceedings*, 1995, 301; Raymond J. Robertson, *A History of the Iron Workers Union* (Washington, D.C.: IABSOIW, 1996), 19, notes that Georgine joined the Iron Workers in 1995, and George M. Cross, *The Complete Iron Workers Directory* (Washington, D.C.: IABSOIW, 2002), 57, notes that when the Lathers joined the Carpenters, the New York City local joined the Iron Workers as Local 46 L.

24. Georgine's address, BCTD *Proceedings*, 1995, 320–21.

25. Ibid., 324, 326.

26. Georgine to the General Presidents, Nov. 28, 1995, box 33, General Presidents' Correspondence, RAG Files, BCTD Records, GMMA; report of the Governing Board of Presidents, BCTD *Proceedings*, 2000, 135–36, 149–50; unpublished notes on Lois Gray's report provided by the author; Boyd interview.

27. "Building & Construction Trades Department Welcomes Two New Key Staff Members," *The Builders* (Jan. 1997): 2; report of the Governing Board of Presidents, BCTD *Proceedings*, 2000, 142–44; Robert Ozinga to Grace Palladino, July 18, 2003; "Why We're Restructuring Our Department," *The Builders* (Sept. 1996): 4 (quotation).

28. Report of the Governing Board of Presidents, BCTD *Proceedings*, 2000, 156–57; RAG to the General Presidents, Mar. 27, 1996, General Presidents' Correspondence, box 33, RAG Files, BCTD Records, GMMA; "Solidarity, Not Censure," *Engineering News-Record*, Apr. 29, 1996, 10 (LexisNexis; quotations).

29. Unpublished notes on Lois Gray's report; "Training, Cooperation May Produce a 'New' Industry," *Engineering News-Record* (Jan. 27, 1997): 84 (LexisNexis); "The New Unionism," *Engineering News-Record* (Sept. 1, 1997): 28 (LexisNexis).

30. "Why We're Restructuring Our Department," *The Builders* (Sept. 1996): 1; Jerry Monahan comments, BCTD *Proceedings*, 1995, 369–70; COTAP [Construction Organizing Training and Action Program] Proposal, 1996, in General Presidents' Correspondence, box 34, RAG Files, BCTD Records, GMMA; "Building Trades Organizing Efforts Showing Success," *America@Work* (June 2001) (online); Weil, "Market Recovery Strategies," 36–37.

31. "Court Backs Unions' On-Job Organizing; Unanimous Decision Allows 'Salting,'" *Washington Post*, Nov. 29, 1995, F3 (quotation); RAG to the International Presidents, Dec. 1, 1995, General Presidents' Correspondence, box 33, RAG Files, BCTD Records, GMMA. The case, *National Labor Relations Board v. Town & Country Electric, Inc.* (516 US 85) was decided on November 28, 1995; Ozinga interview; report of the Governing Board of Presidents, BCTD *Proceedings*, 2000, 173–74; Grabelsky interview.

32. Report of the Governing Board of Presidents, BCTD *Proceedings*, 2000, 173–74; Ozinga interview; Grabelsky interview.

33. Grabelsky interview; RAG to Frank Caine et al., Oct. 1, 1996, box 34, General Presidents' Correspondence, RAG Files, BCTD Records, GMMA (quotation).

34. "Building Trades Organizing Efforts Showing Success," *America@Work* (June 2001) (online); "The Big Push," *Las Vegas-Review Journal* (Sept. 1, 1997) (online); RAG to Charles Jones, Sept. 25, 1996, box 34, General Presidents' Correspondence, RAG Files, BCTD Records, GMMA.; Grabelsky interview; "BTOP," *The Labor Educator* (Apr. 1999) (online).

35. John J. Sweeney to RAG, Nov. 6, 1996, General Presidents' Correspondence, box 34, RAG Files, BCTD Records, GMMA; report of the Governing Board of Presidents, BCTD *Proceedings*, 2000, 174–76; "Why We're Restructuring Our Department," *The Builders* (Sept. 1996): 1 (quotation).

36. "The Big Push" (quotation); "Organizing Campaign Is Up and Running," *The Builders* (Mar. 1997): 1.

37. "Building Trades Organizing Efforts Showing Success," *Workday Minnesota* (June 7, 2001) (online) (reprint from *America@Work* [June 2001]); report of the Governing Board

of Presidents, BCTD *Proceedings*, 2000, 178; Grabelsky interview. The complaint comment is based on my conversation with Mike Lucas, Apr. 7, 2003.

38. "Unions Keep the Heat Up in Las Vegas Organizing Drive," *Engineering-News Record*, Nov. 3, 1997, 17 (LexisNexis); "The New Unionism," *Engineering-News Record*, Sept. 1, 1997, 28 (LexisNexis); Jeffrey Grabelsky, "Comprehensive Campaigns: A Building Trades Case Study," in my possession.

39. "The Big Push"; "Unions Keep the Heat Up in Las Vegas Organizing Drive," 17; Stan Smith, "Editorial," *Organized Labor* (Oct. 13, 1997) (online; quotation); "Construction Union Organizers Run Infomercials," *Las Vegas Review-Journal* (Nov. 20, 1997): D2 (Lexis-Nexis); "Scarcity of Skilled Workers Will Put Brakes on Growth," *Engineering News-Record* (Jan. 26, 1998): 95 (LexisNexis; quotation).

40. "The Big Push"; "Concrete Company under Fire," *Las Vegas Review-Journal* (Aug. 7, 1997): 1D (online).

41. "The Big Push"; "Keep Las Vegas Free and Open," *Engineering News-Record* (Sept. 8, 1997): 97 (online); "Concrete Company under Fire," 1D.

42. Report of the Governing Board of Presidents, BCTD *Proceedings*, 2000, 179–81; Grabelsky interview.

43. "Lesson from Las Vegas—Organizing Works When There's Respect, Commitment," *The Building Tradesman*, Sept. 17, 1999 (online). This interpretation was drawn from conversations with various Department members. Report of the Governing Board of Presidents, BCTD *Proceedings*, 2000, 180 (quotation).

44. "Las Vegas Launches Phase 2 of Organizing Drive," *The Builders* (Apr./May 1998): 5; Ozinga interview.

45. Ozinga interview; "Strikers Told to Picket Peacefully," *Las Vegas Review-Journal* (Aug. 18, 1998) (online; quotation); "Building Trades Organizing Efforts Showing Success," *Workday Minnesota*, June 7, 2001 (online) (reprint from *America@Work*, June 2001); "Las Vegas Project Organizes 7,000," *The Labor Educator* (Apr. 1999) (online).

46. "Las Vegas Launches Phase 2 of Organizing Drive," 5; "Workers Sue to Stop Deductions," *Las Vegas Review-Journal* (May 6, 1998): D1 (online).

47. "Workers Sue to Stop Deductions," D1; handbills are included in Grabelsky, "Comprehensive Campaigns."

48. The website and the campaign are described in Grabelsky, "Comprehensive Campaigns."

49. Grabelsky, "Comprehensive Campaigns"; "Willis Roofing Reaches Settlement with Union," *Las Vegas Review-Journal* (June 25, 1999): 1D (LexisNexis); "When Contractors Are Organized," *Engineering-News Record* (Dec. 20, 1999): 30 (LexisNexis); "Vegas Unions Say They've Signed Big Nonunion Roofing Firm," *Engineering-News Record*, July 7, 1999, 16 (LexisNexis).

50. "BTOP Closes Shop in Las Vegas; AFL-CIO Claims Pilot Project a Huge Success," *Nevada Employment Law Letter* (Oct. 1999) (online); "Celebrating 90th Birthday with Speeches, Workshops, Exhibitions," *The Builders* (Apr./May 1998): 2 (for motto); this interpretation was drawn from conversations with various Department members.

51. Grabelsky interview; Ozinga interview. The limitations of bottom-up organizing are discussed in Weil, "Market Recovery Strategies," 27, 45–46.

52. Boyd interview; "Building Trades Organizing Efforts Showing Success," *Workday Minnesota* (June 7, 2001) (online) (reprinted from *America@Work* [June 2001]); "BTOP Closes Shop in Las Vegas," *Nevada Employment Law Letter* (Oct. 1999) (online).

53. "Building Trades Membership Continues to Grow," *The Builders* (Feb. 1998): 1 (quotation); "'Milestones to Organizing' Unveiled at Conference," *The Builders* (Apr./May 1998): 1 (quotation); Grabelsky interview.

54. " 'Milestones to Organizing' Unveiled at Conference," 1, 8 (quotations); report of the Governing Board of Presidents, BCTD *Proceedings,* 2000, 182–83.

55. "Building Trades Target Seattle," *Engineering News-Record* (Mar. 22/29, 1999): 39 (LexisNexis); report of the Governing Board of Presidents, BCTD *Proceedings,* 2000, 185–86; Georgine is cited in *AFL-CIO Work-in-Progress* (Apr. 26, 1999) (online).

56. "Building Trades Georgine to Retire," *AFL-CIO Work-in-Progress* (Jan. 24, 2000) (online); "Unions Pulling Together," *Engineering News-Record* (Apr. 17, 1995): 14 (Lexis-Nexis); "Robert A. Georgine Retires from Building Trades, Continues to Head ULLICO Inc.," ULLICO press release, Jan. 24, 2000 (online); "Georgine to Leave Building Trades," *Engineering News-Record* (Jan. 31, 2000): 14 (LexisNexis; quotations).

57. "A Tribute to Bob Georgine Topping Out 29 Years of Dedicated Leadership to the Building Trades," souvenir booklet, Apr. 2, 2000 (NEW ad at 43; Italian American ad at 70); sponsors based on the list of guest tables included in "Bob Georgine's 'Topping Out' Party"; the "My Way" anecdote is based on my notes of the proceedings; "Temps and Union Mergers Vex Georgine as He Leaves Trades," *Engineering News-Record* (Apr. 10, 2000): 15 (Lexis-Nexis) (quotation).

58. Sullivan is quoted in "Temps and Union Mergers Vex Georgine as He Leaves Trades," 15; my sense of Georgine's leadership and the merger question are drawn from conversations with a variety of Department members.

59. "Temps and Union Mergers Vex Georgine as He Leaves Trades," 15.

60. BCTD *Proceedings,* 2000, 281 (quotation), 283 (quotation), 433–36, 442–43.

Epilogue

1. "Construction Wages and Union Density Drop in 2002," *AGC Human Resource & Labor News* (Apr. 30, 2003): 1–2 (online).

2. Douglas J. McCarron to members, Apr. 9, 2001, published by Construction Workers News Service (online); "BCTD and the Struggle for the Soul of Organized Labor," *Engineering News-Record* (Apr. 29, 2002): 78 (LexisNexis).

3. "Carpenters Quit AFL-CIO over Focus" (Apr. 9, 2001): 10 (LexisNexis); John J. Sweeney, Memo: United Brotherhood of Carpenters, Mar. 2, 2001, published by Construction Workers News Service (online); "Building Trade Unions in Turmoil," *Engineering News Record* (June 25, 2001): 14 (LexisNexis); John Judis, "Labor's Love Lost," *New Republic,* June 25, 2001 (online); "Reacting to Carpenters' Withdrawal from Federation," *International Operating Engineer Newsletter,* Apr.–May 2001 (online; quotation); "Carpenters Deny Split Prompted by Wall-to-Wall Organizing Plan," *Washington State Labor Council Reports* (July 11, 2001) (online; quotation); "Councils Support Sullivan's Decision to Reject Carpenters' Reaffiliation Terms," *Construction Labor Report* (Mar. 6, 2002): 5 (quotation). Although Judis reported that carpenters make up about 60 percent of the workforce on any given job site, Department officials say that the figure is closer to 20 percent.

4. "Carpenters Quit AFL-CIO over Focus," 10 (quotation); "National Construction Association Kicks Off 'Building to Victory for Bush' Campaign," *PR Newswire,* Oct. 2, 2000 (online); "Open Shop Flexes Politically and Targets 2002 Senate Races," *Engineering News-Record* (Mar. 11, 2002): 11 (LexisNexis; quotation); "Probe Targets Ironworkers," *Engineering News-Record* (Apr. 3, 2001): 15 (online); "Big Labor's Enron," *National Review Online,* Aug. 13, 2002; "Painters' Monroe Bashes Sullivan," *Engineering News-Record* (Apr. 22, 2002): 10 (LexisNexis; quotation).

5. "Building Trades' Leaders Vote to Ask Carpenters to Reaffiliate," *Engineering News-Record* (Jan. 28, 2002): 12 (LexisNexis); "BCTD's Sullivan Calls Carpenters' Terms for Re-

joining Building Trades Unacceptable," *Construction Labor Report* (Feb. 27, 2002): 1433 (quotation); Douglas J. McCarron to Edward Sullivan, Feb. 21, 2001, and BCTD to the General Presidents, Feb. 21, 2002, published by Construction Workers News Service (online); Edward C. Sullivan to Secretaries and CEOs of the State, Provincial, and Local Councils, Mar. 11, 2002, in my possession; "Councils Support Sullivan's Decision to Reject Carpenters' Reaffiliation Terms," 6.

6. "Building Trades' Leaders Vote to Ask Carpenters to Reaffiliate," 12 (LexisNexis; quotation); Edward Sullivan interview, July 1, 2003.

7. "Carpenters Fill Out the Lineup in Reunified Building Trades," *Engineering News-Record* (Dec. 9, 2002): 11 (LexisNexis; quotations); "Building and Construction Trades Department Leadership Adopts Sweeping Change on Jurisdiction Issues," *PR Newswire*, Oct. 17, 2002 (online); "Carpenters on Verge of Re-affiliating with AFL-CIO," *Workday Minnesota* (Nov. 16, 2002) (online; quotations).

8. President Sullivan's address, BCTD legislative conference, Apr. 7, 2003 (BCTD website); "Helmets to Hardhats: IBEW and NECA Support New Program to Recruit Military Veterans for Construction Careers," *IBEW Journal* 9 (Oct. 2002): 6 (online); Sullivan interview.

9. BCTD and CURT (Construction Users Roundtable) Joint Press Release, "Construction Industry Leaders Form Tripartite Initiative," Jan. 18, 2003; "Owners Initiate Collaboration," *Engineering News-Record* (Jan. 27, 2003): 13 (online); Sullivan interview (sentence order transposed for clarity).

10. President Sullivan's address, BCTD legislative conference, Apr. 7, 2003 (quotations); "A Message from the President," May 2003 (BCTD website).

INDEX